1941

This book may be kept

DUKE · UNIVERSITY · PUBLICATIONS

Machiavelli's *Prince*
and Its Forerunners

FORTUNE AND VIRTUE

From a copy of Carolus Bovillus, *Liber de Intellectu. . . . Liber de Sapiente,* etc., Paris, 1510, owned by E. P. Goldschmidt and Co., 45 Old Bond Street, London. The reproduction is reduced in size.

The plate illustrates Machiavelli's conception of Fortune and Wisdom or Virtue as it appears throughout *The Prince,* especially in chapter 25. The figure to the right is indicated on the scroll as *Sapientia,* but on her seat she is denominated *Virtus;* such double meaning is quite in harmony with Machiavelli's conception of *Virtù.* Her seat is four-square, to signify firmness. In her hand she holds the mirror commonly assigned to Prudence; the book of advice to rulers is sometimes called *Speculum regis* or the King's Mirror.

Fortune sits on the ball common in allegorical pictures of Fortune; it indicates her uncertainty, since it turns hither and thither without reason. Before her she holds her wheel, on the summit of which is seated the king, the man most favored by Fortune; as the wheel turns he must yield his place to those now below him. Her eyes are blindfolded, for she deals with men without seeing their deserts.

From the mouth of the foolish man pictured on the medallion above Fortune comes a scroll with the words: "Fortune, we make you a goddess and place you in the heavens," (Juvenal 10.365). From the mouth of the wise man comes a similar scroll inscribed: "Trust in Virtue; Fortune is more fleeting than the waves."

FORTUNE AND VIRTUE

From a copy of Carolus Bovillus' *Liber de Intellectu, . . . Liber de Sapiente*, etc., Paris, 1510, owned by E. P. Goldschmidt and Co., 45 Old Bond Street, London. The reproduction is reduced in size.

The plate illustrates Machiavelli's conception of Fortune and Wisdom or Virtue as it appears throughout *The Prince*, especially in chapter 25. The figure to the right is indicated on the scroll as Sapientia, but on her seat she is denominated Virtue: such double meaning is quite in harmony with Machiavelli's conception of *Virtù*. Her seat is four-square, to signify firmness. In her hand she holds the mirror commonly assigned to Prudence; the book of advice to rulers is sometimes called *Speculum regis* or the King's Mirror.

Fortune sits on the ball common in allegorical pictures of Fortune; it indicates her uncertainty, since it turns hither and thither without reason. Before her she holds her wheel, on the summit of which is seated the king, the man most favored by Fortune; as the wheel turns he must yield his place to those now below him. Her eyes are blindfolded, for she deals with men without seeing their deserts.

From the mouth of the foolish man pictured on the medallion above Fortune comes a scroll with the words: "Fortune, we make you a goddess and place you in the heavens" (Juvenal 10.366). From the mouth of the wise man comes a similar scroll inscribed: "Trust in Virtue; Fortune is more fleeting than the waves."

FORTUNE AND VIRTUE

Machiavelli's *Prince* and Its Forerunners

The Prince as a Typical Book *de Regimine Principum*

By

ALLAN H. GILBERT

The king-becoming graces
As justice, verity, temperance, stableness,
Bounty, perseverance, mercy, lowliness,
Devotion, patience, courage, fortitude.
—*Macbeth* 4.3.

DUKE UNIVERSITY PRESS
DURHAM, NORTH CAROLINA
1938

A DUKE UNIVERSITY CENTENNIAL PUBLICATION

This book, by a member of the faculty of Duke University, is one of a group published in connection with the Duke University Centennial, celebrating in 1938-1939 the anniversary of the origin of Trinity College, from which Duke University developed.

PREFACE

THE important books of the world should be studied for their universal significance and as ultimately important for that alone. But they may also receive historical consideration because they are phenomena in the life of mankind; indeed, their universal meaning is likely not to be altogether plain when their historical position is not clear. By the present work I hope to make Machiavelli somewhat more useful to the present age by showing what he meant in his own day. While he has in many ways been admirably studied, no extensive attempt has been made to see whether in *The Prince* he used the language of other books of advice to rulers circulated in his time. If his work appear as the representative of a type, it cannot be historically intelligible until its typical qualities are clear, nor can the original contribution of the author be estimated. My attempt is to give something of the atmosphere in which *The Prince* was written by means of quotations from treatises having the same purpose as *The Prince,* books that may be assigned to the genus called *the prince* or *de regimine principum.* Many of my quotations may have been accessible to the Florentine secretary, and I do not doubt that some of them came under his eye, yet I do not present them specifically as his sources. Rather they represent the background against which an educated reader anywhere in Europe would have thrown *The Prince* when it appeared. What words, formulas, or ideas in it were familiar to Machiavelli because he had already met them in works of advice to monarchs circulated in his own city, Naples, Paris, Vienna, Toledo, or London?

This hardly can be demonstrated without direct quotations, in whatever language written. Respect for Machiavelli's *patria* requires that what is Italian should remain Italian, and regard for the renaissance demands that Latin shall remain Latin. Indeed, the study is properly an international one. Yet its international character does not forbid but rather welcomes English, for that language has also its works on the governance of princes both earlier and later than Machiavelli, and the English-speaking peoples share in the common heritage.

[v]

My plan has been to take up *The Prince* chapter by chapter, attempting to illustrate whatever can be explained from other books on the conduct of rulers by both quotation and comment. The quotations are commonly in chronological order, with some notion of showing the steady presence of the idea in question from the time of Aquinas to the sixteenth century. It may, however, be suggested that many works from Greek and Latin antiquity and from the middle ages were printed and circulated in the renaissance as working manuals; their steady appearance in new editions ensured the steady absorption of their ideas, even had new works based on them not appeared. To books on the conduct of princes composed after the death of Machiavelli I have given but a subordinate place, since I wished to explain him and his work without being involved with Machiavellism. Perhaps my quotations from later works will suggest that the urge to advise princes was so strong as to continue for many years after the death of Niccolò, especially since some of them are from books that seem in no way indebted to *The Prince*.

To secure fuller statement of some ideas undeveloped in *The Prince* itself, I have used parallels from the other writings of its author, but only as the subject seemed to demand it, without attempt to duplicate work such as that of Burd for his edition of *The Prince;* nor have I repeated unnecessarily citations from Aristotle and other classical authors.

In considering *The Prince* as one among others rather than as *sui generis* I have been led into various opinions not in accord with some at least of the older views still widely circulated. Rejection of much of the common tradition is, it appears, a measure of actual study of the writings of the Florentine secretary, if one may judge from such different studies as those of Burd, Tommasini, Ercole, and Chabod. My endeavor has been to get at the truth, without troubling about the novelty or lack of novelty of the various opinions I have come to hold. Some of my conclusions appear in a brief summary on page 2.

The bibliography presents the books I have actually employed, with such comments as seemed to be required. The section of it containing works *de regimine principum* shows, I hope, that I have used most of the highly important representatives of the type and a considerable number of others. It is altogether made up of such books as I have been able to read; others which I should like to have seen I could not find in libraries or secure from second-hand dealers, but I believe my list sufficiently representative for my purpose. My complete record of books which certainly or apparently—judging from such facts as I have obtained about them—are to be assigned to the class is so extensive as to require separate publication. A similar long list, doubtless containing many additional titles, has been made by Dr. Lester K. Born. My own is still growing.

I have attempted to make the material in the volume easily accessible. Whatever is pertinent to any chapter of *The Prince* appears in the section devoted to that chapter; the main headings are briefly indicated in the table of contents. I assume always that the reader has the text of *The Prince* before him. While treatment by topics rather than according to Machiavelli's own arrangement might at times have appeared more systematic, his method is of the essence of *The Prince* and of its type. The effect I desire demands that it be kept. When, as sometimes happens, the same topic appears in more than one chapter, cross-references are used, and the material is attached to the most important reference. The index has been prepared with the ambition of making it possible to find easily anything in the volume, whether a topic, a significant word, the name of an author, or a passage from one of Machiavelli's other writings.

My obligations to other writers appear in the bibliography and footnotes. Dr. Lester K. Born has assisted me by personal suggestion as well as by his publications. To the authorities of Duke University I owe thanks for the sabbatical leave during which some of my studies were carried on and for appropriations enabling me to obtain essential books for the university library. I wish to thank the officials of the library for their aid in making the books immediately accessible. The librarians at Cornell University and other American institutions have also been most helpful. I am also glad to express thanks to the authorities of the Biblioteca Nazionale at Palermo for their kindness in assisting me with the books in their splendid collection. Without the long-continued support of the Research Council of Duke University my work would have been impossible. I wish also to express my gratitude to the Duke University Press.

TABLE OF CONTENTS

ILLUSTRATIONS

Machiavelli's *Prince*
and Its Forerunners

BRIEF STATEMENT OF SOME OF THE CHIEF IDEAS OF THE VOLUME

1. Machiavelli's first interest was the good of the people of Italy (see the index under *common good*).

2. Machiavelli advised a prince because he believed Italy could be delivered only by a single person, not by a republic (see pages 36 ff., and the index under *kingly hand*).

3. The work is addressed not to a tyrant but to a good ruler (see the index under *tyrant*).

4. Though Machiavelli's prince will be moral when possible, he is under no detailed moral restraint whatever; he has, however, the ultimate obligation to rule well (see pages 77 ff., and the index under *morality*.)

5. *The Prince* is designed for the deliverer of Italy and is a unit (see pages 222 ff.).

6. Though manifesting independence of mind, *The Prince* is not a unique work but a representative—the greatest—of a type familiar to Machiavelli (see pages 5, 80, and *passim*).

ON THE HISTORY OF BOOKS OF ADVICE TO PRINCES

NEAR the dawn of the age of modern parliaments Sir Philip Sidney, through the wise Euarchus, spoke of "the Princes persons" as "in all monarchall governmentes the very knot of the peoples welfare, and light of all their doinges to which they are not onely in conscience, but in necessitie bounde to be loyall,"[1] and yet earlier Jean-Juvenal des Ursins had written of the king as "l'âme, le principe de la vie, de la chose publique."[2] Diminish the contrasts between earlier and modern government as we will, show to the utmost the essentially similar character of men's hearts and institutions, it still remains that the renaissance monarchs held a central place on the stage that can now hardly be understood. Nor can it be supposed that their central place is to be explained from the mental attitude of their subjects. However necessary it may be to recognize that checks have operated in restraint of the most absolute monarchs, it is yet true that the personal qualities of mediaeval and renaissance sovereigns could tremendously influence the well-being of their subjects. Whether there should be war or peace, religious freedom or persecution, economy or extravagance in managing public funds, prudence or dishonesty in the control of the coinage, encouragement of commerce or hostility to it—on all these the individual ruler could exercise a great and perhaps controlling influence. Though in practice his actual power over such matters might be variously reduced, they were still generally admitted to fall within his prerogative and were managed as though by him. The accession of a new monarch was much more important than that of a modern political party because there was no machinery for ridding a country of his administration. He might occupy the throne in some fashion for half a century in spite of rebellion, as did Henry VI of England; free-

[1] *Arcadia,* bk. 5, p. 175.
[2] "The soul, the source of life of the state." Ernest Lavisse, *Histoire de France* 4.2.207 (by Ch. Petit-Dutaillis); the quotation is from the first *Epistre au roi.* Péchenard, *Jean-Juvenal des Ursins* (p. 276), quotes a similar passage from the *Remonstrances,* 2d consideration.

[3]

dom from the utmost abuses of kingly power lay only in the miseries and uncertainties of warfare. Even a ruler who acted under the stimulus of conscience might cause great misery, as did Philip by his persecutions in the Netherlands.

In this condition of the great influence and direct power of the monarch and attention on him as the focus of the activities of government, men properly sought to deal with the problem of government at the centre. What will secure good government? asked every public-spirited man, monarchs as well as nobles, scholars, and public officials, Charles V of France or Johannes Frobenius in Basel. The first answer was to decide what the ruler should be and do if he was to preside over an *agatharchia,* a perfect state.

The answer was at hand in every collection of books, such as that formed for Charles V[3] or later for the young James VI of Scotland.[4] It was to be found in the volumes on the conduct of princes entitled *De regimine principum, De institutione principum, De officio regis, Il principe,* or *The governal of princes.* Between the years 800 and 1700 there were accessible some thousand books and large, easily distinguished, sections of books telling the king how to conduct himself so that he might be "clear in his great office." The more popular of the early examples, such as that by Egidio Colonna, were often recopied and translated, and after the invention of printing went through various editions, living an active life of three or four centuries as standard manuals. The same may be said in its proportion of those composed in the age of printing, for example, the *De regno et regis institutione* of Franciscus Patricius. He who would learn how a king should conduct himself need never have been at a loss for a handbook on the subject.

The scholasticism and classicism of the majority of these authors, taken together, has hidden their import from the modern world, even from professed students of politics. Our forgetfulness of the relation of ethics and politics, our unfamiliarity with systematic ethics, our assumption that citations from classical authors are merely pedantry, our demand for historical analysis rather than practical advice from students of the renaissance, our concern with economic law rather than human volition, our distance from the personal influence of kings—such things have allowed us to suppose that the books of advice to rulers that casually come to our

[3] Ernest Lavisse, *Histoire de France* 4.1.190.

[4] *Publications of the Scottish History Society* XV (1893), pp. xxxi-lxxv (identical with vol. I of the *Miscellany* of the Society).

notice were always as lifeless as they now appear. They have been studied for incidental reasons, such as their peculiarities of language, with little thought of their primary reason for being.

And that there was an enormous number of such works has, it appears, but recently been recognized, though short lists of titles have appeared in such places as the introduction to Roger Bacon's edition of the *Secretum secretorum* by Mr. Robert Steele. The first systematic study of the book of advice to princes appeared in 1928.[5] In its simplest form, the book of this type is easily recognized because it aims to tell the ruler what sort of person he should be and what personally he should do. It is not necessary to swell the number of treatises *de regimine principum* with works of general information useful to rulers as educated men, or with treatises on government and its theory, or with pedagogical works on the instruction of the young children of rulers; the books we have in mind are concerned with the actual king, and with his conduct in office. They were, it is evident, suitable reading for young men who expected to be kings, such as the young Philip the Fair, for whom Egidio Colonna wrote, or the young James VI, who had in his Scottish library several books of the type. But they are on the whole intended for the perusal of men actually on their thrones.

So popular were these books, in their various editions, throughout western Europe for centuries that it is difficult to imagine a renaissance library wholly without them. Considering the composition of new works and the reprinting of old ones, one may suppose, however, that rather more than the average number of them were to be had in Italy during the lifetime of Machiavelli. Be this as it may, it is incredible that the Florentine secretary had not seen many examples, both of the classical books assigned by his age to the genus and of those composed in the centuries immediately preceding his own. Machiavelli's knowledge of classical writers on public affairs has been much studied, though with some tendency to forget that the sixteenth century looked on the classics as more practical than we are likely to, and with slight consideration of the specific problems of *The Prince*. But there has been little recognition of his reading in later books addressed to princes;

[5] Lester K. Born, *The Perfect Prince*, in *Speculum* III (1928), 470. See also his *Erasmus on Political Ethics*, in *Political Science Quarterly* XLIII (1928), 520. Dr. Born has now brought together much of his material in *The Education of a Christian Prince*, by Desiderius Erasmus, translated with an introduction on Erasmus and on ancient and mediaeval political thought, New York, 1936.

Villari mentions Johannes Jovianus Pontanus and Poggio Bracciolini with the purpose of showing that their writings on princes are not Machiavellian.[6] Tommasini, however, is of a different belief, writing of the *De principe* of Pontanus: "È innegabile, per chiunque lo percorra, che il trattato del Pontano, per quanto diverso dal *Principe,* à esercitato pur esso grande potenza sulla mente del Machiavelli."[7] On the *De infelicitate principum* of Poggio he speaks to the same effect.[8] Persico, while not asserting that Machiavelli borrowed from the Neapolitan books on the duties of princes, yet says of *I doveri del principe* by Diomede Carafa:

Ci dà il Carafa una sintesi viva ed efficace, anticipando i risultati delle indagini del Machiavelli; ma con maggior determinatezza di fatti, che rivelano in lui l'uomo esperto nella materia.[9]

While Persico nowhere speaks of absolute borrowing by Machiavelli, whom he does not avowedly treat, the reader infers that he would have presented the Florentine, like the Neapolitan Tristano Caracciolo in his advice to King Alphonso in 1494, as reflecting "in buona parte, le idee che circolavano allora nel pubblico, delle quali però erano stati seminatori e propagatori il Carafa e il Pontano."[10]

Like many writers to princes in his age, Machiavelli mentions no one of his immediate predecessors; his general references include classical works only, though he seems to have his contemporaries quite as much in mind. More than once he plainly refers to works of the sort. In the *Discorsi* (3.20) he discusses *umanità;* in addition, he mentions also *integrità, carità, castità,* and *liberalità.* Toward the end he writes: "Vedesi ancora, questa parte quanto la sia desiderata da' popoli negli uomini grandi, e quanto sia laudata dagli scrittori; e da quegli che descrivano la vita de' principi, e da quegli che ordinano come ei debbano vivere."[11] "Quegli che

---

[6] *Niccolò Machiavelli* 2.16.

[7] "Though the tractate of Pontanus is quite unlike *The Prince,* no one who goes through it can deny that it nevertheless had great influence on the mind of Machiavelli" (*La Vita di Machiavelli* 2.114, and n. 1).

[8] Ibid., 112, n. 2.

[9] "In his living and powerful synthesis Carafa anticipates the results of Machiavelli's investigations, but as a man expert in his material the former better delimits the facts" (*Gli scrittori politici napoletani,* p. 87).

[10] "In great part the ideas that were then generally circulating and of which Carafa and Pontanus were the disseminators and propagators" (ibid., p. 101).

[11] It can be seen, then, how much the people desire great men to have this trait and how much it is praised by writers, both those who describe the lives of princes and those who give directions for their conduct" (*Discorsi* 3.20, p. 229b).

ordinano" are the writers *de regimine principum;*[12] Machiavelli assumes his reader is sufficiently familiar with them to know that the virtues he has been considering are among their commonest topics. Some pages farther on Machiavelli discusses still further the virtue of *umanità,* in contrast with *durezza:* "Quegli che scrivono come uno principe si abbia a governare, si accostano più a Valerio che a Manlio" (i.e., to humanity rather than to harshness).[13] From the word *governare* in this passage, one may pass to the dedication of *The Prince,* where is the sentence: "Nè voglio sia reputata presunzione se uno uomo di basso ed infimo stato ardisce discorrere e regolare e' governi de' principi."[14] The sentence implies that the work in hand is one of those telling how a prince ought to govern himself. Words related to *governare* were widely used in various forms in various languages in this connection. A Middle English translation of the *Secretum secretorum* was called *The Governance of Princes,* as a translation of the title *De regimine principum* applied to that work.[15] In the fifteenth chapter of *The Prince,* which alludes to many moral qualities commonly discussed in books for princes, Machiavelli writes: "Resta ora a vedere quali debbano essere e' modi e governi di uno principe con sudditi o con gli amici. E perchè io so che molti di questo hanno scritto, dubito, scrivendone ancora io, non essere tenuto prosuntuoso, partendomi massime, nel disputare questa materia, dagli ordini degli altri."[16] The *molti* of this passage are the various writers on the regimen of princes, those who teach

[12] Gio. Battista Pigna in his *Il principe* (Venice, 1561, p. 44), later than Machiavelli but apparently uninfluenced by him, writes: "Quel Principe che io vò formando è tale nella mia mente, che vorrei vederlo un Monarca di tutto questo mondo."—"I have such a mental picture of the prince I am forming that I should like to see him monarch of all the world."

[13] "Those who write on how a prince should conduct himself lean rather to Valerius than to Manlius" (*Discorsi* 3.22, p. 233a).

[14] "I do not wish it to be thought presumptuous that a man of lowly and humble station should dare to consider and give rules for the conduct of princes."

[15] Gilbert, *Notes on the Influence of the Secretum secretorum,* in *Speculum* III (1928), 84. Gower (*Confessio Amantis* 7.1650) uses "the governance of kinges" to express *magestas in suo regimine* in the marginal Latin.

[16] "It remains now to see of what sort ought to be the manners and conduct of a prince in dealing with subjects or with friends. And because I am aware that many have written of this, I am afraid, when I also write of it, that I shall be thought presumptuous because in discussing the matter I depart very widely from the paths followed by the others" (*Prince* 15, first sentence).

In explaining the word *governo,* Tommaseo's *Dizionario,* in the section headed *di portamento mor. e soc.,* quotes part of the following: "Fu questo duca, come i

the vertus whiche are assissed
Unto a kinges Regiment.[17]

While some editors now prefer to call Machiavelli's work *De principatibus,* it is traditionally *Il principe;* indeed, in the *Discorsi* the author himself refers to it as "nostro trattato De Principe."[18] This is a conventional title. Pontanus, for example, called his work *De principe.* Twenty-nine years after the publication of Machiavelli's book, Gio. Battista Pigna published his *Il principe;* if there be anything Machiavellian in this work describing "come debba essere il Principe Heroico," it is successfully concealed. With a feeling for the generic, in his dedication he speaks of the book as "un Principe"; its purpose is "di formare un vero Principe," who "ha in sua mano il governarsi con prudenza."[19] Machiavelli apparently had the same feeling for the generic in regard to his work.[20] The title *De principatibus* also has generic suggestion. For

---

governi suoi dimostrorono, avaro e crudele; nelle udienze difficile, nel rispondere superbo; voleva la servitù, non la benivolenza degli uomini; e per questo più di essere temuto che amato desiderava."—"As his conduct showed, this duke was avaricious and cruel; hard to speak with, proud in his answers; he wished subservience, not good will from men; for this reason he desired to be feared rather than to be loved" (*Istorie Fiorentine* 2.37, p. 439b). These are the *governi* of the traditional bad prince. Cf. *Prince* 10, p. 22b for the *governi con li sudditi*—conduct with respect to his subjects—recommended by Machiavelli; *Prince* 7, p. 16b, for the *governi* he admired in Duke Valentino; *Prince* 14, p. 30a, for the ways rulers *si sono governati* in war.

[17] Gower, *Confessio amantis* 7.1718-9. In Villari we read: "E qui allude non tanto agli antichi, quanto agli scrittori del Medio Evo, come Egidio Colonna e Dante Alighieri; agli eruditi del secolo XV, come il Panormita, Poggio, il Pontano ed altri molti, i quali avevano sostenuto che il sovrano deve aver tutte le virtù, e ne avevano fatto un ritratto ideale di religione, di modestia, di giustizia e di generosità."—"Here Machiavelli alludes not so much to the ancients as to the writers of the middle ages, such as Egidio Colonna and Dante Alighieri, and to the scholars of the fifteenth century, such as Panormita, Poggio, Pontano and many others, who had held that the sovereign ought to have all the virtues, and from them had made an ideal portrait of religion, modesty, justice, and generosity" (2.143). It is probable, however, that Machiavelli's reference is too specific to include Dante's *De Monarchia.* For other possible references to such works see pp. 18, 67, 119, 122, 186, below.

[18] *Discorsi* 3.42, p. 257a.

[19] "To form a true prince" who "is attempting to govern himself with prudence" (lib. 1, p. 1).

[20] The same generic feeling appears in respect to *Dell' arte della guerra;* see Tommasini 2.221-4. Writers on warfare ("coloro che alla guerra hanno data regole") think that soldiers should be taken from temperate climates, but this, Machiavelli says, may be impossible; the prince must draw from his own lands, wherever situated (*Arte della guerra* 1, p. 275a, cf. *Discorsi* 1.1, p. 58b). The subject is discussed by Egidio Colonna (*De regimine* 3.3.2) with a reference to the first book of Vegetius.

instance, Philippus Beroaldus (1453-1505) wrote a short work entitled in the Basel edition of 1513 *De optimo statu,* but entitled in full *De republica, deque optimo statu et principe.* He frequently uses the word *principatus,* meaning *form of government.*[21] Or to give an earlier instance, the *De regimine principum* of Aquinas bears the alternative title *De rege et regno.*

Against this background of many volumes *de regimine principum* appears Machiavelli's opinion that in writing *The Prince* he was doing something that would be immediately understood because of the number of books already written on the subject; "scrivendone ancora io,"[22]—"I too writing on the subject"—he says. To be sure he indicated he would pursue a different method, but it is common for writers of partly conventional works to justify themselves by showing where they have departed from the beaten track. At any rate, a person who will use a new method must know the old one he is superseding; his immersion in the old precedes and conditions his desire to improve it, and in his familiarity he easily uses it to give definition to his better ideas. However revolutionary, such a writer is so deeply impressed by the older works which for years have been forming his mind that his emancipation, little as he may suspect it, is not wholly complete. Even its steps may sometimes be traced, as has been suggested by Tommasini in commenting on Machiavelli's early and later view of liberality.[23] From the court of the Emperor Maximilian he wrote:

Che l'Imperadore abbi assai soldati e buoni nessuno ne dubita; ma come li possa tenere insieme, qui sta il dubbio: perchè non li tenendo lui se non per forza di danari, e avendone da un canto scarsità per sè stesso, quando non ne sia provveduto da altri (che non si può sapere); dall'altro sendone troppo liberale si aggiugne difficultà a difficultà; e *benchè essere liberale sia virtù ne principi, tamen* e' non basta satisfare a mille uomini, quando altri à bisogno di ventimila; e la liberalità non giova dove la non aggiugne.[24]

For Machiavelli's reading in the theory of war see L. Arthur Burd, *Le Fonti . . . nell' arte della guerra.*

[21] E.g., "Est principatus unius quam monarchiam vocant. . . . Tu primus in domo tua efficito principatum popularem."—"There is a principate of one man which they call a monarchy. . . . You first establish in your own house a popular principate" (pp. 123 *verso*-124 *recto*). Machiavelli, however, distinguishes republics from principates (*Prince* 1).

[22] P. 7, above.   [23] *Vita di Machiavelli* 1.418-9.

[24] "No one doubts that the Emperor has enough good soldiers; the doubtful thing is how he will be able to hold them together. For he holds them only by

In its charge of too great liberality this passage contains the germ
of one of the ideas that Machiavelli later brought forward against
those held as axiomatic by writers on republics and principates
who imagine states "che non si sono mai visti nè conosciuti essere
in vero."[25] As Tommasini indicates, in his remarks on the Emperor
he is already undermining the maxim that the prince ought in
all circumstances to be liberal; if this is true of rulers in general,
it should be especially true of the Emperor, yet even there Machiavelli doubts it. In coming to see, as a result of his observation of
Maximilian, that liberality might be objected to, he developed
his theory in the direction of *The Prince*. With probability Tommasini imagines that the Italian agents gathered at the court
of the Emperor passed some of their time in theoretical discussion
of the liberality proper to a prince, considering the prodigality of
the King of the Romans, the parsimony of Pope Julius, and the
stinginess of the King of Spain. From such contradictions the
thought of Machiavelli on liberality may have issued completely
shaped to the form it takes in *The Prince;* to some one who objected that the behavior suitable to a pope or a king of Spain was
hardly proper to a Caesar, he may have answered in such words as
he was later to write of the ancient Caesar, the proper norm for
those who asserted that they had inherited rights to his name:

Cesare era uno di quelli che voleva pervenire al principato di Roma;
ma se, poi che vi fu venuto, fussi sopravvissuto e non si fussi temperato
da quelle spese, arebbe destrutto quello imperio.[26]

Maximilian's conduct had shown no such change, for Machiavelli
saw him as an "uomo gittatore del suo sopra tutti gli altri che a'
nostri tempi o prima sono stati: il che fa che sempre ha
bisogno, nè somma alcuna è per bastargli in qualunque grado la

---

dint of payment, and yet on one hand he has very little money unless some one
(and one cannot imagine who) provides him with it, and on the other hand he
joins difficulty to difficulty by being too liberal with it. And though liberality is a
virtue in princes, it is not enough to satisfy a thousand men when one has need of
twenty thousand; for liberality does no good where it does not reach" (*Legazione
all' imperatore,* let. 6, VII, 186—Italia, 1813. The text is that given by Tommasini,
1.418, who says that the letter, ostensibly by Vettori, was written by Machiavelli.)
For a story illustrating Maximilian's liberality, see Bandello, *Novelle,* parte 2, nov.
46.   [25] *Prince* 15, p. 30b.
[26] "Caesar was one of those who wished to attain the principate of Rome, but if,
when he had attained it, he had survived and had not become more temperate in
his expenses, he would have destroyed his empire" (*Prince* 16, p. 32a).

fortuna si trovi."[27] Machiavelli quotes with approval a strong censure of the Emperor's liberality: "Queste due parti la liberalità, e la facilità che lo fanno laudare a molti, sono quelle che lo ruinano."[28] Machiavelli's own suggestion, however, is merely that the Emperor modify—"temperasse"[29]—his habits. Such tempering of liberality is on the way toward the *miseria* or stinginess advised in the sixteenth chapter of *The Prince,* yet is verbally at least still far from it; its kinship is rather to the avoiding of prodigality by adopting the Aristotelian mean in giving, as the "molti" had for many years been advising; Gower, for example, writes:

> A king after the reule is holde
> To modifie and to adresce
> Hise yiftes upon such largesce
> That he mesure noght excede:
> For if a king falle into nede,
> It causeth ofte sondri thinges
> Whiche are ungoodly to the kinges
> (*Confessio Amantis* 7.2152-8).

Machiavelli's Maximilian surely suffered enough of the "ungoodly" because of his excessive expenditure. Altogether one gains the impression that Machiavelli was at the time of his mission to the Emperor not yet ready in discussing the *governi* of a prince to depart greatly from the *ordini* of his many predecessors, and that a *Prince* then attempted would have been more like that of Pontanus, for example, than is the composition of 1513.

Yet, while the facts of time and place make it probable that Machiavelli had read Pontanus' work on the prince, I am unable to agree with Tommasini that such reading is undeniable; indeed, *The Prince* probably would not have been different if Pontanus had never lived. Similarities there are, but they are features common to the type, not the necessary result of contact between the two works. What modern books *de regimine principum* Machiavelli had certainly read is unknown; apparently he mentions none of them, and internal evidence must be looked upon with suspicion. Such failure to mention recent authors is normal. It

[27] "He is a man who wastes his substance more than does any one else of our times or of preceding times; hence he always is in need and no sum is able to suffice him in any condition in which he may happen to be put" (*Discorso sopra le cose di Alamagna,* in *Opere,* Italia, 1813, IV, 174).

[28] "These two habits of liberality and facility which make him praised by many are the ones that ruin him" (*Rapporto della magna,* ibid., p. 166).

[29] Ibid., p. 168.

can hardly be asserted that when composing their works *de regimine principum* Beroaldus, Pontanus, Erasmus, and Pigna were all without knowledge that they were walking a well-beaten path, yet none of them gives a direct indication that he has read other than classical works on the subject. The day when one's immediate predecessors were to be named in the text or in marginal notes had not yet come.[30] The remote predecessors of the works just referred to are about the same; Aristotle's *Politics,* Xenophon's *Cyropaedia,* and Isocrates' oration *To Nicocles* are shared with one or more of the others by *The Prince.* This community of classical sources is one thing that marks *The Prince* as conventional. Erasmus asserts that his work called *Institutio principis Christiani* is founded on the oration by Isocrates, of which he published a translation under the title of *De regno administrando,* or *De institutione principis.*[31] While claims perhaps too extreme have been made for the influence of Isocrates on *The Prince,* there are surely traces of it, and the probability that Machiavelli knew it is strengthened by its normal inclusion among important works of advice to monarchs. Of it Franciscus Patricius Senensis (1412-94) writes in his *De regno et regis institutione:*

Supernatarunt tamen duo [libri de regno], et in Italiam emerserunt, iamque ab omnibus leguntur Isocrates, scilicet et Dio Prusensis. . . . Fuit enim Isocrates vir et dicendi et vivendi disciplina peritissimus cuius ex ludo (ut ait oratorum maximus) tanquam ex equo Troiano innumeri principes exiere. . . .[32] Hic libros duos ad Nicoclem Cypri Regem reliquit, in quorum altero praecepta regi tradit, in altero autem his qui ab eo reguntur.[33]

[30] Andrés Mendo's *Principe perfecto y ministros ajustados* (first ed. in 1657) gives hundreds of marginal notes to authors of all ages.

[31] In 1514, at Vienna, the translation of *To Nicocles* by Martinus Phileticus was published under the title of *De regno gubernando ad Nicoclem.* The translation of Bernardo Giustiniano, under the title of *De institutione principis,* was first published at Venice in 1492. The copy of the Paris, 1511, edition in the Biblioteca Nazionale at Florence is bound with Poggio Bracciolini's *Dialogus de infelicitate principum.*

[32] *Innumeri* is now read *meri;* Cicero, *De oratore* 2.22.94.

[33] "Two books on kingship kept afloat and appeared in Italy; now they are read by every one, to wit, Isocrates and Dio Prusensis. . . . Isocrates was a man thoroughly experienced in the science of speaking and living, from whose school (as the greatest of orators says) as from the Trojan horse innumerable *Princes* have come forth. . . . He left two books addressed to Nicocles, king of Cyprus, in one of which he gives advice to the king, in the other to his subjects" (*De regno* 1.4).

Dio Prusensis, i.e. of Prusa (died about 120 A. D.), called Chrysostomus and Cocceianus, wrote in Greek five orations *De regno* (nos. 1, 2, 3, 4, 56), one *De*

As might be expected Patricius frequently refers to Isocrates. Erasmus wrote with the *Cyropaedia* in mind,[34] and made a translation of Xenophon's *Hieron, sive Tyrannus,* to which Machiavelli refers as *De Tyrannide*.[35] Pontanus says that the Cyrus of Xenophon "omnium . . . regiarum virtutum exemplum fuisse creditum est," and, citing his liberality, writes to Alphonso of Calabria that he desires the prince especially to imitate him.[36] Examples of this use of the *Cyropaedia* can easily be multiplied.[37] Machiavelli's references to it are like those of the others; he read and quoted what everyone interested in the conduct of the prince was familiar with. In considering these and other Greek and Latin writings, it

---

tyrannide (no. 6), and one *De regno et tyrannide* (no. 62). The first edition of the Greek text appeared in 1476; no copy is extant. The first Latin translation is of 1555. Dio probably did not influence Machiavelli.

[34] *Institutio principis Christiani,* chap. 3, 592 E. For Xenophon and other sources of Erasmus' work see Erasmus, *The Education of a Christian Prince,* translated by Lester K. Born, New York, 1936.

[35] *Discorsi* 2.2, p. 140a.   [36] *Opera,* Basel, 1566, I, 257, 267.

[37] Beroaldus, *De optimo statu,* in *Orationes et opuscula,* Basel, 1513, pp. 125 verso, 130 recto. Platina (1421-81), *Principis diatuposis, passim.* In 1521 gli Heredi di Philippo Giunta published the Italian translation of the *Cyropaedia* made by Iacopo di Messer Poggio from the Latin of his father, Messer Poggio Bracciolini. In his dedication to Alphonso of Aragon, the father wrote: "La hystoria di Xenophonte della vita di Cyro . . . contiene in se, e ci dimostra quale debba essere uno principe iusto. . . . Questa [lectione] certo è quella che supera tutte laltre, descrivendosi in questa opera uno Re che habbia à essere exemplo di virtu à ciascuno, il quale imitassino quegli che reggano, lo stato de subditi sarebbe in migliore conditione non è."—"Xenophon's account of the life of Cyrus contains within itself and shows us what a true prince ought to be. This kind of reading is certainly superior to every other, since in this work is described a king who can be an example of virtue to every one. If those who rule would imitate it, the state of their subjects would be better than it is."

In 1470, at the court of Burgandy, Vasco Fernandez, Count of Lucena, translated the *Cyropaedia* after the Latin of Poggio (Petit de Julleville, *Histoire de la langue et de la littérature française* 2.269). As dauphin, Louis XI provided himself with a translation, according to one of his letters: "Nous avons ordonné à maistre Jehan de Templo . . . la somme de trente escus d'or, pour avoir par nostre ordonnance pieçà translaté de latin en françois le livre de Xenophon le philosophe, contenant huit volumes, iceluy avoir fait escripre en parchemin, enluminer et relier, et à nous envoyé en la ville de Geneppe en Brabant, lors nous estant illec."—"We have decreed for Master Jehan de Templo the sum of thirty *escus* of gold because according to our command he some time ago translated from Latin into French the book of Xenophon the philosopher, containing eight volumes, and had it written on parchment, illuminated, and bound, and sent it to us in the town of Geneppe in Brabant, where we then were" (*Lettres de Louis XI* 10.162; because of the mention of Geneppe the editor assigns the date of 1461).

For the present worth of the *Cyropaedia* as "le bréviaire du haut commandement" see General Arthur Boucher, *Les lois éternelles de la guerre* 1.72; 2.239-49.

should be remembered that they were not because of their antiquity set apart from sixteenth-century life; the assumption that the classics are of little immediate and practical value and concern only professional students is a recent one. In the age of Machiavelli the best manual on any subject was assumed to be the classical treatise on the matter. Aristotle, Isocrates, and Xenophon[38] were considered those best fitted to give instruction to a prince of the renaissance; most men would have agreed with Charles V in holding that the *Politics* and the *Economics* of Aristotle were to a king "très nécessaires et pour cause."[39]

But though the classical influence on Machiavelli and Erasmus is great, it is far from accounting for them; even to use the classics as they did is in the mediaeval spirit; in his twelfth-century *De principis instructione liber* Giraldus Cambrensis made full use of all the ancient material available to him. A glance at the very chapter headings used by Erasmus and Machiavelli shows that they were classifying their matter in the mediaeval fashion. Some of the headings used by Vincent of Beauvais, for example, are as follows:

Quo 'iure regna quondam usurpata liceat retinere.
Quod [rex] eciam debet alios in sapiencia precellere.
Quod debet esse sapiens in amicis et consiliariis et officialibus eligendis.
Quod similiter debet esse sapiens in facultatibus dispensandis.
Quod eciam in raciociniis precavendis et in bellis exercendis.
De detractoribus et adulatoribus qui conversantur in curiis.
De adulatoribus ac dectractoribus repellendis.[40]

Engaged on their works about the same time, Erasmus and Machiavelli, notwithstanding the vast differences between them, yet employ chapter headings of the same type, showing that their interests are in part coincident and expressed in harmony with the same tradition. With the *De adulatione vitanda principi* of Erasmus may be compared the *Quomodo adulatores sint fugiendi* of

[38] *Prince* 6, p. 13a; 14, p. 30a; 16, p. 32a; 26, p. 50a.
[39] Ernest Lavisse, *Histoire de France* 4.1.190 (by A. Coville).
[40] "How crowns that have been usurped may legally be held.
That a king should excel all others in wisdom.
That a king should be wise in choosing friends, advisers, and officials.
That he should likewise be wise in bestowing riches.
Likewise in taking in advance precautions about his affairs and in carrying on war.
On the detractors and flatterers who live at courts.
On repelling flatterers and detractors" (from a rotograph of Merton MS 110, of *De morali principis institutione*).
Arpad Steiner and Allan H. Gilbert are now preparing an edition of this work.

Machiavelli; with *De vectigalibus et exactionibus, De liberalitate et parsimonia;*[41] with *De beneficentia principis, Quod principem decet ut egregius habeatur* and *De his rebus quibus homines et praesertim principes laudantur aut vituperantur;*[42] with *De magistratibus et officiis, De his quos a secretis principes habent;* with *De foederibus, Quomodo fides a principibus sit servanda;* with *De bello suscipiendo,* several chapters on war.[43] Erasmus would probably have appeared to Machiavelli one of those who wrote on imaginary rather than real principalities; the differences in tone are obvious enough, but individual characteristics have not submerged typical resemblances.[44]

It is evident, then, that the book entitled *The Prince* or something of the kind was familiar to the educated men of the sixteenth century and well recognized as a type. Important classical works were its prototypes, yet there were some three centuries of tradition of such writing by modern authors, based on the classics but adapted to their own circumstances; Italy of the fifteenth century had produced in abundance works addressed to the ruler. The superficial appearance of Machiavelli's production is that of volumes obviously belonging to the type, and his own references to his opuscule make evident that he thought of it as continuing the tradition in form, though departing from many of its ideas and substituting for them new and better conceptions of the conduct proper for the head of a state. It remains to see in what further respects Machiavelli conformed to the general example and what new truths he uttered.

[41] Erasmus quotes the proverb: "Magnum vectigal parsimonia est."—"Parsimony is a great source of income" (*Institutio* 4, 594 D).

[42] The general moral application is mediaeval; for example, in the *De regimine principum* of Egidio Colonna "universa de moribus philosophia continetur"—"universal philosophy on morals is contained" (title-page of the Rome, 1556, edition).

[43] ERASMUS	MACHIAVELLI
On the prince's avoidance of flattery	In what way flatterers are to be escaped
On taxes and exactions	On liberality and parsimony
On the good deeds of the prince	What a prince should do that he may be held excellent
On magistrates and their duties	On those things because of which men and especially princes are praised or blamed
	On those whom princes choose as secretaries
On treaties	In what way faith is kept by princes

[44] If there were contact of any sort between Erasmus and Machiavelli, the evidence for it is not apparent in the two works under discussion.

WITHOUT a detailed survey, the relation of *The Prince* to its predecessors, contemporaries, and successors can hardly be understood. Hence the chapters will be taken in order, with comment on matters relating to the tradition of works *de regimine principum* and parallels from representative examples. In no instance does a quotation imply that the quoted work is the source of a passage in *The Prince;* while it can hardly be doubted that Niccolò had read a number of the works mentioned, some of the parallels are from earlier writings that he would have been unlikely to see and a few from later authors. The purpose is not to establish indebtedness, but to show to what extent his thought followed and where it departed from traditional lines.

Various students have seen reason to think that this dedication is modeled in part on the address of Isocrates to Nicocles; if they be right, Machiavelli is here proceeding somewhat as did Erasmus in following one of the chief classical works *De regimine principum.* Considering what has been said on Isocrates, one can hardly assert that such imitation is impossible; the oration to Nicocles would have been a normal part of Machiavelli's reading of the classical authors on politics.[1]

Works on the "governi de' principi" are commonly dedicated to some particular prince, usually in much more flattering language than Niccolò employs; he suggests that Lorenzo can really become greater by taking his advice, while it is more conventionally said that the ruler addressed is quite without need of suggestion; for example, Petrus Bizzarus wrote in the dedication of his *De optimo principe* to Queen Elizabeth of England: "Tibi vero (Serenissima Regina) supervacanea est huiusmodi exhortatio, cum nihil unquam praetermittas quod ad veram ac legitimam gubernationem pertinere animadvertas, adeo ut potius caeteris Regibus ac Principibus bene regendi quaedam (ut ita dixerim) forma ideaque sis, quam ut aliorum praeceptis et cohortatione indigeas."[2] More frankly than is usual in such dedications, Machiavelli asserts his own qualifications for the giving of advice. This fits with his feeling that he was a political expert, able to speak on the realities of politics as those hardly could hope to do who had not combined long reading with a life of practical experience. Normally reading alone

[1] Tommasini, *Vita di Machiavelli* 2.110-1, in refutation of the earlier writers, holds that there is no imitation of Isocrates here. He connects the matter, however, with Machiavelli's knowledge of Greek, a consideration not, I take it (see p. 12, above), in point here. The idea of a present to a king appears in the dedications of Clichtoveus and Budè mentioned just below.

[2] "For you (Most Serene Queen) exhortation of this sort is superfluous, since you never neglect anything which you think pertains to true and legitimate rule, so that you are rather for other kings and princes a kind of form and idea (if I may so express it) of ruling well than in need of the precepts and encouragements of others."

Petrarch gives much praise to Francisco Carrara, in *De republica optime administranda,* addressed to him. Erasmus wrote to Charles, in his dedication: "Tuae Celsitudini nihil opus esse cujusquam monitis."—"Your eminence does not need the admonitions of any one" (*Institutio,* col. 559).

is mentioned, as by Machiavelli's contemporary Iodocus Clichtoveus in the dedication of his *De regis officio* (1519): "Libellum inquam de regis officio ac institutione disserentem: et quid regem agere quidve declinare oporteat ex sacrarum literarum promptuario illustriumque virorum sententiis et exemplis edocentem."[3] Writing to give his prince expert advice, rather than diversion,[4] Machiavelli had sound reason to make himself appear as expert as possible, especially since he intended to disagree with the majority. Part of this disagreement and his practical purpose appears in his avoidance of the ornaments "con li quali molti sogliono le loro cose descrivere e ornare."[5] The "molti" here are presumably other writers of advice to princes, though the phrase may apply to authors in general. A phrase in Clichtoveus' dedication seems to confirm Machiavelli's feelings: "Imitatus item et plerosque alios egregios authores: qui de regimine institutioneque principum luculenter et splendide scripserunt."[6] Machiavelli might have added that he differed also from most of his predecessors and many of his successors in writing in a vulgar tongue rather than in Latin.

[3] "A little book, I say, treating the duty and training of a king, and from the repository of the sacred scriptures and the wise sayings and examples of famous men teaching what a king ought to do and to avoid."

[4] Of the purpose of Guillaume Budé in his *Institution du prince* we read: "Il songe à distraire le roi plus encore qu'à l'instruire" (Louis Delaruelle, *Guillaume Budé* 1.202).

[5] "With which many are accustomed to depict and ornament their things" (*Prince*, dedication, p. 3b).

[6] "I have also imitated many other excellent authors who have written excellently and splendidly on the training of princes" (*De regis officio*, dedication). Cf. Petrus Bizzarus, *op. cit.*, dedication: "Sunt, et fuerunt perplures, qui non minus erudite, quam luculenter atque ornate de his quae ad Principis regimen spectant, disseruerunt."—"There are and have been many who have written not less learnedly than excellently and splendidly on those things which pertain to the regimen of princes."

Chapter 1

Quot sint genera principatuum et quibus modis acquirantur.
(The number of types of principates and the way in
which they may be acquired.)

The short first chapter is marked as un-Aristotelian by its
division of governments into two kinds, republics and principates; this is a normal division of Machiavelli's time, and
may be traced historically to Roman history, or in contemporary affairs to the republic of Venice on the one hand and to
the rule by families, such as the Sforza family, on the other.[1] By
principate Machiavelli obviously means monarchy, *regnum*. The
novelty is his emphasis on the new principate, possibly a Tacitean
touch verified in Machiavelli's own experience; it announces what
sort of principate would receive most attention in his work.[2]

[1] The twofold division is essentially that used by Franciscus Patricius Senensis
(1412-94) in his *De regno et regis institutione* 1.1 and his *De institutione reipublicae*
1.1, though he is not ignorant of Aristotle.

[2] To Giuseppe Toffanin (*Machiavelli e il "Tacitismo,"* Padova, 1921) I leave
the discussion of Machiavelli's relation to Tacitus.

Chapter 2

De principatibus hereditariis.
(Of hereditary principates.)

Machiavelli explains that he will not deal with republics because he has elsewhere considered them at length, an obvious reference to the *Discourses on Livy*.[1] The shift from the republicanism of the *Discorsi* to the monarchism of *The Prince* has sometimes been charged to mere willingness to flatter those who had places to give. But in considering the two forms he was not without precedent; in the first chapter of his *De regno et regis institutione* Patricius explains that it is not strange he should compose that work after writing *De institutione reipublicae*. Many of their fundamental principles, he believes with Plato, are the same; "non igitur hoc mihi vitio dandum erit si utrunque tentavero, quum possim superiores testes et complures etiam alios citare qui identidem quoque factitarunt."[2]

Discussion of the advantages of hereditary monarchy is not a new thing. Egidio Colonna in the preface of his *De regimine principum* indicates that he is to be concerned with the principate that is "perpetua"; what should be the conduct of the ruler whose power will endure not merely for his own lifetime but for that of his family? As Machiavelli sets forth the advantages of the hereditary ruler, "il principe naturale," Egidio writes:

Consuetudo est quasi altera natura: propter quod regimina ex consuetudine efficiuntur quasi naturalia. Populus ergo si per diuturnam

[1] Professor Mazzoni holds "che l'opuscolo non è se non una parte di un'opera, o piuttosto della materia per un'opera, cui insiem con esso appartengono *i Discorsi sopra la prima Deca di Tito Livio*."—"The little book is as it were part of a work, or rather part of the material for a work to which the *Discorsi* also pertain" (*Tutte le opere di Machiavelli*, p. xl). Cf. p. 37, below. My quotations on pp. 6-8 go to show that Machiavelli himself recognized the relationship of the works. In the *Discorsi*, however, there seems to be very little suitable for *The Prince* that has not been carried over in a word or a phrase. In the present work I cite passages from the *Discorsi* only when they advance my argument, without attempting to present parallels merely as such. Doubtless I have sometimes read passages in the shorter work in the light of the exposition in the longer one.

[2] "It should, therefore, not be counted a fault in me if I have attempted both, since I am able to cite witnesses in earlier times and many others as well who have indulged in the same practice."

consuetudinem obedivit patribus, filiis, et filiorum filiis, quasi naturaliter
inclinantur ut voluntarie obediant: quare cum omne voluntarium sit
minus onerosum et difficile, ut libentius et facilius obediat populus
mandatis regis, expedit regiae dignitati per hereditatem succedere.[3]

This "natural" rule is the easier because the hereditary prince
is not forced to offend his people by severe measures in order to
maintain himself. The new ruler, however, is inevitably obliged to
new-model the state, even though "non è cosa più difficile a trattare,
nè più dubia a riuscire, nè più periculosa a maneggiare, che farsi capo
a introdurre nuovi ordini; perchè lo introduttore ha per nimici tutti
quelli che degli ordini vecchi fanno bene."[4] He may even have to resort to violence and cruelty, such as Machiavelli is to discuss in chapter eight. But lapse of time allows men to forget these cruelties and
the advantages of their older government, and finally they acquiesce
in an established power, as did the Spaniards in the Roman dominion (*Prince* 4). According to Machiavelli, Tommaso Soderini made
the arguments for heredity his reasons for rejecting the chief power
in Florence and urging the continuance of Medicean rule:

Se volevono che in Firenze si vivesse unito e in pace, e dalle divisioni
di dentro e dalle guerre di fuori securo, era necessario osservare quelli
giovani [Lorenzo e Giuliano de' Medici] e a quella casa la reputazione
mantenere; perchè gli uomini di fare le cose che sono fare consueti mai
non si dolgono: le nuove, come presto si pigliano, così ancora presto
si lasciano; e sempre fu più facile mantenere una potenza la quale con
la lunghezza del tempo abbia spenta la invidia, che suscitarne una nuova
la quale per moltissime cagioni si possa facilmente spegnere.[5]

[3] "Habit is as it were another nature; hence by custom various kinds of government are made as it were natural. Therefore if through daily habit the people has
obeyed fathers, sons, and the sons of sons, it is as though by nature inclined to
voluntary obedience. Hence, since anything voluntary is less onerous and difficult,
if the people is to obey freely and easily the commands of the king, it is expedient
that successions to the kingly dignity should be hereditary" (*De regimine* 3.2.5).

[4] "There is nothing more difficult to discuss, more doubtful of success, nor more
perilous to manage than to carry out the introduction of new customs, because the
introducer has as his enemies all those who profit from the old customs" (*Prince*,
chap. 6, p. 13b).

[5] "If they wished peaceful and united life in Florence, secure from divisions
within and from wars without, it was necessary to respect those young men [Lorenzo
and Giuliano de' Medici] and to maintain the reputation of their house. For men
are never pained by doing the things to which they are accustomed, but new
things are laid down as quickly as they are taken up; therefore it has always been
easier to maintain a power which in the course of time has ceased to inspire envy
than to bring to life a new one which for many reasons can easily be destroyed"
(*Istorie Fiorentine* 7.24, p. 580b).

The same thing was clear to Egidio, who broke from his normal subjection to Aristotle in suggesting that a hereditary ruler has less need for exertion to maintain his power than a new one:

Si quis super aliquos de novo principari coepit, quia contra talem principatum facilius insurgitur; ne cives insurgant in principem, et ut magis unanimiter obediant, incutiendi sunt illis timores de extrinsecis periculis imminentibus; sed si regnum diu in statu perstiterit, et dominus ille sit naturalis, ita quod quasi non sit in memoria hominum ex quo ille et antecessores sui obtinuerunt huiusmodi principatum, tanta cautela non magnam utilitatem habere videtur.[6]

And in the fifteenth century Patricius asserted:

Optabit igitur rex sobolem ex se genitam similem sibi esse non modo effigie, verum virtute, ac moribus, ut rex non decessisse, sed iunior factus esse videatur.

Filius quidem sine periculo regnat, qui optime antecedentis parentis vestigia conterit.[7]

While Patricius' emphasis is chiefly moral, the last sentence hints at wider application; at least it implies that the hereditary ruler who departs from the track of his predecessor rules with peril. The essence of heredity for Machiavelli is in continuance without change; a natural successor who follows an unbeaten path, as did Ferdinand of Aragon according to the twenty-first chapter of *The Prince,* is to be classed with new princes.

Differences between *The Prince* and its predecessors are partly to be explained by the author's deliberate purpose of dealing with a new ruler who will need to establish himself in defiance of custom, though aided, as Machiavelli allows in the twenty-fourth chapter, by the attraction of novelty. Had he been dealing with a hereditary monarch who was to limit himself only to his ancestral do-

[6] "If any one begins anew to rule over others, he should remember that it is rather easy to rebel against such a principate, and therefore, lest the citizens rise against the prince, and that they may more unanimously obey, he should inspire them with terror of imminent perils of foreign attack. But if the kingdom has been long established and its lord is a natural one, so that no one as it were remembers how he and his predecessors obtained the principate they have, so great caution seems not to have much use" (*De regimine* 3.2.15). The ultimate source of the idea of inspiring fear is Aristotle's *Politics* 5.1308a 25 ff.; the application to hereditary and new rulers is not Aristotelian.

[7] "A ruler will desire the offspring he begets to be like himself not merely in appearance but also in virtue and habits, in order that the king may seem not to have died but to have been made younger. For the son reigns without peril who treads exactly in the footsteps of the parent who preceded him" (*De regno* 9.22).

mains, for whom it would be enough "seguire le vestigie del padre,"[8] his treatise would have been more conventional. Most of the works *de regimine principum* are based on settled hereditary rule, with no specific problem of enlarging the kingdom before the ruler. Had Niccolò been considering such conditions, he would have written more in the vein of the others. Castiglione, for example, differs from his contemporary in his conception of the monarch partly because he gives him a much easier problem. But the new ruler who is to form Italy into a new state must have advice suited to the difficulty of his attempt. Moreover, Castiglione and most of the others were generally writing for any ruler, even a weak one; our author, however, started with the assumption of a prince prudent and strong enough to be held equal—when properly advised—to the difficult task before him. To such a man it is hardly necessary to give the elementary instruction required by a young and incapable scion of an established house.

[8] "To walk in the footsteps of his father" (*Prince* 19, p. 39b).

Chapter 3

De principatibus mixtis.
(Of mixed principates.)

This is the first chapter of a group dealing with the new prince—a subject not much considered by writers on the conduct of princes. Wycliffe was conscious that kings might desire such a "mixed principate" as Machiavelli writes of, and cautioned them: "Cum rex debet per se regnum appetere propter opus meritorium, quod non debet duo regna appetere conquirendo, nisi forte, pro destruendis dei hostibus, specialem revelacionem ad illud habuerit."[1] Vincent of Beauvais recognized the practical fact of usurpation of kingly power, even as something that might sometimes receive divine approval.[2] Though Egidio normally considers the established monarch, the new prince once emerges—as though he were familiar enough in practical life—in the chapter entitled *Quae sunt quae salvant dominium regium, et quot oporteat Regem facere ut se in suo principatu conservet.*[3] The "cautela" of waging foreign war is useful for a "principatui in quo quis noviter principari coepit."[4] But in writers nearer Machiavelli the new ruler does not appear.

The present chapter is characteristic of Machiavelli in recognizing that "il tempo si caccia innanzi ogni cosa, e può condurre seco bene come male, e male come bene."[5] With his eye on Time's winged chariot, the wise prince will regard not merely present but also future events and make every effort to forestall them—"quelli con ogni industria obviare." Foresight will enable him to cure ills

[1] "Though a king should desire a kingdom in and for itself for the sake of a meritorious work, yet he should not desire two kingdoms, and attempt a conquest, unless he has a special revelation commanding him to do it that he may destroy the enemies of God" (*De officio regis*, cap. 12, p. 262).

[2] *De institutione morali* chap. 4, "*Quo iure regna quondam usurpata liceat retinere.*"—"How kingdoms that have been usurped may lawfully be retained."

[3] "What are the things that make secure the rule of kings, and how many things it behooves a king to do to preserve himself in his principate" (3.2.15).

[4] "A principate in which some one has newly begun to govern" (3.2.15). See pp. 22, above, and 165 ff., below.

[5] "Time gets ahead of everything, and is able to take along with it good as well as evil, and evil as well as good" (*Prince* 3, p. 8b).

of the state that if neglected will grow beyond the power of medicine.[6] The success of Cosimo de' Medici—who exemplified for Machiavelli many qualities of the prudent ruler—was in part attributable to this foresight: "Sendo prudentissimo, cognosceva i mali discosto, e perciò era a tempo o a non gli lasciare crescere, o a prepararsi in modo che, cresciuti, non lo offendessero."[7] This was high praise, as a later reference to the subject makes plain:

La poca prudenzia degli uomini comincia una cosa, che, per sapere allora di buono, non si accorge del veleno che vi è sotto: come io dissi, di sopra, delle febbre etiche.

Pertanto colui che in uno principato non conosce e' mali quando nascono, non è veramente savio; e questo è dato a pochi.[8]

The prudent Duke Valentino overwent this precept when he considered "che potessi nascere, morendo el padre";[9] yet even he had been unable to imagine all the possible circumstances.[10] On the contrary the Duke of Athens—as a typical foolish ruler—though he

[6] This is one of the many sentiments taken from *The Prince* by Francis Quarles. He renders it: "It is more excellent in a Prince, to have a provident eye for the preventing future mischiefes, then to have a potent arme for the suppressing of present evills: Mischiefes in a State are like Hectique fevers in a body naturall; In the beginning, hard to be knowne, but easily to be cured: but being let alone a while, more easy to be knowne, but harder to be cured" (*Observations Concerning Princes and States* 57). Except for slight verbal differences, the same thing is found in his *Enchyridion* 1.52.

[7] "Being very prudent, he knew evils afar off, and therefore he was in time either to keep them from increasing or to prepare himself in such a manner that when they had increased they did not annoy him" (*Istorie Fiorentine* 7.5, p. 565b). Other passages that exemplify or inculcate foresight, some of them mentioned by Burd, are *Discorsi* 1.32, p. 100b; 33, p. 101a; 51, p. 121b; 3.18, p. 227a; 49, p. 262a. In one instance Cosimo failed; though he foresaw that the Pazzi would be dangerous to the Medici and acted to forestall the danger, his measures proved ineffective (*Istorie Fiorentine* 8.2, p. 591a). See also p. 52, below.

Piero Soderini also possessed prudence enough to foresee a danger to the state, but failed in the policy he adopted to avert it (*Discorsi* 3.3, p. 197b).

[8] "The slight prudence of men commences a thing which, because it presents at first the appearance of good, does not reveal the poison beneath the surface, as I said above about the hectic fever.

"Therefore he who in a principate does not recognize evils when they are concealed is not truly wise; and this power is given to few" (*Prince* 13, p. 28b). The last clause here and the similar one in chapter 3, page 8a ("il che non è dato se non a uno prudente") come from the *Politics* 5.1308a 34; cf. also, for the beginning of an evil, *Politics* 5.1303b 27-31. Machiavelli refers to a prudent rather than a foresighted man perhaps because foresight or *providentia* was part of prudence; see, for instance, Egidio 1.2.8; Aquinas considered it the principal part of prudence (*Summa Theologica* 2.2.49.6, *ad* 1), though he refused to identify the two.

[9] "What could happen if his father died."

[10] *Prince* 7, p. 17b.

feared the hatred gathering against him, had no capacity to provide against it. When in desperation he attempted remedies, they
were "tardi e fuori di tempo, perchè erano forzate e senza grado."[11]

In his demand for foresight, Machiavelli is in harmony with
the tradition. Petrarch, for example, wrote in his *De republica
optime administranda:*

Verum optimus ac providentissimus princeps, non quid delectaret, sed
quid prodesset attendit. Haec nimirum cura frumentaria, tam principum
propria est, ut eam malis quoque et inertibus fuisse comperiam, ex quo,
quanta bonis esse debeat, pronum sit advertere. . . . Consilium est
tamen, ut in prosperis quoque paratus sit animus ad adversa, et velut e
specula, non quid est tantum, sed quid esse possit vigili cogitatione
prospiciat, ne qua eum inopina mutatio rerum turbet.[12]

In the next century Patricius devoted to *providentia* a chapter of his
De regno et regis institutione:

Chilo Lacedaemonius dicebat futurorum providentiam prudenti viro
quadam ratione animi occurrere pro virtute quam in se habet, ut
ostenderet tantum cuique prudentiae esse, quantum virtutis in se fuerit.
. . . Optime quidem fabulati sunt veteres poetae, qui dicunt primam
filiarum summi Dei providentiam extitisse. . . . Haec quidem virtus
in regibus, imperatoribus, ducibus, principibus, magnisque viris maxima
esse videtur, et adeo admiranda, ut quasi divinos eos putemus, qui hoc
providentiae munere praediti sunt.[13]

[11] "Tardy and out of season, because they were forced and ungracious" (*Istorie
Fiorentine* 2.37, p. 439a); cf. *Discorsi* 1.32, 51, and especially *Prince* 8, last sentence.
[12] "But the prince who is most excellent and foresighted observes not what may
please but what may profit. Indeed this care about the grain supply is so proper to
princes that I find it has been exercised even by the evil and slothful; from that
it is easy to conclude how much attention the good should give it. . . . It is
prudence, then, that in prosperity the mind should be prepared for adverse things,
and as though in a mirror not merely should see what is, but by wakeful cogitation
should foresee what can be, that in no way an unexpected change of circumstances
may disturb him" (*Opera*, Basel, 1554, 1.427). See Arpad Steiner, *Petrarch's
Optimus Princeps*, in *The Romanic Review* XXV (1934), 99-111.

The *Secretum secretorum* has a section *De regis providencia contra famem fu-
turam* (cap. 17, p. 55, in *Opera Rogeri Baconi*, Oxford, 1920, Vol. V) and also one
De regis providencia (cap. 10, p. 48). Egidio discusses foresight under prudence,
saying, for example: "Decet [regem] habere providentiam futurorum: quia homines
providentes futura bona, excogitant vias, per quas faciliter illa adipisci valeant."
—"It is well for the king to be able to foresee future events, since men who foresee
future good things think out ways by which they may be able easily to obtain them"
(1.2.8). It also appears under *prudentia* in the *De principe* of Nifo (Firenze, 1521).

[13] "Chilo the Lacedaemonian was accustomed to say that foresight of future
events was presented to the prudent man by reason of a certain faculty of mind in
proportion to the virtue he had in himself, in order that he might show that each
man had as much prudence as he had virtue. . . . Certain ancient poets have

The foresight of this chapter is partly that enabling a prudent ruler to understand what particular conditions in his state portend. It is also the foresight which requires the prince to prepare for possible misfortune of any sort, perhaps quite unpredictable by the wisest man but certain to come because of the variable nature of the world. This general preparation requires from the ruler incessant industry, the opposite of the *ignavia* of the Italian princes who foolishly believed prosperity would be indefinitely prolonged.[14] Presentation of the good ruler as a hard-working man was usual, as may be inferred from the words of Leon Batista Alberti:

Affermava essere veramente cosa difficilissima il reggere uno Imperio a coloro poi che se lo hanno acquistato. Conciosia che quando tu sarai arrivato a quel grado, che ei ti bisogni, che ei dependa dalla sola cura tua, e dalla tua diligentia, la quiete, e la tranquillità di molti, e che ella si mantenga, qual cosa si puo trovare nella vita, che sia piu difficile, o piu faticosa? Aggiugneva a questo che tutte le facende publiche, erano totalmente difficili, e piene di impedimenti, nelle quali se tu ti vorrai affaticare solo senza compagno, tu non sarai bastante a poterlo fare, e se tu ti vorrai servire di altri in metterle ad effetto, incorrerai in infiniti accidenti, e pericoli: e il non ne tener conto, oltre a che saria cosa vergognosa, e da dapochi, ridunderia ancora in tua calamità, e rovina.[15]

Even the medical metaphor, frequent in Machiavelli,[16] of the

---

fabled excellently who say that Foresight came into being as the first of the daughters of the most high God. . . . This virtue appears greatest in kings, emperors, dukes, princes, and great men, and is to be admired to such an extent that we may judge them as though divine who are distinguished by this gift of foresight" (6.12).

[14] *Prince* 24, p. 47b; cf. also 14, pp. 29a, 30b; *Arte della guerra* 2, p. 302b; 7.366b.

[15] "He affirmed that certainly it is a very difficult thing for those who have acquired a state to rule it. For since you will have come to such a condition that the quiet and tranquility of many, and the permanence of their tranquility, is your responsibility and depends on your care alone, what thing can be found in life which is more difficult or more fatiguing? He added to this that all matters of public business are very difficult and full of impediments, and if you wish to labor in them alone without company you will not be sufficient to accomplish it, and if you wish to make use of others in putting them into practice you will run into an infinity of accidents and perils; and if you do not take account of it, besides that that would be a shameful thing, and conduct worthy of worthless persons, the result will be your calamity and ruin" (*Del principe* 2, p. 42, line 11). On the tribulations ("molti affanni") of the ruler see also pp. 81, 94, 101, 228, below.

[16] Tommasini (*Vita di Machiavelli* 2.39) refers to various parts of Machiavelli's work; I have indicated the passages that he seems to have especially in mind. *Prince* 6, p. 13a: "La virtù dello animo loro si sarebbe spenta."—"The virtue of the soul would be exhausted." *Prince* 7, p. 16a: "Purgare gli animi,"—"to purge

prince as the physician of an ailing state, is still more prevalent
among his predecessors than is suggested by Tommasini, who refers to a passage in the *De regimine principum* of Egidio Colonna.[17]
Beroaldus, for example, writes at some length on the prince as physician of the state:

Malos si a malicia revocare non potest per indulgentiam, poena coerceat
per saeveritatem: sic secreti sint a bonis mali. . . . Faciat quod medicus
qui interdum urit, secat, abscindit in corpore membrum quod insanabile
est ne pars integra contagione serpente pariter corrumpatur: iuxta illud
castatissimum: Immedicabile vulnus ense recidendum est, ne pars
sincera trahatur. Consimiliter princeps aliquando secet, amputetque de
corpore civitatis membra putrida: hoc est cives sceleratos, perfidiosos,
turbatores publici commodi; et molitores rerum novarum exterminet,
tollatque de medio. Medici officium est, ut dicebat Asclepiades: et a
Cornelio Celso repetitum est, ut cito, ut tuto, ut iucunde curet: tamen
quandoque austeriore medicina uti cogitur: ad vim morbi gravioris
retundendam profligandamque. Itidem principis officium est ut molliter,
ut delicate, ut indulgenter subditos foveat, curet, tueatur. Nonnunquam
tamen curatione mordaci et austerula utetur. Causticaque adhibebit ad
edomandos duriores civium morbos et omnia molliora malagmata
recusantes.[18]

---

the souls." *Prince* 7, p. 17b: "Rimedio,"—"remedy." *Discorsi* 1.1 passim, on *virtù*
and the effects of climate. *Discorsi* 2.5, p. 147a, on purgations. *Discorsi* 2.30,
p. 189a, the heart. *Discorsi* 3.1, p. 193, a saying of doctors of medicine. Cf. also
Discorsi 3.49, p. 261ab, on the physician and the diseases of the state. Tommasini
refers also to the continuation of the *De regimine principum* (4.23) of Aquinas,
for the organic theory of the state. In the same work (1.2) Aquinas himself com-
pares the prince to a physician. For the subject in earlier times see, e.g., Cicero,
Epistles to Atticus 2.1.7; Seneca, *De clementia* 1.9.6; 1.17.

[17] 3.2.3; cf. 3.2.24.

[18] "If he is not able to bring back the sick from their malady with indulgence,
he should coerce their pains with severity; thus the evil may be separated from the
good. . . . He should proceed like the physician who sometimes burns, cuts,
and takes away a member of the body which is incurable lest the sound part
be equally corrupted by creeping infection, according to that most holy saying: An
incurable wound is to be cut away with the sword lest the healthy part be affected.
The prince in like manner sometimes should cut and amputate from the body of
the state diseased parts; that is, citizens who are wicked, perfidious, and disturbers
of the public good, and he should exterminate those who attempt innovation and
remove them from the midst of the state. It is the function of the physician, as
Asclepiades said and Cornelius Celsus repeats, to cure quickly, safely, and pleasantly,
yet he is sometimes forced to use a more severe remedy to restrain and conquer the
force of a more dangerous disease. So it is the duty of a prince to be gentle, delicate, and indulgent in nourishing, curing, and protecting his subjects. Yet he sometimes uses a means of cure that is biting and rather harsh. He will apply caustics
to eat away the infections of the citizens that are most dangerous and that refuse

se dignũ eſt agit,ſi magiſtratus ſuas obeunt parteis,ſi ple
bes itẽ bonis legibus,& integris magiſtratib⁹ obtempat.
At ubi ſuũ negociũ agit priceps,& magiſtrat⁹ nihil aliud
c̃ɜ cõpilãt populũ,ubi plebes nõ obtempat honeſtis legi
bus,ſed principi ac magiſtratibus utcũ cɜ res tulerit adula/
tur,ibi turpiſſima quædam rerũ confuſio ſit oportet.

Primum ac ſummũ principis ſtudium opoɜtet eſſe , ut
c̃ɜoptime mereatur de republica. At nõ alia re melius po-
teſt mereri,c̃ɜ ſi curet,ut magiſtrat⁹ & officia uiris integer
rimis ac publici cõmodi ſtudioſiſſimis cõmittantur .

**Priceps me
dicus reip.** Princeps qd aliud eſt c̃ɜ medicus reipublicæ ⁊ At medi/
co nõ ſatis eſt,ſi miniſtros habeat peritos,niſi ſit ipſe peri/
tiſſimus ac uigilantiſſimus.Ita principi non ſufficit, ſi magiſtratus habeat probos,niſi ſit ipſe probiſſimus, per quẽ
illi & deliguntur & emendantur .

**Priceps ſũ/
ma ɒs reip.** Vt animi ptes nõ oẽs pinde ualẽt , ſed quædã impant.
aliæ parent,& tñ corpus tantũ paret. Ita princeps ſumma
reip.pars,plurimũ ſapere,& ab oibus craſſis affectib⁹ alie
niſſimũ eſſe oportet.Ad hũc ‚pxime accedẽt magiſtrat⁹,q
partim parẽt,partim impant,parẽt pricipi, impant plebi .

**Magiſtrat⁹
pure creãdi** Ergo præcipue reipublicæ felicitas in hoc ſita eſt, ut pu
re creẽtur magiſtratus,& pure mandentur officia.Deinde
ſit actio male geſti muneris,quemadmodũ antiquis erat
actio repetundarum. Poſtremo ſtatuatur in hos ſeueriſſi
ma animaduerſio, ſi conuicti fuerint .

**Q ſi pure
creãtur ma
giſtratus.** Pure creabunt magiſtratus,ſi princeps eos aſciſcat, nõ
q plurimo emant,nõ qui improbiſſime ambiant,non qui
cognatione cõiunctiores, nõ qui ad illius mores aut affe-
ctus cupiditateſcɜ maxime ſint accõmodi, ſed q moribus
ſint integerrimis,& ad fũctione mãdati mũeris aptiſſimi.

Sig. Pı *verso* from the copy of Erasmus' *Institutio Principis
Christiani,* Basel, 1516, in the library of Duke University.

Machiavelli's contemporary Erasmus inquired: "Princeps quid aliud est quam Medicus Reipublicae?"[19]

Developing his theory of the personal oversight of the ruler in his remark that by residing in a conquered province the conqueror can keep the people from being despoiled by officials, Machiavelli touches on a matter he might be expected to deal with at some length, since it is primary in his theory that a prince who would establish himself cannot have oppressed subjects. Perhaps it is because, in his emphasis on personal rule, he assumes that there will be no independent officials; unlike Alberti, quoted just above, he believes that the prudent monarch will be adequate to manage affairs himself. The ministers Machiavelli later considers are essentially advisers rather than administrators. Such a deputy as Remirro de Orco is exceptional, chosen for a carefully considered purpose and carrying on unpleasant duties which might make the ruler himself unpopular.[20] A prince, however, is likely to be judged from the acts of his deputies unless he restrains them, as Borgia did and as the Emperor Maximinus did not.[21] Niccolò's passing remark on restraining greedy officials would have been easily caught by his contemporaries because it was one of the subjects often written on by advisers of kings. The *Speculum regis* of Simon Islip is almost wholly devoted to oppression of the people by the officers of the king. Nor was there less interest in the matter among Machiavelli's contemporaries. Erasmus, in his chapter entitled *De magistratibus et officiis,* wrote as follows:

Primum ac summum Principis studium oportet esse, ut quam optime mereatur de Republica: at non alia re melius potest mereri, quam si curet ut magistratus et officia viris integerrimis ac publici commodi studiosissimis committantur. . . .

Prudenter admonet in Politicis Aristoteles, super omnia cavendum esse, ne ex magistratibus lucra proveniant iis, qui ea gerunt: alioqui geminum incommodum hinc sequi. Nam primum hac ratione fieri, ut avarissimus quisque et corruptissimus ambiat, imo occupet et invadat magistratum, et populus duplici discrucietur molestia, tum quod ab honoribus excluditur, tum quod lucro privatur.[22]

---

all pleasanter remedies" (*De optimo statu,* folio 128). For an example from Patricius see p. 139, note, below, and for one from Erasmus see p. 40.

[19] "What is the prince other than the physician of the state?" (*Institutio,* cap. 7, col. 601).

[20] See pp. 156 ff., below.   [21] *Prince* 19, p. 40a.

[22] "The first and greatest ambition of the prince should be to deserve as well as possible of the state, and by nothing can he obtain greater merit than by taking care

Clichtoveus, like Gower, told the old story of Cambyses, who flayed an unjust judge and used his skin as a seat for his successors that they might take warning.[23]

At the end of this third chapter Machiavelli gives "a general rule": "Chi è cagione che uno diventi potente, rovina; perchè quella potenzia è causata da colui o con industria o con forza, e l'una e l'altra di queste due è sospetta a chi è diventato potente."[24] In his note on the passage Burd (p. 200) explains it from Aristotle's *Politics* 1315 a:

It is a precaution which is taken by all monarchs not to make one person great; but if one, then two or more should be raised, that they may look sharply after one another. If after all some one has to be made great, he should not be a man of bold spirit; for such dispositions are ever most inclined to strike.

Aristotelian advice to Lorenzo de' Medici against allowing Iacopo Pazzi (with his family) to grow great is found in *Istorie Fiorentine* 8.2, p. 591a. This, with the account in the *Discorsi*[25] of conspiracies by men who have become so great that they lack nothing but official authority—"se non il regno"—suggests Machiavelli's knowledge of this bit of Aristotelian precept.

But the immediate circumstances of this chapter are somewhat different. The author is dealing not with a subject made great by a ruler, but with foreign affairs in which one potentate owes his position to another. It is true that Machiavelli did not hesitate to apply the same general principle to both internal and external affairs.[26]

that the magistracies and public offices are committed to men of firm integrity and thoroughly desirous of the public good. . . .

"Aristotle prudently advises in the *Politics* that it should above all be avoided that money should come from the magistracies to those who are entrusted with them; otherwise a twofold abuse will result. For first it will come about that for this reason every man who is very avaricious and corrupt will strive for, nay will seize and usurp a magistracy, and the people will be tortured with double pain, being both excluded from honors and deprived of money" (*Institutio* 7.601-602). Cf. in Nifo's *Libellus de principe* the chapter entitled *Quod optimi principes bonis ac iustis ministris uti debeant.—That the best princes should employ good and just ministers.*

[23] Clichtoveus, *De regis officio,* cap. 13, p. 49; Gower, *Confessio Amantis* 7.2889 ff. See also the quotation from Erasmus on p. 40, below.

[24] "He who is the cause that a man becomes powerful ruins himself; for he causes that power either through industry or through force, and both of these are objects of suspicion to him who has become powerful" (*Prince* 3, p. 10a).

[25] 3.6, p. 202a. Cf. the quotation from Egidio on p. 173, below.

[26] E.g., pp. 48, 136, 147, 175, below.

Yet here he is not dealing with the making great of one single person and is quite against the elevation of two. The words "acresciuto in Italia potenzia a uno potente"[27] are to be paired with "messo in quella uno forestiere potentissimo,"[28] as is indicated by the later sentence: "La grandezza, in Italia, di quella [la Chiesa] e di Spagna è stata causata da Francia, e la ruina sua causata da loro."[29] Two have been made great and both have contributed to ruin. In the general rule (chi è cagione che uno etc.) *uno* may be interpreted in the sense of *alcuno, anyone*,[30] rather than as a numeral. One ruler who makes another powerful is likely to be ruined because the recipient of favors fears that the industry and force of his patron will be turned against him; suspicion is inevitable when power rests "semplicemente in sulla voluntà e fortuna di chi lo ha concesso loro, che sono dua cose volubilissime e instabili";[31] fearing a change in the will or fortune of his patron, the creature endeavors to secure himself from his creator without regard for gratitude.

That a weak state is a normal and potential enemy of a powerful one that it suspects of designs on it is elsewhere asserted by Machiavelli: "Ogni città, ogni stato, debbe reputare inimici tutti coloro che possono sperare di poterle occupare el suo, e da chi lei non si può difendere. Nè fu mai nè signoria nè republica savia che volessi tenere lo stato suo a discrezione d'altri, o che, tenendolo, gliene paressi aver securo."[32] With respect rather to an able minister than another prince as the cause of greatness, we read in the *Capitolo dell' Ingratitudine:*

[27] "Power in Italy accumulated in the hands of one powerful man" (*Prince* 3, p. 9b).
[28] "Placed in that a very powerful foreigner" (*Prince* 3, p. 9b).
[29] "The greatness in Italy of the Church and of Spain was caused by France, and the ruin of France was caused by them" (*Prince* 3, p. 10a).
[30] Cf. chap. 12, p. 25a: "se uno tiene lo stato."
[31] "Simply on the will and fortune of him who has conceded it to them, and they are two things most shifting and uncertain" (*Prince* 7, p. 14b).
[32] "Every city, every state, ought to reckon as enemies all those who can hope to have the power to take it as their own, and from whom it cannot defend itself. There never was a wise lordship or republic which wished to hold its organization at the discretion of others, or that when so holding it seemed to have it secure against them (*Parole sopra la provisione del danaio*, p. 789ab).
Cf. the letter to Vettori (*Lettere familiari* 38, p. 163): "Li minori potenti, e che hanno paura di te, subito corrono sotto il vincitore, e danno a quello occasione d'offenderti."—"The lesser rulers and those who are afraid of you quickly run to the protection of the conqueror and give him occasion to act against you."

E vedrai come e' mutator di stati
E donator di regni sempre mai
Son con esilio o morte ristorati.

Perchè, quando uno stato mutar fai,
Dubita chi tu hai principe fatto,
Tu non gli tolga quel che dato gli hai;

E non ti osserva poi fede nè patto,
Perchè gli è più potente la paura
Ch' egli ha di te, che l'obligo contratto.[33]

Castruccio Castracani went even further in his conduct to a private citizen to whom he owed his rise:

Avendo fatto morire uno cittadino di Lucca, il quale era stato cagione della sua grandezza, ed essendogli detto che egli aveva fatto male ad ammazzare uno de' suoi amici vecchi, rispose che e' se ne ingannavano, perchè aveva morto uno inimico nuovo.[34]

Castruccio believed that the man who had aided him realized that those raised to high place were natural enemies[35] of their benefactors; hence, by still a further step, the former friend, fearing Castruccio, had become an enemy. The *regola generale* of this chapter is, then, an application of the axiom of chapter seven: "Gli uomini offendono o per paura o per odio."[36] Those who fear one are as a matter of course to be considered as enemies.

[33] "You will see how the changers of governments and the givers of kingdoms are always rewarded with exile or death. Because, when you have changed a government, the man you have made prince always suspects that you will take away from him what you have given him; and he will not observe either faith or contract, because his fear of you is more important than the obligation he has contracted" (lines 169-77, p. 844). For the minister who is feared, cf. pp. 183-4, note, below; for the obligation erased by fear, p. 54, below.

[34] "After he had put to death a citizen of Lucca who had been a cause of his rise to power, it was said to him that he had done an evil deed in killing one of his old friends. But he answered that the facts were quite different, because he had killed a new enemy" (*Vita di Castruccio,* near the end, p. 762b).

[35] "Debbono offendere" (*Prince* 7, p. 17b). Note the use of *dovere* in this connection in the quotations on pp. 43, 54, below.

[36] "Men injure others either because of fear or because of hate" (p. 17b). See p. 47, below. A modern expression of the notion that the former patron can be a cause of ruin is found in words attributed to Matthew S. Sloan, when president of the Brooklyn Edison Company: "Don't forget the people who made you, in the days of your prosperity. They can break you."

Chapter 4

Cur Darii regnum quod Alexander occupaverat a successoribus suis
post Alexandri mortem non defecit.
(Why the realm of Darius which Alexander had occupied did not fall
away from his successors after the death of Alexander.)

This chapter continues the third, in order to dispose of an argument from history. It exhibits the author's combination of the
narratives of contemporary writers, including himself, with those
of historians.[1] Its effect is to show that the problem of a new
prince in Italy would be difficult, requiring more virtue than suf-
ficed Alexander for the conquest of all Asia. By implication, however, the task in Italy is not impossible to the right sort of prince,
if he will take to heart Machiavelli's advice. Italy would offer a less
difficult problem than France, where permanent occupation by a
new ruler would be impossible, for however vigorous he might be,
he could not hope to retain control in time of stress. But the reorganization of Italy, according to Machiavelli's estimate, is not
beyond the power of a wise and courageous leader.

[1] Note Machiavelli's *Ritratto di cose di Francia.*

Chapter 5

Quomodo administrandae sunt civitates vel principatus, qui, antequam
occuparentur, suis legibus vivebant.
(In what way one should administer states or principates that, before
they were occupied, lived under their own laws.)

This chapter is quite out of the path of the normal work *de
regimine principum* because it is dependent on an idea not fully
presented until the last chapter of *The Prince,* but dominant
throughout, that of uniting and delivering Italy. Machiavelli's new
prince, as in his reorganization he attempts to bring the whole
peninsula under his control, must conquer or in some way secure
not merely the states of other princes but also free republics. Before
the latter necessity the statesman, though inclined to favor free institutions, does not hesitate. The management of states recently
free is a highly difficult task demanding a prince of prudence and
courage, ready to learn from competent advisers, such as the Florentine secretary believed himself to be.

Chapter 6

De principatibus novis qui armis propriis et virtute acquiruntur.
(Of new principates which are acquired by one's own arms and ability.)

This chapter, on new princes who have conquered their states,
is more obviously related to the parts of Aristotle's *Politics* dealing
with tyrants than what preceded. Aristotle's ideas were well known
long before Machiavelli; Egidio, for example, gives to a chapter depending directly on *Politics* V the title: *Quae et quot sunt cautelae,
quibus tyrannus nititur se in suo dominio praeservare.*[1] Egidio, as
might be supposed, wholly disapproves of the tyrant. After Machiavelli's time there was a change; Frachetta, for example, in his
Prencipe (1597), devotes a chapter to the conquering prince: *"Qual
sia maggior difficoltà ò acquistare uno Stato, ò conservarlo; e se sia
meglio attendere alla conservatione, ò all' ampliamento."* One is
tempted to think of Frachetta as a pupil of Machiavelli; if so, he is
a concealed pupil, for the passages in his work that seem Machiavellian are assigned, with propriety, to Tacitus, Polybius, and other
classical authors.[3]

Asserting that new princes in order to establish themselves—
"per fondare lo stato loro e la loro securtà"[4]—are forced to introduce new laws and methods of government, Machiavelli yet develops this necessity for innovation as one of the things that makes
the position of the new ruler precarious because of the offence that
his changes will inevitably give. Duke Valentino, as an able ruler,
was successful in his innovations.[5] Changes in law and customs
may be either for the benefit of the public or to maintain the
ruler; in the practice of the prudent king the two would generally

[1] "What and how many are the precautions with which a tyrant strives to preserve himself in his dominion" (*De regimine* 3.2.10).

[2] "Whether there is more difficulty in acquiring a state or in keeping it; and
whether it is better to attend to its preservation or to its increase" (1.21).

[3] Perhaps Frachetta wished to appear classical. Both Erasmus and Machiavelli,
as is remarked on p. 12, above, neglect their contemporary indebtedness. In his
Seminario de' governi di stato, however, Frachetta makes acknowledged use of
Guicciardini and others not far removed in date; he may have been unwilling to
appear a Machiavellian. For something on Frachetta see Toffanin, *Machiavelli e il
"Tacitismo,"* pp. 157-8.

[4] *Prince* 6, p. 13b.   [5] *Prince* 7, p. 17b.

correspond, as in the reforms demanded for the establishment of a citizen army founded on the well-organized state. In extreme cases reorganization, to be effective, must be so cruel as to lead a humane man to retire to private life rather than attempt to carry it through. But though the prudent ruler will give the state the new laws and customs required by necessity, he will proceed with caution, disturbing as little as possible the minds of his subjects.

Without the prince a state is unlikely to be reformed; at least, "egli è necessario essere solo a volere ordinare una republica di nuovo, o al tutto fuor degli antichi suoi ordini riformarla."[6] Sufficiently farseeing and influential citizens to urge reform may be lacking and the people are sluggish, and, in proportion as they are corrupt, opposed to betterment.

Da tutte le soprascritte cose nasce la difficultà, o impossibilità, che è nelle città corrotte, a mantenervi una republica, o a crearvela di nuovo. E quando pure la vi si avesse a creare o a mantenere, sarebbe necessario ridurla più verso lo stato regio, che verso lo stato popolare; acciocchè quegli uomini i quali dalle leggi, per la loro insolenzia, non possono essere corretti, fussero da una podestà quasi regia in qualche modo frenati. E a volergli fare per altre vie diventare buoni, sarebbe o crudelissima impresa o al tutto impossibile.[7]

Corrupt Italy, thought Machiavelli, was in need of complete reorganization. The curse of mercenary soldiers, for example, could be removed only by fundamental changes in the habits of the citizens. Military virtue was lacking in the land because "gli ordini antiqui di essa non erano buoni, e non ci è suto alcuno che abbi saputo trovare de' nuovi."[8] They can be found only by a powerful and prudent prince who will devise and enforce new laws to make men good.[9]

[6] "Only an absolute ruler can expect to give a republic a new organization and make a complete reformation of its old laws" (*Discorsi* 1.9, title).

[7] "From all the things mentioned above rises the difficulty or impossibility of maintaining a republic or of creating one anew in a city that is corrupt. And when you have laid on you the task of creating or maintaining it, you will find it necessary to bring it more toward the kingly than toward the popular organization, in order that men who because of their insolence cannot be corrected by the laws may be in some fashion restrained by a power like that of a king. And to wish to make them become good in other ways would be either a very cruel attempt or wholly impossible" (*Discorsi* 1.18, p. 88b). For cruelty see also *Discorsi* 1.26.

[8] "Its old regulations in military matters were not good and no one has arisen who has known how to find new ones" (*Prince* 26, p. 50b).

[9] *Discorsi* 1.3. Cf. p. 43, below.

It thus appears that Machiavelli's treatise on the prince is to be
explained by his concern with the *verità effettuale* of Italian life
and not by any abandonment of his republican preferences.[10] If
he had felt that a republic could reform Italy, doubtless he would
have preferred such a government, but here as elsewhere he is willing to accept something not ideally desirable but yet possible, rather
than by untimely perfectionism to forgo hope of improvement.
There need be no recourse to the traditional explanation of abandonment of conviction in the hope of personal advantage.

In a review of Federico Chabod's *Del Principe di N. Machiavelli*,
G. Solari writes:

Non si comprende come il Machiavelli, segretario della repubblica
fiorentina, vittima della restaurazione medicea, ammiratore di Livio e
di Roma repubblicana, abbia potuto quasi contemporaneamente, nel
1513, esaltare nei *Discorsi* i governi popolari e fare nel *Principe* l'apologia
della monarchia e della tirannide. L'antica dottrina invocava secrete
mire, ragioni di interesse personale a spiegare la duplice contradizione,
psicologica e dottrinale, tra i *Discorsi* e il *Principe*. Nella critica più
moderna mentre si attenuano le ragioni d'interesse che potevano spingere
il Machiavelli a cercare il favore dei Medici (a cui il *Principe* è dedicato),
si rivela la tendenza a risolvere la contraddizione dottrinale in una
fondamentale coerenza e unità, per cui le due opere avrebbero identica
l'ossatura e comune il fondo, cioè la virtù, che si ordina variamente
in rapporto alla materia del soggetto.

. . . Sotto la pressione degli avvenimenti, in seguito ad un più
sereno apprezzamento della realtà, egli siasi indotto ad abbandonare i
suoi ragionamenti sulle antiche repubbliche incompatibili collo stato
di corruzione in cui trovavasi l'Italia, ed abbia invocato per la sua
salvezza un principe virtuoso che facesse per essa ciò che altri principi
virtuosi avevano fatto ad es. per Francia e Spagna, ciò che il Valentino
aveva tentato per l'Italia. La contraddizione più che nel Machiavelli
era nelle cose. Chi aveva vissuto l'anacronismo di un governo popolare
in Firenze con tutte le sue debolezze e insufficienze, e aveva assistito
alla restaurazione incontrastata dei Medici, doveva nella solitudine
dell' esilio porsi la domanda: repubblica o monarchia? E la risposta
nelle particolari condizioni d'Italia non poteva esser dubbia per il
Machiavelli che non aveva l'idolatria delle forme di governo e queste
considerava come mezzo per attuare lo Stato forte. Non crediamo che
l'autore abbia tenuto nel debito conto la dottrina machiavellica della
necessità, la quale sottrae la scelta dei mezzi all' arbitrio dell' individuo
ed esprime la ragion di Stato. Le ragioni di tornaconto personale non

---

[10] See also p. 43, below.

furono estranee, ma perdono di valore di fronte a quelle che scaturivano della stessa realtà storica e dalla esperienza vissuta dal Machiavelli.[11]

With the presentation of kingship as abstractly the best form of government, sanctioned by God and "in rebus inanimis et brutis animantibus impressa legi,"[12] frequent in works *de regimine principum* Machiavelli would not have agreed, but under certain circumstances he did consider it superior to republican forms. He could not have echoed, with Beroaldus, the condemnation of Cicero: "Non est consilium in vulgo: non ratio: non discrimen: non diligentia."[13] Yet he was familiar with the arguments for kingship advanced by his predecessors and in the Italy of his day was willing to say with them, after Homer: "Unus sit dominus, unus rex."[14] He

[11] "It is not understood how Machiavelli, secretary of the Florentine republic, victim of the restoration of the Medici, admirer of Livy and of republican Rome, still could almost at the same time, in 1513, exalt popular governments in the *Discorsi* and in *The Prince* present an apology for monarchy and tyranny. The old theory invoked secret aims and reasons of selfish interest to explain the double contradiction, both psychological and in their ideas, between the *Discorsi* and *The Prince*. In more recent criticism, while less is made of the reasons of interest that were able to stimulate Machiavelli to seek the favor of the Medici (to whom *The Prince* is dedicated), a tendency is revealed to resolve the contradiction of idea into a fundamental coherence and unity, through which the two works would have an identical framework and a common background, that is *virtù*, which is variously handled in relation to the matter of the subject. . . .

"Under the pressure of events, after a calmer estimate of the reality, he was influenced to abandon his beliefs on ancient republics as inharmonious with the state of corruption in which Italy was placed, and invoked for her salvation a virtuous prince who would do for her what other virtuous princes had done, for example in France and Spain, and what Valentino had attempted for Italy. The contradiction was not so much in Machiavelli as in the facts. After he had seen the anachronism of a popular government in Florence with all its weakness and inadequacy, and had been present at the uncontested restoration of the Medici, he might in the solitude of exile ask himself: republic or monarchy? In the special conditions of Italy the reply could not be doubtful for Machiavelli, who did not idolize the forms of government and considered them as means for giving reality to the strong state. It seems that insufficient weight has been given to the Machiavellian doctrine of necessity, which takes the selection of means from the judgment of the individual and expresses the reason of the state. Reasons of personal profit were not extraneous but they lose value in comparison with those which rise from deep historical reality and from the experience that Machiavelli has lived through" (*Rivista Storica Italiana*, XLIV, 1927, 42-4). For the King in France and Spain, see *Discorsi*, 1.55, p. 126b.

[12] "To be seen written in inanimate things and in brute beasts" (Clichtoveus, *De regis officio*, cap. 1, p. 6).

[13] "In the multitude there is no discretion, no reason, no judgment, no diligence" (Beroaldus, *De optimo statu*, folio 124 recto).

[14] "There should be one lord, one king" (ibid., verso). Cf. Machiavelli, *Discorsi* 1.9.

could see reason in the opinion of Guicciardini who, though uphold-
ing free institutions, yet admitted:

Da altro canto si può considerare (presupponendo che lo stato della
repubblica sia in uno termine che non si riparando la conduca in una
ruina certa, nè si possi per le corruttele della Città o divisione de'
cittadini darli rimedio se non col costrignerlo) che gli è pure meglio
provvedere con modo estraordinario alla salute pubblica, che lasciarla ire
in perdizione. Le leggi medesime, se le potessino parlare, consentirebbono
in questo caso di essere violate una volta per cavare di questa violenza
la sua perpetua conservazione; le quali tutte sogliono in ogni proibizione
eccettuare i casi della necessità. E certo non si può dire che guardi le
leggi quello che per non contravvenire loro le lasci rovinare, nè si può
dire amatore della libertà chi, perchè la non sia violata, la lascia perdere.
Denominansi tutti li atti delli uomini, o buoni o mali, secondo il fine
loro; e però non si potrà dire se non buona e lecita forza quella che si
fa a fine di levare la forza.[15]

In wishing new laws and yet seeing danger in them Machiavelli was not himself an innovator. With an Aristotelian basis
Egidio discussed the matter in a chapter entitled *Quod quantum
possibile est, sunt leges patriae observandae, et quod cavendum
assuescere innovare leges.*[16] Holding that bad laws should be ex-
tirpated, he concludes: "Decet ergo reges et principes observare
bonas consuetudines principatus et regni, et non innovare patrias
leges, nisi fuerint rectae rationi contrariae."[17] Like most of his opinions, this gained currency. Léon Batista Alberti gave innovation
a place in a brief account of the office of the prince:

[15] "From the other side one can consider (on the supposition that the condition
of the state is such that if it is not reformed ruin will certainly ensue, and that
because of the corruptions of the city or division of the citizens there is no remedy
except in force) that it is better to provide for the public safety in some extraordinary
manner than to let it go to ruin. The laws themselves, if they were able to speak,
would consent in these circumstances to be violated once in order to derive from
this violence their permanent preservation. All such laws are accustomed in every
prohibition to make exception of cases of necessity. And surely he cannot be said
to keep the laws who in order not to break them lets them go to ruin, nor can
he be called a lover of liberty who, that it may not be violated, permits it to be
lost. All the acts of men, good or bad, are named according to their ends; therefore a force which is employed with the purpose of removing force cannot be
called anything other than a good and permissible force" (*Delle buone leggi e della
forza, Opere inedite* 10.380).

[16] "That as much as is possible the laws of one's country are to be kept, and
that a ruler should avoid forming the habit of making new laws" (*De regimine*
3.2.31).

[17] "Therefore it is fitting for kings and princes to observe the good usages of a
principate or a kingdom, and not to make anew the laws of their lands, unless
the old laws are contrary to right reason" (ibid.).

Astengasi dallo innovare delle cose, se gia la molta necessità di mantenere la degnita dell' imperio, non lo forzasse à questo, o che non se gli offerisse una certissima speranza di accrescere la gloria.[18]

However different in temperament, Erasmus would have seen much truth in Machiavelli's opinion that "non è cosa più difficile a trattare, nè più dubia a riuscire, nè più periculosa a maneggiare, che farsi capo a introdurre nuovi ordini,"[19] though at the same time he would have agreed that innovation is sometimes imperative:

Ut in morbis non sunt tentanda nova remedia, si veteribus succurri malo possit: ita non sunt condendae novae leges, si veteres ministrent aliquid, quo malis Reipublicae medearis.

Leges inutiles si sine magno malo non queant abrogari, paulatim sunt antiquandae, aut certe corrigendae. Nam ut periculosum est temere novare leges, ita necesse est ut curationem pro corporum ratione, sic leges ad praesentem Reipublicae statum accommodare; quaedam salubriter instituta, salubrius abrogantur.

Multae leges recte quidem sunt institutae, sed eas officiorum pravitas ad pessimos usus detorsit.[20] Nihil autem perniciosius bona lege, ad malas res deflexa. Ab his igitur tollendis aut emendandis, non oportet Principem fisci jactura deterreri. Nec enim compendium est, quod sit cum honesti dispendio conjunctum, maxime cum sint ejus generis, ut plausibilis etiam sit earum abrogatio. Neque vero sibi blandiatur, si leges hujusmodi compluribus in locis invaluerunt, ac diutina jam consuetudine inveteratae sunt. Nec enim hominum numero constat honesti natura, et hoc diligentius est tollendum, quo magis inveteravit malum.[21]

[18] "He should abstain from making things over, unless strong necessity for maintaining the dignity of his rule forces him to it, or unless it offers him a sure hope of increasing his glory" (*Del principe* 4.119, line 25). Cf. *Prince* 26, p. 50b: "Veruna cosa fa tanto onore a uno uomo che di nuovo surga, quanto fa le nuove legge e li nuovi ordini trovati da lui."—"Nothing brings so much honor to a man who rises to new power as do the new laws and new ordinances that he devises."

[19] "There is nothing more difficult to treat, nor more doubtful in its issue, nor more perilous to manage than to succeed in introducing new laws" (*Prince* 6, p. 13b).   [20] See p. 29, above.

[21] "As in diseases new remedies are not to be experimented with if it is possible to help the trouble with old ones, so new laws are not to be established if the old ones furnish anything with which you may medicate the ills of the state.

"If useless laws cannot be abolished without much trouble, they are little by little to be allowed to fall into disuse or at least are to be corrected. For as it is dangerous to make new laws rashly, it is yet necessary to adapt the laws to the present condition of the state, as it is to fit the treatment of a disease to human bodies; laws which it was praiseworthy to establish it may be more praiseworthy to abolish.

"There are many laws which were rightly enacted, but which the wickedness of officials twists to the worst uses. Nothing is worse than a good law twisted to evil

One part of the chapter is conventional enough, that on the imitation of the famous. Beroaldus, for instance, says he will proceed by example—"per exempla maximorum principum decurrentes";[22] he refers to Alexander, Antonius [sic] Pius, Augustus, and Trajan. Petrarch writes to Francesco Carrara: "Quoniam te non nisi bonis et illustribus comparatum velim, hos imitare obsecro, atque horum exempla complectere, qui rebus ac verbis, claram laudem iustitiae meruerunt."[23] He gives as examples Antoninus Pius, Constantine, and others.

Here, as frequently, Machiavelli touches on the relation of virtue and fortune to the success of princes. Beroaldus had already accepted the success of the Romans as resulting from virtue and fortune, for "virtus et fortuna plaerumque alioquin dissidentes mutuo concordiae nexu convenerunt."[24] This was necessary to the prosperity of the republic, because "virtus enim sine fortuna manca est et mutila."[25]

---

purposes. The prince, therefore, should not be deterred from canceling or emending these by a diminution in revenue, for that is no saving that is linked with loss of honor, especially when the laws in question are of such a sort that their abrogation is worthy of applause. Nor should the ruler be allured into keeping laws of this kind, even if they have come into use in many places and grown old in long-established custom. For the nature of the honorable is not determined by numbers, and in proportion as an evil becomes more venerable it is the more diligently to be removed" (Erasmus, *Institutio principis* 6.599 B-C). See also ibid. 3.592 B, where the margin gives "Novitas omnis periculosa." This is translated by Spenser's "All change is perillous, and all chaunce unsound" (*Faerie Queene* 5.2.36), and "All Innovation is perilous" (*View of the Present State of Ireland*, p. 649, Globe ed.).

[22] *De optimo statu*, folio 125 recto.

[23] "Although I should not wish you to be compared except with good and illustrious men, I beseech you to imitate and wholly follow the example of those who by deeds and words show that they deserve high praise for their justice" (*De republica optime administranda*, p. 427). Cf. p. 75, below.

[24] "Virtue and fortune came together in the mutual connection of concord, though usually they act differently by dissenting" (*De optimo statu*, folio 133 verso).

[25] "Virtue without fortune is incomplete and defective" (ibid.).

Chapter 7

De principatibus novis qui alienis armis et fortuna acquiruntur. (Of new principates which are acquired by alien arms and by fortune.)

This characteristic chapter shows Machiavelli's independence of the usual advisers of the prince; he illustrates from his own experience and shows the importance to the new ruler of prudence, capacity, and courage. While perhaps making his hero Caesar too great,[1] he is willing to admit a defect even in his prudence. Above all, he recognizes the limits of human forethought; even a magnified Caesar is not complete master of human affairs, but must yield to Fortune at her worst—"una estraordinaria ed estrema malignità di fortuna."[2] Though he is Machiavelli's model prince, he is in some respects also the good prince of most writers *de regimine principum*. His people love and respect him, he is approachable, magnanimous, and liberal. Apparently these qualities are here accepted by Machiavelli as showing the good ruler, however much he later modifies his approval of them. On the other hand he exemplifies qualities not generally praised by the advisers of princes, as in the use of fraud.

One of the methods of Valentino, elsewhere approved in *The Prince,*[3] was that of gaining friends by honoring men of importance—"di condotte e di governi."[4] Long before, Egidio, following Aristotle, had recommended the politic use of the same method:

Secundum praeservans politiam et regnum regium, est bene uti iis qui sunt in regno, introducendo eos ad aliquos principatus, honorando eos, et non iniuriando eis. Nam ut innuit Philosophus in politicis bene uti civibus non solum praeservat politiam rectam, sed etiam principatus ex hoc durabilior redditur, dato quod in ipso sit aliquid obliquitatis admixtum.[5]

[1] See Gaetano Mosca, *Saggi di storia della scienza politica* 1.10, pp. 67 ff. For Remirro de Orco, see p. 156, below.   [2] *Prince* 7, p. 15a.
[3] Chaps. 9, 21.   [4] *Prince* 7, p. 15b.
[5] "A second preservative of the government and rule of kings is to treat well those who are in the kingdom, putting them in places of authority, honoring them, and not doing injury to them. For as the Philosopher says in the *Politics,* proper treatment of the citizens not merely preserves a political organization of the best form, but a principate, even though it have some admixture of imperfection, is made more durable by it" (*De regimine* 3.2.15).

Quomodo noui Principatus, qui fortuna acquiruntur conſeruentur. Cap. VII•

Qvi uero fortuna ſolum fauente ex priuatis Reges euadunt,facile quidem tolluntur,repente ueio ruunt.Nam ludens fortuna aliquibus plerunq; initium facile,finem uero per diſſicilem facit, euenit autem hoc iis plerunq;qui gratis,aut præcio,aut fauore , principatum accipiunt,ueluti in Græcia a Romanis ducibus in Ionia,atq; Helleſponto nonnulli ciues Principatum acceperunt,Romæ etiam uiri humiles,& priuati a militum turba nonnunquam corruptione,atq;fauore imperatores creati ſunt,poſtmodum breui tempore ſublati,nec ab ratione quidem , nam cum priuate uixerint,bene regere nec poſſunt,nec ſciunt. Nihil enim difficilius(ut Diocletianus dicere ſolebat)ĝ bene imperare, nec minor (ut Ouidius) uirtus eſt parta tueri ĝ noua comparare caſus ineſt illic . Hic erit artis opus,difficultatem uero auget, quia hi,qui eos crearunt,fideles plerunq; non habent•Præter ea in naturæ operibus cernimus,ut quæ celeriter creſcunt, ce leriter pereant. Vnde & prouerbium eſt nimium feſtinata non eſſe diuturna.His igitur,qui fortuna fauente ad imperium adnolant,ut ſe ſeruēt,hoc unum remedium eſt (ut uirtutem fortunæ ſociam quo ad poſſunt) adhibeant•Sic enim agendo, difficultates,quæ poſtea ſuccedunt,facillime ſuperabunt. Stabilito uero his artibus imperio,quæ ſibi obſtare uidebuntur, deleant•Milites,qui mutabiles erant,deponant• Proprios autem creent.Cæteraq; ea ratione diſponant,qua regno ſecuritas • Ciuium uero tranquillitas comparetur . Huius rei teſtes ſunt Franciſcus Sfortia,ac Cæſar Borgia ,ille quidem fortuna fauente, Mediolanenſium . Hic uero patris fortuna urgente multorum principatu potitur. Verum Franciſcus ſua uirtute, atq; prudentia ſe ſecurauit.Borgia uero patris fortuna reflāte, regnum amiſit.Cauſa autem eſt Nam Frāciſcus uirtutem atq; prudentiam cum fortuna coniunxit.Borgia uero crudelitate, atq; ſcelera.

In condemning the bad government of the princes of the Romagna, Machiavelli charges that they had not "corrected"[6] their subjects, in contrast with the admirable conduct of Caesar who when he obtained power exchanged "con nuovi modi gli ordini antiqui."[7] To this correcting of subjects Machiavelli elsewhere refers, going so far as to assert: "Gli uomini non possono e non debbono essere fedeli servi di quello signore da el quale e' non possono essere nè difesi nè corretti."[8] Correction here represents the administration of justice often linked with defense as one of the chief duties of the ruler.[9] As in the instance of the ambitious and oppressive nobles mentioned in *Prince* 19, p. 37a, anyone restrained by the laws from improper conduct or punished for it is said to be corrected. Sometimes the word hardly means more than *organize;* for example, in speaking of the common people in revolt, Machiavelli declares: "Una moltitudine così concitata, volendo fuggire questi pericoli, ha subito a fare infra sè medesima uno capo che la corregga, tenghila unita e pensi alla sua difesa."[10] It may be applied to the salutary effect of laws which act on rulers as a "freno che gli può corregere."[11] The tyrant is the ruler not corrected by law.[12] Princes, like ordinary men, are made good by the laws. As Beroaldus puts it, "lex . . . vitiorum emendatrix."[13] When the correcting and restraining power of the laws is inadequate, the power of a single ruler is needed: "Quegli uomini i quali dalle leggi, per la loro insolenzia, non possono essere corretti, fussero da una podestà quasi regia in qualche modo frenati."[14] Apparently the Italy of

[6] *Prince* 7.16a.

[7] "The old rules for new ways of conduct" (*Prince* 7.17b).

[8] "Men cannot be and ought not to be faithful servants to a lord by whom they can be neither defended nor corrected" (*Parole da dirle sopra la provisione del danaio,* p. 789b). See also *Discorsi* 1.18, p. 88b; 3.1, p. 196a; 3.49, pp. 261b-262a; *Provisione prima per istituire milizie:* "per poter raffrenare e correggere i sudditi." —"through having power to restrain and correct the subjects" (*Opere,* 1813, IV, 428).

[9] Cf. Aquinas, *De regimine principum* 1.15.

[10] "A multitude thus agitated, which wishes to escape these perils, must immediately constitute within itself a head that can correct it, hold it united, and think on its defence" (*Discorsi* 1.57, p. 130a). Possibly here, as apparently in Dante's *Inferno* 5.60, *correggere* means no more than *to rule over,* but seemingly this meaning is not usual in either Latin or Italian.

[11] "A bridle that can correct them" (*Discorsi* 1.58, p. 130b).

[12] See pp. 138, 200, below.

[13] "The law the emender of vices" (*De optimo statu,* folio 130 verso).

[14] "Such men as on account of their insolence could not be corrected by the laws were in some fashion bridled by a power like that of a king" (*Discorsi* 1.18, p. 88b). Cf. ibid. 1.55, p. 127b. See p. 36, above.

Machiavelli's time in his opinion was in a condition demanding royal power—"una mano regia"—for its reform; hence his treatise on the prince, in spite of republican prejudices.[15]

Such correction of individual subjects and through them of the state of which they are members is obviously much the same as the medicating of the state of which our author speaks. The new ruler unable to deal with subjects too desirous of personal advantages is said to be unable to use "medicine forti,"[16] what Beroaldus calls "austerior medicina" in applying the medical figure to the proper government of the state.[17] In speaking of the work of priests, Guicciardini brings together correcting and medicating in the phrases "con lo esempio buono della vita, e col correggere e medicare i costumi trascorsi."[18] In politics the example of the prince is a means of correcting, as Machiavelli implies in the chapter of the *Discorsi* entitled *Che gli peccati de' popoli nascono dai principi,* in which he deals with *correcting.*[19] In conclusion he gives two lines of a passage in which Lorenzo il Magnifico had indicated the example of the ruler as a potent means of correction:

> Sappiate che chi vuole il popol reggere,
> debbe pensare al bene universale;
> e chi vuol altri dagli error correggere,
> sforzisi prima lui di non far male:
> però conviensi giusta vita eleggere,
> perchè lo esemplo al popol molto vale,
> e quel che fa il signor, fanno poi molti,
> ché nel signor son tutti gli occhi vòlti.[20]

Clichtoveus entitled one of his chapters *Quod principem legibus subditum esse decet: et suo exemplo vitaeque probitate subditos ad*

---

[15] See pp. 37 ff., above.

[16] "Strong medicines" (*Prince* 3, p. 6a). See pp. 27, 40, above.

[17] *De optimo statu,* folio 128 verso.

[18] "With the good example of their lives and by correcting and medicating habits that have gone to excess" (*Storia d'Italia* 11.8, p. 257, *anno* 1513).

[19] "The sins of peoples arise from their rulers" (*Discorsi* 3.29). For the example of the prince, see pp. 197 ff., below.

[20] "You should know that he who wishes to rule the people ought to think of the general good, and he who wishes to correct the errors of others should first compel himself not to do evil; therefore it befits the ruler to choose an equitable life, for his example has a great influence on the people, and what the lord does, many then do, because on the ruler all eyes are turned" (*La rappresentazione, Opere* 2.100).

virtutem inducere.[21] Hence Sir Philip Sidney's praise of a good ruler:

> Shepherd of shepherds, whose well setled order
> Private with welth, publike with quiet garnished.
> While he did live, farre, farre was all disorder;
> Example more prevailing then direction,
> Far was homestrife, and far was foe from border.
> His life a law, his looke a full correction.[22]

The corrective function of the monarch also requires at times innovation in the laws and in the *costumi* or habits on which the laws depend for their vitality and which in turn are preserved by the laws. In order "a frenare una universale corruzione,"[23] the prince must be thorough, displacing old habits and customs and substituting new ones, as in the last chapter of *The Prince* Machiavelli urges the new ruler to do.[24] The corrective function of the ruler extends to the complete observation of justice and the development of all that is needed for the production of good citizens in the Aristotelian sense.

In the older writers the prince is exhorted to be a moral corrector; Aquinas held this view, writing in the chapter where he makes it part of the duty of the king "quid inordinatum est corrigere,"[25] as follows: "Cura imminet regi . . . ut suis legibus et praeceptis, poenis et praemiis homines sibi subjectos ab iniquitate coerceat, et ad opera virtuosa inducat, exemplum a Deo accipiens, qui hominibus legem dedit, observantibus quidem mercedem, transgredientibus poenas retribuens."[26] But it must not be supposed that Aquinas lost sight of the practical function of the king, even though less willing than Machiavelli to think that the ruler should have in mind the good citizen, rather than the good man as such.

[21] "That the prince should be subject to the laws and by his example and the probity of his life influence his subjects toward virtue" (cap. 5).

[22] *Arcadia* 4, fourth eclogues.

[23] "To bridle a universal corruption" (*Discorsi* 1.18, p. 86b). *Frenare* in this sense equals *corregere;* see p. 43, note, and *Discorsi* 1.18, quoted on p. 43.

[24] See pp. 35 ff., above.

[25] "To correct what is grown to excess" (*De regimine principum* 1.15).

[26] "It is the king's responsibility . . . by his laws and instructions, by rewards and punishments, to keep from iniquity the men subject to him, and influence them toward virtuous deeds, taking his example from God, who gives law to men, and bestows a reward on those who observe them and penalties on those who transgress" (ibid.).

In expressing one function of the ruler by the word *correct,*
Machiavelli followed a respectable tradition going back to Cicero.[27]
John of Salisbury used it in connection with the medical metaphor
for describing the ruler and showed that his continued power depended on his corrective and curative activity:

Princeps enim tenetur de omnibus et omnium auctor esse videtur quia,
cum omnia possit corrigere, eorum merito particeps est quae noluit
emendare. Cum enim potestas publica sit, ut praediximus, omnium
vires exhaurit et, ne in se deficiat, incolumnitatem omnium debet pro-
curare membrorum. Quot autem in administratione principatus extant
officia, tot sunt principalis corporis quasi membra. Dum autem singulorum officia in integritate virtutis et suavitate opinionis conservat,
quandam quasi membris sanitatem procurat et decorem.[28] Cum vero
ex negligentia aut dissimulatione potestatis circa officia sit virtutis aut
famae dispendium, quasi in membra eius morbi et maculae incurrunt.
Nec diu subsistit incolumitas capitis, ubi languor membrorum in-
valescit.[29]

Egidio wished the king to be able "corrigere volentes insurgere, et
turbare pacem regni."[30] Erasmus felt that when something is in-
tolerably amiss in the state, "id erit corrigendum, sed arte ac
paullatim. . . . Quod si populus erit intractabilis, et suo ipsius
bono repugnans, tum aut obsecundandum erit ad tempus, et
paullatim ad tuum institutum inducendus, vel arte quapiam, vel

---

[27] See p. 198, below.

[28] Cf. *Prince* 24, p. 47a: "Di avere dato principio a uno principato nuovo; e
ornatolo . . . di buone legge."—"To have given origin to a new principate and orna-
mented it with good laws." Cf. the preface of the *Institutes* of Justinian: "Im-
peratoriam maiestatem non solum armis decoratam, sed etiam legibus oportet esse
armatam."—"The imperial majesty should not merely be decorated with arms but
also armed with laws."

[29] "For the prince is held responsible for everything and seems to be the author
of everything because, being able to correct everything, he is properly a partaker of
those things which he is unwilling to emend. For since authority is public, as we
have already said, it draws on the forces of all and, lest it should fail in itself,
should procure the safety of all the members. Whatever the number of the offices
that appear in the administration of the principate, so many are as it were the members of the chief body. So while the prince preserves the offices of single men in
integrity of virtue and agreeableness of reputation, he procures a sort of sanity and
beauty of the member. Yet from the negligence or neglect of the authority in the
matter of offices there may be a loss of virtue or fame, as diseases and blemishes
come upon the members of it. Nor does the security of the head long endure when
weakness gets the better of the members" (*Policraticus* 4.12, 538 cd). For *corrigere*
see also p. 100, below.

[30] "To correct those wishing to rebel and to disturb the peace of the kingdom"
(*De regimine* 3.2.6; see also 3.2.8).

fuco salutari."[31] Similarly Machiavelli held that "quando uno inconveniente è cresciuto o in uno stato o contro a uno stato, è più salutifero partito temporeggiarlo che urtarlo."[32] For this slow correcting Erasmus relied partly on education: "Hac ratione fiet, ut non sit opus multis legibus, aut suppliciis, nimirum, civibus suapte sponte, quod rectum est, sequentibus."[33] Machiavelli also held that "buoni esempli" sprang from "buona educazione."[34]

What Machiavelli says on the laws and on the execution of justice in *The Prince* is smaller in amount than might be expected considering the great importance of the subject to him and the space it commonly occupies in works *de regimine principum*. Clichtoveus, for example, gives two chapters to justice, showing "iustitiam in rege summopere requiri."[35] But Machiavelli, in the twelfth chapter of *The Prince,* seems to dismiss laws entirely because they depend on arms.[36] Yet if one brings together what he says on correcting, medicating, and restraining, and on *costumi* and *ordini,* there appears a body of material somewhat similar to the discussions of justice normal in exhortations to the monarch.[37]

Near the end of this seventh chapter is presented the mistake of Valentino in allowing power to men who had reason to fear him,

[31] "It should be corrected, but artfully and a little at a time. . . . Because if the people is intractable and set against its own good, then either the time must be complied with and the people little by little led to your design, or cured by some art or health-bringing deception" (*Institutio* 3, 592 B-594 A).

[32] "When an inconvenience has grown great in a state or against a state, the more health-bringing plan is to temporize with it than to use violence against it (*Discorsi* 1.33, title, p. 100b).

[33] "If this method is followed, it results that few laws or punishments are needed, for assuredly the citizens follow what is right of their own motion" (*Institutio* 3, 592 E).

[34] *Discorsi* 1.4, p. 63b; see Ercole, *La politica di Machiavelli,* pp. 251 ff.

[35] "Justice is in the highest degree required in a king" (*De regis officio,* cap. 13; see also cap. 14).   [36] *Prince* 12, first paragraph, p. 24b.

[37] Some pages of the *Rosier des Guerres* of Louis XI are devoted to justice; one paragraph runs: "Un Roy ne doit corriger tout à la rigueur les faultes des hommes, car les hommes ne se peuvent pas du-tout garder de faillir, par quoy il convient aucunefois pardonner les erreurs, et si convient de necessité faire punicion, il doit monstrer, qu'il le fait plus comme contràint de la dreçer, et non pas en semblant de vengeance."—"A king should not correct the faults of men with the utmost rigor, for men cannot completely guard themselves from doing wrong; therefore it is sometimes proper to pardon errors, and if necessity requires that punishment be inflicted, the king should make clear that he does it because he is constrained to rectify matters and not with the appearance of taking vengeance" (chap. 3). For a parallel with the last words see the quotation from Carafa, pp. 52-3, below.

In his *Remonstrances* to Charles VII, Jean Juvénal des Ursins puts all the king's duties under two heads, warfare and doing justice in peace (Péchenard, *Jean-Juvénal des Ursins,* pp. 277-8).

for they would certainly be his enemies and "offend," that is injure him. As here applied to foreign affairs, the principle is the same as that stated at the end of chapter three. It is deduced from the axiom of the day that those who fear one are to be feared, often discussed by the writers *de regimine principum* in relation to prince and subjects.[38]

The chapter closes with Borgia's mistake in thinking that new benefits would erase old injuries, thus removing hatred as a cause of offense. Machiavelli states this principle as though refuting wrong theory: "Chi crede che ne' personaggi grandi e' benefizii nuovi faccino dimenticare le iniurie vecchie, s'inganna."[39] If however, the matter was commonly discussed in writings by advisers of princes, the passages have escaped me, except that in which Louis XI advised his son: "Sur tout bien se doit garder de ennemy reconsilié, car tel, s'il pouvoit une fois veoir le temps de soy venger, il ne se pourroit saouller de son sang."[40]

Possibly Machiavelli developed it from a passage of Tacitus: "Proclivius est injuriae, quam beneficio vicem exsolvere, quia gratia oneri, ultio in questu habetur."[41] With respect to the memory, the remark of Seneca is somewhat closer: "Ita natura comparatum est, ut altius injuriae quam merita descendant; et illa cito defluant, has tenax memoria custodiat."[42] From some such passage Machiavelli may have elaborated the positive statement of *The Prince*.

However arrived at, it perhaps represents his own reflection more than any borrowing. Its evolution may be traced. On April 29, 1513, he wrote to Vettori, in discussing the relations of the kings

[38] See pp. 32, above, 149, 161, 183, below.

[39] "He who believes that new benefits cause great personages to forget old injuries deceives himself" (*Prince* 7, p. 18a).

[40] "Above all a king should guard himself from a reconciled enemy, for such an one, if he can once see the right time to avenge himself, can sate himself with the king's blood" (*Rosier des guerres,* cap. 3).

[41] Anyone is more inclined to make requital for an injury than for a benefit, because thanks are considered a burden but revenge an advantage" (*Hist.* 4.3). Quoted by Machiavelli in *Discorsi* 1.29, p. 96b.

[42] "It is arranged by nature that injuries sink deeper than favors; the impression of the latter quickly passes away, the former memory holds tenaciously" (*De beneficiis* 1.1.8). Cf. Seneca, *Epistulae Morales* 11.2 (81). This work is frequently quoted by Aquinas in his treatment of gratitude (*Summa Theologica* 2.2.106, 107). Cf. Guicciardini, *Ricordi* 24: "Non è la più labile cosa che la memoria de' beneficii ricevuti: però fate più fondamento in su quegli che sono condizionati in modo che non vi possino mancare, che in su coloro quali avete beneficati."—"There is nothing more fleeting than the memory of benefits received; therefore place more reliance on those so situated that they cannot get on without you than on those you have benefitted."

of France and Spain: "Ci vedeva una perdita manifesta per se stesso, perchè si sarebbe accostato ad un Re, facendolo potente, che ogni volta che ne avesse occasione ragionevolmente, si doveva ricordare più delle ingiurie vecchie, che de' benefizi nuovi."[43] Perhaps it is implied that the procedure of the king is exceptional. At any rate, on August 10, 1513, Niccolò wrote: "I benefizi nuovi sogliono far sdimenticare le ingiurie vecchie."[44] In his reply Vettori does not reject the principle, though he makes the difficulty that the benefits conferred would by others be looked on as injuries to themselves.[45] From this Machiavelli passes to the strong statement in *The Prince,* the composition of which he mentions in yet another letter to Vettori dated in December of the same year. In the *Discorsi* it is again affirmed that "mai le ingiurie vecchie furono cancellate da' beneficii nuovi";[46] Piero Soderini is made an example of a man who failed partly because he did not understand that "la malignità non è doma da tempo nè placata da alcuno dono."[47] The notion that benefits cancel injuries was apparently one of those commonly circulated pieces of wisdom which, as Machiavelli meditated on *The Prince,* came to appear to him quite false.[48]

[43] "It seems to me a damage manifest in itself, because it involves allying oneself with a king and making him powerful, though that king, whenever he has reasonable occasion for it, is likely to remember better the old injuries than the new benefits" (*Lettere familiari* 20, pp. 79-80; the text from Cambiagi's edition, Florence, 1783, vol. 6). See Tommasini 2.86 note. The quotation also suggests the ruin of oneself by making another powerful, as mentioned in *Prince* 3, end, p. 10a.

[44] "New benefits usually make men forget old injuries" (*Lettere familiari* 24, p. 95).

[45] In Machiavelli, *Opere* (Italia, 1813), 8.85. Cf. Guicciardini, *Ricordi* 25: "Guardatevi da fare quelli piaceri agli uomini che non si possono fare sanza fare equale dispiacere a altri; perchè chi è ingiuriato non dimentica, anzi reputa la ingiuria maggiore; chi è beneficato non se ne ricorda, o gli pare essere beneficato manco che non è."—"Beware of doing favors to some men which cannot be done without equal disfavor to others; for a man who is injured does not forget but rather thinks the injury greater than it is; but a man who is benefitted does not remember it or he appears to himself to be benefitted less than he is."

[46] "Never were old injuries cancelled by new benefits" (3.4, p. 198a).

[47] "Malignity is not subdued by time nor placated by any gift" (*Discorsi* 3.3, p. 198a). The ruler who conquers a free state should remember that "el nome della libertà e gli ordini antichi . . . nè per la lunghezza de' tempi nè per benefizii mai se dimenticano."—"The name of liberty and the ancient laws are never forgotten because of length of time or benefits received" (*Prince* 5, p. 12a).

[48] See Tommasini 1.143 for traditional maxims rejected by Machiavelli: "L'oro essere il nerbo delle guerre."—"Gold is the sinew of war" (*Discorsi* 2.10, p. 153a). "La cavalleria giovar nelle battaglie più che i fanti."—"Cavalry accomplishes more in battles than infantry" (*Discorsi* 2.18, p. 167a). "Esser Pistoia a tener colle parti, Pisa colle fortezze."—"Pistoia is to be held with factions, Pisa with fortresses" (*Discorsi* 3.27, p. 238b; *Prince* 20, p. 41b). "Fondare sul fango chi fonda sul

Among later writers something of Machiavelli's sentiment appears, though without sign of direct influence; for example, Saavedra writes on broken friendship: "Nec satis sunt ulla beneficia ad eam firmandam, quia injuriae memoria nunquam ex animo deletur penitus. . . . Injuriae locis paludosis sunt similes, quae licet exsiccentur, facile tamen aquas iterum hauriunt."[49]

popolo."—"He who builds on the people builds on sand" (*Prince* 9, p. 21b). "Convenirsi godere i benefici del tempo."—"It is proper to enjoy the blessings of the day" (*Prince* 3, p. 8b). In refuting the maxim on recent benefits, Machiavelli might have added to *chi crede* (*Prince* 7, p. 18a) the words *secondo che è la comune opinione.*—"According to the usual belief" (*Discorsi* 2.10, title). For modified and accepted proverbs, see pp. 54, 160, 177, below.

[49] No benefits are great enough to make this firm, since the memory of an injury is never fully erased from the mind. . . . Injuries are like swampy places which though they may dry up yet easily take the waters back again" (*Idea principis . . . simbolis expressa,* no. xci).

Chapter 8

De his qui per scelera ad principatum pervenere.
(Of those who have attained a principate through crimes.)

If the preceding chapters on the new prince are beyond the usual
scope of Machiavelli's predecessors, this one is yet more so, as dealing not merely with a new prince but even with one who came to
his throne by wickedness—wickedness, moreover, which Machiavelli himself condemns. The modern world seems not to have discussed this theme until after Machiavelli's time. Frachetta, for example, considers the problem of rulers who have gained their posi-
tions wickedly—"con sceleratezze"—and explains how such a person may legitimate his rule.[1] Machiavelli dealt with the subject because he thought that principates were sometimes unjustly gained
and that yet, in the complexity of human life, they might be retained with advantage to the subjects. With the wickedness of the
prince may be mingled cruelty well used to the *utilità* of the realm.
If there can be such a principate, the author as a scientist must discuss it; yet further, he must state its laws as they should be known
to the prince himself. In making the choices necessary to human
life, he would prefer the rule of a man who had come unjustly to
his place but who could provide stable government to that of a
prince whose observation of the moral virtues was so unyielding as
to ruin his country. Imprudent wickedness is, however, as likely
to be ruined in hard times—*tempi avversi*—as is imprudent goodness; any successful ruler, wicked or pious, must so live with his
subjects as to be provided against a change of fortune.[2]

This eighth chapter depends on the necessity for foresight,
already presented in chapter three. Only the prince who can look
ahead will be able to exercise necessary cruelty at one stroke and
then to embark on a course of benefits; the unprovident prince
will carry on a policy of continual cruelty, and, like the Duke of
Athens,[3] will defer benefits until they are unable to bring pop-

[1] *Il Prencipe* 1.22. Tacitus and Polybius both appear in the marginal notes of
this chapter.
[2] See also pp. 24 ff., above, and pp. 64, 69, 136, below.
[3] See p. 26, above.

ularity, such as well-used liberality can secure. This foolish ruler
also held his dagger in his hand and kept the minds of his subjects disturbed—"sospesi e paurosi"—by continual offences, as once
the Roman plebeians did those of the patricians.[4] Cosimo, on the
other hand, was wiser; he approved wholesale banishments, on his
return from exile, with his proverb: "Meglio città guasta che
perduta";[5] he sanctioned the efforts of his party who set to work
without showing any favor—"senza alcuno rispetto"—to establish
themselves. But on the other hand, some effort was made to let
initial severity suffice: "Spogliata adunque la città de' nimici o
sospetti allo stato, si volsono a benificare nuove genti per fare più
gagliarda la parte loro."[6] They were humane and did not make
themselves hated in any sinister manner. The murder of Baldaccio,
as Machiavelli interpreted it, is not to be taken as an exception to
this policy; on the contrary, it is an example of cruelty well used
which, with its sequel, brought authority and reputation to the
Medicean party. Possibly Machiavelli intended the reader to see in
this action an example of the foresight for which he praises Cosimo,
though responsibility for the assassination is not laid on that powerful man. To Machiavelli the personal policy of Cosimo was that of
gaining friends by liberality, and he was too prudent to keep the
state unsettled by continued injuries.[7]

Direct presentation of suitable conduct for a man who has
made himself ruler "per scelera" is hardly to be looked for aside
from the influence of Aristotle's discussion of the policy of the
tyrant. Tyranny in general is often warned against, but Machiavelli
is considering not oppression in general, but cruelty for the sake
of preserving power. However, the evil of keeping the minds of
subjects uncertain and timid—"sospesi e paurosi"—under any conditions is at least related to the theme of this chapter. That had
attracted the attention of Diomede Carafa, who advised the prince
against illegal seizure of the property of some of his subjects because of its effect on the minds of them all: "At si quando mulctandi

[4] *Discorsi* 1.45, p. 116a.
[5] "Better a city laid waste than a city lost" (*Istorie Fiorentine* 7.6, p. 566b).
[6] "After the city was cleared of enemies, open or suspected, of the administration,
they turned themselves to benefit new persons in order to make their party more
powerful" (ibid. 5.4, p. 502a). Perhaps related is the attempt of Luca Pitti and
his followers "dare principio a quello governo con terrore"—"to give a beginning
to their administration with terror" (*Ist. Fior.* 7.3, p. 563b).
[7] The material of the paragraph is from *Istorie Fiorentine* 7.6; 5.4; 7.1; 6.7. On
well-used severity see also pp. 104 ff., below.

erunt aliqui, ostendere oportebit servandae justitiae gratia id fieri, non pecuniae aviditate.[8] Nam cum pauci sunt, quibus auferri bona contigat, apud caeteros tamen ea res odiosa esse consuevit."[9] Such disturbance of mind over finances will lead to poverty in the state, because subjects will leave the country or hesitate in the pursuit of wealth.

In his advice that injuries should be inflicted at one blow— "a un tratto"—Machiavelli seems to combat some well-established opinion which an ill-advised prince might be inclined to follow. As though to continue his attack on such a theory, he explains that not injuries but, on the contrary, benefits ought to be given gradually. In Aristotle's *Politics* is found such advice as he objects to, in respect to the ruler's procedure against a man who has grown powerful: "If any one is to be deprived of his power, let it be diminished gradually, not taken from him all at once."[10] But Machiavelli apparently agreed with Rinaldo degli Albizzi, who setting forth the mistake his party made in dealing with Cosimo,

[8] Cf. p. 47, n. 2, above.

[9] "But if it is necessary to lay fines on some, it will be well to make plain that this is done for the sake of keeping justice, not because of desire for money. For though there are few who actually have their goods taken away, yet this is usually looked on with displeasure by the rest" (*De regentis et boni principis officiis*, pt. 1, p. 649). The Italian of the last clause runs: "Despiace alo resto" (Persico, *Diomede Carafa*, p. 267).

Guicciardini believed in keeping subjects secure of their ruler: "La più parte de' mali che si fanno nelle terre di parte, procedono dal sospetto; perchè gli uomini dubitando della fede l'uno dell'altro sono necessitati a prevenire; però chi le governa debbe avere el primo intento, e essere sollecito a levare via le suspizione."—"The major part of the ills that parties do in cities come from suspicion; because in their doubt of each other's faith it is necessary for men to forestall trouble; therefore he who governs them ought to be careful to get rid of suspicions" (*Ricordi* 120).

In his *Discorsi sopra Cornelio Tacito* (1584) Scipio Ammirato begins a chapter: "Non si tengono a freno i popoli, se un Principe non è temuto; ma tenere i popoli in continuo timore solo è opera di tiranno, ma è ancor cosa poco sicura."—"The people cannot be held in check if a prince is not feared, but to hold the people in continual fear alone is the work of a tyrant, and is also an insecure measure" (17.5). In addition to his Tacitean basis, he refers also to the passage in Livy (45.28) that tells how Aemilius Paulus avoided raising apprehensions in the minds of the allies in Greece, and mentions a passage in Caesar's *Gallic War* (8.38) suggesting Machiavelli's opinion: "Quod praecipue eos [Carnutes] propter conscientiam facti timere animadvertebat, quo celerius civitatem timore liberaret, principem sceleris illius et concitatorem belli, Gutruatum ad supplicium depoposcit."—"Especially because he knew that the Carnutes were afraid on account of their knowledge of what had been done, in order that as quickly as possible he might free the state from fear, he demanded for punishment Gutruatus, the principal in that evil deed and the one who had stirred up the war."

[10] *Politics* 5.11, 1315a 13; cf. 1308b 15.

asserted: "Gli uomini grandi o e' non si hanno a toccare, o, tocchi, a spegnere."[11] This appears to be rather Machiavelli's theory than messer Rinaldo's opinion. Yet one is inclined to think the value of Aristotle's advice may have been the subject of some sort of *disputà* in Machiavelli's time. Evidence, however, is lacking, unless a late echo may be found in verbal similarities in a paraphrase of the *Politics* published by Figliucci in 1583: "Se ancora si harà da scemar o annullar la potenza o la grandezza di qualcheduno che troppo sia cresciuto, ciò *si dee far a poco a poco,* e non levarglila tutta in *un tratto;* imperoche cosi si esacerbano troppo, e non possono patirlo, dove a quel modo non se ne accorgendo vengono a sminuire, e ad agguagliarsi a gli altri.[12]

At the end of chapter eight are a few words related to the subjects of foresight and the giving of benefits, what may be called liberality prudently employed.[13] The foresighted man will confer benefits so early that they appear not forced but freely given, for benefits do not advantage the giver if the recipients think them forced—"reputano che siano fatti quasi per obligo."[14] They judge "non avere quel bene da te, ma dagli avversari tuoi; e dovendo temere che, passata la necessità, tu ritolga loro quello che hai forzatamente loro dato, non arà teco obligo alcuno."[15] The subject

[11] "Great men are not to be touched, or if they are touched they are to be ruined" (*Istorie Fiorentine* 4.30, p. 495a).

[12] "If it is a matter of diminishing or annulling the power or the greatness of some one who has grown too great, this should be done little by little, and it should not be taken away at one stroke; if the latter mode is used they are too much angered and cannot endure it, but by the first method they are diminished and equalled to the others without realizing it" (*De la politica,* lib. 5, folio 189 verso).

[13] See pp. 24 ff., 52 ff., above. Of this sort is the munificence recommended in *Prince* 21, near the end, p. 45a. See p. 177, below.

[14] Guicciardini, *Ricordi* 24, Cf. *Istorie Fiorentine* 2.37, p. 439a; *Discorsi* 1.51, p. 121.

[15] "That they do not have that benefit from you, but from your adversaries, and having reason to fear that when the necessity is past you will take back what you have been forced to give them, they will have no feeling of obligation to you" (*Discorsi* 1.32, p. 100b). Here appears also the fear and enmity of the creature toward the interested patron. See pp. 31 ff., above. On a different aspect of forced giving, Machiavelli writes: "Il tutto consiste in domandare audacemente, e mostrare mala contentezza non ottenendo; e i principi facilmente si piegano a fare nuovi piaceri a quelli a chi eglino hanno fatto de' vecchi, anzi temono tanto, disdicendo, di non si perdere i benefici passati, che sempre corrono a fare de' nuovi, quando e' sono domandati in quel modo che io vorrei che voi domandassi questo. Voi siete prudente."—"The whole consists in demanding boldly and showing oneself malcontent at failure to obtain; and princes easily bend themselves to give new favors to those to whom they have given old ones. In fact they so much fear that by refusal they will lose the results of their past benefits that they always run to

of giving freely, "per liberalità" as Machiavelli expresses it,[16] had been treated by Patricius under the heading of *magnificentia:* "Hilaritas Caesaris in elargiendo gratior erat civibus, quam ipsa munerum erogatio. Prudenter quidem locutus est Dionysius Halicarnasseus, quum ait, *Dona voluntaria dantibus gratiora sunt, quam coacta, accipientibus autem firmiora.*"[17] The quotation is close to the opinions of Machiavelli in both wording and idea.

---

confer new ones, when they are asked for in the manner in which I wish you to ask for them. You are prudent" (to Guicciardini, without date, *Lettere familiari* 60, p. 215).   [16] *Discorsi* 1.51, title.

[17] "The cheerfulness of Caesar in giving was more pleasant to the citizens than the bestowal of the gifts themselves. Of a certainty Dionysius of Halicarnassus spoke prudently when he said, 'Voluntary gifts win more favor for those who give than do forced ones, and they are more reliable for those who receive them' " (*De regno* 7.11, p. 304).

Chapter 9

De principatu civili.
(Of the rule of a citizen.)

This chapter, with modifications, is much in the spirit of Aristotle's treatment, in *Politics* 5, of the overthrow of various forms of government from within, particularly in the discussion of the people and the grandees.[1]

The position of the ruler with respect to the great on the one hand and the plebeians on the other is set forth with Machiavellian frankness and represents the new rather than the traditional in the history of advice to princes.[2] Curiously enough, something of it appears in the advice of St. Louis of France to his son:

A ce dois tu metre t'entente coment tes genz et ti sougiet puissent vivre en pais et en droiture desouz toi, meesmement les bones villes et les bones citez de ton roiaume. Et les garde en l'estat et en la franchise ou ti devancier les ont gardées; et se il i a aucune chose à amender, si l'amende et adresce et les tien en favor et en amor. Quar par la force et par les richesces de tes bones citez et de tes bones villes, doteront li privé et li estrange à mespenre envers toi, especialment ti per et ti baron. Il me sovient bien de Paris et des bones villes de mon roiaume qui me aidierent contre les barons quant je fui novellement coronez.[3]

This advice to employ the force of one of the estates of the realm against another obviously sprang from the experience of the king, as Machiavelli's advice came from his observation. On the whole,

[1] See also p. 112, below.
[2] The great and the many in the state appear in *Prince* 8, 19, 24; *Discorsi* 1.5, 40; *Istorie Fiorentine* 2.34; 3.1; 4.8; 5.8; 7.23; *Decennale Secondo* 99.
[3] "It should be your purpose to enable your people and your subjects to live in peace and justice under your rule, likewise the good towns and the good cities of your realm. And preserve them in the condition and in the liberty in which your predecessors have kept them; and if there is anything to reform, reform and change it, and keep your people favorable and loving to you. For on account of the power and wealth of your good cities and your good towns both natives and foreigners hesitate to undertake anything damaging to you; this is especially true of your peers and your barons. I remember clearly Paris and the good towns of my realm for the aid they gave me against the barons when I had just been crowned" (*Enseignements de Saint Louis a son fils* 21, in Bibliothèque de l'École des Chartes XXX, 1872, p. 433).

however, as might be expected, St. Louis is of the pious school of advisers of the prince.[4]

In suggesting that the great should be dealt with according to their necessary dependence on the fortunes of the ruler, Machiavelli has been partially anticipated by Diomede Carafa, who applies the same test both to other rulers and to subjects:

Tam quos tibi, si eveniat, auxilio futuros speres; quam de quorum erga te voluntate dubites: immo etiam de his, qui nec amici, nec inimici sunt, consultandum erit; hoc enim exploratum habeas et in Italia, et apud exteras nationes; sicut et in ipso regno tuo tres, quas retuli animorum varietates reperiri: totius autem fere orbis Reges, populosque in gubernandi status sui deliberationibus commoda sua sequi: et ea tam generis, quam affinitatis, et amicitiae vinculis anteponere solere. Quare hi tibi pluris facendi erunt, quorum fortuna cum tua conjuncta est, quam qui tibi aut cognatione aut alia quavis necessitudine devincti sunt, praesertim si ad eos aliqua ex calamitatibus tuis perventura sit utilitas.[5]

Such connection of the subject with the fortune of the ruler falls under the principle of the dependence of the subject stated by Machiavelli at the end of this ninth chapter of *The Prince*. The safe prince is one whose subjects have need of him, as in the instance of the newly conquered republic do the few who rule because supported by the conqueror; he must rely on something more secure than the obligations of friendship to keep men loyal when they see advantage for themselves in his ruin.[6]

[4] "Nor is it mere accident that the exhortations of King Louis the Saint to his son Philip re-echo the ideas of this monograph *De regimine principum* of Thomas" (Grabmann, *Thomas Aquinas*, trans. Michel, London, 1928, p. 163). Since Vincent of Beauvais was closely associated with St. Louis, his *De morali principis institutione* is a more obvious source.

[5] "So you should take thought of those who, you hope, would aid you in need, as much as of those whose disposition toward you is in doubt, and certainly also about those who are neither friends nor enemies. You should investigate both in Italy and among foreign nations, and in your own kingdom itself, the three varieties of disposition which I have said are to be found. For generally kings and peoples everywhere in the world in their deliberations on the conduct of their affairs follow their own interests, and are in the habit of putting it before the bonds of family, relationship, and friendship. Wherefore those are to be thought of more value to you whose fortunes are joined with yours than those who are bound to you by kindred or any other necessary link, especially if from your calamities some advantage can come to them" (*De principis officiis*, pt. 1, p. 649).

[6] Cf. *Prince* 5, pp. 11b-12a; 17, pp. 33a, 34a.

Chapter 10

Quomodo omnium principatuum vires perpendi debeant.
(In what manner the forces of all principates should be estimated.)

In this chapter Machiavelli seems to have chiefly in mind his theme of the new prince, though his advice is applicable to the defense of any principate, old or new, not well provided with military resources. It is, then, proper to expect greater resemblance than before to the older works *de regimine principum*. In them advice to prepare for war, in the fashion attributed to the German cities, is often found. Egidio, for example, writes on *Qualiter aedificanda sunt castra aut civitates, ne per pugnam ab obsidentibus facilius devincantur,* and on *Quomodo muniendae sunt civitates et castra et universaliter omnes munitiones, ut ab obsidentibus difficilius capiantur.*[1] Characteristic of Machiavelli is the insistence that a ruler who is not hated can maintain himself behind proper fortifications;[2] the more usual statement is that the ruler who will be sustained by his people in need must win their love.[3] Hoccleve makes it a ruler's resource when in need of money:

> And swich a kyng is naght prudent ne wys,
> That of his peple purchaseth hym hate,
> ffor loue excedith al tresour in prys;
> So hath it ben, and so be wole algate,
> Whan that richésses ebben & abbate,
> If loue endure, it may hym restore,
> And loue is goten by prudénces lore.[4]

Pontanus also speaks of the secure position of the loved ruler:

Omnium autem primum studere oportet, ut ab iis potissimum amere, quibus corporis, ac rerum familiarium curam permiseris, quod faciens vives securior, et amor iste cum inter familiares altius egerit radices, latius postea evagatus, non modo inter populares, subjectosque, sed

---

[1] "In what way castles and cities should be built that they may not too easily be taken by besieging armies.

"In what manner cities and castles and universally all fortifications are to be strengthened that they may be taken with difficulty by attackers" (*De regimine* 3.3.20, 21).　　　　　　　　　[2] *Prince* 10, p. 22b.

[3] For more on this subject see chap. 20, below.

[4] *Regement of Princes* 4824-4830, stanza 690.

externos quoque diffundetur. Quem enim quisque amat, eum si fieri possit, vivere perpetuo expetit, nullique minus exercitu opus est, quanquam haud scio an ulli maiores sint copiae quam ei, qui plurimum ametur.[5]

The tendency of preceding writers to imagine the prince as prosperous rather than driven to the last ditch renders them less specific than is Machiavelli.

The well-prepared ruler has on his side the uncertainty in worldly matters that so impressed the Florentine secretary. If forethought has provided against a year's siege of a city, it is hardly probable that an antagonist will come so well provided against the uncertainty of fortune as to continue so long in his attempt at capture.[6]

[5] "First of all you should take pains that you may be as much as possible loved by those to whom you entrust the care of your body and your intimate affairs, for by doing this you may live more securely, and when this love has struck deep root among those nearest you, it will then extend more widely and be diffused not merely among your people and subjects but also among foreigners. For when any one loves a person he desires him to live forever, if it is possible, and no one has less need for an army, nor do I know whether any one has greater forces, than the king who is greatly loved" (*De principe*, pp. 266-7).

[6] *Prince* 10, pp. 22b-23a.

Chapter 11

De principatibus ecclesiasticis.
(Of ecclesiastical principates.)

The theme of the new principate underlies this chapter also; aside from the fascination of the subject, desire for completeness seems to have caused its inclusion. Machiavelli is as willing to advise a politically minded pope as another prince, perhaps thinking it possible that the liberation of Italy might come from a prince of the church. As advice to an ecclesiastical politician, the chapter is without precedent in works *de regimine principum*.

Pope Julius is praised because he acted for the sake of strengthening the church, and not for private ends. Machiavelli does not feel that he was more immediately successful for this reason, but rather that his actions were so much the more praiseworthy—"con tanta più sua laude."[1] This suggests the traditional distinction between the good king and the tyrant, as expounded, for example, by Egidio:

Tangit autem Philosophus V Politicorum quatuor differentias inter tyrannum et regem. Prima est, quia rex respicit bonum commune: tyrannus vero bonum proprium. Nam regnum est principatus rectus, tyrannis vero est dominum perversum. Cum ergo bonum gentis sit divinius bono unius, perverse dominatur qui spreto bono communi intendit bonum proprium. Ex hac autem differentia prima sequitur secunda, videlicet quod tyrannus intendit bonum delectabile: rex vero bonum honorificum. Nam sicut inenarrabile est quanto quis delectatur in bono proprio, sic quasi inenarrabile est quantus honor sequitur, et quanto honore est dignius intendens commune bonum.[2]

[1] *Prince* 11, p. 24a.

[2] "In the Fifth Book of the *Politics* the Philosopher touches on four differences between the tyrant and the king. The first is that the king is concerned with the common good, the tyrant with his individual good. For monarchy is a proper form of government, but the rule of a tyrant is a perverse form. Since therefore the good of the people is more divine than the good of one man, he rules perversely who, despising the common good, looks out for his personal good. And from this first difference rises the second, namely that the tyrant is intent on a good that brings pleasure, but the king on a good that is honorable. And just as it is indescribable how much anyone takes pleasure in his personal good, it is likewise indescribable how much honor follows the ruler who is intent on the common good and how much more worthy of honor he is" (*De regimine* 3.2.6).

And still more suggestive of the moral desires of the older works is Machiavelli's hope that Pope Leo will, by his goodness and other virtues, make the church great and worthy of veneration. Egidio had made true religion the first duty of the king:

Quicunque principatur, sive regnat, sit divinum organum, sive sit minister dei. Quare si minister suam mercedem, et suum praemium debet ponere in suo domino, et debet eam expectare ab ipso, decet regem, qui est dei minister, suam felicitatem ponere in ipso deo, et suum praemium expectare ab ipso.[3]

The reward that the good ruler receives from God perhaps also has some relation to the true and unworldly "laude" of Julius.[4] It is characteristic that Machiavelli is interested in the goodness of a pope and not of a king or a duke.[5]

[3] "He who acts as a ruler or a king should be a divine instrument or a minister of God. Hence if a minister ought to put his reward and his profit in the hands of his lord and ought to await them from him, so the king, who is the minister of God, should put his felicity in the hands of God and await his recompense from him" (*De regimine* 1.1.12).   [4] See p. 228, below.

[5] I am not considering Machiavelli's sincerity in his remarks on Pope Leo. *Bontà* (*Prince* 11, p. 24b, at end of chapter) is sometimes interpreted as *capacità, bravura* (*Il Principe*, introduzione e note di Manfredo Vanni, Milano, 1927); following the explanation of Professor Ercole (*La Politica di Machiavelli*, pp. 39 ff.) I interpret it as *bontà morale;* Professor Ercole does not, it should be added, cite this particular passage.

Chapter 12

Quot sint genera militiae et de mercenariis militibus.
(The different kinds of military forces and of mercenary soldiers.)

In this chapter Machiavelli turns away from new principates and considers a matter applicable to those of any age or condition; at times he goes beyond the limits of his subject to consider, as he does in the *Discorsi,* the policies of republics, evidently with the feeling that what he says is of general application. His treatment of the mercenary soldier is a mark of his interest in what went on before his own eyes, though he may have been stimulated also by his immediate Italian predecessors. Diomede Carafa advises the ruler to train his own people rather than to employ soldiers who may not be trustworthy.[1] Patricius wrote:

Exercitatio rei militaris, in his qui animi virtute, et corporis robore praestant, secundum disciplinas gratissima principibus semper esse solet. Vera enim Galbae Caesaris sententia, qui dicere solebat optimum esse milites diligere, non autem emere. Tunc quidem principes militem emunt quum ex civibus suis non habent quem describant, et exercitum conducere coguntur. Mercennarii militis fides ex fortuna pendet, qua quoque inclinante ad hostes plaerumque ipsi spem, atque animum eo inclinant. . . . Facile est intelligere, quam tutior, praestantiorque sit propria civium nostrorum manus, quam externa militia.[2]

Platina believed that if proper measures were taken the Italian princes could raise soldiers in their dominions and develop military

---

[1] *De regentis et boni principis officiis,* pt. 1, p. 652. Influence on Machiavelli is suggested by Persico in *Diomede Carafa,* pp. 157, 275.

The same opinion appears in Antonio Brucioli's dialogue *Della republica* (Delio Cantimori, *Rhetoric and Politics in Italian Humanism,* in the *Journal of the Warburg Institute* I (1937), 95-6.

[2] "Military training, according to discipline, for those who excel in vigor of spirit and strength of body is usually very acceptable to princes. For Caesar Galba spoke truly in the maxim he was accustomed to pronounce, namely that it was best to choose soldiers and not to buy them. Princes buy a military force when they do not have one made up of their own citizens which they may assign to duty and are yet forced to assemble an army. The faith of mercenary soldiers depends on Fortune, and if she inclines to the enemy, they commonly incline their hope and inclination in the same direction. . . . It is easy to understand how much safer and more effective would be one's own army, made up of one's own citizens, than foreign troops" (*De regno* 9.15).

power "quem si erit opus externis opponamus."[3] But Machiavelli obviously went far beyond his predecessors in his discussion of mercenaries.[4]

More general treatment of military matters is normal; from the *Secretum secretorum* onward, the book of advice to princes assumes that the prince will act as his own general. Egidio defines the relation of the prince to military affairs, in a passage which also gives the reason for the professional soldier, and describes his qualities as quite unlike those Machiavelli attributed to the mercenary:

Hanc autem prudentiam, videlicet militarem, maxime decet habere regem. Nam licet executio bellorum, et removere impedimenta ipsius communis boni, spectet ad ipsos milites, et etiam ad eos quibus ipse rex aut princeps voluerit committere talia: scire tamen quomodo committenda sint bella, et qualiter caute removeri possit impedientia commune bonum, maxime spectat ad principantem. Ex hoc ergo patere potest, quales sint ad militiam admittendi. Nam militia videtur esse quaedam prudentia operis bellici, ordinata ad commune bonum, videntur enim se habere milites in opere bellico, sicut magistri et doctores in scientiis aliis. Quare sicut nullus efficiendus est magister in aliis scientiis, nisi constet ipsum esse doctum in arte illa: sic nullus assumendus est ad dignitatem militarem, nisi constet ipsum diligere bonum regni et commune, et nisi spes habeatur quod sit bonus in opere bellico; et quod velit secundum iussionem principantis impedire seditiones civium, pugnare pro iustitia et pro iuribus, removere quaecunque impedire possunt commune bonum.[5]

[3] "Which in need we might oppose to foreigners" (*Principis Diatuposis* 3.5, 6). This work was composed before 1481.

[4] Among his successors Frachetta entitles a chapter of his *Prencipe* (2.10): *Dei Soldati proprii, mercenarii, et ausiliarii, quali sieno più da pregiare:* etc.—"Of one's own soldiers, mercenaries, and auxiliaries, and which are to be commended."

[5] "It is especially appropriate that the king should possess this kind of prudence, namely that relating to military affairs. For although the carrying on of wars and the removal of impediments from the common good is the function of the soldiers themselves and of those to whom the king himself or the prince wishes to entrust such duties, yet to know how wars should be carried on and how skilfully he can remove the things impeding the common good is one of the chief functions of him who rules. From this therefore it is possible to see what sort of men should be admitted to military service. For military skill seems to be a certain prudence in the activity of war, ordained to the common good, for military men seem to be in the same condition in warlike activity as masters and doctors in other branches of knowledge. Therefore as no one can be made a master in other branches of knowledge unless he can make it certain that he is qualified in his subject, so no one should be received into a place of military responsibility, unless he makes it certain that he respects the good of the kingdom and the common good, and unless there is expectation that he will be good in warlike activity, and that he wishes in accord with the orders of the ruler to impede seditions of the citizens, to fight for

In the first paragraph of chapter twelve Machiavelli states his oft-repeated idea that good laws or justice and good arms are the foundations of states.[6] He has, he says, dealt with the subject above; apparently he refers to chapter seven, in which he shows how Duke Valentino developed his military power and gave good government to the country under his control, thus establishing foundations shaken only by a most extraordinary blow of fortune.

That justice and the sword were fundamental to states was clear to mediaeval writers *de regimine principum*. Egidio shows how without justice and the good laws that embody it the state cannot exist:

Quocunque tamen modo sumatur iustitia, sine ea civitas vel regnum durare non potest. Bene ergo dictum est quod dicitur I *Magnorum moralium,* cap. de iustitia, quod iustum est quoddam proportionabile, et continet urbanitates. Nam sicut anima continet corpus, qua recedente ea corpus dissolvitur, et marcescit: sic iustitia continet urbanitates idest civitates et regna, quia sine ea dissolvitur civitas, et non possunt regna subsistere. . . . Sine ea [iustitia] civitates, et regna durare non possint.[7]

In its proper place he adds military power:

Nam regimen regni, et civitatis, si sit rectum et ordinatum, assimilatur iis quae videmus in uno et eodem homine. Sicut ergo quilibet homo habet duas virtutes animae. Unam per quam sequitur bonum et fugit malum. Et aliam per quam aggreditur, et resistit prohibentibus. Sic quaelibet civitas et regnum indiget duplici virtute, et duplici prudentia, videlicet legum positiva et militari, ut per legum positivam tota civitas et totum regnum prosequatur proficua, et fugiat nociva: per militarem vero et per operationem bellicam aggrediatur, et superet impedientia et prohibentia. Militaris ergo est quaedam species prudentiae, per quam superantur hostes et prohibentes bonum civile et commune. Ex hoc autem apparet ad quid sit militia instituta. Nam sicut leges (ut supra ostendebatur) principaliter respiciunt commune bonum, sic et militia

---

justice and for the laws, and to remove whatever can conflict with the common good" (*De regimine* 3.3.1).

⁶ Cf., for example, *Discorsi* 1.4, p. 63b; 1.21, p. 90b; 3.31, p. 244a.

⁷ "In whatever way justice is understood, without this a state or a kingdom cannot endure. Therefore what is said in the First Book of the *Magna Moralia,* in the chapter on justice, is well said, namely that what is just brings about proper proportion, and contains what is necessary to life in society. For exactly as the soul contains the body and when the soul departs the body is dissolved and decays, so justice contains what is necessary to life in society, that is states and kingdoms, since without this a state is dissolved and kingdoms cannot subsist. . . . Without justice states and kingdoms would not be able to endure" (*De regimine* 1.2.11, 12).

principaliter instituta est ad defensionem communis boni, ut civitatis, aut regni.[8]

St. Thomas had spoken to much the same effect on what enables the state to endure—"permanere":

Igitur . . . triplex cura imminet regi. Primo quidem de successione hominum. . . . Secundo autem ut suis legibus et praeceptis, poenis et praemiis homines sibi subjectos ab iniquitate coerceat, et ad opera virtuosa inducat, exemplum a Deo accipiens, qui hominibus legem dedit, observantibus quidem mercedem, transgredientibus poenas retribuens. Tertio imminet regi cura ut multitudo sibi subjecta contra hostes tuta reddatur. Nihil enim prodesset interiora vitare pericula, si ab exterioribus defendi non posset.[9]

But while arms and laws together may be accepted as foundations, Machiavelli's assumption that good arms mean good laws, and that therefore he need not discuss the laws, has caused some difficulty to his commentators. Erasmus, it may be noted, held no such opinion but gave a chapter to *De legibus condendis aut emendandis*. Guicciardini is less extreme than Machiavelli in believing that the defense of the state must be attended to before internal reforms are considered.[10] How can good laws result from good arms? Machiavelli assumed, as will appear on the pages to

[8] "The regimen of a kingdom and a state, if it is good and well-ordered, is like those which we see in one and the same man. Therefore just as any man has two virtues of the spirit, one through which he follows what is good and flees from evil, and another through which he attacks and resists what hinders him, so every state and kingdom needs a twofold virtue and twofold prudence, to wit the established virtue and prudence of the laws and military virtue, that through the established virtue of the laws the whole state and the whole kingdom may follow what is profitable and flee what is injurious, and that through military virtue and warlike operations it may attack and conquer what impedes and restrains it. Military prudence therefore is a sort of prudence through which enemies and those hostile to civil and common good are overcome. From this appears why military forces are set up. For as the laws (as we showed above) principally have to do with the common good, so a military force is established chiefly for the defence of the common good, as of a state or a kingdom" (*De regimine* 3.3.1). See also the quotation on p. 63, above.

[9] "Therefore the king has a triple responsibility. First, for the succession of heirs. . . . Second, that by his laws and precepts, punishments and rewards, he should keep from iniquity those who are subject to him and direct them to deeds of virtue, following the example of God, who has given law to men, and rewarding those who live virtuously but punishing those who transgress. The king's third responsibility is that he should render the multitude subject to him secure against enemies. For there is no advantage in shunning perils from within if there is no defence from those without" (*De regimine principum* 1.15).

[10] *Del reggimento di Firenze*, book 1, in *Opere* 7.72. See André Otetea, *François Guichardin*, p. 232.

follow, that a prince prudent enough and strong enough to prepare good arms—that is, an army made up of his own loyal citizens
—would be prudent enough to make good laws. Lack of military
capacity would mean the lack of most of the qualities essential to
a distinguished peace. As Ruskin put it for England in the time
of the Crimean War, "truly it is time for us to bear the penalty
of our baseness, and learn, as the sleepless steel glares close upon
us, how to choose our governors more wisely, and our ways more
warily. For that which brings swift punishment in war, must have
brought slow ruin in peace."[11] Certainly the ruler able to defend
his country is not hated for injustice,[12] and poor arms indicate an
imprudent prince:

È piu vero che alcuna altra verità, che, se dove è uomini non è soldati,
nasce per difetto del principe, e non per altro difetto o di sito o di
natura. Di che ce n'è un esempio freschissimo. Perchè ognuno sa, come
ne' prossimi tempi il re d'Inghilterra assaltò il regno di Francia, nè prese
altri soldati che popoli suoi; e, per essere stato quel regno più che trenta
anni sanza fare guerra, non aveva nè soldati nè capitano che avesse
mai militato: nondimeno, non dubitò con quelli assaltare uno regno
pieno di capitani e di buoni eserciti, i quali erano stati continovamente
sotto l'armi nelle guerre d'Italia. Tutto nacque da essere quel re prudente
uomo, e quel regno bene ordinato.[13]

Unless a prince is prudent enough in making and enforcing laws
to win the approbation of his people, he cannot raise and maintain
an army of loyal subjects, secure in his prudence as captain, as an
army that is to succeed must be. A wise ruler who sought only for
military power would be obliged to labor for a good internal organization as a support for his army. Good arms are a symptom
of good government, as Machiavelli indicates in his discussion of
the Roman state. The laws and internal conduct of the republic
were good, he maintains against those who call it tumultuous; in

---

[11] *Modern Painters*, 4.18.36.   [12] *Prince* 10, p. 22b; 20, p. 41b.

[13] "It is more true than any other truth that if in any place where there are
men there are not soldiers, it comes about through the incapacity of the prince, and
not through any defect in the position of the city or in human nature. Here is a
very recent example, for every one knows that only a short time ago the king
of England assailed the kingdom of France without employing other soldiers than
his own people, and that because England had been more than thirty years without war he had neither soldiers nor captain who had ever been in service. Yet
nevertheless he did not hesitate with his forces to assail a kingdom full of captains
and good armies which had been continually under arms in the wars of Italy. It
all came from the king's being a prudent man and his kingdom well regulated"
(*Discorsi* 1.21, p. 90b).

addition to his other evidence, he indicates that the opponents have overlooked the truth that military power results from good government: "Costoro non si avegghino, che, dove è buona milizia, conviene che sia buono ordine."[14]

In the *Proemio* of the *Art of War,* Machiavelli is less sure of this; at least he admits that well-ordered military power can maintain badly-ordered civil organization. If on the other hand there could exist a state well-ordered for peace but with defective military power it would not long endure, for its good organization would rapidly disappear, as in a superb and regal palace deprived of its roof all would fall into ruin. The comparison carries us back to Machiavelli's theory; the protective roof is essential to the house.

In speaking of foreign conquest in Italy, Machiavelli attributes it to the sins of the princes, not, however, those sins commonly mentioned, but those of which he has spoken in *The Prince* and comprised under lack of political prudence. His opponents in this instance are possibly such persons as the followers of Savonarola, who would hold calamity to be the punishment of God for moral wickedness. Or is it possible that they are writers *de regimine principum* who held that a ruler would be overthrown by God as a punishment for moral wickedness? Giraldus Cambrensis, for example, has a chapter entitled *De tyrannorum obitu et fine cruento,*[15] in which he explains that the loathsome disease of which Herod died was the result of divine vengeance; indeed, all the misfortunes of wicked rulers are similarly explained.

At the end of the twelfth chapter of *The Prince* Machiavelli discusses and objects to the excessive use of cavalry in Italian warfare. Patricius recognized its importance, "praesertim nostris temporibus, quibus maxima ex parte equestri pugna decernitur."[16] But he and his contemporaries offer no hint of the Machiavellian theory of infantry.

[14] "They do not perceive that where there is good military organization it is necessary that there be good government" (*Discorsi* 1.4, p. 63b).

[15] "On the destruction and bloody end of tyrants" (*De principis instructione* 1.17).

[16] "Especially in our times when for the most part battles are decided by cavalry combat" (*De regno* 3.2).

Chapter 13

De militibus auxiliariis, mixtis et propriis.
(Of auxiliary armies, mixed forces, and those wholly one's own.)

This, like the preceding chapter, is unusual in advice to a prince, since there was as little assumption that he would wage war by means of auxiliary as by means of mercenary troops. Yet seeing it as one of the methods actually used by rulers, Machiavelli undertook its discussion as essential to his purpose of giving practical advice. Because the sway of Fortune is especially obvious in warfare, Machiavelli here pointedly alludes to her, showing how Pope Julius succeeded through her aid even though his conduct was not governed by reason.[1]

In the matter of arms Machiavelli here reaffirms his belief that the ruler must rely on himself if he is to be secure and the amplifying of his realm genuine.[2] Indeed, the monarch who does not direct his own army is wholly under the control of fortune; he has no *virtù*. Moreover, use of the wrong soldiers makes impossible development of military power required for defense of the state such as would warrant the obedience of subjects.[3] In indicating that a ruler had better fail in war than conquer through the aid of others, Machiavelli is not giving a counsel of chivalry but one of prudence. A ruler who loses a battle with his own army is not certainly ruined; like the Romans, he has foundations such that he is still formidable; at the worst, if he is driven out his people will be likely to aid his return.[4] But one who depends on an ally cannot hope for genuine victory; on the contrary,

Debbe, dunque, un principe o una republica pigliare prima ogni altro partito, che ricorrere a condurre nello stato suo per sua difesa genti ausiliarie, quando al tutto e' si abbia a fidare sopra quelle; perchè

---

[1] For the fortune of war, see p. 207, below.

[2] Cf. *Prince* 6, p. 13b; 7, p. 17a; 24, p. 47b; *Discorsi* 1.21, p. 90b; 30, p. 98a; 43, p. 114b. See pp. 154 ff., below. Even the observation of treaties by other princes is in the hands of the armed prince: "Fra e' signori la [fede] fanno solo osservare l'armi"—"Among lords arms alone make faith observed" (*Parole sopra la provisione del danaio*, p. 790a).   [3] See p. 43, above.

[4] *Discorsi* 3.31, p. 243a; 37, p. 252b; *Prince* 24, p. 47b. The last two give the strength of Philip, "uomo militare," even against the Romans.

[68]

ogni patto, ogni convenzione, ancora che dura, ch' egli arà col nimico gli sarà più leggieri che tale partito.[5]

As Machiavelli probably expected his reader to recall from the preceding chapter, there is still another aspect of the reliance of the ruler on his own subjects as soldiers. This cannot be except the country is well ruled, for good arms indicate good laws and good customs, and a people united, physically vigorous, mentally courageous, and so loyal to the prince that they are willing to die for him.[6] The ruler supported in war by his own subjects must in peace have conducted himself properly and prudently, as did Machiavelli's model, Duke Valentino, when in the Romagna he gained the love and reverence of his people.[7]

While the hereditary prince might profit by this advice of Machiavelli, it is written especially for the new ruler who should owe his power to his own *virtù*, not to fortune or the aid of others: "Colui che è tanto ambizioso che, non solamente per difendersi ma per offendere altri, chiama simili aiuti, cerca d' acquistare quello che non può tenere, e che, da quello che gliene acquista, gli può facilmente essere tolto."[8] The influence of the spirit of the concluding chapter of *The Prince* is here paramount, as elsewhere; the deliverer of Italy must conquer with his own devoted soldiers, who, like him, will combat for true glory as their fit reward. Earlier writers to princes, less bent on a specific and difficult purpose, were under less obligation to advise against hired soldiers.

For the methods according to which these soldiers are to be trained, Machiavelli may be said for the moment to remit his reader to his predecessors. Egidio Colonna, for example, employed in the section on warfare of his *De regimine principum* some of the Latin writers from whom Machiavelli borrowed for his own *Arte della guerra*.[9]

[5] "A prince or a republic, then, ought to adopt any other plan rather than resort to bringing auxiliary troops into his country for its defence, when he is obliged to rely entirely on them, for any treaty, any agreement, however hard, that he may make with the enemy will be less irksome than such a plan" (*Discorsi* 2.20, p. 172a).

[6] *Discorsi* 1.43, p. 114a.   [7] *Prince* 7, p. 17b.

[8] "He who is so ambitious that not merely to defend himself but to attack others he calls in foreign aid seeks to acquire what he is unable to hold and what will easily be taken away from him by the foreigner who gained it for him" (*Discorsi* 2.20, p. 172ab).

[9] L. Arthur Burd, *Le Fonti letterarie di Niccolò Machiavelli nell' arte della guerra*.

Chapter 14

Quod principem deceat circa militiam.
(What the prince ought to do in military affairs.)

In advising his prince to be prepared for war, Machiavelli follows in the footsteps of all the more practical of the advisers of the ruler. There are, to be sure, some who like St. Thomas and his continuator in his *De regimine principum* gave attention to the morals of the ruler and his civil duties without discussion of warfare,[1] but others, like Egidio Colonna, thought it their duty to prepare the prince for both peace and war; each work normally contains a section, borrowed chiefly from the classics, in which specific advice on warfare is given.[2] Much of the matter is such as appears in Machiavelli's own *Art of War*. Other writers give only a general exhortation to be prepared, as in the translation of Isocrates' *Ad Nicoclem* or *De regno administrando* by Erasmus: "Esto bellicosus rei militaris scientia, ac belli apparatu."[3] The opinion of Beroaldus was that "princeps non minus sit rei militaris quam civilis administrationis gnarus consultusque, nec minus bellica laude quam urbica praepollens."[4]

Machiavelli's advice on hunting comes from Xenophon,[5] to

[1] In the light of the passage quoted on p. 65, above, it seems probable that Aquinas, if he had finished his work, would have dealt with warfare.

[2] Egidio devotes to it one of the three parts of his third book. Hoccleve discusses it under the heading of Magnanimity. Frachetta divides his *Prencipe* (1599) into two sections, one on affairs of peace, the other on warfare; the second is longer than the first, but that is unusual.

[3] "Let him be ready for war in his knowledge of military matters and in material equipment for war" (*Opera Omnia* 4, 614 A). Erasmus gives to a chapter of his *Institutio principis* the title *De bello suscipiendo;* it gives no advice for warfare but discourages the prince from undertaking conflict. Peraldus in the last book of his *De eruditione principum,* once attributed to Aquinas, does something of the same sort.

[4] "The prince should not be less intelligent and well-versed in military affairs than in civil administration, nor less strong in military than in civic reputation" (*De optimo statu,* folio 132 recto).

[5] Cf. Platina (*Principis Diatuposis* 3.2), who speaks of hunting as a sort of simulacrum of war, "ea enim bellicae arti omnino persimilis est."—"For this is in every way very similar to warfare." Throughout his book he leans heavily on Xenophon, "tota enim eius historia ad instituendum principem, tum domi, tum foris, pertinet." "For all his narrative pertains to the instruction of a prince, both at home and abroad" (ibid. 3.7).

whom he refers in telling its value to a general in *Discorsi* 3.39, and his associated emphasis on topography is by Burd assigned to Plutarch.[6] Machiavelli is unusually emphatic on the observation of topography, though other writers do not omit it. Platina, for example, writes: "Oportet ducem esse solertem ad omnia prae-cavenda. Quod percommode fiet, si regiones, si vias, si montes, si convalles, si flumina nota habuerit."[7] Patricius writes a chapter *De peregrinationis utilitate, de geographia, cosmographia, et pictura mundi, ac regionum in quibus bellum geritur.*[8]

Egidio had written: "Hanc autem prudentiam, videlicet mi-litarem, maxime decet habere regem."[9] And quite as emphatically Patricius:

Nulla enim disciplina aut exercitatio magis utilis, ac necessaria est, quam rei militaris ac bellicae, cui longe tutius confidere debet, quam omnibus opulentiis, ac copiis.[10] Rex enim qui ocio gaudet, et armorum strepitum, ac laborem exhorret, fortunam suam ut in consilio habeat oportet, quae ei caveat, polliceaturque perpetuam pacem.[11]

Machiavelli is yet more emphatic in his exhortation that a ruler acquire military competence, both in mind and body, as indeed is required by the emphasis laid on "good arms" as being the ruler's own and not those he can hire.[12] The military art is that in which the ruler should become expert and the only one about which he

[6] Burd's edition of *Il Principe*, p. 280. Philipoemon's method of proposing prob-lems is like that used by Admiral Mahan in the Naval War College (Mahan, *Armaments and Arbitration*, p. 214).

[7] "The general should be skilful in guarding beforehand against all contingencies. He may do this easily if he has become acquainted with districts, roads, mountains, valleys, and rivers" (*Principis diatuposis* 3.8, *de itinere militari*).

[8] "On the utility of travel, and on geography, cosmography, and the use of maps of the world and of countries in which war is carried on" (*De regno* 3.14). Cf. p. 209, below.

[9] "It is especially desirable that the prince should possess this type of wisdom, namely military skill" (*De regimine* 3.3.1).

[10] Cf. *Discorsi* 2.10, title: "I danari non sono il nervo della guerra, secondo che è la comune opinione."—"Money is not the sinew of war, according to the common opinion." Machiavelli was not ignorant of the importance of money in war, admitting among independent rulers those able through wealth—"abundanzia di . . . danari" (*Prince* 10, p. 22a)—to put an army in the field, but he be-lieved that the proverb magnified its importance.

[11] "No discipline or activity is more useful and necessary to him than that in soldierly and warlike matters, in which he can confide much more safely than in the most abundant wealth. For a king who delights in idleness and dreads the confusion and labor of arms must needs have Fortune as it were on his council, that she may protect him and promise him perpetual peace" (*De regno* 8.12).

[12] *Prince* 12, first paragraph, and p. 25b.

should seriously concern himself; through this alone he may hope
to retain his principality. Similarly Castiglione's courtier is to have
"in effetto per sua principal professione l'arme."[13] The vigor of
Machiavelli's assertion at the beginning of chapter fourteen that
the ruler should make arms his profession is such that he appears
to be combatting those who had assigned other professions to the
ruler.[14] An example is furnished by Clichtoveus, who quoted with
approval the saying of Vegetius: "Nullus est quem oportet vel plura
vel meliora scire quam principem: cuius doctrina debet omnibus
prodesse subiectis."[15] To Clichtoveus this expresses not the difficulty of the royal office, but what the ruler should actually strive
to attain. The king should be familiar with scripture, he should
understand law, he should be a literary man, as were Augustus and
Trajan; like Alphonso of Castile he may apply himself to astron-
omy. But Machiavelli would answer that such a prince would ruin
himself and his country. The neglect of military affairs was for
him about as serious when it resulted from the attempt to become
"professo" of some other art as when it resulted from love for
"delicatezze."[16] This opinion is the result of observation; Francesco
Sforza became prince because he was a successful soldier, not because of other attainments.[17] In order to present to the ruler a workable scheme Machiavelli abandons the laudable but impossible re-
quirements of the older writers for one that can be realized, namely
that the head of the state should be by profession a soldier. In in-
sisting on a limited field, he was perhaps influenced by a conception of the specialized character of military knowledge, such as
Egidio held (p. 63, above). His advice also depends on preoccupation with the uncertainty of life; if times are not likely to change,
the ruler can safely learn the art of agriculture,[18] but since change

[13] "In truth to have arms as his chief profession" (*Il cortegiano* 1.44).

[14] Osorius, Bishop of Sylves, in his *De regis institutione et disciplina* (Lisbon,
1571) discusses the knowledge of various professions suitable to a ruler. One of
the speakers in the dialogue asserts that empires are gained by arms, not by elo-
quence and learning (lib. 1, p. 24). The bishop was perhaps influenced by Machiavelli.

[15] "There is no one who ought to know more or know it better than the prince,
whose knowledge should profit all his subjects" (Iodocus Clichtoveus, *De regis
officio opusculum*, chap. 6).   [16] *Prince* 14, p. 29a.

[17] Cf.: "Diceva che la Militia gli era parsa molto commoda . . . perche
mediante lei si fanno i Principi de gli huomini."—"He said that military skill appeared to him very convenient because through it princes are made of men" (Leon
Batista Alberti, *Del principe* 2.40.27).

[18] Cf. Osorius, op. cit., bk. 7, p. 229; Patricius, op. cit. 3.8.

is certain—as Machiavelli means by saying "when" not "if" fortune changes,[19] the ruler must learn the only art through which he can hope to hold his position. The exhortation to military activity as a preparation for a change of fortune is in harmony with the words of Patricius already quoted (p. 71), and with the following:

Tunc Rex veluti bonus gubernator tranquillo aequore futurae tempestati se praeparat, arma levat, oppida munit, fossas ducit, arces, muros, et reliqua munimenta instaurat, tunc etiam militiam scribit, ut quando usus fuerit, omnia sint parata.[20]

The paragraph second from the end of this fourteenth chapter of *The Prince* shows the faith of the humanists in the practical value of history.[21] Yet Machiavelli was not the only practical man

[19] *Prince* 14, p. 30b.

[20] "Like a good pilot the king in tranquil weather prepares for the tempest to come; he gets together arms, fortifies towns, digs ditches, builds citadels, walls, and other fortifications; then too he enrolls soldiers, that when there is need all things may be prepared" (*De regno* 9.3). Cf. "non fare conto, nella bonaccia, della tempesta,"—"not to take account, in fair weather, of the tempest" (*Prince* 24, p. 47b).

[21] "Mais vous pouués auoir vne grande Maistresse, qui equipolle toute seule à plusieurs grands Precepteurs ensemble, & si enseigne par grand plaisir & doulceur ceulx, qui s'addonnent à sa doctrine. Et se nomme ceste maistresse que vous aurés au lieu de Maistres, Histoire. . . . Les exemples & faicts memorables sont extraicts de vertus, dont les scintilles sont par Nature engendrées es nobles coeurs, qui ont amour & inclination à poursuiure les choses honnestes & vertueuses.

"Parquoy, si vostre plaisir s'addonne a ouyr ceste Maistresse, auec ce, qu'elle vous donnera passetemps, quand vous serés ennuyé de la presse. Et si d'aduantaige vous monstrera la façon, & vous fera acquerir & garder grand honneur, & hault renom en vostre vie, par toute la Chrestianté, & si loing que la renommée de France s'estend: & moyen aprés la mort de laisser de vostre nom, de vostre regne: digne, honorable, ioyeuse, & recommandable vertu."—"But you are able to have a great mistress who alone equals several great teachers put together and indeed teaches with great kindness and gentleness those who give themselves over to her instruction. And this mistress whom you have in place of masters is called History. . . . The examples and memorable deeds are drawn from virtues of which the sparks are engendered by Nature in noble hearts, which have desire and inclination to pursue things honorable and virtuous.

"Hence you will get great pleasure in listening to this mistress and in addition she will furnish you with recreation when you are wearied with the crowd. And indeed she will admirably show you how to acquire and aid you in gaining and keeping great honor and high renown during your life throughout Christendom and as far as the reputation of France extends, and she will provide you means of leaving after your death your name and reign with the fame of worthy, honorable, happy, and commendable excellence" (Guillaume Budé, *De l'institution du prince*, p. 43). This work is assigned by Delaruelle (*Guillaume Budé*, p. 201) to the year 1519.

Patricius speaks in much the same strain (*De regno* 2.10).

who had faith in the value of reading; Philippe de Commynes asserted, with war especially in mind:

Est grant advantaige aux princes d'avoir veü des hystoires en leur jeunesse, èsquelles voyent largement de telles assemblées et de grans fraudes et tromperies et parjuremens que aucuns des anciens ont fait les ungs vers les autres et prinz et tuéz ceulz qui en telles seüretéz s'estoient fiéz. Il n'est pas dit que tous en ayent usé, mais l'exemple d'ung est assez pour en faire saiges plusieurs et leur donner vouloir de se garder.

Et est, ce me semble (ad ce que j'ay veü par experience de ce monde, où j'ay esté autour des princes l'espace de dix huit ans ou plus, ayant clère congnoissance des plus grandes et secrètes matières qui se soient traictées en ce royaulme de France et seigneuries voysines), l'ung des grandz moyens de rendre ung homme saige d'avoir leü les hystoires anciennes et apprendre à se conduyre et garder et entreprendre saigement par les hystoires et exemples de noz predecesseurs. Car nostre vie est si briefve qu'elle ne suffit à avoir de tant de choses experience.[22]

Machiavelli perhaps began the paragraph with the plan of showing that through reading generals have gained help for specific military situations.[23] But he turned rapidly to matter applying to the

[22] "It is a great advantage to princes to have perused histories in their youth, for in them they read at length of such assemblies and of the great frauds and deceptions and perjuries which some of the ancients have practised on one another, and how they have taken and killed those who put their trust in such security. It is not to be said that all have used them, but the example of one is sufficient to make several wise and to cause them to wish to protect themselves.

"(According to what I have seen in my experience in this world, where I have been around princes eighteen years or more, having clear knowledge of the greatest and most secret matters which were transacted in this kingdom of France and the neighboring countries) it seems to me that one of the best means in which a man can make himself wise is to read history and learn from the histories and examples of our predecessors to conduct himself and act cautiously and undertake enterprises wisely. For our life is so short that it does not permit us to have experience of everything" (*Mémoires* 2.6, pp. 128-9). For Machiavelli's knowledge of the work of Commynes see p. 184, and note, below.

[23] Sir Philip Sidney illustrates this in the *Arcadia* (1.6, pp. 39-40): "Whereupon, the councel of the chiefe men was called, and at last, this way Palladius (who by some experience, but especiallie by reading Histories, was acquainted with stratagemes) invented, and was by all the rest approoved: that all the men there shoulde dresse themselves like the poorest sorte of the people in Arcadia, having no banners, but bloudie shirtes hanged upon long staves, with some bad bagge pipes in stead of drumme and fife, their armour they should aswell as might be, cover, or at least make them looke so rustilie, and ill-favouredly as might well become such wearers; and this the whole number should doo, saving two hundred of the best chosen Gentlemen, for courage and strength, whereof *Palladius* him selfe would be one, who should have their armes chayned, and be put in cartes like

general tradition of the type. Scipio's imitation of Cyrus was well known to writers for princes, and the *Cyropaedia* was frequently alluded to.[24] The four historical characters mentioned by Machiavelli are often used as examples in books of advice to princes, perhaps Scipio most of all, in the famous story of his chastity.[25] The qualities Scipio learned from Cyrus, according to Machiavelli, are those conventionally assigned to good princes, as will soon appear. Here Machiavelli seems to accept them all as though he were in conformity with the tradition, though later, in a more characteristic passage (*Prince* 17, p. 33b), he censures Scipio for his *pietà* (i. e., *umanità,* humanity) which again becomes laudable in the *Discorsi* (3.21), though it caused various inconveniences.

The concluding paragraph of chapter fourteen, though characteristically Machiavellian in its unusual insistence on an inevitable

---

prisoners. . . . They sent a cunning fellow, (so much the cunninger as that he could maske it under rudenes) who with such a kind of Rhetorike, as weeded out all flowers of Rhetorike, delivered unto the Helots assembled together, that they were countrie people of Arcadia, no lesse oppressed by their Lords, and no lesse desirous of liberty than they, and therfore had put themselves in the field, and had alreadie (besides a great number slaine) taken nine or ten skore Gentlemen prisoners, whom they had there well and fast chained." By this stratagem, like that of the Greeks in the Iliad, the forces of Palladius are enabled to enter the city of their enemies. Cf. Machiavelli's use of the Roman expedition to Parthia, in the *Arte della guerra* 2, p. 288b.

[24] Iacopo di Messer Poggio [Bracciolini] in the dedication to Ferdinand of Aragon of his Italian translation (Firenze, 1521) of his father's Latin translation of the *Cyropaedia* of Xenophon, writes: "Perche adunque me pare Serenissimo Re, che molte opere della tua inclita virtu, sieno simili à quelle di Cyro, ho iudicato conveniente in tuo nome tradurre la vita sua, accio che imitando Scipione Aphricano superiore, elquale haveva consumato tutte le carte del libro, per la assiduita dal leggierlo, interamente conosca la tua maesta, come debba esser fatto un degno e perfetto Signore, e quali opere sieno mezo, à fare lui immortale, e li popoli sottoposti al suo governo felicissimi."—"Because it seems to me, Most Serene King, that many works of your famous ability are like those of Cyrus, I have judged it proper to translate his life in your name in order that, imitating Scipio Africanus, who had worn out all the leaves of the book by the assiduity of his reading, your majesty may know entirely how a worthy and perfect ruler should be made, and what works are the means to make him immortal, and the people beneath his rule perfectly happy." The same story is told by Castiglione, *Il Cortegiano* 1.43; he apparently derived it from Cicero, *Epist. ad Q. Fratrem* 1.1.8 (23), as did also Patricius, *De regno* 5. proemium. With slightly different wording the fact is related by Cicero in *Tuscul.* 2.26.62. For the *Cyropaedia* see the index.

[25] Hoccleve (stanzas 526-30) tells the story at some length. In touching on the virtue of chastity—normally recommended in the works de reg. pr.—Milton mentions
    How hee sirnam'd of Africa dismiss'd
    In his prime youth the fair Iberian maid
                                    (*Paradise Regained* 2.199-200).

change of fortune, is conventional in its exhortation to prepare for war in time of peace.[26] Giraldus Cambrensis, for example, writes:

Nec solum ad vivendum, verum etiam ad secure feliciterque tempus agendum, plurimum providentia valet. Urbes enim muris claudere, cingere fossatis, turribus erigere, armis atque alimentis copiose munire, ad haec etiam civium animos libertatibus extollere, crebris excitare donariis, ipsam juventutem martis exercitio negotiis erudire, et tanquam ad bella saeva praeludiis quibusdam non inutilibus sub pace formare, providae mentis est et sapientis. Scriptum est enim, "Beata civitas quae in pace bellum cogitat."[27]

[26] For a late example, one may consult the *De optimo principe* (Venice, 1565) of Petrus Bizzarus, p. 13.

[27] "Prudence is a great assistance not merely in living but even in passing one's time securely and happily. It is the work of a foreseeing and wise intellect to shut up cities within walls, to encircle them with moats, to make them formidable with towers, and to furnish them plentifully with arms and food, and in addition to elevate the spirits of the citizens with liberties, to stimulate them with frequent gifts, to exercise the youth in warfare, and in peace to form them as though for difficult wars with certain valuable preparatives. For it is written, 'Blessed is the state which in peace thinks on war' " (1.12).

Chapter 15

De his rebus quibus homines et praesertim principes
laudantur aut vituperantur.
(Of those things for which men and especially princes are
praised or blamed.)

In the preceding chapters Machiavelli has discussed topics traditionally important to advisers of princes, and has written according
to his own theories of politics, with some implied disagreement
with traditional notions. He has not, however, avowedly come to
grips with his predecessors by stating his own theory and defend-
ing it as truth over against falsehood. The break properly comes
with the discussion of the ethical problem: what view of the world
is to control the *modi e governi* of the prince? A ruler holding any
moral theory might decide to employ native or foreign soldiers,
but on such matters as liberality or veracity there was, according
to the tradition, but one decision to make. Consequently at this
point, Machiavelli, after some slight apology, asserts that he is going to depart far from the procedure of other writers—"dagli ordini
degli altri."[1] Let no reader suppose he is once more to peruse the
commonplaces of the Aristotelian or Biblical writers on the subject. Diverging from their method, that of presenting a prince
morally perfect, but such as man has never seen, Machiavelli will
take facts as they are and attempt to write a book that can guide
a prince in the practical conduct of affairs. Imaginary perfect states
are well enough in their places, but in a world of woe it is not
possible to conduct oneself as though in Utopia; he who attempts
it ruins himself. Hence a prince who expects to rule successfully
must learn to thwart the plans of powerful and unscrupulous enemies; at times he may be able to do this by acting in complete accord with the moral virtues, but at others he must descend to the
level of his enemies or perish. If he decides to remain a ruler, he
must do anything that is necessary to maintain himself, without
respect to ethical teaching. His conduct must be determined by the
demands of present conditions and future probabilities.

Yet Machiavelli uses some caution in his disagreement. His contemporary Clichtoveus asserted in the preface of his *De regis officio*

[1] *Prince* 15, p. 30b.

that a virtuous life would bring everlasting renown and that wickedness would result in unending opprobrium. Machiavelli has observed that praise and blame do actually come to rulers because of certain qualities.

A ruler may be praised as	A ruler may be blamed as
liberale	misero
donatore	rapace
pietoso	crudele
fedele	fedifrago
feroce e animoso	effeminato e pusillanime
umano	superbo
casto	lascivo
intero	astuto[2]
facile	duro
grave	leggieri
religioso	incredulo
e simili	e simili[3]

While these lists may be taken to represent Machiavelli's observation of the reputations of rulers, they are made up also of the qualities conventionally praised and blamed by those who have told how a ruler should conduct himself to his people—"quali debbano essere e'modi e governi di uno principe con sudditi."[4] Giraldus, for example, gives in the heading of chapters the following virtues, among others: *moderamen, mansuetudo, pudicitia, patientia, temperantia, clementia, munificentia, audacia et animositas, religio ac devotio.*[5] Nor was the habit of using such chap-

[2] See pp. 118 ff., below.

[3]
liberal	miserly
willing to give	rapacious
piteous	cruel
faithful	a breaker of faith
bold and spirited	effeminate and pusillanimous
humane	proud
chaste	lascivious
sincere	selfishly astute
easy of access	harsh
grave	irresponsible
religious	skeptical
and the like	and the like (*Prince* 15, p. 31a).

[4] "What should be the habits and conduct of a prince in dealing with his subjects" (*Prince* 15, p. 30b).

[5] Moderation, clemency, chastity, gentleness, temperance, clemency, munificence, audacity and vigor, religion and devotion.

ters merely a mediaeval convention.[6] It was carried also into the renaissance. Patricius, for example, discusses in separate chapters the longest list of virtues and vices and associated qualities that I have seen; he may be supposed to give all Machiavelli would have included in the words "e simili" at the end of the list. He has, for instance, *magnificentia, misericordia, castitas, fortitudo, constantia, amicitia, religio, humanitas, facilitas,*[7] *fides;*[8] fewer vices appear in the headings of chapters, though *avaritia* and others are there; other vices are treated with the virtues to which they are opposed. Having given his list, Machiavelli, tacitly agreeing with the tradition, says that for a prince to have all these good qualities would be admirable —"laudabilissima cosa."[9] That he was not paying merely lip-service to the convention is apparent in his praise of Duke Valentino, who exhibited some of the qualities listed, being "severo e grato, magnanimo e liberale";[10] on the other hand, he is commended for using tricks *(inganni)* and dissimulating.[11] Because human conditions do not permit, the virtues cannot be altogether observed by any ruler. This is the counterblast to Egidio's assertion that to lack

[6] The method is used by Smaragdus in his *Via Regia* addressed to Ludovicus Pius (reigned from 814 to 840), and occurs in later writers so numerous that they need not be specified.

[7] Cf. Machiavelli's *facile*. "Facilitas virtus est in rege omnium gratissima ad ineundam gratiam, benevolentiamque servandam."—"Facility is the virtue in a king that is most likely to bring him into favor and to preserve the good will of the people" (Patricius, op. cit., 8.19). "E certo una de le lodevoli parti ch' abbia ogni vero prencipe, è esser facile ad udir le querele e supplicazioni de i suoi, et intender ciò che si fa nel suo dominio."—"Certainly one of the most praise-worthy qualities a true prince can have is that of facility in hearing the complaints and supplications of his people and understanding what goes on in his realm" (Bandello, *Novelle*, parte 2, nov. 37, p. 401). Machiavelli's praise of the Emperor makes him *facile* (*Rapporto della Magna, Opere*, Italia, 1813, vol. 4, pp. 166, 168; *Legazione all' Imperatore*, vol. 7, p. 186, letter 6).

In Albrecht Dürer's wood-cut designs for the symbolic triumphal chariot of the Emperor Maximilian, dated 1518-22, the Emperor sits in his chariot attended by the allegorical figures of Iusticia, Clementia, Veritas, Temperantia, Liberalitas, Aequitas, Securitas, Gravitas, Perseverantia, Constantia, Ratio, Providentia, Moderatio, Alacritas, Fortitudo, Inteligentia, Mansuetudo, Bonitas, Fidentia, Prudentia, Oportunitas, Velocitas, Firmitudo, Acrimonia, Virilitas, Audatia, Magnanimitas, Experientia, Solertia; the chariot wheels are Honor, Magnificentia, Dignitas, and Gloria; the reins that guide the horses are Nobilitas and Potentia (Dürer, *Gemälde*, pp. 362-9).

[8] Generosity on a grand scale, mercy, chastity, fortitude, constancy, friendliness, religion, humanity, ease of access, good faith.

[9] *Prince* 15, p. 31a.

[10] "Severe and pleasing, magnanimous and liberal" (*Prince* 7, p. 17b).

[11] *Prince* 7, p. 16a. See also pp. 118, 128, below.

one virtue is to lack all.[12] Abandoning moral exhortation, Machiavelli simply requires that his ruler should avoid being generally accused of such vices as would weaken his hold on his state, by causing men to think that he was dilatory, unpopular, easily deceived, cowardly, without financial ability or military experience, or otherwise unfitted to deal with open enemies or secret conspirators. Vices likely to raise up and encourage enemies must be recognized and, if not abandoned, at least dissimulated. As to vices that will not lead men to belittle the ruler's capacity and resources, they may well be avoided—as the moralists exhort—but if this cannot easily be done there need be few regrets. In this statement Machiavelli announces his independence of the older theory that the ruler should be a perfect character or at least should surpass his subjects in moral excellence,[13] and asserts that nothing matters except what clearly affects his success in his dealings with his subjects, his allies, and his enemies. Still further, the ruler should not hesitate before the reputation or the reality of any vices that will be of assistance to him in maintaining his state; in the light of that end all moral considerations disappear. There is no primary asking concerning good or evil but merely what, all things considered, will result in the security and well-being of the ruler—"la securtà e il bene essere suo."[14]

This chapter depends on certain Machiavellian theories of life: the uncertainty of human affairs, the tendency of men toward evil rather than good, the necessity of prudence, the determining force of an immediate and somewhat limited end, the regard of the here and now. But specifically it shows all these theories in action against the advice normally given to princes. It is written to warn the ruler to whom *The Prince* is addressed to reject much of the counsel in the works *de regimine principum* to be found in his library as apparently good but as conducting straight to temporal ruin. Security and well-being can come to the ruler only through a different plan of conduct; this plan Machiavelli intends to set forth. In other words, the purpose of this chapter is to inform a reader that the work will deal with many of the topics normal in works of advice to rulers, but that in treating them it will be governed by principles

---

[12] *De regimine* 1.2.31.

[13] "Par est eum qui dominatur/ut dignitate subditis praestat: ita virtute eos antecellere."—"It is right that he who rules should excel his subjects in virtue as he surpasses them in dignity" (Clichtoveus, *De regis officio*, chap. 4).

[14] *Prince* 15, p. 31a.

quite unlike those that inspired earlier productions. Since there
may be times when the necessity of maintaining himself will demand from the ruler the practice of moral qualities which are
highly laudable when they do not interfere with the primary functions of the prince, Machiavelli's conclusions will not in all circumstances be unlike those commonly accepted. It is no great exaggera-
tion to state his purpose as that of sifting previous works *de
regimine principum,* with the intention of rejecting the inexpedient
or harmful and retaining the valuable.

Machiavelli's position is sufficiently original and powerfully
stated to justify his reputation; if praise for originality implied ideas
in every respect previously unsuggested, it would never be given
to humanity. While earlier writers can hardly be said to have anticipated his work, they are not without some glimmerings of the
reasons behind his beliefs; possibly they even gave specific assistance to the clarification of his thought. They are not unaware of
the difficulty of bringing together the immediately expedient and
the truth resulting from practical consideration of the "modi e
governi" of the prince. Egidio writes on the difficulties of actual
administration:

Oportet ipsum esse cautum, nam sicut in speculabilibus falsa aliquando
admiscentur veris, propter quod creduntur vera, quae non sunt vera,
sed apparent vera: sic in agibilibus mala multotiens admiscentur bonis,
propter quod creduntur bona, sed non sunt bona, sed apparent bona.
Oportet igitur regem esse cautum, respuendo apparenter bona, et
eligendo bona simpliciter, ad quae debet dirigere gentem sibi com-
missam.[15]

Nor is there complete novelty in Machiavelli's belief that the
reputation for the virtues especially concerning the preservation of
the ruler's position is the essential thing; a passage in the fifth book
of the *Politics* of Aristotle had been interpreted by the continuator
of the commentary of Aquinas as meaning:

Expedit tyranno ad salvandum tyrannidem quod non appareat subditis
saevus, sive crudelis: et ratio hujus est, quia ex hoc quod apparet subditis
saevus, reddit se odiosum eis, ex hoc autem facilius insurgunt in
eum: sed debet se reddere reverendum propter excellentiam alicujus

[15] "He should therefore be cautious, for as in what we see the false is mingled
with the true in such a way that those things are believed true which are not true
but appear true, so in what we do evil oftentimes is mingled with good, so that
things are believed good which are not good but appear so. The king therefore
should be cautious, rejecting the apparently good and choosing what is truly good,
toward which he should direct the people committed to him" (*De regimine* 1.2.8).

boni excellentis; reverentia enim debetur bono excellenti: et si non habeat illud bonum excellens, debet simulare se habere illud.[16]

Figliucci interpreted the passage thus: "Debbano attendere a le virtù e, se non possono acquistarse tutte, almeno apprendano la virtù politica, e si mostrino civili in ogni loro azzione, la quale se pur non possono acquistar, studinsi almeno di dare ad intender al popolo d'haverla, et di far nascer nel populo una tal' opinione verso di lui."[17] Such a concession was unacceptable to Egidio (1.2.33); he abandoned Aristotle for Macrobius and Plotinus, who make the "virtutes politicae" lowest in the scale, and demand the highest or exemplary virtues from the true ruler. An interpretation of Aristotle more pleasing to the typical writer *de regimine principum* is that of Erasmus: "Aristoteles in Politicis suis, quid tamen exigit a Principe vir Ethnicus? num Nerei formam, aut Milonis vires, num Maximini proceritatem, num Tantali talenta? Nihil horum. Quid igitur? Summam et absolutam virtutem, in privatis contentus mediocritate."[18] He is referring to a passage in the *Politics,* where we read: "We answer that the good ruler is a good and wise man. . . . If

[16] "It behooves a tyrant that for the preservation of his tyranny he should not appear to his subjects savage or cruel; the reason for this is that if he appears savage to his subjects, he renders himself hateful to them, and thereupon they more easily rebel against him. But he ought to make himself revered by his excellence in some excellent good quality, for reverence is paid to an excellent good quality; and if he does not possess that excellent good quality, he should pretend that he has it" (*Commentary on the Politics,* lib. 5, lectio 12). In the Oxford Aristotle the passage in the *Politics* itself is rendered: "Whatever virtues he may neglect, at least he should maintain the character of a great soldier, and produce the impression that he is one" (1314 b 22).

[17] "They should give attention to the virtues, and if they are not able to acquire all of them, at least they should learn political virtue and reveal in every act that they consider the good of the state. And if they are not able to acquire political virtue, they should at least endeavor to make the people think they possess it and to have such an opinion about them spring up among the people" (*De la politica,* folio 188 verso). This work was composed about 1550 at the "studio celebre di Padova"; it seems unaffected by Machiavelli and perhaps represents the teaching of the university. Of the Aristotelianism of the earlier part of the century at Padova Tommasini says: "When Campanella wrote: 'Machiavellism is derived from Aristotelianism,' he had in mind the Aristotelianism of the university of Padova, to wit, that of Pomponazzi and Andrea Cesalpino and perhaps as well that of Nifo" (*Machiavelli* 2.24, note 4). Since Pomponazzi is said to have believed in the general dissemination of Aristotelian views (Flamini, *Il cinquecento,* p. 474), Figliucci's book may exemplify the teacher's theory.

[18] "What does Aristotle, though a heathen, demand from the prince in his *Politics?* the beauty of Nereus, the physical strength of Milo, the stature of Maximinus, the riches of Tantalus? None of these. What then? Complete and absolute virtue, though he is content with mediocrity in private citizens" (*Institutio* cap. i, col. 583 B).

then the virtue of a good ruler is the same as that of a good man, and we assume further that the subject is a citizen as well as the ruler, the virtue of the good citizen and the virtue of the good man cannot be absolutely the same, although in some cases they may be."[19] This suggestion of a standard other than moral in politics was honestly interpreted by Aquinas, who writes in his commentary: "Relinquitur ergo, quod non sit eadem virtus boni civis et boni viri."[20] Concerning the prince Aquinas assigns to Aristotle the opinion: "Non enim dicitur aliquis esse bonus princeps, nisi sit bonus per virtutes morales et prudens. Dictum est enim in sexto *Ethicorum* quod politia est quaedam pars prudentiae; unde oportet politicum, idest rectorem politiae, esse prudentem, et per consequens bonum virum."[21] The concession as to the citizen was distasteful to him, it appears, for we read in his commentary on the *Ethics*: "In tertio enim libro *Politicae* ostenditur quod non est idem simpliciter esse virum bonum, et esse civem bonum, secundum quamcumque politiam. Sunt enim quaedam politiae, non rectae, secundum quas aliquis potest esse civis bonus, qui non est vir bonus; sed secundum optimam politicam non est aliquis civis bonus, qui non est vir bonus."[22] He is alluding to the kind of state which, Machiavelli thought, existed only in imagination, but for which most advisers of princes had written.

But whatever allowances are made for preceding opinion, for Machiavelli to say that it is essential for a prince who will maintain himself to be sometimes deliberately evil—"imparare a potere essere non buono"[23]—is a contradiction of all the preceding writers on the relations of princes to their subjects.

[19] *Politics* 3.4, 1277a15-24.

[20] "It follows, therefore, that the virtue of the good citizen and of the good man are not the same" (*Commentary on Politics,* lib. 3, lect. 3).

[21] "No one can be called a good prince unless he is good in the moral virtues and prudent. For it is said in the sixth book of the *Ethics* that political ability is a special part of prudence; hence it is necessary that the politician, that is the ruler of a well-ordered state, should be prudent, and consequently a good man" (ibid.).

[22] "In the third book of the *Politics* is shown that it is not the same without qualification to be a good man and a good citizen, in any political organization. For there are certain political organizations, not properly organized, in which one can be a good citizen without being a good man; but in the best political organization one is not a good citizen who is not a good man" (Lib. 5, lect. 3). Figliucci expresses the same opinion: "Può essere per certo che in una perfetta Republica sia qualche buon cittadino ancora buon huomo, e per il contrario qualche buon huomo se ritruovi, che sia buon cittadino."—"It can certainly be true that in a perfect state every good citizen can also be a good man, and on the contrary whoever is a good man is a good citizen" (*De la politica,* lib. 3, folio 86 recto).

[23] "To learn to be able not to be good" (*Prince* 15, p. 30b).

Chapter 16

De liberalitate et parsimonia.
(Of liberality and parsimony.)

It is easy to imagine that Machiavelli put liberality first in his list of kingly virtues because of all the supposed virtues of the king, it was, in the opinion of the Florentine, that on which most non-sense had been written.[1] A further reason is, possibly, that Machiavelli himself had once held the common opinion, as has been suggested above,[2] and wished considerably to dissent from it. Because of the vigor of Machiavelli's opposition to the current opinion, it is easy to miss various qualifications. As throughout *The Prince,* prudent adaptation to circumstances is the ruling principle. If liberality can be practised without destroying itself, it need not be discouraged, and may even be highly commended.

Such liberality is that which takes not from the stores of the prince himself but from those of others, as in the instance of the conqueror who gives freely to his soldiers from the goods of his enemies. This principle explains, we may suppose, Machiavelli's approval of the huge expenditure of Cosimo de' Medici. He was very liberal;[3] his liberality, moreover, is mentioned with approval in a panegyric in which the writer imitates royal biographers—"quelli che scrivono le vite de' principi."[4] Machiavelli intends to show that, as in loans and building operations, it reached that quality of *suntuosità* or *magnificenza* which brings reputation.[5] High

---

[1] As an extreme instance, in the treatise *de reg. pr.* imbedded in the romance of *Lancelot of the Laik,* generous giving receives far more than its proportionate attention. Arthur is almost overthrown by his failure in liberality and prospers when he adopts a liberal policy. The adviser tells him, for example:

Who gladly iffith, be vertew of larges
His tresory encresis of Richness (1767-68, ed. of the Scottish Text Society, Edinburgh, 1912).　　　　　　　[2] Pp. 9 ff.

[3] *Istorie Fiorentine* 4.26, p. 490b; 27, p. 492a; 7.5, p. 565a; 8.10, p. 598b.

[4] Ibid. 7.6, p. 567b.

[5] *Prince* 16, p. 31b. In his treatise on *Magnificentia* (caps. 10, 11) Pontanus praises that virtue in Cosimo, as for instance: "Ad Cosmi autoritatem addidere plurimum tum villae diversis in locis ab ipso aedificatae singulari cum magnificentia, tum domus, in qua condenda pervetustum atque obliteratum iam structurae morem modumque revocavit, qui mihi id videtur egisse, ut discerent posteri, qua via aedificarent."—"A great addition to the dignity of Cosimo was made by the villas

position was reached by Cosimo partly because of his liberality; this, as in the instance of Caesar and Pope Julius, Machiavelli would allow; but the sumptuousness of Cosimo did not cease as long as he lived. The key to Machiavelli's approval is to be found in the word *prudenza,* usually linked with *liberalità* in his praise of the *Pater Patriae.* The sumptuousness of the banker-prince did not destroy his power to be liberal. In other accounts of Cosimo, Machiavelli does not dwell on his financial prudence, perhaps thinking it too well known to all the world, but merely says that the property left by the father was by the son not merely maintained but increased.[6] He implies the same thing by writing—in an aside more vivid than a direct statement—that the men who managed his affairs throughout Europe shared in his prosperity.[7] The money so freely poured out in Florence and in her interests was not taken from the pockets of the citizens, but came from the profits of business in distant cities where Cosimo's banking houses were to be found: London, Paris, Bruges, Lyons, Genoa, or Naples. Since his lavish presents came from the resources of others, there could properly be applied to him the Machiavellian saying: "Non debbe lasciare indrieto parte alcuna di liberalità."[8]

In truth Machiavelli in this sixteenth chapter is objecting to imprudent lavishness, not to liberality properly so-called, "se la [liberalità] si usa virtuosamente e come la si debbe usare, la non fia conosciuta, e non ti cascherà la infamia del suo contrario."[9] True to his principle of dealing not with moral goodness but with what will help maintain the ruler, he has no interest in the Christian virtue of liberality, but only in a liberality that will be of political service by gaining the ruler a reputation, as it did for Pope Julius,

---

he built in various places with extraordinary magnificence, as well as by the houses in the construction of which he brought back the ancient and forgotten custom and manner of building; he seems to me to have done this that he might teach posterity how they should build."

[6] *Istorie Fiorentine* 4.16, p. 482b. Cf. the following: "Cosimo de' Medici inherited in 1429 his share of his father's estate of 179,221 gold florins; and by his business operations was enabled in thirty-five years to give away to the public a half million florins, and still leave a property behind him more than double all his father had accumulated" (Walter B. Scaife, *Commerce and Industry of Florence during the Renaissance,* in Annual Report of the American Historical Association for the Year 1891, p. 307).   [7] *Istorie Fiorentine* 7.6, p. 566a.

[8] "He should not neglect any part of liberality" (*Prince* 16, p. 32a).

[9] "If liberality is used virtuously and as it ought to be used, it will not be known and you will not escape the infamy of its contrary" (*Prince* 16, p. 31ab).

Cosimo de' Medici, and Duke Valentino.[10] This is verbally insisted on throughout the chapter in the discussion not of mere liberality, but of a reputation for liberality—of being "tenuto liberale" and of having the "nome di liberale." But to secure the name of being liberal, virtuous liberality is of no consequence; a ruler must needs be sumptuous, munificent. To those who benefited from it, the lavishness of the ruler would appear liberality, as Vettori knew: "Interviene che, de' cento che usano le corti, ve ne sono novantanove bisognosi, e che in loro piaceri vogliono spendere più che non possono: e perchè il Principe a dare loro inclini; a uno Principe rubatore e prodigo, danno il nome di liberale; a uno astinente di quello d'altri, e vero liberale, danno il nome di avaro."[11]

Such distinction in words Machiavelli may have derived from reading traditional works *de regimine principum,* whence he learned what liberality meant according to the theory founded on the *Ethics* of Aristotle. This is set forth by Egidio:

Si igitur in faciendo sumptus convenit deficere, quod facit avaritia: et superabundare, quod facit prodigalitas, quia utrunque est contra rectam regulam rationis, oportet dare virtutem aliquam mediam inter avaritiam, et prodigalitatem: huiusmodi autem virtus est liberalitas. Patet ergo quid est liberalitas. . . . Liberalitas quia est media inter avaritias et prodigalitates, ideo est virtus reprimens avaritias, et moderans prodigalitates. Consistit autem haec virtus in recto usu pecuniae. . . . Spectat autem ad liberalem non usurpare alios redditus, et cus-

---

[10] Valentino is praised for liberality in *Prince* 7, p. 17b. Munificence for the sake of reputation is recommended in *Prince* 21, near the end.

[11] "It happens that of a hundred who resort to a court, ninety-nine are hard-up and wish to spend in their pleasures more than they are able to. So in order that the prince may be inclined to give to them, they give the name of liberal to a prince who is a thief and a prodigal and the name of avaricious to one who abstains from the property of others and is truly liberal" (*Sommario,* anno 1512, p. 316). This accords with the opinion that flatterers always see the prince as virtuous. Poggio puts it thus: "Obsessi ab adulatoribus omni veritatis cognitione privantur, nam si quem iniuria Princeps afficit, id pro summa iustitia assentatores comprobant. Luxuriam dicunt oblectationem naturalem, usu et consuetudine gentium permissam. Avaricia parcitas, prodigalitas liberalitatis nomine appellantur. Crudelitatis culpam leniunt specie saeveritatis. Nullum est tam tetrum facinus, nullum tam nepharium in regibus vitium, quod non adulatores alicuius virtutis detegant velamento."—"Besieged by flatterers, they are deprived of all knowledge of the truth, for if the prince injures some one these sycophants approve of it as complete justice. They call licentiousness natural delight, allowed by the practice and customs of the nations. Avarice is called thrift, and prodigality goes by the name of liberality. The vice of cruelty they soften with the appearance of severity. There is no evil deed so black, no vice so abominable in kings that flatterers do not conceal it with the garment of some virtue" (*De infelicitate principum,* p. 407). See pp. 186 ff., below.

todire proprios. Nam licet liberales non diligat pecuniam secundum
se, sed ut eam ordinet ad debitos sumptus: tamen ut possit debitos
sumptus facere, non debet proprios redditus inaniter dispergere. Ergo
non usurpare redditus alienos, habere debitam curam de propriis, et
ex eis debitos sumptus facere: sunt illa tria circa quae videtur esse
liberalitas. . . . Maior autem laus consurgit in bene expendendo, et
aliis benefaciendo, quam in custodiendo propria, vel in non usurpando
aliena. Liberalitas ergo principalius consistit in debite expendendo, et
benefaciendo aliis. . . . Cum liberales maxime amentur, circa illud
maxime consistit liberalitas, quod quis agendo maxime amatur. Non
autem maxime amatur aliquis, si aliena bona non surripiat, vel si
proprios redditus custodiat. Sed maxime diligitur si ex propriis redditibus
debitos sumptus faciat, et bonis et dignis magna dona tribuat. Quare
in bene expendendo, et aliis bona retribuendo principaliter liberalitas
consistit. . . . Quia liberalitas magis opponitur avaritiae quam prodi-
galitati, declinandum est magis ad prodigalitatem quam ad avaritiam,
et magis debemus superabundare in dando, quam deficere.[12]

With an understanding of liberality as the right use of money,
avoiding both prodigality and avarice, the dangers of any other
policy were easily arrived at; to the mediaeval world they were
familiar from the *Secretum secretorum:*

[12] "Therefore in attending to expenses there can be too small an allowance, which
is caused by avarice, and there can be lavishness, caused by prodigality; but since
either one is contrary to the rule of right reason, there should be some virtue as
a mean between avarice and prodigality; a virtue of this kind is liberality. It is
therefore evident what liberality is. . . . Since liberality is a mean between acts
of avarice and of prodigality, it is therefore a virtue repressing avaricious acts and
moderating prodigal acts. This virtue, then, consists in the right use of wealth.
. . . It is the part of a liberal man not to seize the income of others and to
care for his own income. For though the liberal man does not love money for
itself but only as he assigns it to proper expenses, yet that he may be able to
indulge in proper expenses he ought not idly to scatter his own funds. Therefore
there are three things that seem to fall under liberality: not to seize the property
of others, to take proper care of one's own funds, and to spend suitable amounts
from them. . . . But greater credit is derived from spending well and from
benefitting others than in taking care of one's own or in not taking another's
goods. Hence liberality consists chiefly in spending properly and benefitting others.
. . . Since liberal men are greatly loved, liberality especially has to do with
that the doing of which makes a man loved. For a person is not greatly loved
because he refrains from taking the goods of others or takes care of his own
finances. But he is much loved if from his own income he makes proper expendi-
tures and gives large gifts to good and worthy persons. Therefore liberality principally consists in spending properly and in bestowing good things on others.
. . . Since liberality is opposed rather to avarice than to prodigality, one should
lean rather toward prodigality than toward avarice, and we should rather super-
abound in giving than fail in it" (*De regimine* 1.2.17).

And if thou wille gete larges, biholde and considir thi power and thi ricches, and also the tyme of nede and the deservyngis of thi men. And than owist thou forto yeue mesurably vnto hem that haue nede thereto, and best haue deseruyd it, and he that yevity othir wise passith the rewle of largesse. ffor he that yevith his good to suche as be not worthi, [it] is but lost, and he that spendith his good out of mesure shalle sone be poore, and this makith her enemyes to haue maystrie ouyr hem. . . . And he that dispendith the goodis of his Rewme out of ordir and discrecioun, and yevith suche as be not worthi, ne haue no nede therto, that kyng distroyeth his peple and the comoun good of the Rewme, and is not worthi forto regne, for he is fool large. . . . Kyng Alexandre, y telle the in certeyne that what kyng makith gretter dispences than the profites conteyne that longen to the crowne, he enclyneth him to fool largesse and nought to skarsnes. That kyng without dowt shalle sone be distroyed. . . . Konnyng is a signe of perfeccioun of a kyng, and that previth whan he withdrawith forto take the goodis and possessiones of his sugetis, for that hath ben the cause of distruccioun of many Remes. ffor kyngis that haue made so outrage dispenses, that the Rentis and profetis that longid to him myght not susteyne ne mayntene ther outrage dispenses, And forto mayntene it, they took the goodis and possessiones from her sugetis, for which cause the pepille cried to god, and god herde hem and sent on hem kyngis of vengeaunce. The pepille rebellid ayens hem and were distroyed of alle, and alle her name putt to nought.[13] And ne were the grace of glorious god, that susteneth and helpith the Innocent peple, alle shuld go to distruccioun and into the domynacioun of Alienes for euyr. And therefore kepe the fro outrageous expenses and yeftis.[14]

The presentation of the evils of foolish liberality in these chapters on "largesse" is not unworthy of Machiavelli; even if, notwithstanding the wide circulation of the *Secretum secretorum* for cen-

---

[13] Cf. Shakespeare, *Macbeth* 4.3.76-87:

MALCOLM.   With this there grows
    In my most ill-compos'd affection such
    A stanchless avarice that, were I king,
    I should cut off the nobles for their lands,
    Desire his jewels and this other's house. . . .

MACDUFF.   This avarice
    Sticks deeper, grows with more pernicious root
    Than summer-seeming lust, and it hath been
    The sword of our slain kings.

[14] *Three Prose Versions of the Secreta Secretorum* (Early English Text Society, Extra Ser. LXXIX), pp. 7, 8. I quote from a vernacular version to illustrate the wide circulation of the work. For other vernacular versions, manuscript and printed, see *Opera . . . Rogeri Baconi*, ed. Steele (Oxford, 1920), 5. xxxi-xxxvii. The earliest Italian printed version there listed is of 1538.

De prudencia:

Princeps fit prudens:fciat hiftorias:faltem familiari∕
ter.Habeat fibi coniunctos; qui legant:qui doceant:
qui honefta fuadeant : inhonefta difuadeant:vtilia &
inutilia demonftrent. Q uamuis neminem oporteat
plūra fcire:cp Principem. Sua enim fapiencia fubiec∕
tis omnibus eft profutura.Ad ipfum eciam pertinet
pacis & belli opera moderari : legumcp tenore iufte
diiudicare.De his ad Dialogos remittimus.

De munificencia.

Princeps in hiftriones impudicos & panthomymos
non fit profufus :fed in graues prudentes & beneme∕
tos fit largus & munificus : quemlibetcp ᵱ fua digni∕
tate remuneret.Omnia vero faciat : adiuncta hilari
affabilitate:& comi quadam dulcedine fermonis : ac
iucunda vultus placabilitate.In hoc imitare Patrem
tuū Philippū benigniffimū & fuauiffimū Principem
Nihil enim adeo cōciliat animos hominū:nihil adeo
beniuolenciam omnium captat:nihil adeo promptā
fubditorum obedienciam parit:ficut placabilitas fer∕
monis:& fuauis affabilitas.Id Iulius Cæfar:id Alex∕
der expertus eft.In hofpites eciam dapfilis & larga
manus Principem decet:quæ itidē virtus a Patre tuo
Philippo non eft aliena.

De manfuatudine.

Princeps manfuetus fit:paciens:lōganimis fiue mag∕
nanimus:non mox verbo aut facto cuiufpiam accen∕
datur ad iram : ad animi perturbacionem : ad vindi∕
ctę appetitum:ad furorem fœmineum . Sic enim ra∕
cio & mentis acies nubilatur : fanitas corporis ledi∕
tur: vita breuiatur:facies benigna deformat̄ :magna∕
nimitas pditur:muliebris pufillanimitas induit̄:rectū
iudiciū fubuertit̄:et facinus nōnūcp ab irato cōmittit̄:

Sig. av *recto* from the copy of Jacobus Wimpfeling's *Agatharchia*,
Strassburg, 1498, in the Duke University Library (enlarged).

turies, he had not read it, he can hardly have escaped indirect influence.[15] It is probable also that Machiavelli had read the remarks
on foolish liberality in Cicero's *De officiis* (1.14, etc.), though in
view of the material on the subject accessible to him, it is hardly
necessary to say with Burd that "it is almost beyond doubt that
Machiavelli used" them,[16] if use means employment of one source
to the exclusion of others.

As one of the qualities of the good man, the virtue of liberality
was continually urged on kings, who should excel all men in virtue,
even to the extent of presenting an image of the Trinity, as Vincent of Beauvais has it.[17] Egidio has no doubt that the virtues,
liberality among them, are to be urged on kings; the only question
is "quomodo decet reges et principes tales virtutes habere" (1.2.1),[18]
for it was possible, as appears in Machiavelli's contemporary Nifo,
to hold that the king should possess the virtues, and yet that his exercise of them was not like that of ordinary men.[19]

But liberality was especially a kingly virtue, for "the name of
skarste is unconvenient to a kyng, and yville bicometh to his royalle
maieste,"[20] while his good name requires the praise of liberality:

> Next after trouthe the secounde,
> In Policie as it is founde,
> Which serveth to the worldes fame
> In worschipe of a kinges name,
> Largesse it is, whos privilegge
> Ther mai non Avarice abregge.[21]

In spite of all that was said on proper measure in giving,[22] the
weight of exhortation was on the side of free-handedness. Beroaldus
well exhibits this:

Ante omnia princeps si vult laudari probarique, perinde ac optimus
principum, sit munificus ac liberalis. Nam ut inquit epigrammaticus
poeta. Nulla ducis virtus dulcior esse potest. . . . Pacatus in Pane-
gyrico ait: Et rei et famae consulit munificus imperator. Lucratur enim

---

[15] In his *De vita et regimine principum,* Dionysius Carthusianus (1394-1471)
often refers to the *Secretum secretorum.*

[16] Burd's edition of *Il principe,* chap. 16, p. 286.

[17] *De morali principis institutione,* chap. 10.

[18] "In what way it is proper for kings and princes to have such virtues" (*De
regimine* 1.2.1).   [19] *De principe,* caps. 2, 34.

[20] *Three Prose Versions of the Secreta Secretorum,* p. 8.

[21] Gower, *Confessio Amantis* 7.1985-90. Cf. Hoccleve, *De reg. pr.,* stanzas 584-5.

[22] Giraldus Cambrensis, *De principis instructione,* 1.8; "modus in dando."

gloriam, quum det pecuniam reversuram. Quicquid enim in cives
manat a principe, redundat in principem. . . . Augustus de seipso
scripsit haec. Liberalitas mea me ad coelum evehet. Sicut autem nulla
virtus amabilior est liberalitate: ita nullum plane vitium odiosius
tetriusque est avaricia in principibus et rempublicam gubernantibus.
Habere enim quaestui rempublicam (ut inquit verissime M. Tullius)
non modo turpe est, sed sceleratum etiam ac nepharium.[23] Idem non
minus vere quam eleganter tradit amorem multitudinis commoveri
ipsa fama et opinione liberalitatis. Avidius Cassius dicere solebat
avaritiam in imperatore esse acerbissimum malum. Eia habeat bonus
princeps in ore promptum, et in pectore conditum verbum illud
Traiani: qui fiscum principis scitissime lyenem vocabat: Nam ut lyene
crescente reliqui artus et membra tabescunt: ita fisco principis turgente
civitatis corpus una cum membris languescit et intermoritur.[24] . . .
Non queo mihi temperare, quin hoc in loco commemorem documentum
saluberrimum Cyri Persarum regis: quod memorat Xenophon in
Paedia: quod sine dubio dignissimum est memoratu. Scribit enim
luculentus ille scriptor Cyrum inter caeteros fuisse beneficum ac liberale:
adeo ut dictitaret se thesauros habere divitiarum amicos: quos dona-
tionibus divites opulentosque efficiebat. [The story of Cyrus' proof to
Croesus of the value of liberality is told.][25] . . . Nonne principes quum
talia aut audiunt aut legunt, ad liberalitatem exercendam inflammantur?
quae subditos reddit devotos, fideles, obnoxios, qua immortales efficiuntur: quae denique tanti momenti est; ut possit princeps obtentu liberalitatis obumbrare crimina tantum non enormia, et hac una laude
pensare.[26]

[23] Cicero, *De officiis* 2.77.

[24] With this reference to the *fiscus* of the king, compare Machiavelli's assertion
that the foolishly liberal ruler will be obliged at last "essere fiscale." Cf. the quotation from Erasmus, p. 40, above.

[25] Compare Machiavelli's reference to the liberality of the Cyrus of Xenophon
(*Prince* 14, p. 30a).

[26] "Above all things if the prince wishes to be praised and approved of as the best
of princes, he should be munificent and liberal. For, as the epigrammatist says, no
virtue of the leader can be more pleasing. . . . Pacatus says in his *Panegyric*:
The munificent emperor has regard for both practical matters and his fame. For
he gains glory when he gives money that will return to him, for whatever flows
among the citizens from the prince returns to the prince. . . . Augustus wrote
of himself as follows: My liberality raises me to heaven. And just as no virtue is
more lovely than liberality, so evidently no vice is more hateful and blacker
than avarice in princes and heads of a state. To hold a state for advantage (as
M. Tullius truly says) is not merely base but also wicked and impious. The same
writer not less truly than elegantly asserts that the love of the multitude is excited by the very fame and reputation of liberality. Avidius Cassius was accustomed to say that avarice was the most repulsive of vices in an emperor. Assuredly
the good prince should "have at the tip of his tongue and fixed in his breast that
saying of Trajan, who wisely called the tax gatherer of the prince his spleen, for
when the spleen increases, the limbs and other members languish; likewise when the
tax-gatherer of the prince grows rich the body of the state along with the members

With this agrees Patricius: "Concludamus igitur maximam in regibus principibusque virtutem esse magnificentiam. A qua quicunque abest, vix quippiam dignum laude agere potest, et in avaritiae crimen facile incurrit, detrectatoribusque obnoxius redditur."[27] In the same chapter he explains that the virtue of magnificence is suitable for kings and princes only, because the individual can hardly attain even liberality, which is concerned with small and private things, while magnificence concerns great and public things.[28] The resources of the ruler permit magnificence, for

> In as mochil as a welle also,
> At the whiche many folk hir water fecche,
> Nedith to han the larger mouth; right so
> The largesse of a kyng moot ferther strecche,
> If he of his estat any thing recche,
> Than other mennes; for hir impotence
> Strecchith naght so fer as his influence.[29]

On the basis of the fourth book of Aristotle's *Ethics*, Egidio went so far as to entitle a chapter *Quod Reges et Principes quodammodo impossibile est esse prodigos, et quod maxime detestabile est eos esse avaros, et quod potissime decet eos liberales esse.* Part of the chapter is as follows:

Philosophus [*Ethica 4*] ait Tyrannos non esse prodigos, quia non videntur posse superabundare multitudine possessiones, dationis, et ex-

---

grows weak and decays. . . . Nor can I refrain from here alluding to the exceedingly wholesome advice of Cyrus king of Persia, related by Xenophon in the *Cyropaedia*, for it is without doubt most worthy to be remembered. That trustworthy author writes that Cyrus among other things was helpful and liberal, so much so that he said his friends, whom he made rich and prosperous by his gifts, were his storehouses of riches. . . . Will not princes when they hear or read such narratives be inflamed to the exercise of liberality? Liberality is the virtue that renders subjects devoted, faithful, obedient, and that makes princes immortal; finally it is of such importance that with the veil of liberality a prince can conceal any crimes short of the greatest, and with the reputation of liberality outweigh them" (*De optimo statu* 129 verso-130 recto).

[27] "We may therefore conclude that magnificence is the greatest virtue of kings and princes, for one who lacks it can scarcely get praise for anything worthy he does and easily runs into the fault of avarice and becomes liable to detraction" (*De regno* 7.11).

[28] Pontanus (*De magnificentia* 1) adds: "Liberalis utilis esse aliis, et commodus magis studet, cum magnifici plura saepe ad aliorum voluptates faciant, ut cum ludos ac munera in theatris edunt, et publicas venationes in arena exhibent."—"The liberal man endeavors to be useful and in a high degree obliging to others, while magnificent men do more things for the pleasures of others, as when they present plays and spectacles in the theatres and exhibit public combats with wild animals in the arena."

[29] Hoccleve, *Regement of Princes*, stanza 665.

pensis. Quicunque enim tot habet, et tanta recipit, quod dationes et expensae multitudinem possessionum superare non possint, quodammodo prodigus esse non potest. Reges igitur et Principes quia multitudine possessionum superabundant, non solum non possunt esse prodigi, sed vix possunt attingere ut sint liberales. . . . Reges enim et Principes vix possunt deviare a liberalitate in dando plus, quia magnitudo expensarum vix potest excedere multitudinem reddituum.[30]

Here Egidio passes directly from Aristotle's views on the tyrant to his own opinion of what is fitting for a good king. Burd remarks that "Machiavelli's originality consists in his having taken the traditional view of the Greek tyrant [derived from Aristotle], and modified it so that it may become the ideal of a new prince."[31] He is referring to the tyrant as presented at length in the fifth book of the *Politics*. The present instance anticipates the method employed by Machiavelli. Considering the immense circulation of Egidio's work, we may suppose that whatever he did had often been noticed; hence that Machiavelli's adaptation to his prince of advice for a tyrant would not have been wholly new and strange.

Such was the influence of Aristotle and Egidio that in spite of the practical financial difficulties of European monarchs, Pontanus echoes them in saying that in princes liberality "modum non potest excedere."[32] The writers *de regimine principum* pretty well agree with Clichtoveus, who entitled a chapter of his *De regis officio* as follows: *Quod liberalitas et magnificentia in splendore honestorum sumptuum consistens magnopere principem decet.*[33]

Machiavelli has the courage to breast the tide and declare that the prince is wiser to get the reputation of parsimony than to ruin

---

[30] "That in a way it is impossible for kings and princes to be prodigal, and that it is especially detestable for them to be avaricious, and that it is exceedingly appropriate for them to be liberal."

"The Philosopher [*Ethics* 4] says that tyrants cannot be prodigal, since in alienating property and paying out money they appear unable to exceed their vast riches. For he who has so much and receives so great an income that his gifts and expenses cannot surpass his enormous possessions is unable to be prodigal. Kings and princes, therefore, on account of the greatness of their possessions, not merely cannot be prodigal, but can hardly attain liberality. . . . Kings and princes are hardly able to deviate from liberality by excessive giving, since the magnitude of their expenses is hardly able to exceed the multitude of their receipts" (*De regimine* 1.2.18).

In my rendering I follow the Italian translation of 1288, reprinted at Florence in 1858; I suspect it indicates the correct Latin text.

For further discussion of new prince and tyrant, see pp. 127 ff., below.

[31] In his edition of *The Prince*, p. 289.   [32] *De principe*, p. 267.

[33] "That liberality and magnificence consisting in the splendor of honorable expenses is very proper for a prince" (chap. 20).

himself in attempting to gain that of liberality. Cutting through Aristotelian verbiage about tempered liberality, such as he himself recommended for Maximilian, he says plainly what he means.[34] The prince is unlikely to have such resources that he can afford the expenditure necessary to get him the name of liberal. Let him not be swayed by the flatterers who tell him what is consistent with his dignity. *Tutius ei est male audire, quam male pugnare.* Parsimony is less dangerous than poverty. ⸙

To be sure Machiavelli seems to attempt some adaptation to the current view. Though a prince who follows his advice may at the beginning be reproached as miserly, as time goes on he will be held more generous—"sempre più liberale."[35] His subjects will see that without burdening them he is able to defend his state and carry on his various projects. In fact he will be generous to the many from whom he takes nothing away and miserly only to the few to whom he gives nothing. This qualification, though perhaps founded on observation, has a basis in Aristotle's presentation of liberality in *Ethics* 2, for Aristotle made it part of liberality to refrain from the improper taking of valuables;[36] the subjects of Machiavelli's financially cautious prince will come to see that the subordinate but genuine part of liberality involved in abstinence from their goods is exemplified by their ruler. This is affirmed by Vettori in a passage at once Aristotelian and Machiavellian:

Giudico che non si debbe attribuire questo vizio [d'avarizia] a un Principe il quale non grava i sudditi suoi di esazioni estraordinarie; non fa accusare oggi questo domani quello, per estorquere da loro le pecunie ingiustamente; non lascia che li ministri suoi succino le sustanze de' poveri, per spogliarli poi di quelle, quando sono fatti ricchi; e più presto si astiene dal donare a servitori, buffoni, cinedi, ed uomini di simil qualità. Ed uno Principe che vive in questo modo, io non avaro ma liberale chiamerei.[37]

The two friends agree that the good king is not avaricious, in that he is not rapacious, does not "per rapina desidera di avere,"[38] as it is

---

[34] *Prince* 16, end.   [35] *Prince* 16, p. 31b.

[36] For Egidio's presentation of this see p. 86, above.

[37] "I judge that one should not attribute the vice of avarice to a prince who does not burden his subjects with unusually heavy exactions; who does not have an accusation made today against this one, tomorrow against that one, in order to extort money from them unjustly; who does not allow his ministers to suck up the patrimony of the poor, in order to despoil them of it when they have become rich; and who still more abstains from gifts to servants, buffoons, catamites and men of like sort. Now a prince who lives in this way I should call not avaricious but liberal" (*Sommario,* p. 316). For unworthy favorites, cf. Erasmus, *Institutio* 5, par. 2.

[38] *Prince* 15, p. 31a.

put in *The Prince*.   A rapacious prince, as Poggio explained, deserves the name of tyrant:

Est enim impossibile regem fieri avarum. Rex enim ille dicitur, qui est speculator ac procurator publici commodi, cui est cordi utilitas subditorum, qui quaecunque agit refert ad eorum quibus praeest commoditatem: Hic autem avarus esse nulla ratione potest. Quod si secus fecerit, non rex, sed tyrannus dicendus est, cuius est proprium vacare privato emolumento. Hoc enim differt rex a tyranno, quod alter eorum quos regit commodis invigilat, alter suis intentus est.[39]

Commynes was even more extreme on the subject of rapacity, holding that a good king levies taxes only with the consent of the taxpayers: "Y a-il roy ne seigneur sur terre qui ayt povoir, oultre son dommaine, de mectre ung denier sur ses subgectz sans octroy et consentement de ceulx qui le doyvent payer, sinon par tyrannie et violence?"[40] This sixteenth chapter of *The Prince* is, then, not merely advice to a monarch who would maintain himself, but also dissuasion from the conduct of the tyrant written in the spirit of the concluding chapter of the work with the hope for good government in Italy.[41]

On the side of liberality as giving, Dionysius Carthusianus may be held to have anticipated Machiavelli when he wrote of rulers: "Veruntamen esse non debent tam liberales, quin competentem habeant provisionem pro defensione patriae suae, et pro certis oneribus, quae eis incumbunt."[42] But a ruler who followed such advice would still find himself struggling—for the most part in vain —for the reputation of liberality, with constant worrying attempts to cut down demands and enlarge inadequate resources. The Florentine secretary understood that liberality of this kind would

[39] "It is impossible for a king to become avaricious. For that one is called a king who looks after and brings about the public advantage, who has at heart the advantage of his subjects, and who relates whatever he does to the advantage of those whom he stands over, but by no reckoning is he able to be avaricious; for if he has done otherwise he is to be called a tyrant and not a king, who is distinguished by freedom from private emolument. For in this the king differs from the tyrant, namely that he thinks of the advantage of those whom he rules, while the tyrant is intent on his own advantage" (*Historia disceptativa de avaritia*, pp. 21-22). Cf. p. 137, note 79, below.

[40] "Is there a king or lord on earth who has power to lay on his subjects a penny of taxation beyond what belongs to him, without a grant and the consent of those who ought to pay, except by tyranny and violence?" (*Mémoires* 5.19, II, 217).

[41] See *tyrant* in the index.

[42] "Certainly they should not be so liberal that they do not have adequate provision for the defence of their country and for the fixed obligations that rest on them" (*De vita et regimine principum* 1.31). The work was composed before 1471.

normally involve such care in financial matters as to amount to stinginess, and honestly said so. Behind this honesty of speech lies a perception of the truth that could change the attitude of a ruler from hopeless and unavailing effort to calm acceptance of an unpleasant reputation coupled with funds adequate for his needs.

There had been hints even of this clarity before 1500. Giraldus Cambrensis admitted in his *De principis instructione* that *parcimonia* was a virtue, though he hastened to add: "praestantior tamen largitas et laudabilior"[43]—a *largitas,* however, which preserves proper measure, such as, he says, Cicero had recommended in *De officiis*.[44] In his formal work *Dei doveri del principe* Diomede Carafa gave the normal advice on steering properly between avarice and "lo inconveniente de mendicare et vivere ad mal termine" which results from prodigality.[45] Though admitting that generosity befits princes,[46] he has little enthusiasm for it, but much for advising financial care, for many good results come from proper spending—"lo spendere mesurato." Princes are advised to lay up money for emergencies,[47] and told that proper care of their normal incomes will enable them to avoid turning "fiscali"[48] and oppressing their subjects, who will be willing to contribute to a ruler whose expenditure is obviously wise. Sound financial policy observes the maxim: "Chy compera et spende ad quello non have debisognio, li bisognara poy vendere quello ei necessario."[49] The example of such conduct will stimulate subjects to thrift. Carafa's ideal ruler is as careful in financial matters as Machiavelli would have wished, but is not directly advised to be content with a reputation for stinginess. In a memorial to Frederick of Aragon, about to undertake a journey to France that might involve much temptation to lavish expenditure, he goes much farther: "Defecto ei la avaritia et defecto ei la prodigalità quali molti la usano per non sapere admaystrare [*sic*]. Ma ei men male la avaricia" perchè "resta la

[43] "Liberality is more admirable and more praiseworthy" (1.8, p. 29).

[44] *De officiis* 1.14. In Patricius' *De regno* 6.25, *parcitas* or *parsimonia* is a virtue, but not enthusiastically advised.

[45] "The inconvenience of begging and living at extremities" (*Doveri del principe*, pp. 283-5).

[46] See pt. 1 of the Latin translation of the same work, entitled *De regentis et boni principis officiis*, in Fabricius, *Bibliotheca Latina*, p. 649.   [47] Ibid., pts. 1 and 3.

[48] Machiavelli's word in *The Prince*, chap. 16, p. 31b. Quoting the passage from *The Prince*, Tommaseo's Dictionary defines it to mean "chi è minuziosamente tenace nell' imporre pesi e nella loro esazione,"—"one minutely tenacious in imposing burdens and in the exaction of them."

[49] "He who spends his money in the purchase of what he does not need will have to sell what is necessary to him" (*Doveri del principe*, p. 284).

utilità ad casa, che non [si] va mendicando robbe de altrui."[50]
This is almost completely Machiavellian. It is not hard to believe
that the Florentine had seen or heard such an opinion presented
and defended.

Machiavelli's contemporary Erasmus does not plainly advise
the prince to be stingy, though he does quote the proverb, "Magnum
vectigal parsimonia est,"[51] and indicates that the prince should trim
his expenses to fit his income. He weakens the usual exhortation
to liberality by discussing it as a heading under the virtue of
beneficentia, which may take other forms than ordinary liberality.
Though proper giving is commendable, "nec tamen temere col-
locanda est Principis liberalitas."[52] In matters pertaining to his
person the prince will be more frugal and sparing than in public
affairs, and while any of his subjects are in need will avoid travel
and other causes of heavy expense; in matters of state, however, he
will make a splendid appearance "si quae populi causam agant."[53]
The qualification is characteristic of the position of the Dutch
scholar. To extensive liberality he is opposed:

Falluntur et hi qui largitionibus, epulis, prava indulgentia sibi multitudinis animos conciliant. Et paratur hisce rebus nonnulla popularis
gratia potius quam benevolentia, verum ea neque vera, neque duratura.
Alitur interea mala populi cupiditas, quae posteaquam, ut fit, in im-
mensum increvit, jam nihil satis esse putat: et tumultuatur, nisi per
omnia cupiditatibus responsum fuerit: atqui istud est corrumpere tuos,
non conciliare.[54]

Merit exhibited by the prince is the only basis for genuine and lasting love. Erasmus agrees with Machiavelli that liberality is bad

[50] "Avarice is a defect in him and prodigality is a defect in him; many fall into
these because they do not understand administration. But avarice is a lesser evil because its usefulness remains at home, if it does not go begging the property of
others" (Persico, *Diomede Carafa,* p. 164).

[51] "Parsimony is a great source of income" (*Institutio* 4, 594 D). It is found in
Cicero, *Paradoxa Stoicorum* 6.3.49).

[52] "The liberality of the prince is not to be rashly employed" (*Institutio* 5, 595 A).

[53] "If this advances the cause of the people" (ibid. 10, 606 E). Cf. Leon Batista
Alberti, *Del principe* 4.119.28: "Nelle cose publiche dimostri Magnificentia, & nelle
private vadia dietro alla parsimonia."—"In public matters show magnificence, and
in private affairs practice parsimony."

[54] "They also err who by gifts, feasts, and evil indulgence conciliate to themselves
the minds of the multitude. These things bring some popular favor rather than
genuine good will, and even this favor is neither true nor enduring. Meanwhile
the wicked cupidity of the people is nourished, and afterward, when it has greatly
increased, as commonly happens, nothing is judged sufficient for it, and there are
riots unless popular cupidity is fully satisfied. To follow this procedure is to corrupt
your people, not to win their favor" (*Institutio principis* 3, col. 589 F).

policy because it does not furnish the prince with a secure basis. Machiavelli, however, stops there, but Erasmus continues to give moral objections as well. Both feel that giving defeats itself because the demand of the populace cannot be met. They agree that the hold of the prince on the people is measured by his inner qualities—Erasmus with his usual moral emphasis. Yet notwithstanding his independence, Erasmus does not use the word liberality in his advice against what would be popularly thought liberal conduct; he is less positive than the Italian in attacking a respectable and widely circulated error.

But though Machiavelli is honest and unhesitating in his unconventional advice, is he in this matter in possession of the *verità effettuale* or is he led astray by his delight in theory? Possibly the answer may be had from Guicciardini:

Più detestabile e più perniziosa è in uno principe la prodigalità, che la parsimonia; perchè non potendo quella essere sanza tôrre a molti, è più ingiurioso a' sudditi el tôrre che el non dare; e nondimeno pare che a'popoli piaccia più el principe prodigo che lo avaro. La ragione è che ancora che pochi siano quegli a chi dà il prodigo a comparazione di coloro a chi toglie, che di necessità sono molti; pure, come è detto altre volte, può tanto più negli uomini la speranza che el timore, che facilmente si spera essere più presto di quegli pochi a chi è dato, che di quegli molti a chi è tolto.[55]

[55] "Prodigality is more detestable and more harmful in a prince than parsimony, because the first cannot exist without taking away from many and it is more injurious to subjects to take from them than not to give to them. Yet it appears that to the people a prodigal prince is more pleasing than an avaricious one. The reason is that though the prodigal gives to but few in comparison with those from whom he takes away, who necessarily are many, yet, as I have said before, hope is more powerful in men than fear, for they hope to be of the few to whom something is given rather than of the many from whom something is taken away" (*Ricordi politici e civili* CLXXIII). In the *Istoria* (12.19, p. 382—1516) Guicciardini writes: "Accade quasi sempre per il giudicio corrotto degli uomini, che ne' re è più lodata la prodigalitá, benché a quella sia annessa la rapacitá, che la parsimonia congiunta con la astinenza della roba di altri."—"It almost always comes about through the corrupt judgment of men that a ruler is more praised for prodigality, though to it is joined rapacity, than for parsimony accompanied with abstention from the property of others."

A somewhat different interpretation is that of Diomede Carafa: "Si quando mulctandi erunt aliqui, ostendere oportebit servandae justitiae gratia id fieri, non pecuniae aviditate. Nam cum pauci sint, quibus auferri bona contigat, apud caeteros tamen ea res odiosa esse consuevit."—"When some one has to be made to pay a fine, it will be well to show that this is done for the sake of doing justice and not for desire of money. For though they are few to whom it happens that they are deprived of their goods, yet among the rest the thing is generally odious" (*De principis officiis*, p. 649). Fear is stronger than hope. But Guicciardini is thinking of generally spread taxation, while Carafa speaks of action against individuals, without compensating liberality to others.

Chapter 17

De crudelitate et pietate; et an sit melius amari quam
timeri, vel e contra.
(Of cruelty and pity, and whether it is better to be loved
than to be feared, or the reverse.)

The subject of clemency—discussed by Machiavelli as *pietà*—
is almost invariably treated in works *de regimine principum,* with
exhortation to the practice of the virtue. The treatise on the subject
best known to such authors was the *De clementia* of Seneca,
often quoted, as in Giraldus' chapter with the same title. In the
headings of chapters, Gilbert of Tournai uses both words,[1] and
Hoccleve treats the subject as pitee.[2] Giraldus quotes at length from
Hildebert of Le Mans to show that a prince should prefer clemency to cruelty, as for example:

Clementiae plurimum laudis accedit quod pluribus prodest; mitis enim
principatus regnum servat incolume. Hujus profecto virtutis locus est
apud potentes, qui jure parentum, vel vi, vel electionis beneficio, caeteris
principantur; apud populum vero non ita, cui nulla est potestas puniendi.
Ipse autem ex alto crudelitatem detestatur, adhortatur clementiam, quorum alterum feris, alterum hominibus natura docuit assignandum. Ea
sanxit oportet homines mansuescere clementia, timeri feras crudelitate.
Igitur crudelem esse cum feris est habere commercium et hominem
diffiteri. . . . Clementia non ultimum possidet locum, qua, sicut hu-
manitati nihil est affinius, ita nihil gloriosius in principe. . . . "Bonus
princeps sibi dominatur, populo servit, nullius sanguinem contemnit."
. . . Diligentiores facile percipient quantum vel crudelitas obsit vel
prosit clementia potestati.[3]

[1] *Eruditio regum et principum* 3.1-5; composed in 1259.

[2] *Regement of Princes* 2997, st. 429.

[3] "The greatest praise is given to clemency because it is of benefit to many, for
a mild rule keeps the kingdom safe. This virtue is especially appropriate to the
powerful, who by the right of their parents, or by force, or because of the result
of an election rule over others. Among the people, who have no power to inflict
punishment, it is of little importance. God himself in heaven detests cruelty and ex-
horts to clemency, the first of which nature has assigned to beasts, the second to
men. Nature has appointed that men should grow mild as a result of clemency and
wild beasts be made afraid by means of cruelty. Hence to be cruel is to have commerce with wild beasts and to disavow man. . . . Clemency does not occupy the
last place, for as no virtue is nearer humanity so none is more glorious in a

The beginning of Machiavelli's chapter is conventional in senti-ment; but with a quick turn to the more characteristic: "Dico che ciascuno principe debbe desiderare di essere tenuto pietoso e non crudele: nondimanco debbe avvertire di non usare male questa pietà. Era tenuto Cesare Borgia crudele; nondimanco quella sua crudeltà aveva racconcia la Romagna, unitola, ridottola in pace e in fede."[4] The word *crudeltà* here is to be taken as severity, or perhaps bet-ter, the exercise of severity by a ruler which appears cruel to his people; Machiavelli is speaking of being thought cruel rather than of being so.[5] Looking at the matter from the side of the ruler, Sir Philip Sidney writes:

In this . . . plight . . . did the King Euarchus finde his estate, when he tooke upon him the regiment: which by reason of the long streame of abuse, he was forced to establish by some even extreme severitie, not so much for the very faultes themselves, (which he rather sought to prevent then to punish) as for the faultie ones; who . . . coulde not learne to digest, that the man which they so long had used to maske their owne appetites, should now be the reducer of them into order. But so soone as some fewe (but in deede notable) examples, had thun-dred a duetie into the subjects hartes, he soone shewed, no baseness of suspition, nor the basest basenes of envie, could any whit rule such a

_____

prince. . . . 'The good prince is lord of himself, he serves his people, he despises the blood of no one.' . . . The more attentive may easily perceive how much cruelty obstructs power or clemency avails it" (*De principis instructione* 1.7, pp. 25-27). Cf. Petrarch, *De rep. opt. adm.,* p. 428: "Sicut autem nulla re facilius quam clementia, & liberalitate amor quaeritur plurimorum, sic econtra nil potentius ad odium concitandum, quam crudelitas atque cupiditas. . . . Haec duo vitia in-numerabiles tyrannorum ac principum perdiderunt. . . . Ignobilis est enim ac pusilli sibique diffidentis animi, crudelitas, & potestate ultionis oblata, nil inultum linquere, vitium a natura hominis, & praesertim Principis alienum, cui ulciscendi potestas, magna satis est ultio."—"As by nothing is the love of the many more easily obtained than by clemency and liberality, so on the contrary nothing is more powerful in exciting hate than cruelty and cupidity. . . . These two vices have ruined innumerable tyrants and princes. . . . Cruelty is the vice of an ignoble and weak mind without confidence in itself, and when the power of vengeance is conferred on one, to leave nothing unavenged is a vice alien to hu-man nature and especially to the nature of princes, for whom the power to avenge is a sufficiently great vengeance." For more on cupidity, see *avarice* in the index. Giraldus' quotation is from Hildebert of Le Mans, *Epistle* 3 (Migne, *Patrologia Latina* 171.144).

[4] "I say that every prince ought to wish to be considered clement and not cruel; yet he should remind himself not to make bad use of pity. Caesar Borgia was re-puted to be cruel, yet his cruelty brought the Romagna into good condition, united it, restored peace and faith in it."

[5] "Tenuto crudele." See the index under *cruelty*.

Ruler. But then shined foorth indeede all love among them, when an awfull feare, ingendred by justice, did make that love most lovely.[6]

The problem before Sidney's king was not unlike that offered by the Romagna, as Machiavelli describes it in the *Discorsi* (3.29), and in *The Prince* (7, p. 16a), and doubtless his notable and thundering examples of extreme severity appeared cruel to his subjects. They are the very small number of instances necessary to establish good government which the prince must exhibit without caring about being thought cruel—"della infamia di crudele."[7] This sort of conduct is especially necessary to a new prince, which, after his long minority, Sidney's Euarchus essentially was.[8] The value of initial severity seems not to have been commonly recognized among Machiavelli's predecessors; he may, however, have gained suggestion for it from Sallust, who advised Caesar to adopt a firm policy:

Firmanda igitur sunt vel concordiae bona et discordiae mala expellenda.[9] . . . Atque ego scio quam aspera haec res in principio futura sit, praesertim is, qui se in victoria licentius liberiusque quam artius futuros credebant. Quorum si saluti potius quam ludibini consules, illosque nosque et socios in pace firma constitues. . . . Quare capesse, per deos, rem publicam et omnia aspera, uti soles, pervade. Namque aut tu mederi potes aut omittenda est cura omnibus. Neque quisquam te ad crudelis poenas aut acerba iudicia invocat, quibus civitas vastatur magis quam corrigitur, sed ut pravas artis malasque libidines ab juventate prohibeas. Ea vera clementia erit, consuluisse ne merito cives patria expellerentur, retinuisse ab stultitia et falsis voluptatibus, pacem et concordiam stabilivisse, non si flagitis opsecutus, delicta perpessus praesens gaudium cum mox futuro malo concesseris.[10]

---

[6] *Arcadia* 2.6.5. In a letter to Hubert Languet (April 29, 1574) Sidney says he agrees with Machiavelli, "neque inanem . . . speciem clementiae, salutari severitati praeferam."—"Nor should I choose the empty appearance of clemency rather than salutary severity" (III, 91).   [7] *Prince* 17, p. 32b.

[8] See *The Prince* 8, p. 18b, for the principle applied to the genuine cruelty of a wicked ruler.

[9] Cf. Machiavelli's "per tenere li sudditi suoi uniti e in fede"—"to keep his subjects united and faithful"—in the present chapter, p. 32b.

[10] "The good results of concord are therefore to be established and the evils of discord got rid of. . . . And I know how hard this may be in the beginning, especially to those who were thinking that they were going to enjoy victory unrestrainedly and freely rather than severely. If you consult their safety rather than their pleasure, you will establish them and us and our allies in a firm peace. . . . Therefore, I conjure you by the gods, administer the state and break through all difficulties as you are accustomed to do. For either you can remedy everything or everyone must give up the attempt. No one is urging upon you cruel penalties or harsh judgments, by which the state is wasted more than corrected, but merely that

The conventional writers would have approved the conduct of Euarchus, for justice is even more fitting to the ruler than is clemency and must never wholly give place to it. Hoccleve tells the story of a king who was rebuked by his jester when he considered pardoning a second time a murderer whose first offence had been overlooked, and comments on the situation:

> Pitee auailith mochil, but naght there;
> ffor bet it is to sle the mordreman,
> Than suffre hym regnë, for he hath no fere
> His hand to usë forth as he by-gan;
> And in my cónceit, feelë wel I can,
>   That of suche pitee, is the abstinence
>   Of gretter pite, for the consequence (stanza 453)

This is the conduct recommended by Machiavelli, whose just prince "sarà più pietoso che quelli e' quali, per troppa pietà, lasciono seguire e' disordini, di che ne nasca occisioni o rapine."[11]

Clemency was advised by the Neapolitan school of writers *de regimine principum,* such as Pontanus, who wrote: "Clementiam

---

you prohibit to the youth vicious arts and wicked inclinations. It will be thought true clemency to have arranged that citizens shall not be deservedly expelled from their native land, to have restrained them from baseness and false pleasures, and to have established peace and concord, and not, yielding to the wicked, by suffering evil deeds to allow enjoyment for the present with the certainty of evil soon to come" (*De republica ordinanda,* epistola I; or *Ad Caesarem oratio* 5-6).

In the *Basilikon Doron,* which may be called his *Prince,* James I of England refers to this oration in the margin of the following passage: "When ye have by the severitie of justice once setled your countries, and made them knowe that ye can strike, then may ye thereafter all the dayes of your life mixe justice with mercie, punishing or sparing, as ye shall finde the crime to have bene wilfullie or rashlie committed, and according to the by-past behaviour of the committer. For if otherwise ye kyth your clemencie at the first, the offences would soone come to suche heapes, and the contempt of you growe so great, that when ye would fall to punishe, the number of them to be punished, would exceed the innocent; and ye would be troubled to resolve whome-at to begin: and against your nature would be compelled then to wracke manie, whome the chastisement of fewe in the beginning might have preserved. But in this, my over-deare bought experience may serve you for a sufficient lesson. For I confesse, where I thought (by being gracious at the beginning) to win all mens heartes to a loving and willing obedience, I by the contrarie founde, the disorder of the countrie, and the losse of my thankes to be all my reward" (bk. 2, pp. 30-31).

James refers also to Egidio Colonna, and to the *Politics,* the *Cyropaedia,* the *De regno* of Isocrates, and other classical works. Apparently he did not know Machiavelli's writings.

[11] "Will be more truly full of pity than those who, because they have too much pity, permit disorders from which arise murders or rapines" (*Prince* 17, p. 32b).

in quo esse senserimus, illum omnes admiramur, colimus, pro deo
habemus."[12]

With clemency was often linked humanity, as by Patricius, who
in his chapter *De humanitate* defines it, with a reference to Aulus
Gellius, as "benevolentia quaedam ac dexteritas erga omnes homines
promiscam,"[13] called by the Greeks philanthropy. "Ad humanitatem
vox illa maioris Scipionis pertinet, quum ait malle se civem unum
servare, quam mille hostium perdere."[14] And Pontanus says: "Quid
magis alienum a regibus, aut ipsorum securitati minus conducens,
quam quod cum ipsi praebere se caeteris debeant humanitatis exemplum, difficiles et superbos agant? Inhumanitas enim mater est
odii ut superbia crudelitatis, malus utraque et vitae et principatus
custos."[15] Presumably Machiavelli had something of this sort in
mind when he wrote of the Duke of Athens:

Quella severità e umanità che gli aveva finta, in superbia e crudeltà si
era convertita. . . . Fece ancora tagliare la lingua con tanta crudeltà
a Bettone Cini, che se ne morì; . . . la qual cosa accrebbe a' cittadini
lo sdegno, e al duca l'odio. . . . Crebbono adunque questi sdegni in
tanto e questi odi, che, non che i Fiorentini, i quali la libertà mantenere
non sanno e la servitù patire non possono, ma qualunque servile popolo
arebbono alla recuperazione della libertà infiammato. Onde che molti
cittadini, e di ogni qualità, di perdere la vita o di riavere la loro libertà
deliberarono; e in tre parti, di tre sorte di cittadini, tre congiure si
feciono.[16]

[12] "When we have perceived that a man is clement, we all admire him, we honor
him, we look on him as a god" (*De principe,* p. 257).

[13] "A certain benevolence and skill toward all men indiscriminately" (*De regno*
8.18). I have emended the text from Aulus Gellius 13.17. Cf. 5.10.

[14] "To humanity would pertain that saying of the elder Scipio, when he said
that he preferred to preserve one citizen rather than to kill a thousand enemies"
(ibid.).

[15] "What is more remote from the advantage of kings, or conduces less to their
security than when their conduct is surly and proud? For inhumanity is the mother
of hatred as pride is of cruelty, and either of these is a bad guardian of the ruler's
life and position" (*De principe,* p. 268).

[16] "That severity and humanity which he had pretended to were changed into
pride and cruelty. . . . He had the tongue of Bettone Cini cut out with such
cruelty that the victim died of it; . . . this increased the irritation of the citizens
and the hatred they felt for the duke. . . . Then these irritations and hatreds increased so greatly that they would have inflamed not merely the Florentines, who
do not know how to maintain their liberty and cannot endure servitude, but any
servile people to the recovery of its liberty. Consequently many citizens, of every
rank, determined to lose their lives or to recover their liberty, and in three different parts of the city three different conspiracies were made, each by one type of
citizen" (*Istorie Fiorentine* 2.36, pp. 436a-437a).

In the present chapter the prince so severe as to appear cruel can still temper his conduct with humanity.

From the exhortation to clemency on the one hand, and on the other to justice, the bond of human society and the first virtue of the ruler,[17] springs the *disputa:* "s' egli è meglio essere amato che temuto, o e converso."[18] In this seventeenth chapter the meaning of the words used for fear is not perfectly clear. Since the fear of subjects is made a desirable thing, the word inclines toward respect, the "awful fear" in which Sidney says Euarchus was held by his subjects, and which he succeeded, as an ideal ruler, in uniting with love—"il che quanto è più difficile ad osservare, tanto è più laudabile";[19] Duke Valentino, however, attained it in the Romagna,[20] and Lorenzo in Florence.[21] This respect is based on a stronger fear, called at the end of the paragraph *paura;* respect for the just ruler is secured by fear of punishment for any offence. In chapter seven the active fear of men who expect the ruler to injure them for reasons of politics rather than justice is expressed by *paura.*[22] In the Proemio of the *Art of War* the word *paura* is used of the fear inspired by the savage mercenary, while in the context we read of "timore delle leggi e d'Iddio."[23] Similarly in the *Discorsi* is a sentence: "Dove manca il timore di Dio, conviene o che quel regno rovini, o che sia sostenuto dal timore d'uno principe che sopperisca a' difetti della religione."[24] But there is not always the suggestion of approval; we read of the unwise and wicked regiment of the Duke of Athens that to the indignation of the citizens "si aggiugneva il timore, veggendo le spesse morti e le continue taglie con le quali impoveriva e consumava la città."[25] The next sentence

[17] Beroaldus, *De optimo statu,* folio 130 verso: "Iustus esse ante omnia princeps debet."—"The prince should observe justice before all other virtues."

[18] "Whether it is better to be loved than feared, or the reverse" (*Prince* 17, p. 33a).

[19] "Which in proportion as it is the more difficult to bring about is the more worthy of praise" (a fragment of a letter to Vettori, Aug., 1513, *Lettere Familiari* 27, p. 112).

[20] *Prince* 7, p. 17b: "farsi amare e temere da' populi"—"to make himself loved and feared by the people."   [21] Amare e reverire (p. 110, below).

[22] *Prince* 7, p. 17b. See p. 149, below.

[23] "Fear of the laws and of God" (p. 265b).

[24] "Where the fear of God is not present either the realm will go to ruin or it will be sustained by the fear of a prince who supplies what religion lacks" (*Discorsi* 1.11, p. 77b).

[25] "Fear was added, when they saw the frequent executions and the continual taxes with which he impoverished and consumed the city" (*Istorie Fiorentine* 2.36, p. 436b). Cf. the quotation relating to Pope Julius, pp. 111, 144, below.

uses the more expected word: "I quali sdegni e paure erano dal
duca cognosciute."[26] The solution is perhaps furnished by Machiavelli's analysis of the career of Hannibal who, over-desirous to inspire fear—"troppo di essere temuto"—became cruel and inspired
paura and *terrore*.[27] As Machiavelli indicates in the same context,
a slight deviation from the proper mode of inspiring fear makes
the ruler hated. The same observation had been made by Patricius
in his discussion of *severitas,* in a chapter *De legibus:* "Facile in
saevitiam falsa quadam similitudine prolabitur."[28] Nevertheless, he
commends it heartily:

Severitas quidem regem plurimum addecet, majestatem quandam praestat, et dignitatem auget, redditque eum inter mortales quasi divinum
aliquod numen, quod homines non modo venerantur, verumetiam
adorant. Perutilis est haec virtus omnibus in rebus agendis, et praecipue
in jure dicundo, et in plectendis sontibus: vera est enim Menandri
Comici sententia, quum ait: *Salutaris severitas vincit inanem speciem
clementiae,*[29] saevitia autem tyranni est, nec vitium ullam tam tetrum,
tam detestabile, atque inhumanum est quam crudelitas. Improbus est,
qui contra legem peccat, inofficiosus qui contra merita: qui vero

[26] "This irritation and these fears were known to the duke" (ibid.).

[27] *Discorsi* 3.21, pp. 230b, 231a. For "terrore" inspired by a government, see
Ist. Fior. 7.3, p. 563b.

[28] "Severity having a certain false appearance of savagery easily runs over into it"
(*De regno* 8.6).

[29] In the *Aphorismi politici et militares* of Lambertus Danaeus is the passage:
"Ex Tacito: Ex libro Primo Historiarum. Nerva Imp. dicere solebat. Praestat vivere
sub tali Principe, quo regnante nihil licet, quam sub quo omnia licent. Salutaris
enim severitas vincit inanem speciem clementiae. Hinc Cotys Rex Thraciae increpanti
severitatem ejus et ajenti: Furor hic non est regnum: belle respondit, At meus hic
furor sanos subditos reddit: Stobae. de regno.—"The Emperor Nerva was in the
habit of saying that it was better to live in the reign of a prince who permitted
nothing than under one who permitted everything. For salutary severity is better
than the empty appearance of clemency. Hence Cotys the king of Thrace when
some one rebuked his severity and affirmed: This is insanity, not kingly government, cleverly answered: But this insanity of mine makes my subjects sane. Stobaeus,
de regno" (p. 457). Favorinus, who in 1512 became director of the Medici Library
at Florence, translated into Latin the sentences or apophthegms of Stobaeus; his
version was printed at Rome in 1519 (*Biographie Universelle*). One section of Stobaeus is called *Admonitiones de regno,* sermo 147, ed. Frankfort, 1581. See also p.
100, note, above.

The attribution of the saying on salutary severity to Menander is curious, for
the words occur in a letter of Cicero to Brutus 1.2a.2 (5): "Vehementer a te, Brute,
dissentio nec clementiae tuae concedo, sed salutaris severitas vincit inanem speciem
clementiae."—"I vigorously dissent from you, Brutus, nor do I yield to your clemency, but believe that salutary severity is superior to the empty appearance of
clemency." Ammianus Marcellinus quotes it in the form: "Salutaris rigor vincit
inanem speciem clementiae" (29.5.24).

saevus contra deum, contra pietatem, atque humanitatem delinquit, et hominis nomen perdit, efferatique animi vitio in tetram truculentamque beluam convertitur.[30]

The passage helps one to understand why, notwithstanding his admiration for Hannibal, Machiavelli calls his cruelty inhuman,[31] and, in the *Discorsi,* detestable.[32] Guicciardini also realized how easily severity might appear as cruelty: "Non si possono governare e sudditi bene sanza severità, perché la malignità degli uomini ricerca così; ma si vuole mescolare destrezza, e fare ogni dimostrazione perché si creda che la crudeltà non ti piaccia, ma che tu la usi per necessità, e per salute publica."[33]

Yet he still believed in its necessity, as appears in his *Istruzione delle cose di Romagna a suo fratello Iacopo,* a work that may be called Guicciardini's *Prince,* and is one of the most specific examples of the type. He advises his brother as governor:

Cape e fondamento di tutto il bene è l'avere nome e opinione di severità, la quale è necessaria in tutti i governi. . . . Chi manca di questa non può sperare alcuno buono fine; e il modo a conservarla è non solo punire tutti i delitti, e risentirsi nelle cose piccole con qualche demonstrazione che gli uomini temino il fare peccati grandi, non essere parziale, avere le mani nette, nè piegarsi per lettere e intercessione de' Cardinali e gran maestri; ma ricordarsi principalmente che queste cure non si pigliano per acquistare degli amici, per fare de' piaceri e farsi grato a' popoli; e che la facilità e umanità ancora che nel principio sia più laudata, partorisce presto il contempto; dopo il quale viene di necessità lo odio, causato da mali offici che seguitano di questo modo

[30] "Severity is very suitable to a king; it presents a certain majesty, and increases his dignity and renders him as it were a divine being among mortals, not merely venerated but even adored by men. This virtue is very useful in carrying on all kinds of activity, and especially in giving judgment and in punishing offenders; for that aphorism of Menander the comic poet is true, when he says: Salutary severity is superior to the empty appearance of clemency. Yet savageness is to be attributed to the tyrant, nor is there any vice so foul, so detestable, and so inhuman as cruelty. He is wicked who sins against the law; he is undutiful who sins against what is deserving, but he who is savage sins against God, against piety and humanity, and loses the name of man, and by the vice of his fierce spirit is changed into a foul and truculent beast" (Patricius, *De regno* 8.6).

[31] *Prince* 17, p. 33b.   [32] 3.21, p. 231b.

[33] "It is not possible for subjects to be well governed without severity, because the malignity of men requires it, but it is desirable to mix kindness with severity and to present every appearance that may cause the belief that cruelty does not please you, but that you use it of necessity and for public security" (*Ricordi* 307). Cf. 41: "Bisogna fondarsi più in sulla severità."—"It is necessary to rely more on severity."

di procedere, dove la severità, se bene nel principio offende, ha sempre seco la riputazione, e alla fine la benivolenza e le laudi.[84]

But to return to the "disputa" between the means of Scipio and those of Hannibal. Tommasini, to illustrate Machiavelli's words, quotes from the commentary by Aeneas Sylvius on Panormita's *De dictis et factis Alphonsi Aragoniae,* a work somewhat related to those *de regimine principum:* "Quemadmodum superi amari et timeri volunt, ita et reges. Neque enim bene amas nisi timeas."[35] Tommasini says also that the question whether princes ought to be loved or feared finally became a topic for the discussion of academies.[36] Certainly it is in one way or another considered by many of the advisers of princes.[37] Egidio may be taken as fundamental, influential, and representative. One of his chapters bears the title: *Quomodo Reges et Principes debeant se habere ut amentur a populo, et quomodo ut timeantur, et quod licet utrunque sit necessarium, amari tamen plus debent appetere quam timeri.*[38] In like

---

[84] "The head and foundation of all good is to have the name and reputation of being severe, something necessary in governments. . . . He who lacks this cannot hope for any good result, and the method of preserving it is not merely to punish all offences, and to make oneself felt in little things with such demonstrations that men fear to commit serious offences, not to be partial, to have clean hands, and not to be influenced by letters and intercessions of cardinals and great men, but in addition to remember that these duties are not undertaken for the sake of winning friends, doing kindnesses, and making oneself acceptable to the people; one must remember too that the accessibility and humanity which may at the beginning be praised quickly produce contempt, and after that of necessity hatred comes, caused by the bad service that results from this mode of procedure. But severity, though it offends in the beginning, always has reputation with it, and finally good will and praises" (*Opere inedite* 8.393-394).

[35] "Kings wish to be loved and feared in the same way as do the gods. Nor do you love well unless you fear well" (Tommasini, *Machiavelli* 2.115, n. 2). Cf. p. 241, below.   [36] Loc. cit.

[37] Giraldus Cambrensis thinks fear can result from love rather than from coercion, and wishes it to be tempered with love, "nec insolenti rigore violenter extortus timor in tyrannidem convertatur."—"Lest fear violently excited by insolent rigor change into tyranny" (*De principis instructione* 1.2, p. 12). Dionysius the Carthusian writes: "Postremo, quamvis princeps a suis subditis debeat velle diligi ac timeri, magis tamen debet velle amari."—"Finally, though a prince ought to wish to be valued and feared by his subjects, still more he ought to wish to be loved" (*De vita et regimine principum* 3.23). Erasmus wrote: "Tyrannus metui studet, Rex amari."—"The tyrant strives to be feared, the king to be loved" (*Institutione principis,* cap. 1, col. 572 B). Clichtoveus wished the ruler to be loved rather than feared (*De regis officio,* folio 41 recto).

[38] "In what way kings and princes should conduct themselves that they may be loved by the people and in what way that they may be feared, and that if one of the two is necessary they should more earnestly desire to be loved than to be feared" (*De regimine* 3.2.36).

manner Machiavelli recognizes the value of the combination, though feeling that its attainment is possible only in a Cosimo[39] or a Valentino.[40]

The qualities which lead a people to love *(diligere)* princes are put by Egidio under three heads: 1, to be *benefici et liberales;* 2, to be *fortes et magnanimi;* 3, to be *aequales et justi.* In *The Prince* likewise appear not merely "amicizie che si acquistano col prezzo,"[41] but also those gained "con grandezza e nobiltà di animo."[42] Machiavelli, however, seems on the whole to consider, and object to, love acquired through liberality rather than that resulting from sterner qualities. The liberal prince depending on the words of his subjects would be ruined in adversity because men are ungrateful, flighty, covetous, and eager to avoid danger. Egidio had remarked that the strong prince is loved because he secures safety: "Populus valde diligit fortes et magnanimos, exponentes se pro bonis communibus: credit enim per tales salutem consequi."[43]

Egidio states his third point somewhat negatively, as it were, showing, like Machiavelli, how to avoid hatred rather than win love: "Maxime provocatur populus ad odium Regis, si viderit ipsum non observare iustitiam."[44] The justice here in Egidio's mind, as is indicated by his reference to Aristotle's *Rhetoric* 2.4, is that which keeps the ruler from oppressing his people by taking their wealth for improper purposes and in excessive amounts.[45] Machiavelli says that to avoid odium a ruler must respect the property of his subjects as well as abstain from injury to their women, a caution to be found in Aristotle's *Politics* 5.10.[46] Galeazzo, Duke of Milan,

[39] *Istorie Fiorentine* 7.6, p. 567a: "Questa sua prudenza adunque, queste sue ricchezze, modo di vivere e fortuna, lo feciono a Firenze da' cittadini temere e amare." —"So his prudence, his riches, his way of living and his good fortune made him feared and loved by the citizens of Florence."

[40] See p. 103, above.

[41] "Friendships acquired with money" (*Prince* 17, p. 33a).

[42] "With greatness and nobility of mind" (ibid.).

[43] "The people greatly esteems the strong and magnanimous who expose themselves for the public good; for through such men it believes safety is attained" (*De regimine* 3.2.36).

[44] "The people is especially provoked to hatred of a king if it has seen that he does not observe justice" (*De regimine* 3.2.36). In 3.2.6 Egidio says merely: "Si abundet in beneficiis tribuendis, diligetur a populo."—"If he bestows a great many benefits he is loved by the people."

[45] In 3.2.9 Egidio writes that tyrants "bona aliorum rapiunt, et iura regni non observant,"—"take away the property of others and do not observe the laws of the kingdom."

[46] Burd, p. 293, in his note on this chapter of *The Prince* quotes from *Discorsi* 3.26, p. 237b: "Aristotile, intra le prime cause che mette della rovina de' tiranni, è

brought on his assassination by injuries in women and property,[47] and the Duke of Athens, who personifies the bad prince, made the same errors;[48] indeed, he caused, we read, more displeasure by his violence to women than in any other way. In *The Prince*,[49] however, injury to property seems to take the chief place. Campanus also wavers between the two:

Nec ulla res est in administratione imperii flagiciosior et quae magis offendat popularium animos quam injuria libidinis: ut stupra et adulteria et quae sunt eius generis turpidines: ut omnis violatio pudicitiae: quae ita custodienda est: ut nullum omnino libidinis in te vestigium videatur apparere. Haec enim omnia et ab honestate vitae et ab officii gravitate recedunt. Rerum autem omnium nescio an turpissima sit avaricia in Magistratu; quae et odium parit et maximas solet importare calamitates: et detrimenta gignit et perversam opinionem integritatis: Ut quem cupidum pecuniarum homines intelligunt posse eum causis iudicandis integrum esse non putant.[50]

The fear excited by rulers comes, says Egidio, "propter punitiones, quas exercent in subditos,"[51] a statement almost echoed by Machiavelli's "paura di pena."[52] Obviously this fear of justice which keeps men in the right path must be very unlike the fear generated by tyrannous cruelty which leads subjects to rebellion. Three things condition it: the punishment itself, the person punished, and the manner of punishing. As to the punishment, Egidio writes that princes, "in eos qui ultra modum regnum et politiam perturbant,

---

lo avere ingiuriato altrui per conto delle donne, o con stuprarle, o con violarle, o con rompere i matrimonii."—"Aristotle, among the first causes which he lays down for the ruin of tyrants, places injury to others with respect to women, either by strumpeting them, or violating them, or breaking up marriages." Burd quotes from *Politics* 1314b, but 1311ab is more pertinent.

[47] *Istorie Fiorentine* 7.33, p. 587b.

[48] Ibid. 2.36, p. 436b.   [49] *Prince* 17, p. 33.

[50] "There is no more flagrant abuse in the administration of power or one that more offends the spirits of the people than an injury resulting from lust, as defilements and adulteries and base acts of this nature, such as every violation of modesty. These should be so guarded against that no vestige of lust at all shall appear in you. For all these things are remote from honesty of life and the gravity suitable to a high office. But of all things I think perhaps avarice is basest in a magistrate; it both produces hatred and often brings on the greatest calamities and produces damages and a wrong opinion of one's integrity, as when men believe that one whom they know to be eager for money is not trustworthy as a judge in court" (*De regendo magistratu*, p. 728).

[51] "Because of the punishments they inflict on their subjects" (*De regimine* 3.2.36).

[52] "Fear of a penalty" (*Prince* 17, p. 33a). Cf. pp. 103, above, 149 ff., below.

inexquisitas crudelitates exerceant."[53] Secondly, the prince will be impartial: "Imo, ut vult Philosophus, 7 *Politicorum,* decet Reges et potentes ut magis timeantur, et ut virilius observent iustitiam, magis punire, et severius se gerere contra amicos, si contingat eos valde forefacere, quam contra alios."[54] Thirdly, the execution of law will be so thorough that the evildoer cannot hope to escape.

But in spite of the necessity of fear, love is better:

Cum cives et existentes in regno si bene agant, et observent leges, et mandata Regis ex amore honesti, et ex dilectione quam habent ad bonum commune et ad Regem, sint magis boni et virtuosi, quam si hoc facerent timore poenae, et ne punirentur; magis debent appetere Reges et Principes amari a populis: et quod amore boni, populi bene agant, quam timeri ab eis, et quod timore poenae cavere sibi ab actibus malis. Utrumque enim est necessarium, timeri et amari. Nam non omnes sunt adeo boni et perfecti quod solo amore honesti et boni communis,[55] et ex dilectione legislatoris, cuius est intendere commune bonum, quiescant male agere: oportuit ergo aliquos inducere ad bonum, et retrahere a malo timore poenae. Elegibilius tamen est amari, quam timeri.[56]

Debating the same matter under the head of *De thyrannide et crudelitate cavenda,* in 1498, Jacobus Wimpheling decided: "Sic subditorum odium et insidias effugiet, atque se talem exhibebit quod et amari dignus sit a suo populo et timeri. Et si enim utrumque horum necessarium est, quod timeatur et ametur, multo tamen

[53]"On those who immoderately disturb the kingdom and the state, princes may exercise the most carefully-devised cruelties" (*De regimine* 3.2.36).

[54] Nay more, as the Philosopher says in the seventh book of the *Politics,* in order that kings and rulers may be more feared and that they may more vigorously execute justice, they should punish more rigorously and conduct themselves with more severity against their friends, if they should seriously offend, than against others" (*De regimine,* 3.2.36).

[55] Cf. *Discorsi* 3.5, p. 199a: "Egli è molto più facile essere amato dai buoni che dai cattivi."—"It is much easier to be loved by the good than by the evil."

[56] "Since the citizens and those who live in a kingdom, if they act correctly and observe the laws and mandates of the king because they love what is right and have a high regard for the common good and the king, are better and more virtuous than if they did this from fear of a penalty and lest they should be punished, it is proper that kings and princes should desire to be loved by their people, and that the people should act correctly from love of the good, rather than that the rulers be feared by the people and the subjects refrain from evil actions through fear of punishment. For both of the two are necessary, to be feared and to be loved. For not all are so good and perfect that from mere love of what is upright and of the common good, and from affection for the legislator, whose function it is to regard the common good, they cease from doing evil. Therefore it is necessary to lead some toward good and restrain them from evil by fear of punishment. Yet one should prefer to be loved rather than feared" (ibid. 3.2.36).

magis ut ametur quam timeatur conari Principem decet."[57] The opposite conclusion drawn by Machiavelli is in harmony with the
purpose of his work. Asking what will enable a ruler to continue as
ruler in all imaginable circumstances, he answers that fear will be
more effective than love.[58] The conclusion of Egidio depends on
his desire that the ruler—here thought of as secure—shall make his
people morally better; for this love is a better instrument than fear.
But even then love is workable only for the good among his subjects; the wicked must be controlled by fear. Egidio would admit
that such subjects as Machiavelli describes in this chapter, "ingrati,
volubili, simulatori," etc.,[59] would not respond to kindness; since
men are generally such, for Machiavelli, fear must be the general
reliance of the prince who is to control a real rather than an imaginary dominion.

The heart of Machiavelli's contention is to be found not so
much in his choice of love or fear, as in his insistence that the security of the ruler should be in his own hands, "fondarsi in su
quello che è suo,"[60] and not in that of others; for this higher reason
successful leaders can be cited on either side, as Scipio and Hannibal, and Valerius and Manlius; their final reliance was extraordinary ability—"una virtù istraordinaria."[61] From the virtue of
the ruler may spring a quality between fear and love, namely reverence or veneration. As though to carry out Machiavelli's advice
suggested by the conspiracy against Galeazzo the Duke of Milan,
Lorenzo di Piero de' Medici "fassi in somma e amare e reverire,
piuttosto che temere."[62] On the other hand, this reverence can be

---

[57] "Thus a prince may escape the hatred and plots of his subjects and show himself such that he is worthy to be loved and feared by his people. And if both of the
two, that is to be feared and to be loved, are necessary, it is much more fitting
that the prince should strive to be loved than to be feared" (*Agatharchia*, sig. a5
verso).

[58] *Prince* 17, p. 33a.   [59] "Ingrate, shifty, hypocritical" (ibid.).

[60] "On what is in his own control" (*Prince* 17, p. 34a).

[61] *Discorsi* 3.21, p. 231b; cf. "una virtù eccessiva" (ibid, 3.22, p. 233a).

[62] "In short, he made himself loved and revered rather than feared" (to Vettori,
Aug., 1513, *Lettere Familiari* 27, p. 112). Tommasini speaks of the passage as an
important and perhaps not disinterested character-sketch of Lorenzo (*Vita di Machiavelli* 2.76, n. 5). From Galeazzo's own experience Machiavelli concludes: "Imparino
. . . i principi a . . . farsi in modo reverire ed amare, che niuno speri potere,
amazzandogli, salvarsi."—"Princes should learn to conduct themselves in such a
way that no one who assassinates them can hope to escape" (*Istorie Fiorentine* 7.34,
p. 589b). Cf. *Prince* 6, p. 14a: "essere in venerazione"; *Prince* 19, p. 36a: "eccellente
e reverito da' suoi"; and of Marcus: "molte virtù che lo facevano venerando"
(p. 38a); *Istorie Fior.* 7.5, p. 564b, of Cosimo: "la cui reverenza." The "benivolenzia

combined with fear: "Papa Giulio non si curò mai di essere odiato, pure che fusse temuto e riverito, e con quello suo timore messe sottosopra il mondo, e condusse la Chiesa dove ella è."[63] The cruel Hannibal, we read in this chapter, was both terrible and venerable. Something of the sort is perhaps implied when in praise of Duke Valentino it is said that he made himself "seguire e reverire da' soldati."[64] In his government of the Romagna he gained the reputation of cruelty,[65] and when his soldiers against his desire attempted to sack Sinigaglia, "il duca con la morte di molti represse la insolenzia loro."[66] Apparently reverence is related to "le amicizie che si acquistano . . . con grandezza e nobiltà di animo"[67] though Machiavelli is not to be held for exactly scientific uses of words. Another aspect of the self-dependence of the good ruler has appeared in his belief that it is necessary to convince the citizens that they have need of the state;[68] they then will be faithful, with a fidelity similar to the love which Egidio thought a strong ruler would inspire in his subjects. A similar opinion is expressed by Guicciardini, whether derived from Machiavelli, representing a current opinion, or however arrived at:

Non è la più labile cosa che la memoria de' beneficii ricevuti: però fate più fondamento in su quegli che sono condizionati in modo che non vi possino mancare, che in su coloro quali avete beneficati; perché spesso o non se ne ricordano, o presuppongono e beneficii minori che non sono, o reputano che siano fatti quasi per obligo.[69]

---

populare" of *Prince* 19, p. 36b, as a protection against conspiracy, seems to represent love and reverence. Reverence is opposed to contempt in *Prince* 23, p. 46a. In *Discorsi* 1.10, p. 75b, it is associated with glory as the reward of the prince; cf. p. 228, below.

[63] "Pope Julius did not care if he was hated, if only he was feared and revered, and by the use of this fear he turned the world upside down and brought the Church to her present position" (to Vettori, Dec. 20, 1514, *Lett. Familiari* 38, p. 162). Severus was also "temuto e reverito" (*Prince* 19, p. 39a). In the letter to Vettori of Jan. 31, 1514 (*Lett. Fam.* 41) occurs "riverenza o timore." Egidio writes: "Non severa sed reverenda."—"Not severe but reverend" (*De regimine* 2.3.19); he refers to Aristotle's *Politics* 5.11. Clichtoveus thought the good king "amatur ab omnibus et cum reverentia timetur,"—"is loved by all and with reverence feared" (*De regis officio,* folio 41 verso).

[64] "Followed and revered by the soldiers" (*Prince* 7, p. 17b).

[65] See p. 99, above.

[66] "The duke repressed their insolence by the execution of many" (*Del modo tenuto dal Duca Valentino,* p. 747b).

[67] "The friendly intentions toward one that are acquired through greatness and nobility of spirit" (*Prince* 17, p. 33a).   [68] *Prince* 9, p. 22a.

[69] "There is nothing more perishable than the memory of benefits received. Therefore place more reliance on those who are so situated that they cannot get on

To the same theory of self-reliance attaches Niccolò's remark that "tutti e' profeti armati vinsono, e li disarmati ruinorono";[70] when the people are no longer willing to believe, the prophet must be ready to make them believe by force. Yet Machiavelli is willing to allow something to the people; a strong and prudent ruler who has risen by popular favor will not rely on them in vain, provided he is a prince "che possa comandare, e sia uomo di core nè si sbigottisca nelle avversità, e non manchi delle altre preparazioni, e tenga con lo animo e ordini suoi animato lo universale."[71] This is a very qualified dependence on popular support which emphasizes the self-reliance of the ruler.

Diomede Carafa is on the side of love rather than fear, and seems to feel that this is partly or wholly in the ruler's hands. Since, however, his means of gaining love is that suggested by Machiavelli for avoiding hate, his love is probably equivalent to what Machiavelli characteristically calls *non essere odiato,* to be unhated.[72]

Et omne dì se vede dicti stati se tengono o per amore o per timore, et certo lo melly e lo più laudabile modo e farli tale compagnia ali subditi che ve pongano amore; che in verita facilemente se fa; che non ei vero ch' ala generalità de li subditi li habiati da dare de la robba vostra per che ve ami: basta assay che noli levate la sua iniustamente. Et si puro lo bisogno fosse che le rendite ordinarie non bastassero, se volino requedere in tal modo ve ajutano, che cognoscano la necessita e no la volunta vence induce, Anche fareli cognoscere se fa de mala vollya. Et quando accascano in pene mustrarli che per mantenere la iustitia se fa, Et non per sete de sua robba.[73]

---

without you than on those whom you have benefited; for often the latter either do not remember benefits, or suppose them less than they are, or think they are conferred because one is obliged to" (*Ricordi* XXIV; cf. CCLV, CCLXIV).

[70] "All the armed prophets conquered and the disarmed prophets went to ruin" (*Prince* 6, p. 13b).

[71] "Who is able to command, and is a man of spirit who does not get downcast in adversity, and does not lack other preparations, and keeps the common people animated with his spirit and laws" (*Prince* 9, p. 21b).

[72] *Prince* 10, p. 22b; 19, pp. 36a, 38a; 20, p. 43a. Cf. p. 160, below.

[73] "And every day it can be seen that the said states are held either through love or through fear, and certainly the best and most praiseworthy manner of doing it is to have such relations with one's subjects that they have affection for you; and this is easily done because it is not true that to the generality of your subjects you need to give of your property that they may be your friends; it is enough that you do not unjustly take away theirs. And if necessity should bring about that your ordinary revenues do not suffice you, it is advisable that they be requested to aid you in such a manner that they may know that necessity and not desire induces you to do it, and also that they are made to understand that you do it against your will. And when they become subject to penalties show them that this is done

This passage especially suggests Machiavelli's earlier remark that
a prince who gains his place through favor of the people "debbe
. . . mantenerselo amico; il che li fia facile, non domandando
lui se non di non essere oppresso."[74] Perhaps the statement from
the independent Carafa suggests how difficult it was for a writer to
give up the belief that a prince must be loved by his subjects.[75]
As has been exemplified in discussing chapter ten, it is usual to
insist that a prince who gains the love of his subjects is secure;
Beroaldus writes enthusiastically of the prince he imagines:

Talem cuncti amabunt ut parentem: venerabuntur ut deum. Sub talis
imperio vivent quam beatissimi. Talis charitate civium septus erit: quae
arx inaccessa est, et inexpugnabile munimentum.[76] Melius enim tutatur
principem amor civium quam ferrum lateranum. Nam ut inquit
verissime Claudianus: Non sic excubiae, non circumstantia pila quam
tutatur amor. Non sunt adamantina vincula illa quae Dionysius tyrannus dictitabat: metus, violentia, classis, praesidium decem militum
armatorum: sed benivolentia, gratia, bonitas, innocentia. Da principem
talem qualem libellus iste describit: huic affatim praesto erunt: qui
oculi regum, qui aures principum apud veteres dicebantur. Et quum
iucundissimum sit in rebus humanis amari et amare, hic amabitur et
amabit mutuis affectibus. Hic denique cunctos habebit devotos, fideles,
obnoxios: nec minus de vita principis, quam de suametipsorum inco-
lumitate sollicitos.[77]

---

to maintain justice and not through hunger for their property" (*I doveri del
principe*, pp. 266-7). The Latin advises the ruler so to deal with his subjects "ut
te diligere cogantur,"—"that they are forced to love you" (pt. 1, p. 649).

[74] "Ought to keep it friendly to him; and this is easy, since the people demands
only not to be oppressed" (*Prince* 9, p. 21a).

[75] It is true that Pontanus thought it more important to avoid the vices that
bring destruction than to practice the virtues that bring love, saying: "Non tam
autem studendum est, ut liberalis habeare, atque humanus, quam cavendum ab iis
vitiis, quae ab his virtutibus dicuntur contraria."—"It is not so necessary to make an
effort to be held liberal and humane as it is to avoid those vices which are said
to be contrary to those virtues" (*De principe*, p. 268). Tommasini (2.114, n. 1)
cites this passage to illustrate Machiavelli's warning against the infamy of those
vices which may take away a ruler's position, and says that undeniably the tractate
of Pontanus had great influence on the mind of Machiavelli. Pontanus, however,
does warmly advise liberality and humanity as bringing love. The parallel
seems to me hardly to imply influence.

[76] Misprinted *nutrimentum;* the marginal summary runs: "Amor munimentum
firmissimum." The source is apparently Seneca's *De clementia* 1.19, or Pliny's
Panegyric 49; see pp. 160-1, below.

[77] "All will love such an one as a parent; they will venerate him as a god.
Under the rule of such a prince they will live in the happiest of conditions. Such an
one will be protected by the love of the citizens, which is an inaccessible citadel and
an impregnable fortress. The love of the citizens guards the prince better than

There is no room here for Machiavelli's belief that love will not hold subjects except in peace and prosperity, and even then only until their fickle minds change. In fact, of all the works *de regimine principum* the old *Secretum secretorum* seems most Machiavellian:

O Alexander obedienciam dominacionis (vel dominatoris) quatuor modis attendimus, scilicet in religiositate, dileccione, curialitate, et reverencia. O Alexander, converte ad te animas subditorum, tolle injurias et injusticias ab eis. Noli dare hominibus contra te materiam obloquendi, quia vulgus dicit mala de levi, et quando de jure potest dicere, de facto leviter potest facere. Contine te ergo ita ut nichil contra te possit dicere, et per hoc evitabis eorum facere. Insuper scias quod discrecio maturitatis est gloria dignitatis, et reverencia domini est exaltacio regis et regni. Summa igitur prudencia est et providencia laudabilis, ut tua reverencia cohabitet in cordibus subditorum magis quam dileccio.[78]

Many years later Commynes, speaking of the attitude of the subject to the good ruler, does not mention love at all, but only fear. Possibly his decision that fear was what the king should desire led him to write:

Mais si nostre roy ou ceux qui le veulent eslever ou agrandir disoyent: "J'ay les subgectz si très bons et loyaulx qu'ilz ne me reffusent chose que je leur demande et suys plus crainct et obéy et servy de mes subgectz que nul autre prince qui vive sur terre et qui plus patientement en-

---

Lateran iron. For as Claudian most truly says: Not the guards, not the spearmen stationed about secure safety as does love. Fear, violence, a fleet, a guard of ten [thousand] armed men are not chains of adamant, as the tyrant Dionysius affirmed, but these chains are benevolence, grace, goodness, innocence. Granted a prince such as this little book describes, on such an one will surely be in attendance those who by the ancients were called the eyes and the ears of the king. And since among human things it is one of the most pleasant to be loved and to love, this prince will be loved and will love his people with mutual affection. He then will have subjects who are devoted, faithful, and obedient, and not less concerned for the life of the prince than for their own safety" (*De optimo statu,* folio 133). The passage from Claudian is *De quarto consulatu Honorii* 281-2. It is quoted by John of Salisbury, *Policraticus* 5.7.555b. See also p. 161, below.

[78] "Alexander, we expect obedience to rule in four ways, to wit, because of religious duty, love, courtliness, and reverence. O Alexander, draw to yourself the spirits of your subjects, remove injuries and injustices from them. Do not be willing to give men matter for speaking evil of you, for the common people speak evil for trifling reasons and when they have good reason for speaking, they easily turn to action. Restrain yourself, therefore, so that it is possible to say nothing against you, and by this you will avoid doing what causes reproach. Above all you should know that the discretion of maturity is the glory of dignity, and reverence for the lord is the exaltation of the king and the kingdom. Therefore the greatest prudence and foresight are praiseworthy, that reverence for you may dwell in the hearts of your subjects rather than affection" (*Secretum secretorum,* pt. i, chap. 15, p. 53).

durent tous maulx et toutes ruddesses et à qui moins il souvient de leurs dommaiges passéz," il me semble que cela luy seroit grant loz et diz la verité.[79]

In making clear the dependence of the wise prince on his own capacities and resources, this chapter emphasizes a topic which pervades *The Prince*.[80] If Machiavelli had been dealing with a ruler whose family had been well established, or if the little book had not had an immediate purpose, he might have said less of the personal demands on the head of the state, but he is influenced by the problem of his last chapter, that of delivering Italy and organizing it into a lasting and well-ordered kingdom. For such an accomplishment only the most completely adequate abilities could suffice, and they only if favored by fortune. Cesare Borgia had displayed much of the necessary capacity, but had made at least one error sufficient to ruin him, considering the malignity of fortune. He, moreover, had been obliged to learn by experience, something Machiavelli's deliverer cannot give time to do, for the conqueror of Italy must begin his career as the responsible head of his own army, prepared mentally and physically for all the accidents of the field. Ferdinand of Spain exemplified enough of the qualities of the ideal prince to enable him to found a great new state, but he too was inadequate, in that he thought too little of the good of his people; he also failed in the treatment of his officers, as appears in the career of Consalvo.[81]

To say that Niccolò demanded the impossible is easy; nor did he suppose that he was asking other than the very difficult. Only the fullest political wisdom could suffice. In his own day a man sufficient for the task did not arise; a later age, it is often said, provided Cavour and Garibaldi to conquer difficulties in part by the methods of Machiavelli.

But while Machiavelli emphasizes the personal capacity of the prince far more than other writers *de regimine principum,* he is giving vitality to what they take for granted rather than presenting

[79] "But if our king or those who wish to exalt or aggrandize him should say: 'I have subjects so very good and loyal that they refuse me nothing which I ask of them and I am more feared and obeyed and served by my subjects than any other prince who lives on the earth, and there are no subjects who more patiently endure all ills and all afflictions and who less remember their past injuries,'—that, it seems to me, would be high praise and speaks the truth" (*Mémoires* 5.19, pp. 218-9).

[80] E.g., chaps. 3, 4, 5, 6, 7, 8, 9 (last sentence), 12, 13, 14, 19, 21, 22 (ministers are good or bad according to the prudence of the ruler), 23, 24, 26.

[81] See pp. 119, 134, 166 ff., 183 note, below.

a new conception. The whole series of works addressed to princes on their *governi* is a symptom of the importance of the prince and his responsibility for the rule of his state. As lovers of humanity the authors essay to improve the condition of mankind by the obvious method of improving the monarch as the centre of the government. As active ruler the prince they present can do much as he pleases without restraint. If he wishes good ministers, he can choose them; there is no clear statement that the prince may be incapable of doing so. If he sets out to be loved by his subjects, all will be smooth; there is no emphasis on the possibility of an ungrateful people. Difficulties with the nobles are hardly recognized. We seldom read of danger from ambitious neighboring princes or dependence on them. The problems of the conqueror are not treated. That a king can be imprudent is asserted, that he can be overthrown for bad government is emphasized by those who do not flatter, that the labors of a king are very heavy is generally asserted. But that a sovereign may gain enmity for acts good in intention, that his soldiers may not submit to discipline, that a virtuous ruler may be driven from his throne, that, in short, success is not on the whole in the monarch's own hands is seldom or never admitted, even when flattery does not unduly exalt the king's power and ability. Even allowing much to the body of Niccolò's predecessors, one can still feel that they do not realize the complexity of the sovereign's task and the difficulties it involves, that, in comparison with our author, they usually deal with the smooth paths of imaginary rulers rather than with things as they are. The analysis in detail of conditions necessary to reveal the difficulties of the ruler is lacking. To such analysis, based on his unusual experience, Machiavelli was stimulated by his practical and immediate desire for the deliverance and reform of Italy. So limited and so stimulating a problem was not given to his predecessors.

Properly realizing the enormous importance of the prince, above all in Italy where a republic on a grand scale could not then exist, Machiavelli was equally impressed by the restrictions of his sovereign power and freedom of action. Yet the limitations he saw were not constitutional; on the contrary, constitutional forms, such as the French parliament, seemed to him to strengthen the king as the head of a body politic designed for the common good. The prince in Machiavelli's eye was limited by quite other things. He might rely on the good will of subjects conciliated by presents rather than consciously owing their prosperity to an administration which alone could enforce beneficial laws and protect them from rapacious nobles or invading foreigners; such citizens would not fight for the ruler in time of need. Nobles might support the king only as their selfish interest directed and not because the military capacity of their lord made disloyalty the road to ruin. Or the prince might rely on worthless mercenary soldiers or the arms of some ambitious and grasping foreign potentate. Ministers not recognized as incompetent or disloyal might hold state secrets in their hands. The monarch himself might rely on the seeming prosperity of the times and neglect the right sort of preparation by giving his attention to agriculture instead of to military training. Such limitations as these, Machiavelli saw, made the position of a well-intentioned ruler a precarious one, instead of the secure throne normally assumed by literary advisers of princes. Yet on the policy of the prince in the midst of limiting conditions depended the well-being of his people.

How could the indispensable ruler free himself from such limitations in order that he might exercise his full capacity for the good of Italy? How might a prince of *virtù,* with good fortune, be absolute except in the obligation to rule well? be absolute that he might adopt the methods of the constitutional monarch, as did Romulus in Rome? To this the answer is given in a policy of unswerving self-reliance: "Debbe uno principe savio fondarsi in su quello che è suo, non in su quello che è d'altri."[82]

[82] "A wise prince will lay his foundation on what belongs to himself and not on what belongs to someone else" (*Prince* 17, p. 34a).

Chapter 18

Quomodo fides a principibus sit servanda.
(In what way faith should be kept by princes.)

In the opening paragraphs of this chapter Machiavelli, in harmony with his usual procedure, represents full adherence to traditional morals as worthy of praise, and yet immediately asserts that necessity does not always permit it, but that reprehensible means must at times be employed. Since he wrote with good government ever in view,[1] he might have attempted to make the conduct he thought necessary appear moral. He probably knew that St. Thomas, for instance, holding to the Biblical prohibition against the shedding of blood, affirmed the justice of wars carried on for the common good; in these wars a restricted amount of deception is allowed.[2] On some such basis Machiavelli could have rested a moral justification of his ruler. But his method is much simpler and more direct, even to allowing to brutishness more than is required. He makes no attempt to justify his prince; the question of the common good is left implicit; the ruler is required only to maintain his state, with perhaps an implication that more than maintenance—that is, conquest—is permitted.[3] Though faith, Christian charity, humanity, and religion are genuinely good things, the ruler need not regard them; his commanders are "the winds of fortune and the variations of things."[4] He need not consider what ethical justification he can give for his conduct or whether there are limits beyond which ethics does not permit him to go; freed from the need for such perplexing considerations, he can devote all his energies to empirical decisions, with a clear conscience.

In speaking of the quality of *astuzia* Machiavelli apparently has in mind Ferdinand of Spain, again referred to, it is usually supposed, at the end of the chapter; among the other contemporary princes who have exhibited astuteness would doubtless have been that greatest of feigners—"grandissimo simulatore"—Duke Valen-

[1] Francesco Ercole, *La politica di Machiavelli*, p. 58.
[2] *Summa Theologica* 2.2.40 (*de bello*).
[3] For the meaning of the word *stato* in Machiavelli, see Ercole, *La politica*, pp. 65 ff.   [4] *Prince* 18, p. 35a.

[118]

tino.[5] Though obviously approving the use of *astuzia* in necessity, our author asserts here, as in chapter fifteen, that it is not laudable, as every one knows—"ciascuno lo intende."[6] Among those who knew this were some of the writers *de regimine principum,* to whom Machiavelli perhaps intends to refer. Patricius asserted: "Scita est enim Agesilai Regis sententia, *qui ait regiae dignitati non astutiam, sed bonitatis excellentiam convenire.*"[7] Platina also writes of it:

Tollendae igitur astutiae sunt: eaque malitia quae vult quidem videri prudentia cum absit ab ea distetque plurimum: Mentiri enim emolumenti sui causa, criminari, fallere, praeripere, in bonum virum cadere non potest: sagaces eos sane velim non tamen astutos et callidos. Est enim sagacitas (ut Aristoteli placet) rerum agendarum scientia circa principia: eosdem enim ut sagaces et bonos dicit. Si (inquit) in deliberando intentio sit honesta vis illa laudabilis est. Sin improba, astutia nuncupatur. Fieri ergo non potest: ut quispiam prudens sit habendus; nisi idem sit bonus: cum virtus sit habitus ratione determinatus: et ipsa recta ratio prudentia nuncupetur.[8]

This idea was widely spread, it appears.[9] It perhaps determined the form of Machiavelli's assertion about Ferdinand in April, 1513. "Spagna parse sempre mai a me più astuto e fortunato, che savio e

[5] *Del modo tenuto dal Duca Valentino,* p. 744b. Cf. *Prince* 7, p. 16a; 18, p. 34b.

[6] Cf. pp. 7-8, note 17; 67; 77 ff., above.

[7] "The opinion of Agesilaus is well known, who says that not astuteness but excellence of goodness befits the kingly dignity" (*De regno* 3.13).

[8] "Astuteness is therefore to be put away, and this malice which pretends to be prudence when it is as different and remote from it as possible. For to lie for the sake of gain, to commit crimes, to cheat, to seize violently cannot be proper for a good man. Indeed I could wish good men sagacious, but yet not astute and artful. For sagacity (as Aristotle holds) is the understanding of how to do things according to principles, for he thinks that men who possess that power are sagacious and good. If, he says, in making plans one's intention is honest, that ability is laudable, but if one's intention is dishonest his ability is called astuteness. Hence it cannot be that any one can be considered prudent unless he is good, since virtue is a habit determined by reason, and right reason itself is called prudence" (*De optime cive,* lib. 2, folio lxxxix verso-xc recto).

[9] Cf. Dante, *Convivio* 4.27.5: "Non è da dire savio uomo chi con sottratti e con inganni procede, ma è da chiamare astuto."—"He is not to be called wise who proceeds by means of shady schemes and deceptions, but is to be called astute." Tommaseo's *Dizionario* quotes a Tuscan proverb: "Senno vince astuzia."—"Brains surpass astuteness." It quotes also from Buti's comment on *Inferno* 17.1: "Astuzia è intendimento in mal fine, con mali mezzi, ma con simulazione e apparenza di bene."—"Astuteness is intention directed toward a bad end, with bad means, but with the simulation and appearance of good." Cf. pp. 134, 166, below, for further illustration of *astuzia* and for Ferdinand's simulation of good.

prudente."[10] It is possible that in the months following this letter, while composing *The Prince,* Machiavelli came to think more highly of *astuzia.* My impression, however, is that he felt a ruler might be astute without being wise and prudent, but that a wise ruler would when necessary be able to practice astuteness. Machiavelli's admiration for Ferdinand was limited; at least he refrains from such praise of his government as that of Duke Valentino receives.[11] Ferdinand's clever tricks were in themselves worth imitating, but he was incapable of any other sort of conduct, whereas the wise prince when he can holds to the good, and turns to *inganno*[12] only in necessity. The king of Spain lacked the qualities of prudence and virtue that would entitle him to true glory as a ruler whose acts, whether marked by *astuzia* or *lealtà,* were directed to the promotion of the common good.

Considering the importance of warfare in the scheme of Machiavelli, as revealed in *The Prince,* chapter fourteen, and in *The Art of War,* and the importance to the soldier of prudence, as presented by Egidio Colonna,[13] for instance, it is an example of Machiavelli's ruthlessness in making the path of the ruler clear that war is thrown wholly to the side of the beast.[14] Nor is the lion here the lion accompanying the virtue of Fortitude, as at the portal of the cathedral of Amiens; it is the lion of inhuman cruelty such as might typify Hannibal, who succeeded by detestable measures.[15]

---

[10] "The king of Spain always seems to me more astute and fortunate than wise and prudent" (to Vettori, undated but apparently April, 1513, *Lettere Familiari* 20, p. 74). The idea is repeated in the same letter. Cf. also: "Con improntitudine e astuzia, più che con ingegno e prudenzia."—"With effrontery and astuteness rather than with ability and prudence" (to Vettori, April 9, 1513, *Lettere Familiari* 18, p. 67).

[11] Cf. *Prince,* chap. 21, p. 43a, with chap. 7; see pp. 42-3, above, 166, below.

[12] *Capitolo dell' ambizione* 39. *Inganno* (fraud) is one of the vices accompanying ambition, a trait of Ferdinand's.   [13] *De regimine* 3.3.1.

[14] Possibly Machiavelli influenced the following lines by Milton:

> Nor is it aught but just,
> That he who in debate of Truth hath won,
> Should win in Arms, in both disputes alike
> Victor; though brutish that contest and foule,
> When Reason hath to deal with force, yet so
> Most reason is that Reason overcome (*Paradise Lost* 6.121-6).

[15] Cf. Erasmus, *Institutio principis* 1, 573 A: "Si Tyranni quaeris imaginem, leonem, ursum, lupum, aut aquilam cogita, quae laniatu vivunt ac praeda: . . . nisi quod horum quoque saevitiam superat Tyrannus."—"If you wish an image of the tyrant, think of the lion, the bear, the wolf, or the eagle, which live by mangling and spoil: . . . unless the tyrant shows more savagery than even these."

But the concern of Machiavelli is not so much with force as with another sort of brutish conduct, characterized by craft.

Violence and fraud, as Dante thought of them in planning the *Inferno* (11.24), are both inhuman as opposed to conduct in harmony with law—founded on justice—which represents man at his best, in the exercise of reason.[16] Aristotle had explained that in distinction from the rest of creation man is the social animal, who in his perfection lives according to justice. In an adaptation in his *Discorsi*[17] of the pertinent passage from the *Politics,* Machiavelli explains that in the beginning men lived like beasts, but that ultimately they entered into society and acquired the understanding of justice. But Aristotle had said that men who rejected the social order remained beasts; as Egidio put it, "quicunque non civiliter vivit . . . est bestia et sceleratus et sine iugo."[18] Ezekiel, quoted by Aquinas in showing that rapine is opposed to justice, had said that rulers who spoiled their subjects were wolves.[19] In the language of Machiavelli men who abandon justice for force or fraud are properly lions or foxes.[20] If men were good, only truly human conduct would be suitable— even expedient—but in a wicked world animal-like conduct is the price of survival. Something of the atmosphere of Machiavelli's thought of the inhuman character of breaking faith and otherwise opposing justice, though without his approval of it, appears in Dante:

Avvegna che ciascuna vertù sia amabile ne l'uomo, quella è più amabile in esso che è più umana, e questa è la giustizia, la quale è solamente ne

[16] Cf. Aquinas, *Summa Theologica* 2.1.31.7; 90.1.

[17] *Discorsi* 1.2, p. 60a; based on Aristotle, *Politics* 1.2.

[18] "Whoever does not live in society is a beast both acursed and without a yoke" (*De regimine* 3.1.3). About the middle of the sixteenth century Figliucci put as follows Aristotle's remark on the man outside society:

"Questo tale adunque è tristo, e inhumano, ne da giogo alcuno ritenuto, a guisa che molti uccelli rapaci, e ingordi vediamo, come è l'Aquila, l'Avoltore, il Nibbio, e somiglianti, li quali da gl' altri divisi, e solinghi se ne vanno; fuggendo adunque costui il praticare con gl' altri huomini, mostra insieme d'esser desideroso di discordie, e di risse, e di apprezzare poco la pace, e la compagnia humana."—"Such an one then is wicked and inhuman and not held by any yoke, just as we see many rapacious and greedy birds, such as the eagle, the vulture, the kite, and the like, which are in the habit of going apart from the others and solitary; so that man, fleeing contact with other men, shows that he is at once desirous of discords and disputes and puts a low value on peace and human company" (*De la politica,* folio 8 verso).

[19] Ezekiel 22.27, quoted in *Summa Theologica* 2.2.66.8.

[20] *Prince* 18, p. 34b. For similar use of these animals in Dante (*Inferno* 27.75) and other authors, see Tommasini, *Vita di Machiavelli* 2.117, n. 1.

la parte razionale o vero intellettuale, cioè ne la volontade. Questo è tanto amabile, che, sì come dice lo Filosofo nel quinto de l'Etica, li suoi nimici l'amano, sì come sono ladroni e rubatori; e però vedemo che 'l suo contrario, cioè la ingiustizia, massimamente è odiata, sì come è tradimento, ingratitudine, falsitade, furto, rapina, inganno e loro simili. Li quali sono tanto inumani peccati, che ad iscusare sè de l'infamia di quelli, si concede da lunga usanza che uomo parli di sè, sì come detto è di sopra, e possa dire sè essere fedele e leale.[21]

As the words of Dante would lead one to expect, in this chapter Machiavelli is in opposition to the moral and religious writers of advice to princes. He was well aware of his departure from their methods; possibly the opening sentence is intended to refer to them; their works, it implies, are so widely circulated that everyone is acquainted with them; moreover, they are right in the abstract, but composed for imaginary republics in which, as is suggested later in the chapter, all men are good; for the *verità effettuale* of things they are useless or positively harmful.[22]

Early among the works of advice to princes that inculcate maintenance of faith is the *Secretum secretorum,* in which we read:

O clementissime Imperator, cave ne infringas datam fidem et federa confirmata, quoniam hoc convenit infidelibus, juvenibus, et meretricibus. Serva fideliter promissam fidem, quoniam omnem infidelitatem consequitur finis malus. Et si in federa fringendo aliquid boni eveniat, tamen quando ipsa species mala est, exemplum erit reprobum, et de genere malorum.

[21] "Though every virtue is lovely in a man, that is most lovely in him which is most human, and this is justice, which resides solely in the rational or intellectual part, that is in the will. This is so lovable that, as the Philosopher says in the fifth book of the *Ethics,* its enemies love it, such as thieves and robbers. Therefore we see that its contrary, that is injustice, which appears in betrayal, ingratitude, falsity, theft, rapine, deception, and the like, is especially hated. These are such inhuman sins that to excuse himself from the infamy of them a man is permitted by long-established custom to speak of himself, as has been said above, and can say that he is faithful and loyal" (*Convivio* 1.12.9-11).

[22] It is possible that Machiavelli had encountered a concession to things as they are by the historian Menander Protector, also an adviser of princes:
"Ὅτι οὐχ ὅστις ἀντεπιβουλεύει τοῦ δικαίου κατόπιν ὀφθήσεται, ἀλλ' ὃς ἐπιβουλεύει τῶν χαλεπῶν ὑπόθεσις γίνεται."—"Not the man who makes a counterplot against crafty enemies, but the man who makes the first plot is the originator of evil" (*Ex historia excerpta* 32). Cf. *La mente di un uomo di stato* 2.11: "Non quello, che prende prima le armi, è cagione degli scandoli, ma colui che è primo a dar cagione, che le si prendino."—"Not the man who first takes arms is the cause of scandals, but he who is the first to furnish the cause for taking them" (Machiavelli, *Opere,* Italia, 1813, VIII, 246, from *Ist. Fior.* 7.16, p. 574b).

Scias itaque quod per fidem fit hominum congregacio, civitatum inhabitacio, virorum communio, regis dominacio; per fidem castra tenentur, civitates servantur, reges dominantur. Si quidem tollas fidem, cuncti homines ad statum pristinum revertentur, videlicet ad instar brutorum et similitudinem bestiarum.[23]

The position of Machiavelli as to the bestiality of fraud is already affirmed, though his standard of expediency in princely dealings is considered and rejected. In the fifteenth century Patricius urged truth on the king on the basis of the well-known advice of Isocrates to Nicocles:

Isocrates regem suum monet ut veritatem ante omnia colat, idque manifeste semper et indissimulate agat adeo ut cuncti cognoscant iniurato potius regi, quam privatis omnibus iuratis fidem adhibendam esse. Ignavi quidem hominis est mentiri et eius, qui vel alios decipere vult, vel qui opinionem potius sequitur quam veritatem. Hunc enim vel timor compellit quae vera sunt occultare, et simulando vel dissimulando tegere: vel futilis aliqua species in mendacium inducit. Magnanimus quidem verax est, et palam amat, palamque odit.[24]

This is a contrast with Machiavelli's ruler, who is interested in reputation rather than truth, and rejects the open violence of the king of beasts.

As would be expected, Erasmus, in the chapter on treaties in his *Institutio principis Christiani,* urges truth in the foreign relations of the prince. Even he, however, writes especially of agreements between "bonos ac sapientes principes."[25] Though presenting the evils

---

[23] "O most clement emperor, beware lest you infringe the faith you have given and the treaties you have confirmed, since this is conduct expected in infidels, young men, and harlots. Keep faithfully the faith you have promised, since an evil end follows all infidelity. And if some good may result from infringing a treaty, yet when the very species is evil the example will be bad and in the category of evils.

"You should know that through faith comes about the association of men, the inhabiting of states, the communion of men, the authority of the king; through faith castles are held, states are preserved, kings rule. Indeed if you take away faith all men revert to their pristine state, to wit to the fashion of brutes and the likeness of beasts" (pt. 1, chap. 19).

[24] "Isocrates advises his king to cherish truth before everything else and always to practice it manifestly and without dissimulation, to the end that all may know that confidence can be placed in a king who has not sworn rather than in all private men who have sworn. For lying is the part of a slothful man and of him who either wishes to deceive others or who follows opinion rather than truth. For either fear compels him to conceal the things that are true and to cover them by simulating and dissimulating, or some futile appearance leads him into falsehood. The magnanimous man is truthful and loves and hates openly" (Patricius, *De regno* 4.1).

[25] "Good and wise princes" (col. 603 B).

that spring from treaties "inter stultos ac malos,"[26] he has no plan of conduct for the prince obliged to deal with such neighbors. Would the standard of "publica utilitas" which he sets up have forced him to admit that a ruler in the interests of his own subjects might break the faith pledged to the wicked ruler of another realm? He leaves no answer. Somewhat earlier, Platina had made some attempt at that subject, asserting that the first duty of the ruler is to his own people, rather than to foreigners; yet he does not open the gates to the abandonment of treaties, in spite of some allowable breaches of agreement:

Quis enim est qui nesciat plus se patriae, parentibus, liberis, propinquis, civibus debere eiusdem nationis, eiusdem linguae, quam peregrinis et externis? . . .

Servandum enim ius gentium est, servanda fides, non dico praedonibus, aut piratis, qui communes omnium hostes sunt, non perduellis: Iis si pactum pro capite pretium non attulerint cives tui, nulla fraus est, ne si iurati quidem id non facerint.[27]

In Machiavelli's century the possibility of breaking faith for the good of one's country was suggested by one of the speakers in a dialogue by Bishop Osorius of Portugal; possibly this was the bishop's own opinion, derived from his experience with practical politics:

Illud tamen dico, eos Principes, qui cum Reipublicae salus postulaverit, fidem datam neglexerint, summis esse laudibus efferendos, si enim propriae utilitatis ratio facit, ut fides sine dedecore a Regibus violetur; quid eveniet, cum patriae salus atque dignitas eos ad fidem frangendam

---

[26] "Between base and wicked rulers" (ibid.).

[27] "Who is ignorant that he has greater obligation to his native land, to his relatives, his children, his neighbors, to the citizens of the same nation and language than to aliens and foreigners? . . . The law of nations is to be kept, faith is to be kept, I do not say with robbers, or pirates, who are the common enemies of all, not with those with whom one is at war. To them your citizens should not render a price agreed on for a life; they commit no fraud even if the citizens having sworn do not carry out their agreement" (*Principis diatuposis* 2.4, 5); some of the same words are used in *De optime cive*, lib. 2, folio xcii, recto, a work dedicated to Lorenzo de' Medici.

In his note on this chapter of *The Prince* (p. 298) Burd writes: "The idea of the inviolability of public faith is essentially a modern idea; it was not thought of in Machiavelli's day." This hardly follows from the quotations I have given. Indeed, Machiavelli's chapter is in itself evidence that the faith of princes (which I take to be the meaning of "public faith") was considered, by moralists and the general public, as inviolable. In the copy of Burd's edition of *The Prince* from the library of W. H. Hutton, now in my possession, there is a manuscript note on Burd's assertion: "This is not strictly true; many mediaeval instances to the contrary."

impulerit? Quamquam ii, qui ea gratia fidem non servant, ut patriae suae consulant, non fidem produnt, sed inviolatam conservant: magis enim fidem patriae obligatam habent, quam illis ipsis cum quibus foedera percusserunt. Is igitur qui cum patriae peste, atque pernicie fidem servandam putat, multo maius in se perfidiae crimen admittit, quam si fidem omnibus foederibus obligatam violaret. Perfidus namque is maxime putandus est, qui Reipublicae sibi commissae salutem negligit; negligit porro salutem Reipublicae qui fidem tuetur, cum illam fidei constantiam patriae perniciosam fore videt.[28]

Machiavelli himself made an effort to find justification for fraud in one of the classic works of advice to princes, representing a prince who was generally credited with all the virtues:

Mostra Senofonte, nella sua vita di Ciro, questa necessità dello ingannare; considerato che la prima ispedizione che fe' fare a Ciro contro al re di Armenia è piena di fraude, e come con inganno, e non con forza, gli fe' occupare il suo regno; e non conchiude altro, per tale azione, se non che a un principe che voglia fare gran cose, è necessario imparare a ingannare. Fegli ingannare, oltra di questo, Ciassare, re de' Medii, suo zio materno, in più modi; sanza la quale fraude mostra che Ciro non poteva pervenire a quella grandezza che venne.[29]

[28] "I assert that those princes who, when the safety of the state demands it, neglect the faith they have pledged, should be very greatly praised; for if the reason of their own advantage brings it about that faith may be violated by kings without disgrace, what shall we say of conditions in which the safety and dignity of the country impel them to break faith? Yet those who do not regard faith that they may advance the interests of their country do not betray faith but preserve it inviolate, for they have a greater obligation to keep faith with their country than with those with whom they have made treaties. He therefore who thinks that faith must be kept with injury and damage to his country, much more allows in himself the crime of perfidiousness than if he should violate the faith pledged in all his treaties. For he is to be judged especially perfidious who neglects the safety of the state committed to him; moreover he neglects the safety of his country who keeps faith when he sees that constancy in faith will be damaging to his country" (De regis institutione et disciplina, lib. 1, p. 37). The volumes of the Opera of Osorius in the Bibliotheca Nazionale in Palermo are from the old Jesuit library. The most unacceptable parts of the passage I quote are blotted out and on a slip in the volume is written, in an old hand: "Questo libro deve essere prohibito."—"This book ought to be prohibited."

[29] "In his Life of Cyrus, Xenophon shows this necessity for deception, in view of the fact that the first expedition that he has Cyrus make against the king of Armenia is full of fraud, and that he has him occupy his kingdom with deception and not with force; and from this action he does not draw any other conclusion than that if a prince wishes to do great things it is necessary for him to learn to deceive. In addition to this he has him deceive Cyaxares king of the Medes, his maternal uncle, in many ways. He shows that without this fraud Cyrus could not have attained the greatness to which he arrived" (Discorsi 2.13, p. 157a).

The fraud of Agatocle is mentioned in the same chapter, yet he appears to Machiavelli a wicked breaker of faith,[30] while part and perhaps all of the conduct of Cyrus exhibits stratagems such as are pronounced praiseworthy and glorious,[31] and would have been justified by the moralists. Possibly this is the reason why Xenophon does not figure in this chapter of *The Prince,* where Machiavelli is endeavoring to make clear that he is permitting his ruler when compelled by necessity—"necessitato"—not morally defensible stratagem but the most wicked and detestable conduct, "contro alla fede, contro alla carità, contro alla umanità, contra alla religione."[32]

The ruler who can follow Machiavelli's plan must be a prudent man, able not merely to select the conditions under which faith need not be kept, but also to simulate and dissimulate with skill. Such capacities, for other purposes than covering breach of faith, were not uncommended before Machiavelli. Patricius writes:

Magnum siquidem onus inter mortales est personam principis sustinere, atque tueri, quando quidem eam non solum hominum animis, sed oculis quoque inservire debet. . . . Princeps vero morosus, ac tristis aliorum animos perturbat, anxiosque reddit quid acturi sint. Nec quicquam potest in rebus dubiis, atque adversis periculosius, quam ex vultu principis intelligere rem in praecipiti esse discrimine. Proinde simulando, atque dissimulando saepe contraria ut ostendantur oportet.[33]

Still more strikingly Pontanus writes in a chapter entitled *An sit mentiendum reipublicae gratia:*

Sapientis sit, e duobus obiectis malis, minus semper eligere. Licitum ergo fuerit reipublicae, regisque qui patriae pater est, gratia, aliquando et mentiri, quanquam qui pro loco ac tempore, et cum consilio verum obticet, praesertim ubi de regis ac regni, patriaeque salute agitur, non videtur is quidem mentiri: aut si mendacio utitur, non statim mendax

---

[30] *Prince* 8, p. 18b.   [31] *Discorsi* 3.40, p. 255a.

[32] "Against faith, against charity, against humanity, against religion" (*Prince* 18, p. 35a).

[33] "One of the difficult tasks given to mortals is to preserve and maintain the character proper to the prince, since he must keep it up not merely in the hearts but also in the eyes of men. . . . The morose and gloomy prince disturbs the spirits of his subjects and renders them anxious about what they are to do. Nor is anything more perilous in doubtful and adverse circumstances than to learn from the countenance of the prince that affairs are on the very brink of ruin. Hence it is proper that by simulating and dissimulating he should often show the contrary of the truth" (*De regno* 7.10).

videtur, cum prudentis hoc, sit, et utilitatem, necessitatemque cum vero, falsoque pensitantis.[34]

This, however, falls short of Machiavelli's frankness.

Preservation of the appearance of religion and other virtues has its root in the advice of Aristotle to the tyrant. Burd quotes at some length from the continuator of the commentary of St. Thomas on *Politics* 5, where are such sentences as: "Si non habeat illud bonum excellens, debet simulare se habere illud."[35] The Aristotelian Egidio took over the same matter, writing a chapter with the title *Quot et quae sunt illa quae debet operari verus Rex, et quod eadem simulat se facere Tyrannus,*[36] in which, for example, we read:

Bona communia et iura regni debet [bonus rex] maxime custodire et observare. Quod tyranni licet se facere simulant, non tamen faciunt, immo bona aliorum rapiunt, et iura regni non observant. Tertio decet Regem, et Principem non ostendere se nimis terribilem et severum, nec decet se nimis familiarem exhibere, sed apparere debet persona gravius et reverenda, quod congrue sine virtute fieri non potest: ideo verus Rex vere virtuosus existit: tyrannus autem non est, sed esse se simulat. . . . Decet veros reges bene se habere circa divina. Populus enim (ut recitat Philosophus) omnino est subjectus Regi quem credit esse deicolam, et habere amicum Deum: existimat enim talem semper iuste agere, et nihil iniquum exercere. . . . Verus ergo Rex secundum veritatem bene se habet erga divina; tyrannus vero non talis est, sed simulat se talem esse.[37]

[34] "It is the act of a wise man, when two ills are put before him, always to choose the smaller one. Hence it is permissible, for the sake of the state and of a king who is father of his people, sometimes to tell falsehoods; though when time and circumstances require silence about the truth, especially when the safety of the king, the kingdom, and the fatherland is in question, he who prudently keeps still certainly does not seem to be a liar. Or if he uses deception he does not seem straightway to be a liar, since he acts like a prudent man who balances utility and necessity with the true and the false" (*De obedientia* 4.12, p. 107).

[35] "If he may not have that excellent good, he ought to simulate the possession of it" (*Lectio* 12, p. 392). See Burd's edition of *Il principe*, p. 305.

[36] "How many and what are the things the true king should do, and that the tyrant should give the appearance of doing the same things" (*De regimine* 3.2.9).

[37] "The good king should especially guard and attend to the common advantages and laws of the kingdom. Though tyrants simulate that they do this, yet they do not do it, but rather they take away the goods of others and do not observe the laws of the kingdom. Thirdly, it befits the king and the prince not to show himself too terrible and severe, nor is it fitting to show himself too familiar, but he should appear to sustain his part rather gravely and to be worthy of reverence, something that cannot fittingly be done without virtue. Therefore the true king should with good reason be looked on as virtuous, but the tyrant is not virtuous, but simulates he is. . . . It is proper for true kings to conduct themselves properly in divine matters. For the people (as the Philosopher says) is in every way subject to the king whom it be-

In the conduct of the Duke of Athens, Machiavelli saw an attempt to exemplify such behavior:

> Aveva il duca, per dare di sè maggior segno di religione e di umanità, eletto per sua abitazione il convento de' Fra' Minori di Santa Croce.[38]

> Per darsi riputazione di severo e di giusto, e per questa via accrescersi grazia nella plebe, quegli che avevono amministrata la guerra di Lucca perseguitava.[39]

His conduct was so successful that he obtained the rule of the city through the favor of the populace. But once having obtained power, he failed to continue his simulation: "Quella severità e umanità che gli aveva finta, in superbia e crudeltà si era convertita."[40] Losing his reputation, "da ogni parte di essere odiato meritava; onde che in termine di dieci mesi i suoi cattivi costumi gli tolsono quella signoria."[41] Evidently Machiavelli felt that the Duke's short rule

---

lieves to be a holy man and to have God as his friend, and it thinks that such an one always acts justly and does nothing wicked. . . . Therefore the true king according to the truth conducts himself well in religious matters; but the tyrant is not such a person but simulates he is" (ibid.).

Figliucci interprets Aristotle as saying that the tyrant is "simulare e mostrare astutamente di volerlo imitare in modo che il governo paia uno state Regale. . . . Studinsi almeno di dare ad intender al populo d'haverla [la virtù politica], et di far nascer nel populo una tal' opinione verso di lui. . . . Apresso dee il tiranno essere di tali costumi ripieno, e ornato che overo egli mostri esser rivolto e dato a la virtù; overo si mostri almeno alquanto huomo da bene cosi mezanamente, e non apparisca al tutto scelerato, e malvagio: ma non potendo far altrimenti paia mezo tristo e mezo nò. Deono i tiranni ancora esser cosi fatti per durare nel Regno, e per conservarsi lungamente."—"To simulate and show astutely that he wishes to imitate him in such a way that the government may appear a kingly state. . . . He should strive at least to make the people think he has political virtue and to cause to spring up in the people such an opinion about him. . . . The tyrant ought to be provided with such habits, and made attractive by them, that he may seem either to have reformed and turned to virtue, or at least that he is a man half-way good and may not appear altogether villainous and wicked. But if he cannot do otherwise he should appear half wicked and half not. Tyrants must be so constituted in order to last in a kingdom and to protect themselves a long time" (*De la politica*, pp. 188-90).

[38] "To give a stronger indication of his religion and humanity, the Duke had chosen for his habitation the convent of the Minor Friars of Santa Croce" (*Istorie Fiorentine* 2.34, p. 434a).

[39] "To give himself the reputation of being severe and just, and in this way to increase his favor with the people, he prosecuted those who had conducted the war with Lucca" (ibid. 33, p. 433b).

[40] "That severity and humanity he had feigned were changed into pride and cruelty" (ibid. 36, p. 436a).

[41] "He deserved the hatred of every party; wherefore at the end of ten months his wicked habits took away from him that lordship" (ibid. 37, end, pp. 439-40).

was in part the result of his failure to keep up the appearance of princely virtues.

The value of the appearance of piety was not unknown to those who would not have dreamed of inculcating mere simulation; Beroaldus, for instance, in his discussion of the necessity of religion to a ruler writes: "Speciosum haud dubie est principem et esse et videri religiosum, reique divinae cultorem."[42] Half a century before Machiavelli, Campanus, also urging a true piety, is at the same time aware of the outward value of religion:

Non solum qui opes fortunasque contempserint: sed etiam illas qui appetunt: studioseque accumulant: tanto habentur meliores: quanto ad religionem et rem divinam propensiores esse videantur. Gignitur quaedam inde opinio virtutis et modestiae: quibus finitima est: quam praestari maxime oportet; auctoritas rerum gerendarum. Quae cum frequenter a vitae nascatur integritate: nonnunquam ex gloria et admiratione virtutis: tum vero frequentissime a cultu observantiaque rerum divinarum. Quod si nonnulli simulatae probitatis viri falsa superstitione tantum valent ad hominum mentes illiciendas: ut flectere: concitare: lenire: exasperare soleant: quid in his est existimandum quorum est sanctitas vitae probata et aperta: spectata integritas et in medium exposita: quantum in his elucet maiestatis: quantum observantiae et auctoritatis. Denique ita maxima est vis conscientiae: ut praeceptione religionis minime seiungatur, nec ulla res est in tam vario genere virtutum unde plus consequi possis laudis: et auctoritatis: et fidei: a quibus metus et gratia gignuntur: quae duo eminentissima in Republica sunt propugnacula.[43]

[42] "There is no doubt that it is splendid for a prince to be and to seem religious and devoted to religious observance" (*De optimo statu*, folio 131 recto).

[43] "Not merely those who contemn riches and the gifts of Fortune but also those who desire them and eagerly accumulate them are held so much the better in proportion as they seem the more inclined toward religion and divine service. Thence springs a certain reputation for virtue and modesty to which is related, as it is highly desirable should be made known, authority in administering affairs, which though frequently it comes from integrity of life, and sometimes from the admiration of men for splendor of virtue, most frequently comes from a careful observation of the rites and ceremonies of religion. For if some men by excessive but false and pretended regard for probity are so successful in misleading the judgments of men that they can usually prevail on them, rouse them, calm them, and stir them up, what is to be thought of the capacity in these matters of those whose sanctity of life is established and open, their integrity tested and obvious? How striking is the majesty of these, how great is their influence and authority! Then the force of conscience is so great that it can scarcely at all be severed from the precepts of religion; nor is there anything in the varied family of the virtues whence you can gain more reputation and authority and faith. From these are derived fear and favor, which are two lofty bulwarks in a state" (*De regendo magistratu*, pp. 703-6).

The king who will seem religious must guard that unruly member, the tongue, from betraying his true character. While dissimulation is not advised by the older writers, they advise care in speech as one of the virtues conventionally necessary to all good men and especially suitable to kings. In his *Lingua* Erasmus quotes from Plato the belief that the speeches of kings should be "verbis astricta, sed sententiarum pondere efficax,"[44] otherwise they may fall into perilous slips of the tongue and betray their secrets. And Isocrates, as translated by Erasmus, advised the king: "Considera semper quid vel dicas vel facias, ut in errata quam minima incidas."[45] Though advising only virtuous conduct, Giraldus Cambrensis is well aware of the way the words of the ruler will be scrutinized:

Princeps igitur in eminenti specula constitutus tanquam omnium obtuitus in se noverit esse conversos, sic os, sic oculos, sic membra singula gestusque corporis omnes, ut nec unum in tot millibus oculum offendat, regere tenetur et moderari. Cum autem in cunctis sit modus observandus atque modestia, in nullo magis actu humano opus est observantia quam sermone. Quid enim magis familiare sapienti et praecipue principi quam pro locis et temporibus aptare sermones?[46]

With no great relaxation of his desire for truth a prince so carefully guarding his words and adapting them to the surroundings can pass into Machiavellian expression of the sentiments most likely to please his hearers.

In this matter even the prudent Cosimo failed, thus giving opportunity to his enemies to accuse him for irreligion: "Rispose come egli era meglio città guasta che perduta: e come due canne di panno rosato facevono uno uomo da bene; e che gli stati non si tenevono

[44] "Sparing in words, but impressive in the weight of their opinions" (*Opera* 4.673 C; see also 678 B). Mambrino Roseo gives to one of the chapters of his *Institutione del prencipe christiano* the title: *Che il Prencipe deve fuggir la loquacita.* —"That the prince should avoid loquacity."

[45] "Take great care in what you say or do that you may fall into as few errors as possible" (*De regno gubernando* 614 F).

[46] "Therefore the prince, since he knows that he is as it were made into a conspicuous mirror on which the eyes of all are turned, is under obligation so to restrain and control his mouth, his eyes, his individual limbs and all the movements of his body that he may not offend one of the thousands of eyes that gaze on him. But though temperance and modesty should be observed in everything, in no human act is there more need for care than in speech. For what is more appropriate to the wise man and especially to the prince than to adapt his words to places and times?" (*De principis instructione* 1.1). This work gives no sign of Aristotelianism. The references for this passage are Proverbs 10.18, 19; 13.3; 15.1, 2, for example: "He that keepeth his mouth keepeth his life: but he that openeth wide his lips shall have destruction."

co' paternostri in mano; le quali voci dettono materia a' nimici di calunniarlo, come uomo che amasse più se medesimo che la patria, e più questo mondo che quell' altro."[47] Galeazzo at Milan also added imprudently to the hatred generated by his conduct "perchè non solo non gli bastava corrompere le donne nobili, che prendeva ancora piacere di publicarle."[48] Special faults in speech are not charged against the Duke of Athens—almost a typical bad ruler— though he was "nelle udienze difficile, nel rispondere superbo."[49] Had he been wise he would have kept up in his answers the *umanità* which at the beginning he feigned.

Leon Batista Alberti presents dramatically a career of dissimulation when he has Momus plan to give up his harsh and unpopular manners:

Penso che hora sia bene tenere altri modi, e accommodarsi piu commodamente a questi presenti tempi. . . . Allettato dalla speranza, constretto dalla necessità, e da i propostimi premii, potrò pure mentire a me stesso, e accommodarmi a quelle cose, che fiano necessarie. . . . Sdimenticherommi io però quel naturale, e proprio, e quasi meco nato costume dello offendere? Non certamente; ma lo modererò con la taciturnità, e manterrò quella usanza del nuocere a gli inimici, con una certa nuova arte da ingannargli, e da offendergli. . . . Ma che si accommodino a tempi, e simulando, e dissimulando in cosi fatto affare, non manchino mai a se stessi. Ma quasi come se stessino ad una sentinella stieno vigilanti, facendo capitale del parere di ogni uno, e per quali rispetti egli si muova, quel che ei pensi, qual sia il suo disegno, quel che egli habbia di necessità, qual sia la cagione, per la quale ciascuno si muova, e quale la volontà, qual sia la faculità, e il modo del trattare i negocii: Dalla altra parte tenghino astutamente, e artificiosamente ascosi a ciascuno quali si sieno i desiderii, e i disegni loro, simulando sempre, e sempre vegliando, astuti, pronti, e parati, senza lasciarsi uscire occasione alcuna di mano, che se li offerisca da potersi vendicare. . . . Ma che piu ei ci gioverà ricordarsi di nuovo, e da capo, principalmente di questo adombrare, cioè accortissimamente ogni cosa con alcune dimostrationi di bontà, [50] e di innocentia, la qual cosa ci

[47] "He replied that a city laid waste was better than a city lost; that five yards of scarlet cloth made a man of consequence; that states were not held in subjection with paternosters. These sayings gave his enemies basis for calumniating him as a man who loved himself more than his country and this world more than the next" (*Istorie Fiorentine* 7.6, p. 566b).

[48] "Because it was not enough for him to corrupt noble ladies but in addition he took pleasure in telling about it" (*Istorie Fiorentine* 7.33, p. 587b).

[49] "Difficult in his audiences, proud in his answers" (ibid. 2.37, p. 439b).

[50] "I judge that now it is time to use other manners and to adapt myself better to the present times. . . . Nourished by hope, constrained by necessity and by

riuscirà eccellentemente, ogni volta che noi assuefaremo le parole, e i
gesti del nostro volto, e tutte le attioni del corpo in sapersi talmente
assimigliare a coloro, che son tenuti buoni, e di buona natura: ancor
che noi dentro siamo totalmente al contrario di loro. O che cosa ottima è
il sapere coprire, e velare i tuoi segreti pensieri con astuto artificio della
lisciata, e fallace simulatione.[51]

Even though this be interpreted as an attack on *astuzia* and *simulatione,* it is a clear statement of policy, probably based on what its
author had seen in practice or heard recommended in theory. Machiavelli's theory of simulation and dissimulation, according to the
necessity imposed by "the winds of fortune and the variations of
affairs,"[52] evidently has its background, though he perhaps may be
called original in making it the duty of a prince devoted to the
common good.

The simulation and dissimulation which Aristotle and his followers assigned to the tyrant are by Machiavelli urged on the
prince, as they had been exemplified by that "grandissimo simulatore,"[53] Duke Valentino. Is the prince therefore a tyrant in the
true sense of the word? The similarities between the new prince in
Italy and the tyrant in Greece are obvious: their manner of acquir-

---

the rewards put before me, I shall be able to deceive myself and to accommodate
myself to those things which may be necessary. . . . Shall I forget therefore
that natural, individual, and as though innate habit of injuring people? Certainly
not, but I shall moderate it with taciturnity and maintain my custom of injuring
my enemies with a certain new art of deceiving them and harming them. . . .
Those who accommodate themselves to the times by simulating and dissimulating
in affairs of this sort never fail themselves. But as though they stood sentinel they
are vigilant, observing the appearance of every one, for what reasons he acts, what
he thinks, what his intention is, what necessity he is under, what is the cause for
which every man acts, what he wishes, and what is his capacity for and method in
carrying on business. On the other hand they keep astutely and artfully concealed
from everyone their desires and their designs, always simulating and always watching, astute, prompt, prepared, without letting slip from their hands any occasion
that offers a possibility of vengeance. . . . But there is one thing that it will be
a good thing to remind ourselves of anew and to set out from the beginning
as the chief matter, that is in short to do everything with some show of goodness
and of innocence."

[51] "The value of this procedure will appear whenever we succeed in making our
words and the expressions of our faces and all the actions of our bodies resemble
those of men who are thought good and of good nature, even thought we are in our
hearts totally unlike them. O what a good thing it is to be able to cover up and veil
your secret thoughts with astute artifice of smooth and false simulation" (*Del principe*
2.32. 12-33. 19)! For accommodating oneself to the times, see p. 218, below.

[52] *Prince* 18, p. 35a.

[53] "Chiefest of simulators" (*Del modo tenuto del Duca Valentino,* p. 744b). Cf.
Prince 7, p. 16a; 18, p. 34b.

ing power, their lack of historical justification, their problem of maintaining themselves—such likenesses could hardly be missed. But was the transfer from advice to the tyrant to advice to a prince whom he approved a bold stroke by the unshrinking and original Machiavelli?[54] To any who believe that it was, it may be answered that Aristotle himself gave some justification for it in saying that the ways of losing and conserving a kingdom and a tyranny were similar, and that a tyranny could be preserved by approximation to a kingdom, while a kingdom might be lost by approximation to a tyranny. In the *De regimine principum* of Egidio, in connection with warning against tyranny, this suggestion is developed:

Verum quia nullus forte est omnino tyrannus, quia malum seipsum destruit, et si integrum sit, importabile fit, ut dicitur 4. Ethicorum, et forte vix aut nunquam reperitur aliquis, qui sit omnino Rex quin in aliquo tyrannizet; esset enim quasi semideus, si nihil de tyrannide participaret. Inde est ergo quod dominantes aliquid participant de cautelis regiis, et aliquid de versutiis tyrannorum.[55]

Egidio is aware of the limitations of human nature and allows his king—in practice—some of the tricks of the tyrant. He advises kings, however, to be cautious in any necessary tyrannizing: "Reges ergo et principes si volunt suum durare dominium, summe cavere debent ne a iustitia deviantes in tyrannidem convertantur: et si eos aliquo modo tyrannizare contingat, suam tyrannidem pro viribus moderare debent, quia quanto remissius tyrannizabunt, tanto durabilius principabuntur."[56] The chapter following is entitled *Quae sunt quae salvant dominium regium, et quod oporteat Regem facere ut se in suo principatu conservet.*[57] It is made up from the fifth book of the *Politics,* with free handling of the material. The chap-

[54] For Burd's opinion that it was, see p. 92, above.

[55] "Perhaps no one, in fact, is altogether a tyrant, for evil destroys itself, and if it should be unmixed it would be unbearable, as is said in the fourth book of the *Ethics,* and perhaps hardly ever or never is there found one who is in every respect a king and plays the tyrant in nothing, for he would be as it were half divine if he had in him nothing of the tyrant. Thence it is, therefore, that those who rule have a share in the precautions of the king and also a share in the subtleties of the tyrant" (*De regimine* 3.2.11).

[56] "Therefore if kings and princes wish their dominion to last, they should take the greatest care lest deviating from justice they go over to tyranny; and if it happens that they do in any way tyrannize, they should moderate their tyranny according to their strength, since the more mildly they tyrannize, the more durably they rule as princes" (*De regimine* 3.2.14).

[57] "What are the things that protect the dominion of kings, and what a king should do to secure himself in his principate" (ibid. 3.2.15).

ter explicitly recognizes the new prince, and discusses as especially
suitable for him a method assigned by Aristotle to the tyrant,
namely the making of foreign wars.[58] This plan will keep the
minds of the subjects occupied, and will also, Egidio adds, keep
subjects loyal because of their fear of the enemy.[59] The wide circulation of Egidio's work makes probable Machiavelli's acquaintance
with its ideas.[60] With his emphasis on morals, Egidio had no reason to make his king a simulator of religion, but the Florentine,
released from the usual moral bonds, when once he had the notion of the employment of tyrannical policies by the new prince,
was free to advise any method necessary to conservation of the
government.

All the methods of the tyrant are open to the new prince, even
to him who will bring "bene alla università degli uomini"[61] of
Italy. In a wicked world he may be obliged—"necessitato"—to
imitate conduct as disgraceful as that of Agatocle, whom Machiavelli denies a place among the most excellent men on the ground
of his infinite wickedness; the new prince, for example, must be prepared to "operare contra alla fede,"[62] just as Agatocle was faith-
less—"sanza fede." Ferdinand of Aragon, condemned by Machiavelli for his expulsion of the Moors,[63] can nevertheless be a proper
example for a prince who would be approved by Machiavelli;[64]
his cruelty to the Moors, to be censured because it involved the ruin
of unoffending citizens, nevertheless shows skill in government because of its power to strike the imagination of subjects. Such conduct may be justified by necessity, as was the oppression of the
Roman people by the emperors in order to hold the favor of the
soldiers.[65] Ferdinand's conduct did, however, give him the reputa-

---

[58] See the quotations on pp. 22, 24 ff., above, and 166-7, below.

[59] The continuator of the comment of Aquinas on the *Politics* (lib. 5, lectio 11)
adds fear to occupation of mind. It is true that Egidio found the notion of fear, of
an unspecified kind, in Aristotle's general advice on the conduct of public affairs
(1308a 28), but he was well aware that war was advised to the tyrant, as appears in
3.2.10, on the *cautelae* of the tyrant; here he says that the true king will take up
arms only for defense or other just cause. If in suggesting warfare without limitation
he is thinking of the king who is obliged to assume something of the tyrant, the
contradiction is explained.

[60] See p. 92, above, for another instance.

[61] "Good to the generality of the men" (*Prince* 26, p. 49b).

[62] "To act contrary to good faith" (*Prince* 18, p. 35a); for Agatocle see *Prince* 8;
in *Discorsi* 2.13, p. 157a, he is an example of a man who rose by fraud.

[63] *Prince* 21, p. 43b.   [64] See *Ferdinand* in the index.

[65] "Si volgevano a satisfare a' soldati, stimando poco lo iniuriare il populo. Il
quale partito era necessario."—"They wished to satisfy the soldiers, thinking injury

tion of religion. It would, however, seem to fall among deeds such as those of Agatocle which give "imperio, ma non gloria."[66] The good ruler has a right to these rewards of glory, yet circumstances may make conduct that can bring honor incompatible with maintenance of his position; he must then abandon honor, unless he is willing to live a private life.[67] It is also possible that the situation is one in which all is to be sacrificed to the fatherland; then not merely glory, but the soul itself is to be held of little moment, and any means, however tyrannical, will be approved by good men, if we may believe Machiavelli's Rinaldo degli Albizzi.[68] The reformer must be prepared to go very far, yet has a right to approval:

Uno prudente ordinatore d'una republica, e che abbia questo animo, di volere giovare non a sè ma al bene comune, non alla sua propria successione ma alla comune patria, debbe ingegnarsi di avere l'autorità, solo; nè mai uno ingegno savio riprenderà alcuno di alcuna azione straordinaria, che, per ordinare un regno o constituire una republica, usasse. Conviene bene, che, accusandolo il fatto, lo effetto lo scusi; e quando sia buono, come quello di Romolo, sempre lo scuserà: perchè colui che è violento per guastare, non quello che è per racconciare, si debbe riprendere.[69]

---

to the people of little moment. That course of action was necessary" (*Prince* 19, pp. 37b-38a). Opposition to this justification by necessity appears in Milton's *Paradise Lost* 4.389-94:

> Public reason just
> Honour and empire with revenge enlarg'd,
> By conquering this new World, compels me now
> To do what else though damnd I should abhorre.
> So spake the Fiend, and with necessitie,
> The Tyrant's plea, excus'd his devilish deeds.

Satan is familiar with the argument of Machiavelli. The passage does not, however, prove that Milton was an anti-Machiavellian.

[66] "Rule, but not glory" (*Prince* 8, p. 18b). Cf. *Discorsi* 3.40, p. 255b: "Io non intendo quella fraude essere gloriosa, che ti fa rompere la fede data ed i patti fatti: perchè questa ancora che la ti acquisti, qualche volta, stato e regno, . . . la non ti acquisterà mai gloria."—'I do not think that fraud glorious which makes you break faith you have given and treaties you have made; because even if this sometimes acquires for you state and kingdom, . . . it will not gain you glory."

[67] *Discorsi* 1.26, p. 94b.

[68] *Dell' arte della guerra*, lib. 1, beginning. *Istorie Fiorentine* 5.8, p. 504b. In one of his last letters Machiavelli wrote: "Amo la patria mia più dell' anima" (to Vettori, April 16, 1527, *Lett. fam.* 73, p. 246).

[69] "A prudent organizer of a republic and one so minded that he wishes to accomplish something not for himself but for the common good, not for his own descendants but for the native land of all, should give his attention to having the authority in his own hands alone. Nor will good judgment ever censure any one for any extraordinary action that he uses in the course of setting a kingdom in order

Machiavelli's advice to the true prince is precisely that which he gives to the patriotic citizen:

Dove si dilibera al tutto della salute della patria, non vi debbe cadere alcuna considerazione nè di giusto nè d'ingiusto, nè di piatoso nè di crudele, nè di laudabile nè d'ignominioso; anzi, posposto ogni altro rispetto, seguire al tutto quel partito che le salvi la vita, e mantenghile la libertà.[70]

Here, if anywhere, is the essence of Machiavelli's theory.

Good rule, or approximation to kingship, had been recommended by Aristotle as a device for the maintenance of tyranny; turning the matter around, the Florentine throws open to the true prince all the methods of the tyrant, on condition that they are to be used not for personal gratification but for the benefit of the whole body of the people of Italy.

"Tirannici modi"—the ways of the tyrant—are those of the Duke of Athens,[71] who personified for Machiavelli a foolish ruler and might have appeared to the new prince as a warning example. Complete tyranny implied to Machiavelli the violation of all his advice to the prince; only the imprudent are tyrannical; tyrants are "gl' impii, i violenti, gl' ignoranti, i dappochi, gli oziosi, i vili."[72] Because of "ignavia" and "poca prudenzia"[73] Italian princes, even of long standing, lost their states. In fact, a ruler who can hold his position in times of stress cannot be altogether a tyrant; his continuance is proof that at least one *università* in his realm is well-disposed toward him; his conduct has presumably been such that he is not hated by the people, who are more likely to sustain a ruler than are the nobles; as we have seen,[74] the good arms by which a ruler maintains himself are normally an indication of good laws.

---

or constituting a republic. It is proper that though the deed accuses him its effect should excuse him, for he should be condemned who is violent in order to tear things to pieces, not he who is so in order to mend them" (*Discorsi* 1.9, p. 73a).

[70] "When deliberation is wholly concerned with the safety of the country, no weight should be given to considerations of what is just or unjust, merciful or cruel, praiseworthy or ignominious; rather, without regard to anything else, one should wholly follow the course of action that will save the life and maintain the liberty of the country" (*Discorsi* 3.41, p. 256a).

[71] *Istorie Fiorentine* 2.36, p. 437a.

[72] "The impious, the violent, the ignorant, those of little account, the lazy, the worthless" (*Discorsi* 1.10, p. 74a); see also p. 238, below. Clichtoveus wrote: "Recta ratione non ducitur tyrannus."—"The tyrant is not guided by right reason" (*De regis officio,* cap. 5).

[73] "Laziness" and "lack of prudence" (*Prince* 24).

[74] P. 64, above.

At the worst the subjects of the prudent and capable ruler are secured against injury by their fellow-citizens and by foreign enemies; such an extreme case as that of the emperor who was obliged to allow the soldiers to oppress the people is unusual, and even then there is some limitation of oppression. It may be for this reason that in his condemnation of the wicked but "virtuous"[75] Agatocle the word *tyrant* is not used. After this man has established himself through prudent cruelty, his actions "si convertiscono in più utilità de' sudditi che si può," and he is able to have for his state "con Dio e con gli uomini . . . qualche remedio."[76] In proportion as his prudence led him to rule for the good of his people, he ceased to be a tyrant.

As Aristotle had said, the tyrant labors only for himself; in the words of Egidio: "Si vero propter bonum proprium, est perversus, et vocatur tyrannis."[77] But the Machiavellian prince, whatever his conduct, is concerned with the common good.[78] The Florentine secretary would have agreed with the statement of his friend Vettori:

Vorrei che mi fusse mostro che differenzia è dal re al tiranno. Io per me non credo certo che vi sia altra differenzia, se non che quando il re è buono, si può chiamare veramente re; se non è buono, debbe essere nominato tiranno. Così, se uno cittadino piglia il governo della città o per forza o per ingegno e sia buono, e'non si può chiamare tiranno; se sarà tristo, se gli può dar nome non solo di tiranno, ma d'altro che si possa dire peggio. E se noi vorremo bene esaminare come sieno stati i principii de' regni; troveremo tutti essere stati presi o con forza o con arte. . . . E però non si debbe chiamare tiranno alcuno privato cittadino, quando abbi preso il governo della sua città e sia buono: come non si debbe chiamare uno vero signore di una città, ancora che abbi la investitura dallo Imperatore, se detto signore è maligno e tristo.[79]

[75] The *virtù* of Agatocle is twice mentioned in *Prince* 8, p. 18. I do not understand why Alderisio (*Machiavelli,* p. 126) attacks Ercole (*Politica di Mach.,* p. 42) for imputing virtue to Agatocle.
[76] "Change themselves into the greatest usefulness for his subjects that is possible" and he has "with God and with man some means of relief" (*Prince* 8, p. 20a).
[77] "If a man rules for his own benefit, his principate is perverse and is called a tyranny" (*De regimine* 3.2.12).
[78] Ercole, *La politica,* p. 326.
[79] "I wish it was made clear to me what difference there is between king and tyrant. For my part I do not feel sure that there is any other difference except that when the king is good he can truly be called a king, and if he is not good he should be called a tyrant. Hence, if a citizen seizes the government of the city either by force or by skill and is a good ruler, he cannot be called a tyrant; if he is wicked there can be given to him the name not merely of tyrant but any other than can be called

Vettori obviously has in mind the well-known saying in which is employed the logical argument of notation, or the interpretation of a word: "Dicitur enim rex a bene regendo, et non a regnando, quia rex est dum bene regit, tyrannus dum populum sibi creditum violenta opprimit dominatione."[80]

---

worse than it. And if we come to make a good examination of the beginnings of kingdoms, we shall find that all of them were taken with force or with skill. . . . Therefore no private citizen should be called a tyrant because he has taken the government of his city if he rules well, just as he should not be called a true lord of a city, even though he has been invested with it by the emperor, if he is malignant and wicked" (*Sommario della storia d'Italia*, pp. 293 ff.). Cf. Machiavelli, *Istorie Fiorentine* 7.33, p. 587ab: "Il vivere sotto un principe non buono detestava."—"He detested life under a prince who was not good."

John of Salisbury, *Policraticus* 3.14, 512c, after explaining that the tyrant may be killed because he has taken the sword, continues: "Sed accipere intelligitur qui eum propria temeritate usurpat, non qui utendi eo accipit a Domino potestatem. Utique qui a Deo potestatem accipit, legibus servit et iustitiae et iuris famulus est. Qui vero eam usurpat, iura deprimit et voluntati suae leges summittit."—"But this is to be understood of one who usurps it in selfish rashness, not of one who receives from God the power of using it. For he who receives power from God keeps the laws and is the servant of justice and law. But he who usurps power debases the right and submits the laws to his own will."

[80] "He is called king because he uses kingly power well, and not merely because he uses kingly power, while the tyrant oppresses with violent despotism the people committed to him" (Bracton, *De legibus et consuetudinibus Angliae* 3.1.9.3, folio 107b).

Egidio also uses the argument: "Quare si nomen regis a regendo sumptum est, et decet Regem regere alios, et esse regulam aliorum, oportet Regem in regendo alios sequi rectam rationem, et per consequens sequi naturalem legem, quia in tantum recte regit, in quantum a lege naturali non deviat."—"Therefore if the name of the king is taken from his exercise of kingly power, and it is fitting for the king to govern others and to be the rule for others, the king in governing others should follow right reason and consequently follow natural law, since in so far as he uses his kingly power rightly, in so far he does not deviate from natural law" (*De regimine* 3.2.29). In the *Speculum regis Edwardi III* by Simon Islip we read: "Tu, per commissiones tuas, opprimis bonos, et malos sublevas et defendis, et sic, facis contra naturam officii regis, nam rex dicitur qui regit populum sapienter, rem publicam utiliter, et seipsum innocenter. . . . Unde Ysid[orus] libro iij° de summo bono, dicit quod rex vocatur a recte agendo, ideoque recte faciendo, regis nomen tenetur, peccando etiam ammittitur."—"By your commissions you oppress the good and aid and defend the wicked, and thus you act contrary to the nature of the king, for he is called king who rules the people wisely, the state usefully, and himself innocently. . . . Wherefore Isidore in his third book, on the highest good, says that the king is so called from acting rightly, and therefore the name of king is kept by doing rightly and lost by sinning" (cap. 16, pp. 101-2; other instances are mentioned in the notes of Moisant's edition). See also *Rex a recte regendo*, by József Balog, in *Speculum III* (1928), 580; and for the argument from the name, John Milton, *The Art of Logic* 1.24 (*Works*, Columbia Univ. Press, vol. 11).

Patricius treats the etymology as follows: "Non erit igitur importuna definitio illa, qua dicitur rex est vir bonus, cui per generis dignitatem, vel per legitimam electionem concessum sit, ut civitates, populosque regat. *Regere* enim nonnulli in-

Since Machiavelli was inclined to judge by the acts of rulers whether they were moved by concern for the common good or by personal ambition, he had little temptation to imagine tyranny when good government was evident.[81] For him the prince who governs prudently, according to Machiavellian standards, is not a true tyrant, even though necessitated to use the most reprehensible methods. Loosely, it is true, the word might be applied to anyone setting up absolute power, even to such a person as Romulus, who, with the good of the state at heart, observed ruthlessly the principle that "egli è necessario essere solo a volere ordinare una republica di nuovo, o al tutto fuor degli antichi suoi ordini riformarla,"[82] but the essence of tyranny is not in such an absolute governor, for even a "tiranno virtuoso" will not bring "alcuna utilità a quella republica, ma a lui proprio."[83]

---

terpretantur *recte agere,* quae interpretatio si durior fortasse videbitur, relinquatur a lectoribus, et nos lusisse putemur: si enim verbum minus acute exponimus, rem profecto ipsam optime declaramus. . . . Nam sicut medicus languentis utilitati non suae, et gubernator eorum quos vehit consulere debet, sic rex eorum quibus imperat. Aliter rex neutiquam habendus esset, sed Tyrannus [qui]iniuste imperans omnia ad utilitatem suam metitur. Quocirca finis regis est (ut ait Socrates apud Platonem) cives suos ad foelicitatem perducere, quod nequaquam nisi per virtutem assequi posset. Tyranni autem finis est eos quibus dominatur, in voluntatem suam compellere."—"That definition therefore will not be out of place in which is said: The king is a good man to whom on account of the dignity of his family or by legitimate election is conceded the right to rule states and peoples. For some interpret *rule (regere)* as derived from *do rightly (re[cte a]gere);* if this interpretation seems too difficult it may be left to the readers and we may be judged to have been playing; for if we expound the word with little acuteness, we set forth the thing itself as well as possible. . . . For as a physician should consult the advantage of a sick man, not his own, and a pilot that of his passengers, so a king should consult that of his subjects. Otherwise he is by no means to be thought a king, but a tyrant, who, ruling unjustly, measures all things by his own convenience. Therefore the end of a king (as the Socrates of Plato says) is to bring his subjects toward felicity, and this he cannot attain except by means of virtue. But the end of a tyrant is to force to his own desires those he lords it over" (*De regno* 2.1). See also p. 92, above.

The word *dominari* and its cognates is commonly used of the tyrant, as in the quotation from Bracton, in Cicero, *De republica* 1.33 (50), and John of Salisbury: "Est ergo tirannus, ut eum philosophi depinxerunt, qui violenta dominatione populum premit, sicut qui legibus regit princeps est."—"He is therefore a tyrant, as the philosophers paint him, who oppresses the people with violent domination, as he who rules according to the laws is a prince" (*Policraticus* 8.17, 777d). On the tyrant and the laws cf. Machiavelli, *Discorsi* 1.10, p. 75a; 3.5, p. 198b.

[81] *Discorsi* 1.9, p. 73b-74a, approves the apparent tyranny of Cleomenes.

[82] "He who hopes to reorganize a republic or to reform it with complete abandonment of its ancient laws must needs be an absolute ruler" (ibid. title).

[83] "A virtuous tyrant" will not bring "any good to that state but only to himself" (*Discorsi* 2.2, p. 140a). See the index under *tyrant*.

Chapter 19

De contemptu et odio fugiendo.
(Of escaping contempt and hatred.)

This chapter continues the theme of reputation already made so prominent. Contempt and fear are in the minds of other men and are not altogether founded on the possession of excellent qualities by a ruler. In fact, laudable qualities may bring about hatred or contempt—and therefore ruin. Since, then, Machiavelli's concern is immediately with reputation rather than with virtues themselves, none of which are invariably essential to the prince, he can content himself with the treatment already given to the more important excellent qualities and treat the rest under the head of the effect the ruler makes on his subjects. Incidentally it is difficult to avoid feeling that Machiavelli had been somewhat wearied by the long discussions of the virtues and vices given, for example, by Patricius, and felt that any practical rules for conduct must be much briefer.

Hatred and contempt are made by Egidio rather less relatively important than by Aristotle himself or by Machiavelli. In his chapter entitled *Quod summe expedit Regibus et Principibus recte gubernare populum, et cavere ne tyrannizent, quia multis de causis contingit subditos insidiare tyrannis,*[1] he gives six causes for the overthrow of tyrants, while Aristotle makes hatred and contempt the two chief motives, though presenting others as well.

Aspects of the hatred of this chapter have already been discussed in chapter seventeen; it was there remarked that fear can be unaccompanied by hatred, as when a just prince gives his subjects cause to feel that they are safe from injury so long as they keep the laws, though certain to be punished for any infractions of them. This condition is subject to the exception of the present chapter, namely, that the body of persons punished, such as the Pretorian guard, is so large and so licentious that justice will cause a mass of hatred able to overthrow the ruler. In the normal instance Machiavelli would not have denied that some of the wicked who were

---

[1] "That it is advisable above everything else that kings and princes govern their people rightly and beware that they do not tyrannize, since there are many causes that lead subjects to plot against tyrants" (*De regimine* 3.2.13).

punished would hate the ruler, but thought that hatred derived from private offences could be neglected. Dangerous hatred is "universale odio."[2] Chapter nineteen, then, deals with the ruler who excites, by laudable or illaudable conduct, the fear that brings hatred. A man who fears the violence of the king so much as to act against him may be said to hate him; more obvious hatred is that resulting from injury accomplished; there is also that which depends on mere detestation of ferocity and cruelty. Antoninus, son of Severus, roused the last kind in men generally, and both the other kinds in his murderer, one by threatening the man himself, the other by contumelious execution of his brother.

Allied to this fear and hatred is despair, against the exciting of which in the nobles the ruler is warned in this chapter. This is the result of fear which removes hope of escape, except by the most extraordinary measures. This condition of mind makes "uno uomo pericolosissimo per il principe"[3] as was Francesco di Orso to Count Girolamo of Furli after the count menaced him. Fearing to be killed by the count, Francesco decided to deliver himself by the death of the ruler, a matter the easier to accomplish because the people "aveva in odio l' avarizia e crudeltà del conte."[4] Even the timid are made brave by despair, as Egidio well understood:

Prima [causa quare subditi tyrannis insidiantur] est propter timorem, nam multi pusillanimes existentes, cum nimis timent, et non credunt se posse evadere, quasi desperantes invadunt alios, et efficiuntur probi. Unde et proverbialiter dicitur, quod nimis fugans timidum, vi compellit esse audacem. Sic etiam et alia animalia quasi communiter timent hominem, et nisi crederent se laedi ab eo, raro aut nunquam invaderent ipsum: bestiae ergo ut plurimum timore compulsae insidiantur homini et invadunt eum: hoc ergo modo multotiens subditi insidiantur tyranno, et perimunt ipsum tyrannum, timentes se offendi ab eo.[5]

[2] *Discorsi* 3.6, p. 200a.

[3] "A man exceedingly dangerous to the prince" (*Discorsi* 3.6, p. 200b).

[4] "Were full of hatred for the avarice and cruelty of the count" (*Istorie Fiorentine* 8.34, p. 619a).

[5] "The first reason why subjects plot against tyrants is fear, for there are many men apparently poor-spirited who, when they fear too much and believe that they cannot escape, as though they were desperate attack others and are made valiant. Whence it is said in the proverb that he who too fiercely pursues a timid man by force compels him to be bold. Thus also the other animals generally fear man, and unless they think they are injured by him rarely or never attack him. So as beasts when they are driven by fear often lie in wait for man and attack him, in the same way subjects often lie in wait for a tyrant and kill the tyrant himself, since they fear that they will be injured by him" (*De regimine* 3.2.13). For further discussion of the effects of fear see the index.

Egidio here goes beyond the matter furnished by Aristotle in the *Politics* 5. Under stress of necessity those already virtuous become more dangerous as enemies, as Machiavelli illustrates from warfare in the chapter of the *Discorsi* entitled *Come uno capitano prudente debbe imporre ogni necessità di combattere a' suoi soldati, e, a quegli degli inimici, torla,*[6] where we read:

Lo esercito de' Volsci, del quale era capo Vezio Messio, si trovò, ad un tratto, rinchiuso intra gli steccati suoi, occupati dai Romani, e l'altro esercito romano; e veggendo come gli bisognava o morire o farsi la via con il ferro, disse a' suoi soldati queste parole: "Ite mecum; non murus nec vallum, armati armatis obstant; virtute pares, quae ultimum ac maximum telum est, necessitate superiores estis." Sì che questa necessità è chiamata da Tito Livio "ultimum ac maximum telum."[7]

Patricius admitted this as a possible opinion, but denied its normal validity:

Non defuere etiam qui existimant desperationem aliquando ex exiguis fortes viros reddere, quod et Virgilius sentire videtur, quum ait. *Una salus victis nullam sperare salutem* [*Aeneid* 2.354]. Nota est etiam sententia illa qua dicitur. Necessitas efficacior est omni arte, quae non modo usitata praesidia, sed etiam nova, et inaudita adhibet. . . . Atqui verius si recte inspicimus, iudicandum est, desperationem saepius furorem suum in seipsam convertere, quam in hostem. Quot enim duces, imperatores, atque illustrissimos viros legimus desperatis rebus sibiipsis

---

[6] "How a prudent captain should give his own soldiers every sort of necessity for fighting and remove every kind of necessity from those of the enemy" (*Discorsi* 3.12, title).

[7] "The army of the Volsci, of which Vectius Messius was leader, found itself of a sudden shut in between its fortifications, occupied by the Romans, and the other Roman army. Seeing that it was necessary either to die or to gain life with steel, Vectius addressed his soldiers in these words: 'Come with me; there is no wall or ditch in your way, men with weapons are opposed to you who also have weapons; you are equal in courage and superior in necessity, the last and most dangerous weapon.' So this necessity is called by Titus Livius 'the last and most dangerous weapon'" (*Discorsi* 3.12, pp. 220b-221a).

Toward the end of his life Machiavelli still held this opinion: "Con questa tramontana conviene che voi ancora navighiate, e risolvendosi alla guerra, tagliare tutte le pratiche della pace, e in modo, che i Collegati venghino innanzi senza rispetto alcuno, perchè qui non bisogna più claudicare, ma farla all' impazzata: e spesso la disperazione truova de' rimedi che la elezione non ha saputi trovare."—"In this tempest it is still necessary for you to mind the helm, and if you have determined on war you must instantly abandon the deeds of peace, and in such a way that your allies may set to work without any hesitation, because now it is necessary not to waver any more but to go it like mad; and often desperation finds some remedies which choice has not been clever enough to discover" (to Vettori, April 16, 1527, *Lett. familiari* 73, p. 245).

mortem intulisse? qui si diutius vitam produxissent, seque meliori fato reservassent, ulti injurias adversam fortunam superassent.[8]

The last sentence is in accord with Machiavelli's opinion that even in desperate circumstances men should not give up the struggle: "Debbono, bene, non si abbandonare mai; perchè, non sappiendo il fine suo, e andando quella per vie traverse ed incognite, hanno sempre a sperare, e sperando non si abbandonare, in qualunque fortuna ed in qualunque travaglio si truovino."[9] Even those who follow this advice, however, are rendered formidable by conditions in which, even though they make no effort, death is so nearly certain that they can dare the utmost risks without increasing their danger.[10] Such a man is akin to the assassin spoken of in this chapter who, being without fear of death, can hardly be guarded against.[11] The prudent ruler will obviously use measures that if possible will content all his subjects, at least that will not awaken the active hate of desperation; "gli uomini si hanno o accarezzare o assicurarsi di loro; e non li ridurre mai in termine che gli abbiano a pensare che bisogni loro o morire o far morire altrui."[12] In the spirit of Machiavelli is the saying of Guicciardini:

Grande differenzia è da avere e sudditi malcontenti a avergli disperati. El malcontento se bene desidera di nuocerti, non si mette leggiermente

[8] "There are not lacking those who think despair sometimes makes strong men out of feeble ones, as Virgil seems to suppose when he says: 'One means of security to the conquered is to hope for no security.' Well-known also is that maxim that says: Necessity is more powerful than every art, and brings into use not merely customary means of security but also new and unheard-of ones. But if we get a truer view of the matter, we shall conclude that despair more often turns its fury on itself than on the enemy. Of how many generals, rulers, and famous men do we read who in desperate circumstances inflicted death upon themselves! Yet if they had prolonged their lives and reserved themselves for a better fate, by avenging their injuries they would have overcome adverse fortune" (De regno 7.6).

[9] "Indeed they should never abandon themselves, because, since they do not know the end of Fortune and she walks by confused and unknown paths, they should ever hope, and, since they hope, should not abandon themselves, no matter what fortune or hardship they find themselves in" (Discorsi 2.29, p. 187b). Cf. p. 217, below.

[10] Sidney writes of two of his heroes in desperate circumstances: "When they were with swordes in handes, not turning backs one to the other (for there they knew was no place of defence) but making that a preservation in not hoping to be preserved, and now acknowledging themselves subject to death, meaning onely to do honour to their princely birth, they flew amongst them all (for all were enimies) and had quickly either with flight or death, left none upon the scaffolde to annoy them" (Arcadia 2.8.8, p. 200).   [11] Prince 19, p. 39b.

[12] "Not ever to reduce them to such a state that they are forced to think that they must either die or cause the death of the prince" (Discorsi 3.6, p. 206a).

in pericolo, ma aspetta le occasione, le quali talvolta non vengono mai; el disperato le va cercando e sollecitando, e entra precipitosamente in speranza e pratiche di fare novità; e però da quello t'hai a guardare di rado, da questo è necessario guardarti sempre.[13]

In compressing his treatment of the virtues of the ruler into advice to avoid hatred and contempt, Machiavelli mentions the two as though on an equality. Sometimes, however, hatred appears alone, as the chief cause of conspiracy,[14] or in the assertion that not to be hated will be the best defence of a ruler,[15] provided— and the qualification is important—he has prepared himself according to the directions of his adviser; but one so prepared cannot be a subject for contempt as it is conceived by Aristotle. The ruler who neglects military preparations, for example, is despised and overthrown by the ambitious, even though hatred be not involved. It is, however, possible for a hated ruler to maintain himself so long as he is feared. To Vettori, as a sympathetic audience, Niccolò wrote:

Non è cosa più necessaria a un principe che governarsi in modo con li sudditi, e con gli amici e vicini, che non diventi o odioso, o contennendo, e se pure egli ha a lasciare l'uno di questi duoi, non stimi l'odio ma guardisi dal disprezzo. Papa Giulio non si curò mai di essere odiato, pure che fusse temuto e riverito; e con quello suo timore messe sottosopra il mondo, e condusse la Chiesa dove ella è.[16]

[13] "There is a great difference between having subjects malcontented and having them desperate. The malcontented man, even though he wishes to injure you, does not lightly put himself into peril but awaits suitable occasions, which sometimes fail to come. The desperate man goes searching for and hastening after them, and enters precipitately into hopes and acts for bringing about different conditions. Therefore from the malcontent you seldom have to guard yourself, but from the desperate man you must always guard yourself" (*Ricordi* 131). To the same effect is 306.

[14] *Discorsi* 3.6, p. 200a. On the basis of this passage Burd in his note on *Prince* 19 (p. 310) says that "Machiavelli is inclined to consider hatred as far the most important" cause of conspiracies. In the *Discorsi*, however, Machiavelli is dealing with the violently exciting causes; hence he does not mention contempt at all. Yet to one who is contemplating a movement against a prince, either from within or without his country, the contempt of others is even more important than their hatred. As I at once proceed to show, a ruler who is contemned is weak, but a hated ruler may be strong.   [15] *Prince* 10, p. 22b; 20, p. 43a.

[16] "Nothing is more necessary to a prince than to conduct himself in such a manner with his subjects, his friends, and his neighbors that he does not become either hated or contemned. If he has to disregard one of these, he should not care about hatred but should guard himself from being thought negligible. Pope Julius cared nothing about being hated because he was feared and revered, and because of this fear he turned the world upside down and brought the Church to her present state" (to Vettori, Dec. 20, 1514, *Lett. familiari* 38, p. 162).

And he repeats the axiom to the same correspondent: "Voi sapete che l'offizio principale di ogni principe è guardarsi dall' essere odiato o disprezzato: *fugere in effectu contemptum et odium;* qualunque volta e' fa questo bene, conviene che ogni cosa procede bene. E questa parte bisogna osservarla così nelli amici come ne' sudditi; e qualunque volta un principe *non fugit saltem contemptum,* egli è spacciato."[17] Severus is an instance in support of this opinion; "la sua grandissima reputazione lo difese sempre da quello odio ch' e' populi per le sue rapine avevano potuto concipere."[18] Though the prudent ruler will avoid hatred when he can, he may be necessitated to incur it; but to appear personally able is in his own hands; hence "sopra tutto, uno principe si debbe ingegnare dare di sè in ogni sua azione fama di uomo grande e d'ingegno eccellente."[19] Hatred is caused chiefly by tyrannical conduct, particularly by the Aristotelian faults—already mentioned in chapter seventeen—of attacking the honor and property of subjects. As to hatred, then, the present chapter is essentially the discussion of the tyrant normal in works *de regimine principum.* Their chief purpose, indeed, may be stated as an attempt to discourage tyrannical conduct. They urge on the ruler that he can prolong his rule only by ruling well, and thus, as appeared in the discussion of the preceding chapter, deserving the name of king. Petrarch,

[17] "You know that the principal duty of every prince is to keep himself from being hated and contemned; practically to escape contempt and hatred. When he succeeds in this, it follows that everything goes on well. He needs to observe this plan as much among his friends as among his subjects, and whenever a prince does not escape at least contempt he is done for" (to Vettori, Dec. 20, 1514, *Lett. Familiari* 39, p. 167). The Latin words suggest a quotation from some work *de regimine principum,* but I have not identified them. Tommasini, *Vita di Machiavelli* 2.115, n. 1, comments that it may be noted that here Machiavelli cites the Latin text, but explains only that the thought comes indirectly from the *Politics* of Aristotle.

The thought is stated by Francis Quarles as follows: "It is more dangerous for a Prince to be *disdained* by his subjects, then to be *hated: Hatred* admits Feare, and Feare forces *Loyalty.* But disdaine excludes both *Love* and *Feare,* and consequently dissolves *obedience.* That Prince that is hated, is in his high *Road* to Ruine; And he that is disdain'd, is at his *journey's end*" (*Observations concerning princes and states* 21).

[18] "His very great reputation ever defended him from that hatred which the people would have been able to conceive because of his acts of rapacity" (*Prince* 19, p. 39a).

[19] "Above all a prince should devote his ability to obtaining for himself from his every action the reputation of a great man and one of great capacity" (*Prince* 21, p. 44a).

for example, found in cruelty and avarice the chief causes of the odium that accounts for the overthrow of rulers:

Nil potentius ad odium concitandum, quam crudelitas atque cupiditas, quae si invicem conferantur, crudelitas acrior, avaritia communior, crudelitas durius, sed in paucos saevit, avaritia levius est in cunctos: haec duo vitia innumerabiles tyrannorum ac principum perdiderunt, odiosque et infames omnibus saeculis reddiderunt.[20]

The tyrannical king may end his rule through the wrath of God, as in the instance of Herod king of Judea who "divinam ultionem non evasit" but perished through a loathsome disease.[21] Machiavelli, however, does not feel it necessary to seek causes for the overthrow of the tyrant beyond the conspiracies such as appear along with the divine vengeance in Giraldus' chapter *De tyrannorum obitu et fine cruento*.[22] There can be no doubt that Machiavelli would have approved Giraldus' opinion that "percussori vero tyranni non quidem poena, sed palma promittitur. Juxta illud, Qui tyrannum occiderit, praemium accipiet."[23] But in *The Prince* he has no occasion to praise the tyrannicide. When speaking of murders of princes by obstinate men he could hardly have avoided some thought of those mentioned in the *Politics* who despised death because of the honor they would derive from killing a tyrant, as well as of those who

[20] "Nothing is more powerful in exciting hatred than cruelty and cupidity; if they are compared cruelty will be found more bitter, avarice more common; cruelty is more burdensome but its rage injures but a few; avarice presses more lightly on every one. These two vices have destroyed innumerable tyrants and princes and rendered them odious and infamous to all ages" (*De republica optime administranda* 1.428). Campanus also saw in "immanis crudelitas" the cause of "odium tyrannicum" (*De regendo magistratu*, p. 699). Cf. p. 104, above.

[21] "Did not escape the divine vengeance" (Giraldus Cambrensis, *De principis instructione* 1.17, p. 59).

[22] "On the death and bloody end of tyrants" (*De principis instructione* 1.17).

[23] "The slayers of tyrants have cause to expect not punishments but palms, according to that saying: 'He who kills a tyrant should receive a reward'" (ibid. 1.16, p. 56).

See *Discorsi* 1.10, p. 74b-75a; *Istorie Fiorentine* 7.33-4. In *Discorsi* 3.6, p. 201a, Machiavelli quotes from Juvenal:

Ad generum Cereris sine caede et vulnere pauci
Descendunt reges, et sicca morte tiranni.—

To the son-in-law of Ceres few kings descend without
slaughter and wounds, and few tyrants die a dry death
(*Satires* 10, 112-3).

This is twice found in Giraldus' treatment of the tyrant (chaps. 16 and 17). On tyrannicide see Ercole, *Tractatus de tyranno von Coluccio Salutati*, pp. 135 ff.; John Dickinson, *Kingship in the Policraticus of John of Salisbury*, in *Speculum* 1 (1926), 329 ff.; Tommasini, *Vita di Machiavelli* 2.160.

were fearless of death because of their anger.[24] But his virtuous prince, since he is not a tyrant because he rules for the common good, need fear hatred only in exceptional cases; his greatest danger would come when the difficulties of his position forced him to adopt some of the stern measures associated with tyranny. In normal times the ruler can rely on the belief that "gli uomini, quando sono governati bene, non cercono nè vogliono altra libertà."[25]

Against perils from open warfare a prince makes fundamentally the same preparations as against dangers from within, namely that he should have the reputation of a person "eccellente e reverito da' suoi."[26] A monarch who can gain this reputation is presumably a man of *virtù*, both in qualities of mind and in the military preparations also included under *virtù*.[27] If provided with good arms, he will have good friends, that is faithful allies, among neighboring princes, for monarchs, Machiavelli held, are kept to their agreements by arms.[28] Such friends will not lend encouragement and aid to the enemies of a prince among his own subjects, as seems implied in the words: "Sempre staranno ferme le cose di drento, quando stieno ferme quelle di fuora" or "quando le cose di fuora non muovino";[29] there can hardly be a powerful movement against a prince without support from some other potentate. On the other hand, "non mancano mai a' populi, preso che gli hanno l'armi, forestieri che li soccorrino,"[30] but from such foreigners a prince revered by his people is safe. It is always true that an excellent prince, strong in allies and internal resources, is attacked "con difficultà."[31]

Among earlier writers this topic seems to have been discussed in Machiavellian fashion only by Diomede Carafa. He deals with the danger to a ruler of exiles who try to secure foreign aid, and with alliance as affected by military preparation, asserting that good

[24] *Politics* 5.10, 1312a; 11, 1315a 25-31.
[25] "When they are governed well, men do not seek for or wish other liberty" (*Discorsi* 3.5, p. 199b).
[26] "Of ability and reverenced by his subjects" (*Prince* 19, p. 36a). For *reverence* see the index.
[27] *Prince* 13, last paragraph, p. 29a. See p. 68, above.
[28] *Parola sopra la provisione del danaio*, p. 790a. See p. 68, above.
[29] "Things within a country always stand secure when external relations are secure" or "when external things are not in commotion" (*Prince* 19, p. 36a).
[30] "When the people have taken arms, they never lack foreigners to aid them" (*Prince* 20, p. 43a).
[31] "With difficulty" (*Prince* 19, p. 36a); but apparently the word is used in the sense of *dubbio* (see Tommaseo, *Dizionario*, s. v. *difficultà*), implying hesitation as the result of doubt of the issue.

arms "donano temença ad chy volesse malcagniare [introdur cattive novità] et amiano [tirano con l'amo] alli amici."[32]

In this matter also Valentino exemplifies the principle. Discussing the duke's earlier employment of auxiliaries and final adoption of his own arms, Machiavelli concludes:

E puossi facilmente vedere che differenzia è infra l'una e l'altra di queste arme, considerato che differenzia fu dalla reputazione del duca, quando aveva e' Franzesi soli e quando aveva gli Orsini e Vitelli, a quando rimase con li soldati suoi e sopra se stesso: e sempre si troverrà accresciuta; nè mai fu stimato assai, se non quando ciascuno vidde che lui era intero possessore delle sue armi.[33]

Good arms secured general esteem.

The prince who carries out Machiavelli's advice in both internal and external affairs need have no fears; only exceptional blows of fortune against which there is no defense can endanger him. Yet in practice princes must sometimes fear; for example, they may have been unable to complete a reform of the state such as to bring security, and may rule a people that hates its sovereign because it cannot forget free institutions. In such conditions the monarch must adapt himself to the times and provide against the hatred of his people by such precautions as the building of fortresses.[34] Most of the writers *de regimine principum* do not advise a good ruler when to fear because they commonly think of the sovereign as *pater patriae,* loved by his citizens, at least by the good.[35] Egidio, it is true, did say that the king needed to prepare for war partly "impedire omnes seditiones civium.[36] And with respect to the nobles rather than the people the topic is touched

[32] "Cause fear in anyone who wishes to introduce dangerous novelties and fasten the prince to his friends" (*I doveri del principe,* p. 271, quoted from Persico, *Gli scrittori politici napoletani,* p. 80). Persico calls attention to the parallel with Machiavelli, who uses, he remarks, almost the same words.

[33] "It can easily be seen what a difference there is between these two kinds of arms, when one sees what a difference there was in the reputation of the Duke when he had the French alone or when he had the Orsini and Vitelli and on the other hand when he was left with his own soldiers and in personal command. It will be found that his reputation always increased, and that he was never adequately esteemed except when every one saw that he was complete possessor of his own arms" (*Prince* 13, p. 28a).

[34] *Prince* 20, p. 43a; see p. 159, below.

[35] Machiavelli thought it easier to get the love of the good than of the wicked (*Prince* 3, p. 7a; *Discorsi* 3.5, p. 199a). For the fatherly prince see Erasmus, *Institutio* 1.574 E; 2.586 E.

[36] "To impede all the insurrections of the citizens" (*De regimine* 3.3.1). Cf. p. 160, n. 5, below.

on by Commynes. His master was accused of being fearful, but the minister only partly admitted this, showing that various ambitious men who had presumed on it had been ruined, for Louis XI "congnoissoit bien s'il estoit temps de craindre ou non," and conducted himself accordingly.[37]

In discussing the fears of the ruler and giving examples of emperors attacked by subjects who feared them, Machiavelli apparently has in mind the principle stated in chapter seven: "Gli uomini offendono o per paura o per odio."[38] The attack on the ruler because of fear had been observed by Aristotle, who said: "Fear is another motive which . . . has caused conspiracies as well in monarchies as in more popular forms of government.[39] There is also a passage in the De Clementia of Seneca, a work widely circulated before Machiavelli's time:

Tantum enim necesse est timeat, quantum timeri voluit, et manus omnium observet et eo quoque tempore, quo non captatur, peti se iudicet nullumque momentum inmune a metu habeat: hanc aliquis agere vitam sustinet, cum liceat innoxium aliis, ob hoc securum salutare potentiae ius laetis omnibus tractare? errat enim, si quis existimat tutum esse ibi regem, ubi nihil a rege tutum, sed securitas securitate mutua paciscenda est.[40]

[37] "Knew well whether it was time to fear or not" (Mémoires 3.12). Cf. ibid. 1.11; 3.3.

[38] "Men do injury either through fear or through hate" (Prince 7, p. 17b). See fear in the index.

[39] Politics 1311b 37. For part of Egidio's comment on this see p. 198, above.

There is also an earlier passage (Politics 5, 1302b) in which Aristotle speaks on the subject; the comment on it of St. Thomas may be compared with the ideas of Machiavelli: "Dicit quod propter timorem faciunt seditiones. Quando enim aliqui fecerunt injurias timentes quod puniantur et vindicta fiat de eis, movent seditionem, ut per seditionem motam possint evadere, ut non puniantur. Similiter si aliqui sint passuri injusta, vel timeant se passuros propter aliquam causam, antequam patiantur volentes praevenire, movent seditionem et turbant rempublicam, antequam sustineant injurias; sicut contigit fieri in Rhodo insula. Divites enim convenerunt contra populum, timentes sententias, quae debebant dari contra eos, et turbaverunt rempublicam."—"He says that they engage in civil discords because of fear. For when some men have done injuries they fear that they may be punished and vengeance taken for what they have done, and therefore they stir up rebellion that through the rebellion they may be able to escape punishment. Likewise if some men are about to suffer some injustice or fear that they are going to suffer for some reason, they wish to ward off damage in advance, and therefore stir up rebellion and disturb the state before they are injured, as it came about in the island of Rhodes. For the rich men united against the people, because they feared the sentences which were going to be given against them, and upset the state" (Comment on the Politics, liber 5, lectio 2). Cf. Discorsi 1.45, p. 116a.

[40] "For it is necessary that he should fear in the same measure as he has wished to be feared, and that he should watch the hands of all, and that in times when

Hoccleve, for example, alludes to it as follows:

> And Senek also seith as touchyng this,
> The sogett hateth whom he hath in drede;
> And hate is hard, if it his venym schede
>
> (*Regement* 4807-9).

Seneca had dealt with the subject in his tragedies also, as was known to Clichtoveus:

Et hoc ipso rex a tyranno longe dissidet, quod hic timeri velit: cum minime ametur, sed implacabili habeatur odio, neque ipse itidem timoris est vacuus: sed omnia etiam tuta et secura habet suspecta, ut praeclare ait Seneca in Oedipo.

> Qui sceptra duro saevus imperio regit:
> Timet timentes, metus in authorem redit.

Idem alio in loco. Necesse est ut multos timeat, quem multi timent.[41]

---

no one lies in wait for him he should think that he is searched for and should have no moment immune from fear. Can anyone endure to lead this life, when it is possible for him without harm to others, and therefore secure, to exercise the salutary rights of power for the happiness of all. For he is in error who thinks that a king is happy in a country where nothing is safe from the king, for security must be bartered for mutual security" (*De clementia* 1.19).

[41] "In this the king is very different from the tyrant, for the latter desires to be feared, because he is not at all loved but is held in implacable hatred; nor is he himself without fear on his side but is suspicious of all safe and secure things, as Seneca admirably puts it in the *Oedipus*:

> The savage king who rules with heavy sway
> fears those who fear him, and dread returns on its author [705-6].

The same author says in another place: 'It is necessary that he should fear many whom many fear' [*De Ira* 2.11]" (*De regis officio* 11).

Other similar passages are quoted from Seneca on the same page. Cf. Claudian, *De IV cons. Honor.* 290-1:

> Qui terret, plus ipse timet. Sors ista tyrannis
> Convenit.—
> Who frightens others is more in fear himself. That lot befits tyrants.

This is quoted by John of Salisbury, *Policraticus* 8.813b. Cf. also the pseudo-Sallustian speech *Ad Caesarem senem de re publica ordinanda* 3: "Equidem ego cuncta imperia crudelia magis acerba quam diuturna arbitror, neque quemquam multis metuendum esse, quin ad eum ex multis formido reccidat; eam vitam bellum aeternum et anceps gerere, quoniam neque adversus neque ab tergo aut lateribus tutus sis, semper in periculo aut metu agites."—"I judge the cruelties of rulers more bitter than lasting, for no one is feared by the many without terror returning upon him from the many; such a life produces eternal and doubtful war, for you may be safe neither in front, nor behind, nor on your sides; you move always in peril or fear." Cf. also Cicero, *De officiis* 2.7, where he quotes from Ennius: "Quem metuunt, oderunt: quem quisque odit, periisse expetit."—"Whom they fear, they hate: him whom anyone hates he wishes to be undone."

To Louis XI this appeared worth bringing to the attention of his son, who received the advice:

Au monde n'a plus seure chose à deffendre les choses, que estre aymé: et n'est chose plus espoventable que de estre craint, car chascun hayt ce qu'il craint.

Qui vieult estre craint, il est de necessité qu'il craigne celui ou ceulx de qui il vieult estre craint, autrement il est en peril.[42]

The fears of the tyrant, with the implication that they are of his own making, are developed by Pontanus, who quotes from Juvenal the passage later used by Machiavelli,[43] and asserts that cruelty cannot protect a ruler.[44] In his *De infelicitate principum,* Poggio takes an extreme view, representing princes as normally in a state of fear that they will be murdered or overthrown: "Cum inferioribus nulla eis esse potest amicitia. Nam timeri a suis quam diligi principes malunt. Sed quem metuunt, et oderunt, veteri sententia."[45] If Poggio's picture of the prince is realistic, Machiavelli was quite right in thinking the ruler must take every precaution to deliver himself from the results of the hatred and fear of his subjects. While the humanist was probably influenced by his classical reading, he need not be considered as wholly without appreciation of the *verità effettuale* in the Italian courts of his day. Machiavelli differs from him not so much in stating the difficulties of the ruler as in accepting, with his own modifications, the normal belief that the wise prince need not fear, while Poggio gives no hope. In Machiavelli's day Nifo wrote in his *De principe:* "timorem odium sequitur."[46] As though to illustrate the principle of *timet timentes,* Machiavelli wrote of the mutual fears of the Duke of Athens and his subjects: "A che si aggiugneva il timore, veggendo le spesse morti e le continue taglie con le quali impoveriva e

[42] "There is not in the world a more certain way to defend one's state than to be loved; and there is nothing more horrible than to be feared, for every man hates those whom he fears.

"If a man wishes to be feared, it is necessary that he fear that one or those by whom he wishes to be feared; otherwise he is in peril" (*Le rosier des guerres,* chap. 4).

[43] See p. 146, note 23, above.   [44] See pp. 98 ff., above.

[45] "Princes can have no friendship with inferiors for they prefer to be feared rather than loved by their subjects. But according to the old saying, they hate whom they fear" (*De infelicitate principum,* p. 407).

[46] "Hate follows fear" (*De principe,* chap. 9). This work, known in full as *Libellus de his quae ab optimis principibus agenda sunt,* shows no trace of the influence of Machiavelli, though the same writer's *De regnandi peritia* is commonly called a plagiary of *The Prince.* See Tommaso Persico, *Gli scrittori politici napoletani,* pp. 147-75.

consumava la città. I quali sdegni e paure erano dal duca cognosciute e temute."[47] Not knowing, in his fears, how to take precautions, the duke was overthrown by the people who feared and hated him.

As to conspiracies, and hatred and contempt, it is proper to say with Burd that the treatment in chapter nineteen "in its main features follows throughout the eighth [i. e., the fifth] book of the *Politics.*"[48] Machiavelli makes one direct reference to Aristotle's account of the causes "della rovina de' tiranni."[49] Presumably no one would doubt that before he wrote the *Prince* the author had read a Latin translation of the *Politics,* if it were not for passages in his correspondence with Vettori. The latter suggested that he should read "bene la *Politica*"[50] on the subject of divided states, and Machiavelli answered: "Nè so quello si dica Aristotile delle repubbliche divulse."[51] Villari disposes of the opinion that if Machiavelli had been acquainted with the *Politics* he would have known that the subject of a scattered state is not discussed there, saying that he might have forgotten. The admission of ignorance may mean some other sort of incomplete knowledge, such as would have come from a work explaining part of the *Politics,* of the kind that, it may be, is quoted in the letters dealing with hatred and contempt written in 1514.[52] Or is Machiavelli merely answering politely a mistaken suggestion of his friend? Or is the denial of knowledge a rhetorical part of his attack on authority and assertion of the value of experience? Of his knowledge of Aristotle in some way or other Tommasini is so certain that he asserts that this chapter of *The Prince* in its method perfectly corresponds with the pertinent parts of *Politics* 5, though he also observes that none of the examples given by Aristotle are employed.[53] It is hardly likely that Machiavelli's first knowledge of Aristotle's account of

[47] To this was joined fear, because of the frequent executions and continual taxes with which he impoverished and devoured the city. This hatred and these fears were known and feared by the duke" (*Istorie Fiorentine* 2.36, p. 436b). Cf. ibid. 8.34, p. 618b; see p. 141, above. Toffanin (*Machiavelli e il Tacitismo*, p. 62) thinks Machiavelli has in mind the wiser conduct of Nero in moving against senators he had offended; he refers to *Annals* 15; I have not identified the passage.

[48] Burd, edition of *Il principe*, pp. 310-1.

[49] "Of the ruin of tyrants" (*Discorsi* 3.26, p. 237b).

[50] "The *Politics* well" (letter of Aug. 20, 1513, in Machiavelli, *Lettere familiari*, p. 111, n. 6).

[51] "I do not know what Aristotle says of scattered states" (to Vettori, Aug. 26, 1513, *Lett. familiari* 26, p. 107).

[52] P. 145, above.   [53] *Vita di Machiavelli* 2.192, n. 2.

conspiracies, and therefore the idea of this chapter of *The Prince*, is subsequent to Vettori's letter. Secondhand contact with Aristotelian thought could hardly be escaped, and lack of access to the Latin *Politics* in sixteenth-century Florence is improbable.[54]

In the treatment of contempt Aristotle is not followed in details. Sardanapàlus, a stock example of the disprized ruler, is not mentioned, and drunkenness is not discussed.[55] In his brief treatment of what brings contempt Erasmus includes it.[56] Platina writes on the subject:

Facile enim contemnuntur, qui nihil virtutis, nihil animi, nihil nervorum habent, quique nec sibi nec alteri prosunt, ut dicitur, contra vero in admiratione omnium sunt, qui anteire caeteros virtute putantur, atque iis vitiis carere quibus alii non facile possunt obsistere. Hos admirantur populi, hos amant, hos colunt ut Deos, fieri enim non potest, ut eum contemnam, quem video eniti, curare, ut omnes quam beatissime vivant.[57]

Machiavelli is somewhat less elementary and more intellectual in his conception of contempt than are the Aristotelians; the qualities that bring contempt are "essere tenuto vario, leggieri, effeminato, pusillanime, irresoluto," and it may be avoided by "grandezza, animosità, gravità, fortezza."[58] The immediate application of these qualities as the antidotes of contempt is not Aristotelian, though suggested by other remarks of Aristotle on the successful ruler. Even after *The Prince* the narrow tradition—based on the *Politics*—persisted. In 1565 Bizzari wrote:

Contemptus potissimum provenit, si voluptati, luxui, ac intemperantiae dedatur, ex quo etiam fit, ut nascatur odium si quid crudele interseratur,

---

[54] Ibid. 2.24-5.

[55] For Sardanapalus see, for example, Aristotle, *Politics* 5, 1312a; Egidio, *De regimine* 1.2.16; 3.2.13 (he develops Aristotle's account from Justin); Dante, *Paradiso* 15.107; Gower, *Confessio Amantis* 7.4314; Patricius, *De regno* 4.3; Bizzarus, *De optimo principe*, p. 10.   [56] *Institutio* 3.591 C.

[57] "For they are easily contemned who have nothing of virtue, nothing of spirit, nothing of vigor, and who are of no avail either to themselves or to others, as it is put; but on the contrary those who are thought to exceed others in virtue and to lack those vices which others cannot easily resist are admired by every one. The people admire them, love them, revere them as gods, for it cannot be that I should despise a man whom I see exerting himself and taking precautions that all may live as happily as possible" (*Principis diatuposis* 1.12).

[58] "To be held variable, light, effeminate, poor-spirited, irresolute," and it may be avoided by "greatness, courage, gravity, fortitude" (*Prince* 19, pp. 35b-36a).

In his description of the foolish princes of Italy (*Arte della guerra* 7, pp. 366b-367a), Machiavelli puts more emphasis on softness.

si frequentioribus conviviis et lusibus oblectetur, si stultis ac histrionibus faveat, si stupidi sint et amentes, si etiam sint molles ac effeminati, ut olim Sardanapalus, qui ob id Regnum amisit. Auctoritas vero integritate, prudentia, continentia, sobrietate, et diligentia comparatur. His itaque virtutibus praeditum esse decet quicunque a suis aestimari, et auctoritate cupit praecellere.[59]

Another Aristotelian detail is that the prince should gain popular favor or "benevolence" and avoid hatred by giving favors in person and leaving punishments to his officers.[60] In commenting on the *Politics* (1315a) Aquinas had paraphrased Aristotle as follows: "Ad benivolentiam[61] majorem honores debent distribui per ipsum, sed supplicia debent infligi per alios principes et judicia."[62] In Erasmus' translation of Xenophon's *Hiero,* a work known to Machiavelli as *De tyrannide,*[63] it is said:

Attamen functiones mihi videntur, aliae prorsus in odium adducere, aliae rursus cum gratia benevolentiaque peragi. Itaque docere quae sunt optima, et eos qui ea pulcherrime praestant, laudibus et honoribus adficere, haec quidem functio cum benevolentia conjuncta est. Caeterum qui secus quam oportet agit quidpiam, hunc convitiis afficere, cogere, mulctam dicere punireque, nam et haec facere necessitas est, cum odio malevolentiaque conjuncta sunt. Censeo itaque viro Principi sic agen-

---

[59] "Contempt most easily arises if he is given to pleasure, luxury, and intemperance; contempt may give birth to hatred if some cruelty is intermixed, if he is entertained by too frequent banquets and shows, if he favors base men and actors, if he is stupid and foolish, if he is soft and effeminate, as once Sardanapalus was, who because of it lost his kingdom. But authority is kept by integrity, prudence, continence, sobriety, and diligence. He who seeks to be esteemed by his subjects and to possess great authority must be furnished with these virtues" (*De optimo principe,* p. 10, recto).

[60] This advice was later adopted by Frachetta, *Prencipe* 1.1, p. 7; Mariana writes: "Si aliquid negandum est, si severitate vindicanda peccata, per alios faciat."—"If anything is to be denied, if a fault is to be punished severely, let others do it" (*De rege et regis institutione* 3.13).

[61] Cf. "benivolenzia popolare" in this chapter of *The Prince,* p. 36b, and see p. 161, below. In his *Institutio* (3, 589 E) Erasmus writes: "Benevolentiam stultissime quidam incantamentis et anulis magicis sibi conciliare nituntur, cum nullum sit incantamentum efficacius ipsa virtute, qua nihil esse potest amabilius, et ut ipsa vere bonum est et immortalis, ita veram et immortalem comparat homini benevolentiam."—"They are very foolish to attempt to gain popular good will by enchantments and magic rings, since no enchantment can be more efficacious than virtue itself, than which nothing can be more amiable; and as virtue is truly good and immortal, so it furnishes a man good and immortal good will."

[62] "That the prince may have greater popular affection, honors should be distributed by the prince himself, but punishments should be inflicted by other princes and by bodies of judges" (*Commentary on the Politics,* liber 5, lectio 12).

[63] *Discorsi* 2.2, p. 140a.

dum, ut si quid egeat coactione, hoc aliis exsequendum deleget: caeterum quum praemia reddenda sunt his qui rem bene gesserunt, id per se ipsum faciat. . . . Ita fit protinus, ut in his quod gratiosum est, per Principem sit factum: quod vero contra, per alios.[64]

Clichtoveus also deals with the subject:

Aristoteles tamen libro quinto de natura animalium author est, quod ii [reges apum] aculeum quidem habent: sed eo non utuntur, quocirca eos carere aculeo nonnulli existimant. Sed quid aliud eo ipso natura insinuat: nisi reges rerumque publicarum rectores, etsi potentes sunt, eos tamen saevitia uti non oportere; sed clementes potius esse, nec arma nisi per ministros (ubi ius postulat) exercere?[65]

[64] "It seems to me that some of the acts of the prince lead straight on to hatred, and others again can be accomplished in such a way as to win popular favor as their result. Thus to teach the things that are most worthy of praise and to bestow praises and honors on those who are most excellent in them is an act of the prince that can win popular favor. On the other hand, to heap reproaches on him who does other than he should, to use force on him, and to fine him and punish him—for it is necessary to do these things—bring about hatred and malevolence. Hence I judge that a prince should so carry on his affairs that if any matter requires force he may delegate to others its execution; on the other hand when rewards are to be bestowed on those who have carried out their duty well, he should bestow them in person. . . . So it should henceforth be arranged that in such matters what is pleasing should be done by the prince, but what is of an opposite sort should be done by others" (*Hieron* 651 A-B). See also *Institutio* 3.591 E.

[65] In the fifth book *On the Nature of Animals* Aristotle says that the kings of the bees have a sting, but because they do not use it some think that they have no sting. But what does Nature indicate by this very thing if not that kings and rulers of countries, though they are powerful, should not act with savagery, but rather should be clement and use arms when law demands it, only through their ministers? (*De regis officio* 10, p. 36 verso).

Cf. Beroaldus, *De optimo statu*, folio 128 recto: "Igitur principes sine aculeo sint: vel si aculeum habent, eum recondant: et maximum deorum Iovem imitentur: qui missurus fulmen perniciosum advocat in consilium deos: idque ex consilii sententia iaculatur. Quod vero placabile est et prodest, id solus emittit. Hoc philosophi poetaeque rationabiliter finxerunt: quia scilicet Iovem: id est regem prodesse etiam solum oportet: nocere non nisi cum pluribus visum est."—"Therefore princes should be without a sting, or if they have a sting should hide it, and above all the gods they should imitate Jove who when he was going to hurl a destructive thunderbolt called the gods in council, and the bolt was hurled according to the opinion of the council. But what is appeasing and beneficial he sends forth by his own act alone. The philosophers and poets apparently were reasonable in feigning this, since it is right for Jove, that is the king, to act alone in conferring benefits, but not to injure except in company with others." See also Gilbert of Tournai, *Erudito regum* 3.1.

Henry IV said of his minister Sully, who had offended Casaubon: "Never mind Rosny; it is his share of the business to say the disagreeable things; the saying of the pleasant things I keep for myself" (Mark Pattison, *Isaac Casaubon*, p. 236).

It is said of Abraham Lincoln and his secretary of war, Edwin M. Stanton: "Most of the hatred of the time was now transferred to Stanton and Lincoln was left free to monopolize benignancy" (Seitz, *Lincoln the Politician*, p. 283).

Skill in the use of this policy was illustrated by the career of Cosimo de' Medici. For example, "sendo pervenuto al gonfalone della giustizia Luca Pitti, uomo animoso e audace, gli parve tempo di lasciare governare la cosa a quello, acciò, se di quella impresa s' incorreva in alcun biasimo, fusse a Luca, non a lui, imputato."[66]

In the seventh chapter of *The Prince*, the author in his comment on the fate of Remirro de Orco anticipated the counsel of the present chapter that the minister be used as a shield to protect the prince himself from hatred. Duke Valentino, to pacify the Romagna, wished to give it good government.

Però vi prepose messer Remirro de Orco, uomo crudele ed espedito, al quale dette pienissima potestà. Costui in poco tempo la ridusse pacifica e unita, con grandissima reputazione. Di poi iudicò el duca non essere necessario sì eccessiva autorità, perchè dubitava non divenissi odiosa. . . . E perchè conosceva le rigorosità passate averli generato qualche odio, per purgare gli animi di quelli populi e guadagnarseli in tutto, volle mostrare che, se crudeltà alcuna era seguita, non era nata da lui, ma dalla acerba natura del ministro. E presa sopr'a questo occasione, lo fece a Cesena, una mattina, mettere in dua pezzi in sulla piazza, con uno pezzo de legno e uno coltello sanguinoso a canto. La ferocità del quale spettaculo fece quelli populi in uno tempo rimanere satisfatti e stupidi.[67]

The success of the measure made Borgia's condition unlike that of Maximin as presented in the present chapter (19, p. 40a), for the cruelty of the emperor's prefects was considered to reveal his own disposition. In the seventeenth chapter the reputation of cruelty is attributed directly to Cesare, without mention of the minister.[68]

There has been debate over the Duke's treatment of this official; did he make use of him and then sacrifice him to the anger

---

[66] Luca Pitti, a spirited and audacious man, having become gonfalonier of justice, it appeared to Cosimo the time to leave the conduct of affairs to Lucca, so that if anyone was blamed for that undertaking it would be the gonfalonier and not himself" (*Istorie Fiorentine* 7.3, p. 563b). Cf. ibid. 5.31, p. 524b; 6.6, p. 534b.

[67] "Hence he established there Master Remirro de Orco, a cruel and prompt man, to whom he gave complete power. In a little while Remirro pacified and united the country, in a most striking fashion. Then the Duke decided such excessive authority was not necessary, because he thought it might cause hatred. . . . And because he knew the earlier rigor had roused some hatred against him, for the sake of freeing the spirits of the people from it and gaining them wholly to himself, he wished to show that if there had been any cruelty, it did not come from him but from the nature of his minister. And having taken an occasion for it, one morning he had him placed on the public square at Cesena in two pieces, with a piece of wood and a bloody knife beside him. The ferocity of this spectacle put the people into a state of combined satisfaction and amazement" (*Prince* 7, p. 16ab).

[68] First paragraph.

of the people,[69] or was the punishment just, not the result of Remirro's good work but of some offence he committed? Villari accepts the execution as just punishment.[70] Burd seems uncertain of the sincerity of Cesare's charges against the *presidente* (chiefly that he had tampered with the supply of grain), and implies that the ruler at least wished to appear just.[71]

Machiavelli does not invariably attribute success in the Romagna to Remirro's cruelty alone, for, as he wrote to Vettori,[72] one reason for Borgia's winning of the people was that he changed the manner of government, putting the province under one governor (who, it is true, was Remirro) directly representing himself, instead of under a number of apparently independent ones.[73] Wishing the good will of his subjects, Valentino would have desired to punish a deputy who injured them, and as a result the master's reputation, by unwise cruelty. Machiavelli believed the inhabitants were against the minister, writing: "Dubitasi che [il Duca Valentino] non lo sagrifichi a questi popoli, che ne hanno desiderio grandissimo."[74] Though showing no knowledge of specific charges against Remirro, Machiavelli does not say that he was wantonly executed, but rather assumes that the Duke considered the deserts of his servant: "Non si sa bene la cagione della sua morte, se non che gli è piacuto così al principe, il quale mostra di saper fare e disfare gli uomini a sua posta, secondo i meriti loro."[75] Does this refer to genuine merit? If so, the execution is the act of a prince who will not allow his subjects to be distressed by his subordinates.[76]

According to Machiavelli's theory a wanton execution of his minister would not have added to the Duke's reputation, for fame is the result of acting justly and appearing hard to deceive.[77] Valentino did a striking deed, something that would make plenty of admiring talk, but such an act, according to the theory presented in *The Prince*,[78] must be concerned with suitable reward and punish-

---

[69] Sir Francis Bacon deals with the subject in *De sapientia veterum* 3.

[70] *Machiavelli* 2.138.   [71] Note on *Prince* 7, p. 223.

[72] January 31, 1514, *Lett. familiari* 41, p. 176.

[73] *Prince* 7, p. 16a; *Discorsi* 3.29, p. 240a; on union see p. 162, below.

[74] "It is suspected that Duke Valentino will sacrifice him to the people, who very much desire it" (*Legazione al Duca Valentino*, Dec. 23, 1502, *Opere*, Italia, 1813, VI, 329). The date of this and the following letter is much earlier than that of the *Prince*.

[75] "The cause of his death is not well known, except that it seemed good to the Prince, who shows that he knows how to make and unmake men of his own will" (ibid., Dec. 26, 1502, p. 331).

[76] See p. 29, above.   [77] *Prince* 19, p. 36a.

[78] *Prince* 21, p. 44a.

ment. The people of the Romagna, at least, since they were satisfied as well as struck with astonishment by Cesare's act, must have held that their governor received his due reward. Ingratitude to faithful ministers was not approved by the Florentine secretary; a prudent ruler makes his good servants prosperous and honors them.[79] Either, then, Remirro de Orco was justly punished or Borgia violated one of Machiavelli's precepts of wise government. If the latter, it seems it might have been pointed out along with the other errors of the Duke.[80] But perhaps other aspects of the matter are subordinated in the critic's mind to a combination of two, namely the spectacular act of justice or apparent justice, and the use of the official to do necessary work that would not gain popularity. If Borgia was using the latter policy, he carried it very far: not merely did he not appear in person but by punishing the deputy he secured himself from the suspicion, such as attached to Maximin, of having commanded measures disliked by the people.

To the causes of contempt discussed in this nineteenth chapter, Machiavelli seems to have added humble origin as a result of his own reflection. Such a subject is hardly possible except to a writer *de regimine principum* who contemplates a new prince. He is also apparently original among advisers of princes in saying that virtuous attempts to enforce justice, such as those of Pertinax, may give reason for hatred leading to overthrow;[81] this comes from his concern with the hard realities of the world rather than with abstract principles of morality.

---

[79] *Prince* 22, p. 45b; *Capitolo dell' ingratitudine* 157 ff.; see pp. 182 ff., below.

[80] *Prince* 7, p. 17b.

[81] On this matter Pigna writes as follows: "Perchè per esser Heroico, [il Generale] amerà solo il ben publico, e cosi terrà l'arme in sua mano, non solo in su la guerra, ma ancora in tempo di pace, accioche esse non restino in potestà de soldati per modo, che i suoi sudditi desiderosi della quiete, non la possano mai godere, e per loro profitto, amerà anche se stesso, e però non lascierà, che i soldati siano patroni del principato, e che per questa baldanza, fatti licentiosi habbiano in odio le sue buone opere, e che finalmente l'uccidano, come già fecero Pertinace."—"Because he is heroic, the general will love the public good only and will so control his arms, not only in war but also in time of peace, that they will not be in the power of the soldiers to such an extent that his subjects who desire quiet will never be able to enjoy it. And for the profit of his subjects he will love himself also, and therefore will not allow the soldiers to be the masters of the principate and consequently, in the license engendered by their pride, to hate his good deeds and finally kill him as they did Pertinax" (*Il principe* 2, p. 26 verso). This is apparently independent of Machiavelli, though perhaps based on the same sources, as they are indicated in the notes on *The Prince* 19 in Burd's edition, p. 318.

Chapter 20

An arces et multa alia quae cotidie a principibus
fiunt utilia an inutilia sint.
(Whether fortresses and many other devices daily employed
by princes are useful or useless.)

As is observed by Burd,[1] this chapter is in part taken from
Aristotle's discussion of the methods that may be employed by
tyrants, though here too the discussion "is not mainly determined
by classical reminiscence." The guiding principle is that of adaptation to circumstances by a prince prudent and strong enough to
carry through his policy. This especially appears in the discussion
of the value of fortresses, which were admitted to give immediate
power over a city; for example, Machiavelli wrote on the fortification of the hill of San Miniato, overlooking Florence:

La più nociva impresa che faccia una repubblica è farsi in corpo una
cosa forte, o che subito si possa far forte. Se voi vi arrecate innanzi il
modello che si lasciò costì, voi vedrete che, abbracciato San Miniato e
fatto lassù quel baluardo, che una fortezza è fatta, . . . di qualità
che se mai per alcun disordine un potente venisse a Firenze, come
il re di Francia nel 1494, voi diventate servi senza rimedio alcuno.[2]

Niccolò is here writing against those who assume that fortresses
are necessarily and permanently of value to a prince—the position
of Aristotelians such as Egidio Colonna.[3] It is possible that the
present chapter in *The Prince* gave rise to the debate on the subject.
At any rate, Scipio Ammirato wrote a chapter, obviously directed
against the Florentine secretary, which he entitled *Del fortificarsi,
e che le fortezze sono utili, e non dannose.*[4] Pigna, on the other

[1] Edition of *Il principe*, pp. 326-7.

[2] "The most injurious undertaking possible to a republic is to have made within
its body a strong place or one that can quickly be made strong. If you take a look
at the model that was left there, you will see that, if San Miniato is included in the
walls and that fortification is made up there, a fortress is constructed, of such a sort
that if ever in any disorder a powerful man should come to Florence, as did the
king of France in 1494, you would become slaves without any way of escape" (to
Guicciardini, June 2, 1526, *Lettere familiari* 67, p. 235).

[3] Aristotle, *Politics* 7, 1330b; Egidio, *De regimine* 3.3.20, 21.

[4] "On fortifying oneself, and that fortresses are useful and not injurious"
(*Discorsi sopra Cornelio Tacito* 19.4). He does not mention the name of Machiavelli,
though passages from *The Prince* are indicated by quotation marks.

hand, repeated the old ideas without apparent knowledge of any objection to them.[5] Machiavelli's opposition to castles is a sign of his reaction against any policy that can lend itself to the purposes of a tyrant.

In earlier chapters Machiavelli has declared that it is not necessary for a ruler to gain the love of his subjects, though it is highly important not to be hated; a prudent ruler, not hated by his people, need have little fear of invasion.[6] If, however, his people hate or fear him, he must needs fear them and take against them such precautions as the building of strong places.[7] Yet, as is asserted with repetition, the prudent monarch will always remember that "la migliore fortezza che sia, è non essere odiato dal populo."[8] This is Niccolò's modification to suit his belief of a conventional statement, made by Diomede Carafa as follows: "Nulla tamen castella, nullosque muros magis inexpugnabiles fore tibi persuadeo, quam populorum animos, ut antea dixi, tibi conciliatos habere; et subditorum omnium benevolentiam."[9] About the same statement is found in Isocrates and in the *De clementia* of Seneca, a work early familiar to advisers of princes.[10] It finds expression also in another classical work highly esteemed by renaissance writers *de regimine principum:*

Ille tamen, quibus sibi parietibus et muris salutem suam tueri videbatur, dolum secum et insidias et ultorem scelerum deum inclusit. Dimovit perfregitque custodias poena angustosque per aditus et obstructos, non

---

[5] "È necessario [che il Principe fortifichi i suoi luoghi], accioche egli sia rispettato dalli stranieri, e da suoi, e venendo il bisogno possa difendersi da nimici, e castigare i popoli senza sospetto di rebellione."—"It is necessary that the prince fortify his towns in order that he may be respected by strangers and by his own citizens, and that in time of need he may be able to defend himself from enemies and to punish his people without fear of rebellion" (*Il principe* 2, p. 40 verso). See also Egidio's opinion on the value of military preparations, p. 148, above.

[6] *Prince* 10, 17, 19. See p. 113, above.   [7] See p. 148, above.

[8] "The best fortress that can be is not to be hated by the people" (*Prince* 20, p. 43a).

[9] "I assure you that no castles, no walls will be more nearly impregnable than the defence which consists in having the spirits of your people friendly to you, and to have all your subjects wish you well" (*De principis officiis* 1, p. 652).

[10] Both Isocrates (*Ad Nicoclem* 21) and Seneca (*De clementia* 1.19) are quoted by Saavedra (*Idea de un principe,* Empresa 38) in a section that seems otherwise to have been influenced by Machiavelli. Of the earlier writers, Giraldus often refers to *De clementia,* though without mentioning this passage, and Hoccleve (*De regimine* 3375) takes something from the same chapter. Gilbert of Tournai (*Eruditio regum* 3.1) quotes with a slight shift in wording. Pontanus has the spirit of it: "Amorem inermem quidem incedere, dormire tamen loricatum."—"Love walks unarmed and sleeps in armor" (*De principe,* p. 267). For the idea in Beroaldus see p. 113, above.

secus ac per apertas fores et invitantia limina, inrupit; longeque tunc illi divinitas sua, longe arcana illa cubilia saevique secessus, in quos timore et superbia et odio hominum agebatur. Quanto nunc tutior, quanto securior eadem domus, postquam erus non crudelitatis sed amoris excubiis, non solitudine et claustris sed civium celebritate defenditur! Ecquid ergo discimus experimento fidissimam esse custodiam principis ipsius innocentiam? Haec arx inaccessa, hoc inexpugnabile munimentum, munimento non egere. Frustra se terrore succinxerit qui septus caritate non fuerit: armis enim arma inritantur.[11]

Nor did the formula disappear with Machiavelli. In 1568, for example, Viperanus wrote: "Hominem vero homini benevolentiae fides, et probitatis opinio charum facit. Non arce, non stipatoribus, non satellitibus indiget, non venena, non dolos, non gladios formidat, quem civium benevolentia[12] custodit."[13]

[11] "The cruel prince, by means of the bulwarks and walls by which he seems to secure his safety, shuts up with himself craft and plots and the god who revenges impious acts. Vengeance removes and bursts through the guards and rushes through narrow and obstructed approaches as through open doors and welcoming portals. Then his divinity is of no avail, there is no help in those secret hiding places and wild recesses into which he is driven by fear and pride and the hate of men. How much safer, how much more secure is the same house when its lord is defended by guards not of cruelty but of love, not by solitude and fortress walls but by a concourse of citizens! Is it necessary then to show by proof that to harm no one is the most faithful guardian of the prince? The unassailable fortress, the impregnable castle is to have no need for protection. In vain he encircles himself with terror who is not surrounded with love, for arms are roused up by arms" (C. Plinius Caecilius Secundus, *Panegyricus* [Trajani] 49).

Verbal similarities suggest this as the source of the passage quoted from Beroaldus on p. 113, above. Poggio suggests the *Panegyric* as a work *de institutione principum* in his *Epistolarum liber*, epist. Bornio suo Bonien. iurisconsulto, *Opera* 348-9. For fifteenth-century manuscripts of the *Panegyricus* see C. Plini Caecili Secundi *Epistolarum libri novem, recen.* Mauritius Schuster, Lipsiae, 1933, p. xiii; also *Rheinisches Museum für Philologie*, n. folge, 80.404. Agapetus writes on the prince as guarded by love and by his liberality toward the poor in his *De officio regis, ad Iustinianum Caesarem* (p. 95, section 58) which circulated in the sixteenth century. Clichtoveus in his discussion of the matter finds support in Sallust's *Jugurtha* and in Terence, but without specific reference (*De regis officio*, cap. 16, p. 56 verso).

A modern instance appears in the following on Queen Victoria: "At a period when the lives of the continental rulers were in great peril from revolutionists and assassins, the queen on both her fiftieth anniversary and her jubilee rode in an open carriage through many miles of London streets, with millions of spectators on either side pressing closely upon the procession, and there was never a thought that she was in the slightest danger. She was fearless herself, but she had on the triple armor of the overmastering love and veneration of the whole people" (Chauncey M. Depew, *My Memories*, p. 275).

[12] Cf. Machiavelli's *benivolenzia* (*Prince* 19, p. 36b) as apparently a synonym of his *non essere odiato* (*Prince* 20, p. 43a); see pp. 154, 160, above.

[13] "Faith in a man's good will and belief in his probity makes him dear to another man. He does not need a castle, guards, and attendants, he does not dread

This situation is typical of Niccolò's procedure; he holds to the traditional except at the points where the tradition seems to him not to touch the verity of things, or, as we now might put it, where his own theories are not involved. But of abandonment of the traditional for innovation's sake there is none; here, as normally, the traditional and the new intermingle.

One of the obvious qualities of this twentieth chapter is what may be called its un-Machiavellism—in the ordinary employment of the word—in attitude to parties in the state. No finesse of trickery in setting parties against each other is allowed to the ruler who will have a lasting dominion, for the only foundation he can esteem as good is the united support of his people. In quiet times clever "industrie" in making divisions may avail something, but even then they argue the weakness of the ruler unable to hold his state by dint of solid ability—"con forza e con virtù."[14] So important is the united state that the wise ruler will make it his business "constringere i cittadini ad amare l'uno l'altro, a vivere sanza sètte, a stimare meno il privato che il publico."[15] Who does this plants trees in the shade of which he can live in felicity. Such a position is in harmony with Machiavelli's advice that the new prince exercise all necessary severity at the beginning of his rule. So important is it that parties be rooted out of the state that means which appear inhumane may be employed—as they were by the virtuous Romans and by Duke Valentino[16]—without hesitation. This advice against exciting divisions flows from the writer's love for the common good; "da' partigiani nascono le parti nelle cittadi; dalle parti la rovina di quelle."[17]

In this matter part of Aristotle's advice to the tyrant is utterly rejected. On the basis of a short passage in *Politics* 5 (1313b) Egidio wrote:

Volunt enim tyranni turbare amicos cum amicis, populum cum insignibus, insignes cum seipsis. Vident autem quod quandiu cives discordant

---

poisons, stratagems, or swords when the good will of the ciitizens protects him" (*De rege* 17, p. 88).   [14] *Discorsi* 3.27, p. 239a.

[15] "To force the citizens to love one another, to live without factions, to estimate their private affairs as less important than those of the state" (*Arte della guerra* 1, p. 269a).

[16] For the Romans see *Discorsi* 3.27, p. 237b; 1.7, pp. 69-70. For Valentino, *Prince* 7, p. 16a; 17, p. 32b; the letter to Vettori of Jan. 31, 1514, *Lett. familiari* 41, p. 176.

[17] "From partisans spring parties in the state; from parties the ruin of the state" (*Discorsi* 1.7, p. 69b). On factions and unity see also *Discorsi* 1.55, p. 126b; 2.25, p. 181b; *Istorie Fiorentine* 7.1 passim.

a civibus, et divites a divitibus: tamdiu non potest aeque de facili eius potentiae resisti: nam tunc quaelibet partium timens alteram, neutra insurgit contra tyrannum. Verus autem Rex econtrario non procurat turbationem existentium in regno, sed pacem et concordiam: aliter enim non esset verus Rex, quia non intenderet commune bonum. . . . Decima cautela tyrannica, est quod postquam procuravit divisiones et partes in regno, cum una parte affligit aliam ut clavum clavo retundat. Rex autem econtrario non procurat divisiones et partes in regno, sed si quae ibi existunt, eas amovere desiderat.[18]

Patricius likewise believed that discord would overthrow the state:

Hac animi perturbatione [discordia] quicunque civis laborat, inutilis est reipublicae, et in hominum coetu importunus habetur. Dissidet siquidem ab aliis, nemini cedit, omnemque humanam societatem dirimit, Principum aulas perturbat, Seditionibus, ac partibus omnia inficit; hinc conspirationes, coniurationesque oriuntur; hinc caedes, direptiones, veneficia, et pestes illae teterrimae, quae status omnes publicos, privatosque labefactare solent. Crispi quidem Salustii sententia pro oraculo habenda est, quum ait: *Concordia parvae res crescunt, discordia autem maximae dilabuntur.* Per hanc interitum omnibus humanis societatibus parari scribit Xenophon.[19]

As might be expected, Erasmus declared:

Tyrannus gaudet inter cives factiones ac dissidia serere, et simultates forte fortuna obortas, diligenter alit ac provehit, atque his rebus ad suae Tyrannidis communitionem abutitur. At hoc unicum Regi studium

[18] "Tyrants wish to annoy friends with their friends, the people with men of rank, and those of rank with each other. For they see that when citizens are at variance with citizens and rich men with rich men, then correspondingly their power cannot easily be resisted, for since either party fears the other neither one rises against the tyrant. But on the contrary the true king does not procure disturbance among those living in his kingdom, but peace and concord; otherwise he would not be a true king, since he would not have in view the common good. . . . The tenth device of the tyrant is that after he has brought about divisions and parties in the kingdom, he annoys one party with another that he may blunt nail with nail. But the king on the contrary does not bring about divisions and parties in the kingdom, but if there are any he desires to get rid of them" (*De regimine* 3.2.10). Cf. the quotation from Figliucci, p. 165, below.

[19] "If a citizen has his mind perturbed by discord, he is useless to the state and is held dangerous in the society of men. If he disagrees with others he yields to no one, he breaks up all human society, causes disturbance in the courts of princes, infects everything with seditions and factions; thence arise conspiracies and plots, thence come murders, plunderings, poisonings, and those terrible plagues that overthrow all public and private establishments. Indeed the saying of Crispus Salustius should be considered as an oracle, for he said: 'Little things through concord grow great, but great things dwindle away through discord.' Xenophon says that through discord overthrow is prepared for all human organizations" (*De regno* 4.10).

est, civium concordiam alere, et si quid ortum fuerit dissensionis, continuo rem inter eos componere, nimirum, qui intelligat hanc esse gravissimam rerum publicarum pestem.[20]

Even the "tiranno virtuoso" of a city once free, if he increases his dominions, has no choice between the united and the divided realm:

Non può ancora le città che esso acquista, sottometterle o farle tributarie a quella città di che egli è tiranno: perchè il farla potente non fa per lui; ma per lui fa tenere lo stato disgiunto, e che ciascuna terra e ciascuna provincia riconosca lui.[21]

In this matter, it seems, Niccolò would have admitted that the other writers *de regimine principum* had not missed the realities of public life.

The disarming of subjects is also a method of the Aristotelian tyrant rejected—for most conditions—by Machiavelli, chiefly for reasons given in his earlier treatment of mercenaries.[22] It still remained for him the method of the tyrant, not of the true prince: "Ottaviano, prima, e poi Tiberio, pensando più alla potenza propria che all'utile publico, cominciarono a disarmare il popolo romano per poterlo più facilmente comandare."[23] As we have seen, this thought for himself rather than for the public is the distinguishing mark of the tyrant.[24]

[20] "The tyrant delights in sowing factions and dissensions among his citizens, and rivalries that fortune happens to bring about he diligently nourishes and promotes, and these things he abuses for the strengthening of his tyranny. But it is the one effort of the king to nourish concord among the citizens and if any dissension should spring up, steadily to compose it among them, as one who knows that it is surely the worst disease of states" (*Institutio* 1, 572 B-C).

[21] "Nor can he subordinate or make tributary to the city of which he is tyrant the cities he acquires, because to make it powerful is not to his advantage; but it is to his advantage to keep the state disunited and to have each city and each province recognize him" (*Discorsi* 2.2, p. 140a).

[22] *Prince* 12, p. 25b; 13, pp. 27b, 29a. In the *Ghirbizzi scritti in Raugia al Soderino*, p. 879a, Machiavelli writes, apparently with approval: "Lorenzo de' Medici disarmò il popolo per tenere Firenze."—"Lorenzo de' Medici disarmed the people in order to hold Florence."

[23] "First Octavian and then Tiberius, thinking more of their own power than of the good of the public, commenced to disarm the Roman people in order to be able more easily to rule them" (*Arte della guerra* 1, p. 272b). In *Discorsi* 2.30, p. 188b, rulers are said to have caused disarmament "di potere saccheggiare i popoli,"—"in order to plunder the people."

[24] P. 137, above. See *tyrant* in the index.

Chapter 21

Quod principem deceat ut egregius habeatur.
(What a prince must do if he would be thought
an extraordinary person.)

In the first paragraph of the present chapter Ferdinand is represented as keeping the minds of his subjects "sospesi e ammirati . . .
e occupati"[1] by foreign wars. The suggestion that subjects are to
be kept occupied is made in Aristotle's discussion of the tyrant in
the *Politics* (5, 1313ab), and appears in Figliucci as follows:

Si dee ancora studiare e ingegnar il tiranno di concitare e suscitare
guerre e contese, e discordie; cosi tra li sudditi come con altri populi,
accioche cosi sempre sia il populo occupato, e non habbia ozio da
pensare male alcuno contra il tiranno, anzi sempre ritrovandosi in
pericolo habbia bisogno del Principe che lo difenda.[2]

Such conduct appears as normal for the tyrant in the Spanish *Las
Siete Partidas*.[3] Carafa advises the prince to occupy the minds of
his subjects with festal days, as does Niccolò at the end of this
chapter; because "dum hoc ludo erunt occupati vanis cogitationibus,
levioribusque, aut seditiosis negotiis non inquietabuntur."[4] The
idea that the prince should strike his subjects with wonder as well
as occupy their minds does not, so far as I know, appear in
works *de regimine principum* before Machiavelli. While the preceding writers wished their prince to be successful in war, their
religious background hardly permitted them to present conquest
as a means of acquiring reputation. Even Machiavelli himself
seems opposed to wars for reputation, though he would not have
prohibited conquests to his true prince. Indeed, to amplify the
state by foreign wars may become a necessity of national life: "È

[1] "In suspense and wonder . . . and occupied" (*Prince* 21, p. 43).

[2] "The tyrant should also give thought and effort to stirring up and exciting
wars and struggles and discords, both among his subjects and with other peoples,
so that the people may ever be occupied and may not have leisure to think any evil
against the tyrant, but rather, always feeling that they are in peril, may have need
of the prince to defend them" (*De la politica*, folios 186 verso-187).

[3] *Segunda Partida*, titulo 1, ley 10. Cf. pp. 22, 24, 134, above.

[4] "While they are occupied with this sport they are not disquieted with vain
or rather light thoughts or with seditious activities" (*De principis officiis* 1, p. 653).

impossibile che ad una republica riesca lo stare quieta, e godersi la sua libertà e gli pochi confini: perchè, se lei non molesterà altrui, sarà molestata ella; e dallo essere molestata le nascerà la voglia e la necessità dello acquistare."[5] Such wars, however, are to be approved only when necessitated, for Machiavelli approved the sentiment of Livy: "Justum est bellum quibus necessarium."[6] Conquest may be to the advantage of the conquered state, as appeared in the Romagna after Duke Valentino's occupation.[7] The conquests of a tyrant, however, are of no value to his original state, but only to himself: "E se la sorte facesse che vi surgesse uno tiranno virtuoso, il quale per animo e per virtù d'arme ampliasse il dominio suo, non ne risulterebbe alcuna utilità a quella republica, ma a lui proprio."[8] Were Ferdinand's conquests of this type? Though admitting that he possessed astuteness, Machiavelli denied him the virtues of wisdom and prudence—"sapere o prudenzia."[9] He had not, Niccolò wrote to Vettori, made his country rich or his army well organized: "Io ho inteso di buono luogo, che chi è in Spagna scrive quivi non essere danari nè ordine da averne, e che l'esercito suo era solum di comandati, i quali ancora cominciavono a non lo ubbidire."[10] He had also given an example of cruelty to his subjects, "cacciando e spogliando, el suo regno, de' Marrani."[11] His wars, moreover, as is also explained to Vettori,[12] were not made with the right end in view but only to get himself reputation. This was not a proper motive, as Gower knew:

[5] "It is impossible that a republic will succeed in remaining quiet and enjoying its liberty and its narrow confines, because if it does not molest some other state, it will be molested, and from being molested will spring the wish and the necessity of acquisition" (*Discorsi* 2.19, p. 169b). Cf. *Discorsi* 1.6, p. 67b, and see Ercole, *La politica di Machiavelli*, p. 278.

[6] "A war is just for those to whom it is necessary" (*Prince* 26, p. 50ab, quoted from Livy 9.1.10). Cf. *Discorsi* 3.12, p. 220b; *Istorie Fiorentine* 5.8, p. 505a. See also p. 224, below.

[7] *Prince* 7, p. 16a; *Discorsi* 3.29, p. 240. See also pp. 223-5, below.

[8] "And if chance should bring about that there should arise a virtuous tyrant, who through his spirit and his ability in arms would increase his domains, no good would come from it to that republic but to himself alone" (*Discorsi* 2.2, p. 140a).

[9] Letter to Vettori—dated April 29, 1513, by Tommasini, *Vita di Machiavelli* 2.86 —*Lettere familiari* 20, p. 76. See *astuzia* in the index.

[10] "I have learned from a good source that letters from Spain say there is no money there or means of getting it, and that Ferdinand's army is made up only of officers, and that even they were beginning not to obey him" (ibid., p. 78).

[11] "Hunting down the Moors and driving them out of his kingdom" (*Prince* 21, p. 43b).

[12] *Lettere familiari* 20, p. 82.

King Salomon in special
Seith, as ther is a time of pes,
So is a time natheles
Of werre, in which a Prince algate
Schal for the comun riht debate
And for his oghne worschipe eke.
Bot it behoveth noght to seke
Only the werre for worschipe,
Bot to the riht of his lordschipe,
Which he is holde to defende,
Mote every worthi Prince entende.[13]

Yet the wars of Ferdinand were necessary if he was to produce on the minds of men the effects described in *The Prince,* in order to hold his new states. As we have seen, such plea of necessity could be made by a true prince who employed certain devices of the Aristotelian tyrant. But in spite of recognition of the success of Ferdinand, Machiavelli never attributes to the Catholic king good government, but only the reverse, and does not allow him that prudence and wisdom from which good government springs. To lack these qualities is, in Niccolò's opinion, to be on the way to tyranny.[14] The necessity of Ferdinand is, then, possibly that of the tyrant rather than of the good prince. Such an opinion would fit with one by Guicciardini, who, though calling Ferdinand "prudentissimo" and "savio,"[15] yet wrote:

Una delle maggiore fortune che possino avere gli uomini è avere occasione di potere mostrare, che a quelle cose che loro fanno per interesse proprio, siano stati mossi per causa di pubblico bene. Questa fece gloriose le imprese del Re Cattolico; le quali fatte sempre per sicurtà o grandezza sua, parvono spesso fatte o per augumento della fede cristiana, o per difesa della Chiesa.[16]

[13] *Confessio Amantis* 7.3594-3604. For the end of war see p. 225, below.

[14] See p. 136, above. In later times Frachetta wrote: "Il Prencipe non è da chiamar Prencipe senza la prudenza. . . . Di vero non può esser ne' Tiranni vera prudenza."—"A prince should not be called a prince unless he has prudence. . . . Indeed in a tyrant there cannot be true prudence" (*Seminario,* Discorso 12. Cf. p. 120, above).

[15] "Most prudent" and "knowing" (*Ricordi* 77, 273).

[16] "One of the best pieces of good fortune that men can have is to be able to show that they are moved by reason of the public benefit to deeds which they do for their personal advantage. Such good fortune made glorious the deeds of the Catholic King, for though his acts were always for his own security or greatness, they frequently appeared to be intended either for the augmentation of the Christian faith or for the defense of the Church" (*Ricordi* 142).

Cf. the advice on appearing religious in *Prince* 18, p. 35a. Elsewhere Guicciardini

Personal ambition rather than devotion to the public good is the mark of the tyrant.[17]

In the second paragraph of this twenty-first chapter the "rari esempli" which have just been considered in foreign affairs are urged for internal matters. As it is said of the prince in the *Discorsi,* "Nessuna cosa gli fa tanto stimare, quanto dare di sè rari esempli con qualche fatto o detto rado, conforme al bene comune, il quale mostri il signore o magnanimo o liberale o giusto, e che sia tale che si riduca come in proverbio intra i suoi suggetti."[18] The same concern with the common good is implied in *The Prince,* for the ruler is evidently to perform his spectacular actions in giving proper rewards and punishments. The striking deed or saying is also subject to the condition that the ruler in all he does should obtain for himself "fama di uomo grande e d'ingegno eccellente."[19] On these dramatic examples of his power to act is based the reputation that enables a ruler to keep his position even though he has not gained the love of his people.

The gaining of reputation by striking deeds or sayings has not, it appears, been urged on rulers before Machiavelli's time. It had, however, been recognized that a ruler might live for posterity at at least through his proverbial sayings, which perhaps Machiavelli especially indicates by his word *ingegno.* It had been observed also that the pithy remark was often of a political cast. Plutarch's *Apophthegms* were widely circulated in the fifteenth century. Erasmus, as he tells us in the preface, modeled after them the *Apophthegmata lepideque dicta principum, philosophorum, ac diversi generis hominum* which he addressed to the young prince

---

writes of Ferdinand: "Coprì quasi tutte le sue cupidità sotto colore di onesto zelo della religione, e di santa intenzione al bene commune."—"He covered most of his cupidity beneath the color of honest zeal for religion and holy intention to further the common good" (*Istoria* 12.19, p. 383).

[17] See *tyrant* in the index.

[18] "Nothing makes him so much esteemed as striking illustrations of his capacity through some unusual deed or saying, in harmony with the common good, which shows that the ruler is magnanimous or liberal or just, or which is of such a sort that it becomes proverbial among his subjects" (*Discorsi* 3.34, p. 248a). See also ibid., 3.1, p. 195a.

Compare the plan attributed to a duke by James Shirley:

> Then some rare
> Invention to execute the traitor,
> So as he may be half a year in dying,
> Will make us famed for justice (*The Traitor,* I, ii).

[19] "The reputation of a a great man, of excellent ability" (*Prince* 21, p. 44a). Cf. Severus as described in *Prince* 19, p. 38b; see p. 145, below.

William of Cleve. They contain, he says, matter "de Republica administranda, deque bello gerendo."[20] Certain of them are attributed to Alphonso of Aragon, as for example: "Interrogatus quos e civibus haberet carissimos, *Qui magis,* inquit, *pro me metuunt, quam me.* Sentit, illos esse ex animo amicos, qui Principem magis amant quam timent."[21] A larger collection of the sayings of this famous prince is that of Panormita entitled *De dictis et factis Alphonsi regis memorabilibus.* On this Aeneas Sylvius wrote a commentary. In pursuance of his view that the able prince says such striking things as are there recorded, Machiavelli attributes to Castruccio Castracani a considerable number.[22] Cosimo de' Medici also said things worthy to be recorded, but some of them, by appearing opposed to religion and the common good, lowered rather than raised his reputation.[23]

Advice that will aid the ruler to hold a high reputation among his people is common enough in works *de regimine principum,*[24] and sometimes the imagination of the people is considered. In the early *Secretum secretorum* the king is advised to appear once a year in a grand spectacle calculated to strengthen his hold on the people; "hoc igitur modo principaliter publicatur et accrescit fama regis in secreto et in aperto."[25] At this time he is also, to borrow the words of Machiavelli, "dare di sè esemplo di umanità e di munificenzia."[26] In the preceding chapter of the *Secretum secretorum* is advice so to act that "dignitas regis decoretur, potencia non ledatur, et debita reverencia tribuatur."[27] Machiavelli desires

---

[20] "On administering the state, and on carrying on war."

[21] "When he was asked what citizens he held dearest, he answered: 'Those who fear not me but for me.' He understood that they were friends in their hearts who loved the prince rather than feared him" (Erasmus, *Apophthegmata,* bk. 8, Alphonsus Aragonum Rex, no. 11, col. 378 D).

[22] *Castruccio Castracani,* pp. 761 ff. (the last pages).

[23] Cf. pp. 130-1, above.

[24] In a note on chapter twenty-one Burd (p. 340) quotes from Tacitus (*An.* 4.40). and also from Mariana on fame. But Mariana is concerned with the true fame that comes from the absolute goodness of the king: "El mas honesto fruto de las virtudes verdaderas."—"The most honorable effect of the genuine virtues" (*De rege* 2.13). Such a ruler, he thinks, will not be guided by the opinion of the vulgar. Machiavelli, however, is interested in popular effect; his ruler is to be in the mouths of all as an able man; wide or lasting fame is not in question.

[25] "So then this is the chief way in which the fame of the king is spread about and increases in secret and openly" (pt. 1, chap. 12).

[26] "To make himself an example of humanity and munificence" (*Prince* 21, p. 45a).

[27] "The dignity of the king is raised, his power is not decreased, and proper reverence is paid to him" (pt. 1, chap. 11).

also that the king should be careful never to lose "la maestà della dignità sua."[28] His union of dignity and complaisance is that of Egidio, who, after advising the ruler to be "amicabilis," adds: "Quia nimia familiaritas contemptum parit, Reges et Principes, ut in reverentia habeantur, et ne dignitas regia vilescat, maturius se habere debent, quam alii."[29] Patricius also has some thought of an imaginative effect on subjects: "Anaxagoras clazomenius quum Periclem Atheniensem instrueret, dicebat magnificentiam, et animi graviorem quandam elationem, ad popularem potentiam capessendam plurimum valere."[30] Pontanus felt that much could be done to increase the effect of majesty, though nature was also contributory:

Maxime autem opinionem tum subiectorum, tum caeterorum hominum conciliabit ea, quae nunc a quibusdam etiam non indoctis viris, quamvis parum proprie maiestas vocatur. Sed non sit mihi de verbo controversia, vulgus in hoc sequar, in quo veniam mihi dari a te postulo. Est autem ea principum propria, comparaturque arte, et diligentia multa, habetque ortum a natura. Primum igitur oportet teipsum ut cognoscas, intelligasque te gerere principis personam, quod intelligens in omnibus tum dictis, tum factis gravitatem servabis, atque constantiam. Cumque omnis tum consultatio, tum actio sit de consiliis capiendis, aut de rebus publicis aut privatis, in capiendis consiliis oportet multa audire, plurima circumspicere, causas singulorum, quae dicuntur, exquirere: non statim assentiri, nec semper etiam palam improbare oculis, nutuque multa declarare, multa etiam pensitantem animo, vultu prae te ferre, sententias aliorum ita examinare, ut mentes dicentium videare velle introspicere, quod ipse sentias, aut non statim, aut solum paucis aperire, in dicendo cautum et brevem esse: pro rerum tamen qualitate, parce reprachendere, rarenter, et non nisi maxima ex causa obiurgare, laudare cum gravitate, iracundiam cohibere, tamquam maiestatis inimicam, in nullo ita efferri, ut quod agunt, lineam transeas. Ex his igitur, atque aliis, quae natura, tempus, res, et ars docuerit, de quibus nulla certa praecepta tradi possent, nasceretur admiratio quaedam, sine qua maiestas esse nullo modo potest.[31]

[28] "The majesty of his dignity" (*Prince* 21, p. 45a).

[29] "Since too much familiarity breeds contempt, kings and princes, that they may be held in reverence and that the kingly dignity may not grow cheap, should hold themselves more decorously than others" (*De regimine* 1.2.28).

[30] "Anaxagoras of Clazomene, when he gave instruction to Pericles the Athenian, said that magnificence and a certain rather grave elevation of mind were of the greatest value in getting hold of popular power" (*De regno* 7.11).

[31] "But especially the good opinion of subjects as well as of other men is conciliated by that quality which now certain learned men, though with little fitness, call majesty. But that I may not raise controversy over a word, I follow the crowd

L'Autheur traicte,combien est chose necessaire aux Prin
ces, de retenir leur Maiesté, & d'en vser tousiours. Alle-
guant plusieurs exemples des Rommains, qui,par icelle,
ont acquis grande estime & reputation, auec honneur
immortel,   CHAP. XXXVIII.

VIDE DICT, QVE MAIE-
sté fut produicte & procreée de Chaös,auec les elements : & qu'elle feist la discretion des ordres, &
des dignités tant celestielles, comme elementaires. *Maiesté,fil-*
Et que sans son ordonnance, les choses inferieures *re de Chaos*
n'eussent porté reuerence aux superieures : mais eussent voulu occuper le lieu d'icelles.

Et dict, que creincte & reuerence sont assises au Ciel, ou est le do-
micile des Dieux, à l'entour de Maiesté, qui la maintenoit en son *Creincte &*
Throsne. Et que à la semblance & mutation d'elle,touts les Celestes se *reuerice as-*
conforment, pour se faire plus venerables.   *sises au ciel.*

Ces choses bien consyderées, doibuent donner le cœur aux Roys,
& aux grands Monarcques,qui viennent à domination par succesion
legitime, & par ottroy de Prouidence diuine,a conseruer leur Maiesté
en son entier, & aussy celle de leurs Royaulmes, & Monarchies. Pour
laquelle conseruation (comme dict Valere le grand) n'est point tant *Aduertisse-*
requis à vn Prince,de donner grande terreur au peuple,& de luy mon- *ment aux*
strer gens armés à l'entour de luy, ou estre monté en vn hault siege *Princes.*
Royal : comme il luy est mestier d'entretenir son estime & sa reputation, par composition de mœurs, & contenance pleine d'authorité.
Car Maiesté est reuestue d'vn manteau d'admiration,tissu de grandes
vertuz, & d'honnesteté de cœur, dont les signes euidents sont en son
maintien, en son regime, & en touts ses actes.

Valere recite plusieurs exemples sur ce mesme propos,dont l'vn est
de Scipion l'Africain, lequel estant en son exil, à Linterne, ou il se re-
tira,comme courroucé contre le peuple de Romme,entendit que aul- *Exemples.*
cuns Capitaines pillards venoient en sa maison, pour le voler : qui e-
stoit vne maison située aux champs. Au moyen de quoy, Scipion delibera de se fortifier à l'encontre de leur entreprinse qu'il soupçonnoit.
Laquelle chose venue à la congnoissance des Capitaines : ilz feisrent
retirer leurs gens, & laissairent touts accoustremens de guerre : & puis

From the copy of Guillaume Budé's *De Linstitution du
Prince,* Paris, 1547, in the Duke University Library. The
facsimile is smaller than the original.

This passage is in various respects Machiavellian, in addition to the basic similarity in the idea that the reputation for *ingegno* and the appearance of *maestà* can prudently be built up. In the chapter on avoiding contempt—the reverse of acquiring reputation—Machiavelli advises the prince to appear hard to deceive,[32] as Pontanus thinks he should seem to desire to read the minds of those he deals with. And in the same passage Machiavelli counsels against appearing variable, as Pontanus recommends constancy. The earlier writer, too, in remarking that some things cannot be satisfactorily taught in precepts, but that time and conditions must be consulted, touches a favorite theme of the Florentine secretary.

In advising the prince to encourage his people to add to the prosperity of the country,[33] Niccolò opposes another part of Aristotle's plan for the tyrant, who was to keep his people poor and in subjection; the true king, as Egidio and all the others knew, wished his people to have such riches as were consistent with the common good.[34] Machiavelli advised the prince to rely on individual initiative, while Petrarch recommended great public works, such as the draining of marshes, in the attempt to bring prosperity.[35] Diomede Carafa writes at length and with feeling on the encouragement of trade and industry, starting with the declaration: "La vera industria del bon Signore è bene administrare sue intrate iuste, e le industrie far fare ad soi subditi et aiutarencili, chè,

---

in this, in which I beg that you will pardon me. But this is a quality proper to princes which may be acquired by art and great diligence and has its origin in nature. It is first proper therefore that you should recognize and understand that you bear the character of a prince; knowing this, you will preserve gravity and constancy in all your sayings and your acts. Since every consultation and every action relates to taking counsel or to public or private affairs, in taking advice it is proper to hear many things, to examine as many as possible, and to enquire into the causes of single things that are said, not to assent immediately, nor ever openly to disapprove a thing by your expression, to indicate many things with a nod, and weighing many things in your mind, to indicate by your countenance that you so examine the opinions of others that you seem to wish to look into the minds of the speakers, but what you think yourself not to make known immediately or only to a few, and to be cautious and brief in speaking. As for the quality of your words, to blame little and seldom, and to reproach only for a very important reason, to praise with gravity, to bridle anger as hostile to majesty, in nothing to be so moved that, as they say, you step over the line. From these and other things then, which nature, the time, the circumstances, and art teach, and about which no certain precepts can be given, there springs a certain admiration without which majesty can by no means subsist" (*De principe* 271-2).

[32] *Prince* 19, p. 36a.
[34] *De regimine* 3.2.8.
[33] *Prince* 21, last paragraph.
[35] *De republica,* p. 426.

come ho dicto, le industrie fanno arricchire li subditi quando le fanno lloro."[36]

Men who benefit the country are to be rewarded by Machiavelli's prince, as Petrarch, for example, had advised the pensioning of the learned.[37] Such rewards would represent the true liberality—giving to the right persons—of the older writers.[38] Platina felt that honors, mentioned by Machiavelli, were more desirable than more material rewards, as encouragement of merit.[39] That rewards should go to those who merited them by public service was also the opinion of Erasmus, who in speaking of liberality, continues: "Intelligat Respublica iis potissimum expositam Principis benignitatem, qui publicis commodis quam maxime consulant. Virtuti praemium sit, non affectui."[40] The rewards to those who attempt "ampliare la sua città o il suo stato"[41] that is, to make it richer, are possibly connected with the munificence which the ruler is to show at the feasts of the "arte"; in any case they do not transgress Machiavelli's earlier advice against the attempt to gain a reputation for liberality. If the Aristotelian tyrant is to keep his subjects poor, he will not give rewards and honors to those who add to prosperity; indeed, Machiavelli held that he could not: "E se la sorte facesse che vi surgesse uno tiranno virtuoso, . . . e' non può onorare nessuno di quegli cittadini che siano valenti e buoni, che egli tiranneggia, non volendo avere ad avere sospetto di loro."[42] This tyrant is completely Aristotelian; so far is he from raising men

---

[36] "The true industry of the good prince is to administer well his just income and to have his subjects carry on their occupations and to aid them in them, because, as I have said, occupations make their subjects grow rich when they carry them on" (*I doveri dei principi*, p. 287).

[37] Machiavelli, *Prince* 21, last paragraph. Petrarch, *De republica*, p. 433. Cosimo de' Medici did this (*Istorie Fiorentine* 7.6, p. 567a).

[38] See pp. 87-8, above.

[39] *Principis diatuposis* 2.11. Machiavelli approved the Roman triumphs (*Discorsi* 3.28, pp. 239-40).

[40] "The state should realize that the goodness of the prince is especially bestowed on those who most consult the public advantage. There should be a reward for virtue, not for affection" (*Institutio* 5.595 A). Possibly from the *Hiero* of Xenophon, which Erasmus translated and Machiavelli knew; see p. 13, above.

[41] "To make greater his city and his state" (*Prince* 21, p. 45a). Cf. "ampliato nè di dominio nè di ricchezza"—"increased neither in dominion nor in riches" (*Discorsi* 2.2, p. 139b). See also the quotation from the same chapter on p. 166, above.

[42] "If fate should bring about that there should arise a virtuous tyrant . . . he is not able to honor any of those citizens who are courageous and good, whom he is tyrant over, since he does not wish to be obliged to have suspicion of them" (*Discorsi* 2.2, p. 140a). Cf. pp. 30 ff., above.

tending powers,[52] but if that is inavoidable, he had best act with decision in securing friendship and bringing about the victory of an ally who at the worst may think it politic to appear grateful.

If Machiavelli took from the Aristotelians the avoidance of the hatred and contempt of subjects, he apparently made for himself its application to foreign affairs; in one of his letters he treats the reputation of a prince abroad under this head:

Non è cosa più necessaria a un principe che governarsi in modo con li sudditi, e con gli amici e vicini, che non diventi o odioso, o contennendo, e se pure egli ha a lasciare l'uno di questi duoi, non stimi l'odio, ma guardisi dal disprezzo.[53] . . . Ed io vi dico che chi sta neutrale conviene che sia odiato da chi perde, e disprezzato da chi vince; e come di uno si comincia a non tener conto, e stimato inutile amico, e non formidabile inimico, si può temere che gli sia fatta ogni ingiuria, e disegnato sopra di lui ogni ruina; nè mancano mai al vincitore le iustificazioni, perchè, avendo li suoi stati mescolati, è forzato ricevere ne' porti ora questo, ora quello, riceverli in casa, sovvenirli di alloggiamento, di vettovaglie: e sempre ognuno penserà di essere ingannato, e occorreranno infinite cose che causeranno infinite querele; e quando bene nel maneggiare la guerra non ne nascesse alcuna, che è impossibile, ne nasce doppo la vittoria, perchè li minori potenti, e che hanno paura di te, subito corrono sotto il vincitore, e danno a quello occasione d'offenderti; e chi dicessi: —Egli è il vero, e' ci potrebbe essere tolto questo, e mantenutoci quello— rispondo, che egli è meglio perdere ogni cosa virtuosamente, che parte vituperosamente, nè si può perdere la parte che il tutto non triemi.[54]

[52] On self-sufficiency see pp. 110 ff., above; *Prince* 7, p. 17a; 13, pp. 27b, 28b; 24, end.

Perhaps Machiavelli's phrase "lo stare a discrezione di altri" (p. 44b) was a formula. At least Giovan Giorgio Trissino uses it (with the article before *discrezione*) in his *Poetica* (Divisione 5, p. 106), composed by 1529, writing that "it is a fearful thing to stand at the discretion of others."

[53] For the missing part of the quotation see p. 111, above.

[54] "Nothing is more needful to a prince than to govern himself in such a way with his subjects and with his friends and neighbors that he may not become either odious or contemptible, and if he has to let one of these two go, he should not think about hatred but protect himself from being despised. . . . And I say to you that he who remains neutral must needs be hated by the one who loses and contemned by the victor; and as one who begins to be thought of little account and esteemed a useless friend and not a formidable enemy, he can fear that every injury will be done to him and every sort of ruin designed for him. Nor will the conqueror lack justification, for the neutral prince, having his affairs in a mixed condition, is forced to receive within his gates now this one, now that one, to take them into his house, and to supply them with lodging and with victuals. Each one who is received will think he is being deceived and an infinite number of things will occur that will cause infinite complaints. And even though in managing war nothing of the sort arises, which is impossible, it will arise after the victory, because the lesser rulers and those

This makes clear the importance in foreign affairs of a reputation for courage and capacity; in *The Prince*—in spite of the topic of the chapter—the value of reputation is neglected for the discussion of the varying conditions of alliance. The prince who will maintain his state should guard himself against hatred by other rulers, but their contempt is still more dangerous, because it means for him loss of reputation and for them facility in working against him.[55]

A bit of Machiavellian philosophy appears in the statement that no perfectly secure decision can be made, for in avoiding one inconvenience the prince encounters another; prudence consists in the recognition of the various inconveniences and the choice of the least damaging one.[56] This is frequently stated by our author, as in one of his letters to Vettori: "Quando uno è forzato a pigliare uno de' duoi partiti, debbe, intra l'altre cose, considerare dove la trista fortuna di qualunque di quelli ti può ridurre, e sempre debbe pigliare quella parte, quando l'altre cose fussero pari, che abbia il fine suo, quando fusse tristo, meno acerbo."[57] The theme also appears in the writings of Guicciardini, as for example:

Sarebbe da desiderare el potere fare o condurre le cose sue a punto, cioè in modo che fussino sanza uno minimo disordine o scrupolo; ma è difficile el fare questo; in modo che è errore lo occuparsi troppo in limbiccarle, perché spesso le occasione fuggono, mentre che tu perdi tempo a condurre quello a punto; e anche quando credi averlo trovato e fermo, ti accorgi spesso non essere niente perché la natura delle cose del mondo è in modo, che è quasi impossibile trovarne alcuna che in ogni parte non vi sia qualche disordine e inconveniente; bisogna resolversi a tôrle come sono e pigliare per buono quello che ha in sé manco male.[58]

---

who are afraid of you run at once to the protection of the conqueror and give him occasion to injure you. If any one says, 'Neutrality is the best policy; this can be taken away from us and that kept,' I answer it is better to lose everything virtuously than part shamefully, and part cannot be lost without the whole hanging in the balance" (to Vettori, Dec. 20, 1514, *Lettere familiari* 38, pp. 162-3).

[55] *Discorsi* 2.9, p. 151b. Cf. pp. 104-5, above.   [56] *Prince* 21, p. 45a.

[57] "When a person is forced to accept one of two plans, he should, among other things, consider where an unsuccesful issue of either of them may bring him, and always choose that plan, when other things are equal, whose end, if bad, may be less unpleasant" (Dec. 20, 1514, *Lett. familiari* 37, pp. 161-2). Burd (pp. 344-5) cites a number of passages such as *Discorsi* 1.6, p. 67b, and a fragment given by Tommasini (1.661, note 4); from Guicciardini he gives *Storia d'Italia* 12.4. Guicciardini deals concretely with the subject in his *Discorsi Politici* 12 and 15. For his use of Machiavelli's words "partiti securi"—"plans that cannot fail" (*Prince* 21, p. 45a)—see pp. 212, 216, below.

[58] "It would be desirable to be able to carry out or conduct one's affairs with completeness, that is in such a way that they are done without the least disorder or

It is not necessary to suppose Guicciardini derived the thought from Machiavelli; it may have been fairly well known in their circles. At any rate, we read in Diomede Carafa that in his earlier time it was a proverbial saying: "Idcirco dici consuevit: appellandum esse sapientem; non qui bonum a malo secernat; sed qui propositis duobus bonis, utilius; rursusque, qui de duobus incommodis minus eligere noverit."[59]

Machiavelli's exhortation to employ public spectacles and festivities[60] is anticipated by Beroaldus, who writes:

Decet principem imprimis esse magnificum. Est autem magnificus, ut docet Aristoteles in quarto ethicorum: Is qui in publica facit impensas velut in spectaculis: in epulo: in aedificiis. Hinc Plinius in Traiani laudem. At quam magnificus inquit in publicum es. Hinc porticus: inde delubra occulta celeritate properantur.[61]

The quality of magnificence is not the same as munificence, but the two are connected; Patricius mentions munificence in his chapter on magnificence, in which he tells of the spectacles exhibited by Caesar. Magnificence appears especially in public spectacles, and is important "in amicis comparandis."[62] Machiavelli advises munificence on public occasions pretty much for the gaining of friends. Erasmus, usually cautious about expenses, is willing to have his prince spend money in public sports.[63] Niccolò had no doubt that

difficulty, but it is difficult to do that, so difficult that it is an error to busy oneself too much in puzzling over it, because often occasions pass by while you lose time in bringing something to an absolute conclusion, and when you believe you have it worked out and solid, you often learn that it is not at all so, because the nature of the things of the world is such that it is just about impossible to find anything which does not have in every part of it some disorders and inconveniences. It is necessary to make up your mind to take them as they are and to accept as good that which has in itself the least evil" (*Ricordi* 126).

[59] "Therefore it is commonly said that the appellation of wise man should be given not to him who discerns good from evil, but to him who when two good things are put before him knows how to choose the more useful, and again who knows how to select the less of two disadvantages" (*De principis officiis* 1, p. 648).

[60] *Prince* 21, p. 45a.

[61] "First of all it befits the prince to be magnificent. And, as Aristotle teaches in the fourth of the *Ethics*, he is magnificent who goes co expense for the public, as in providing spectacles, feasts, and buildings. Thence Pliny says in praise of Trajan: 'How magnificent you are for the public. As a result, porticoes and secret shrines are prepared with great swiftness'" (*De optimo statu*, folio 128 verso). The quotation is from C. Plinius Caecilius Secundus, *Panegyricus* 51. See p. 198, below, and the index under *Pliny*.

[62] "In gaining friends" (*De regno* 7.11). The edition I follow (Prato, 1531), and the Italian translation of Venice, 1553, attribute friends to magnificence; the Latin edition of Strassburg, 1594, attributes them to munificence.

[63] *Institutio* 10, 606 E.

reputation could be acquired "con giuochi e doni publici,"[64] though, as we have seen, he felt that liberality was likely to be ruinous to the giver. When taken in isolation, however, this exhortation to munificence and humanity is conventional in its character.[65]

[64] "With games and gifts to the public" (*Istorie Fiorentine* 7.1, p. 562a). Cf. ibid. 7.12, p. 571a. For prudent liberality see p. 54, above.

[65] As a parallel with Machiavelli's "raunarsi con loro"—"to mingle with them" (*Prince* 21, p. 45a), Burd (p. 346) quotes from Tacitus: "Augustus . . . civile rebatur misceri voluptatibus vulgi."—"Augustus thought it courteous to mix in the pleasures of the vulgar" (*Annales* 1.54). Pliny, praising Trajan for his expenditure on the circus, continues: "Tum quod aequatus plebis ac principis locus; siquidem per omne spatium una facies, omnia continua et paria, nec magis proprius spectanti Caesari suggestus quam propria quae spectet. Licebit ergo civibus tuis te invicem contueri: dabitur non cubiculum principis sed ipsum principem cernere, in publico, in populo sedentem."—"Then too the seats of prince and people have been put on a level; and indeed if through all the space there is one form and all things are continuous and equal, Caesar as he looks on is as far from having a high seat for himself alone as he is from being the only one to see the performance. It will be possible for the citizens to see you as well as for you to see them; there will be opportunity to see not the private box of the prince but the prince himself sitting among the people in public" (*Panegyricus* 51).

Chapter 22

De his quos a secretis principes habent.
(Of the confidential ministers employed by princes.)

In this chapter Machiavelli deals with a subject important to monarchs from the time of Rehoboam and his two sets of advisers.[1] Commynes writes of normal events in his day: "Le prince tumbe en telle indignation envers Nostre Seigneur, qu'il fuyt les conseilz des saiges et en eslieve de tous neufz, mal saiges, mal raisonnables, flateurs, qui luy complaisent à ce qu'il dit."[2] With such possibilities in mind, Vincent of Beauvais wrote a chapter showing that the king "debet esse sapiens in amicis, consiliariis, officialibus eligendis."[3] Fidelity, prudence, and fitness for the special matter in hand are some of the qualities a ruler should look for. The writer of the *Secretum secretorum* would judge a minister much as would Machiavelli when asking whether the minister thinks "più a sè che a te":[4]

Temptabis eciam bajulos tuos in donis et muneribus faciendis. Quem ergo illorum videris conari et intendere super hiis ultra modum, nullum bonum speres in eo. Et ille bajulus qui anelat pecunie acquirende, et ad thesauros observandos, non confidas in eo, quia ejus servicium est propter aurum, et dimittit pecuniam currere cum sensibus hominum, et est profunditas sine fundo, et non est in eo terminus sive finis, quia quanto magis crescit pecunia crescit intencio acquirendi et sollicitudo.[5]

[1] Used by Clichtoveus (*De regis officio* 6, f. 24 verso) to show that the king should associate with prudent men and not ignorant and pleasure-seeking youths.

[2] "The prince so falls into the displeasure of our Lord that he gives up the counsels of the wise and takes advice only from new advisers, unwise, unreasonable, and flatterers, who say what is acceptable to him" (*Mémoires* 5.19, p. 228).

[3] "Ought to be wise in choosing his friends, counsellors, and officials" (*De morali principis institutione* 12).

[4] "More of himself than of you" (*Prince* 22, p. 45b).

[5] "You will also test your counsellors by making gifts and presents. Then if you see one of them striving for them and setting his heart on them beyond measure, you may hope nothing good from him. And if a counsellor strives to acquire wealth and to give attention to treasure, do not confide in him, for he serves for the sake of gold, and lets money equal the feelings of men, and is a pit without a bottom, and there is no terminus or end in him, since in proportion as his money increases his intention and eagerness for acquiring it increases" (*Secretum secretorum* 3.12, p. 140).

Machiavelli's belief that a ruler may be judged from the capacity of his ministers is the point of a story in Gower's *Confessio Amantis* (7.3994-7):

> Sire king, if that it were so,
> Of wisdom in thin oghne mod
> That thou thiselven were good,
> Thi conseil scholde noght be badde.

In this twenty-second chapter Machiavelli takes for granted the principle of the *Secretum secretorum* that "nichil sine consilio faciendum est,"[6] and that "nec altitudo tui status in temetipso impediat quin semper agreges tuo consilio consilium alienum";[7] in the twenty-third chapter he says: "Uno principe . . . debbe consigliarsi sempre,"[8] and in *Il demonio che prese moglie* the principle is fully presented; calling a council for the purpose "di avere sopra questo caso con tutti gl'infernali principi maturo esamine e pigliarne di poi quel partito che fussi giudicato migliore,"[9] Pluto speaks as follows:

Ancora che io, dilettissimi miei, per celeste disposizione e fatale sorte al tutto inrevocabile possegga questo regno, e che per questo io non possa essere obligato ad alcuno iudicio o celeste o mondano, nondimeno, perchè gli è maggiore prudenza, di quelli che possono più, sottomettersi più alle leggi e più stimare l'altrui iudizio: ho deliberato essere consigliato da voi come, in uno caso il quale potrebbe seguire con qualche infamia del nostro imperio, io mi debba governare.[10]

The tyrannical devil adopts the policy of the true prince, for there is no comedy in keeping laws and taking advice. With a failure to get sufficient advice Commynes connects one of the serious errors of Louis XI:

Toutesfois le sens de nostre roy estoit si grand que moy ne autres, qui fussent en la compaignie, n'eussions sceü veoir cler en ses affaires comme

---

[6] "Nothing should be done without taking advice" (ibid. 3.9, p. 136).

[7] "The height of your position should not keep you from always adding the plan of some one else to your own" (ibid. 3.11, p. 139).

[8] "A prince should always take counsel" (*Prince* 23, p. 46b).

[9] "To make a mature examination of the circumstances with all the princes of hell and as a result to arrive at the plan that should be thought best" (p. 765a).

[10] "Though I possess this realm, my beloved subjects, through divine disposal and the lot of fate, which is in every way irrevocable, and therefore I am not obliged to defer to any judgment either celestial or worldly, nevertheless, because it is the part of prudence for those who possess much to submit themselves to the laws and put high value on the judgment of others, I have determined to be advised by you how I should conduct myself in an affair from which some infamy can result for our dominion" (p. 765ab).

luy-mesmes faisoit: car, sans nulle doubte, c'estoit ung des plus saiges princes et des plus subtilz qui ayt regnè en son temps. Mais en ces grandz matières, Dieu dispose les cueurs des rois et des grandz princes, lesquelz il tient en sa main, à prendre les voyes selon les oeuvres qu'il veult conduyre. . . .

Je diz ces choses au long pour monstrer que, au commencement que on veult entreprendre une si grand chose, que on la doit bien consulter et debattre, affin de povoir choisir le meilleur party; et, par especial, soy recommander à Dieu et luy prier qu'il luy plaise adresser le meilleur chemin; car de là vient tout: et se voyt par escript et par experience.[11] Je n'entendz point blasmer nostre roy pour dire qu'il eust failly en ceste matière, car, par adventure, autres qui sçavoient et congnoissoient plus que moy seroient et estoient lors de l'advis qu'il estoit, combien que riens n'y fut debattu, ne là ny ailleurs, touchant ladicte matière.[12]

The Duke of Burgundy met his death because of his refusal of "saige conseil."[13]

Louis was gifted with that ability to choose his servants which distinguishes the prudent ruler of Machiavelli.[14]

Je ne veulx point dire que tous les princes se servent de gens mal condicionnéz, mais bien la pluspart de ceulx que j'ay congneü n'en ont pas tousjours esté desgarnyz. En temps de nécessité ay-je bien veü que les aucuns saiges se sont bien sceü servir des plus apparens et les cercher sans y riens plaindre.

Et, entre tous les princes dont j'ay eu la congnoissance, l'a le mieulx sceü faire le roy nostre maistre et plus honnorer et estimer les gens de bien et de valleur.[15]

[11] Cf. in the dedication of *The Prince:* "Una lunga esperienzia delle cose moderne e una continua lezione delle antique."—"A long experience in recent affairs and a continual reading of ancient history."

[12] "The intelligence of our king was so great that neither I nor others who were in his company would have had the power to see so clearly in his affairs as he could himself, for without any doubt he was one of the wisest and most subtle princes who reigned in his day. But in these great affairs God disposes the hearts of kings and great princes, whom he holds in his hand, to take their ways according to the actions that he wishes to carry on. . . .

"I speak of these things at length to show that at the beginning when one wishes to undertake so great an affair one ought certainly to consult and discuss, in order to be able to select the best plan, and especially he should commend himself to God and pray to Him that it may please Him to point out the best road, for everything comes from that and can be seen from both literature and experience. I do not at all intend to blame our king by saying that he was faulty in this matter, for, perchance, others who know and understand better than I do will be and were then of the opinion that he held, but rather I blame him that there was no debate, there or elsewhere, on the said matter" (*Mémoires* 5.13, pp. 171-2).

[13] Ibid. 5.8, p. 150.   [14] *Prince* 22, p. 45b.

[15] "I do not at all wish to say that all princes are served by vicious men, but the greater part of those I have known have surely not ever been free from them.

Is it possible that Machiavelli had Louis' minister in mind when he instructed his prince to reward his ministers liberally? The idea is sufficiently obvious and old; for example, in the *Secretum secretorum* we find advice on rewarding the man chosen "ad scribenda secreta tua opera":[16] "Et condecet quod tu remuneres opera sua juxta servicium tibi exhibitum, et juxta terminum imposicionis tue voluntatis ut sit sollicitus in tuo regimine. Pone ergo ipsum in gradu remuneracionis tue, quia ejus veritas tua est, et ejus corrupcio tua est."[17] The wise prince will take this to heart and do all he can to retain good ministers, because "questi si truovano rarissimi,"[18] even in the courts of the ablest and most generous princes. Certainly, "Se e principi, quando viene loro bene, tengono poco conto de' servitori, per ogni suo piccolo interesse gli disprezzano o mettono da canto; che può sdegnarsi o lamentarsi uno padrone se e ministri, pure che non manchino al debito della fede e dell' onore, gli abandonano o pigliano quelli partiti che siano più a loro beneficio?"[19]

The position of the minister is often not an enviable one. Patricius entitled a chapter *Non esse invidendum illis, quibus reges ac principes arcana committunt,*[20] and another *Neque etiam inviden-*

In time of necessity I have seen that some wise princes have known how to employ as their servants the most able men and to seek for them without making any complaint about it.

"And among all the princes with whom I have been acquainted, the king our master has best known how to do it and how most to honor and value men of quality and worth" (*Mémoires* 2.6, p. 130).

Cf. Guicciardini, *Ricordi* 3: "Vedesi per esperienzia che e principi, ancora che grandi, hanno carestia grandissima di ministri bene qualificati; di questo nessuno si maraviglierà quando e principi non hanno tanto giudizio che sappino cognoscere gli uomini, o quando sono sì avari che non gli vogliono premiare."—"It can be seen by experience that princes, even though great ones, have very great lack of well-qualified ministers. No one should be astonished at this when princes do not have enough judgment to understand how to estimate men, and when they are so avaricious that they do not wish to reward them."

[16] "For writing out your secret business" (3.15, p. 146).

[17] "It is also fitting that you reward his works according to the service done you and according to the boundary set by requiring him to fulfil your will, in order that he may be eager to carry out your policy. Put him therefore on your list for reward, since your truth and your corruption are in his hands" (*Sec. sec.* 3.15).

[18] "Such ones are very seldom found" (Guicciardini, *Ricordi* 3).

[19] "If princes, when it suits them, put a low value on their servants, and for any slight reason contemn them and throw them aside, what right has a master to get angry and complain if his ministers not merely lack faith and honor but also abandon him and enter upon plans that are more to their own benefit?" (Guicciardini, *Ricordi* 4).

[20] "Those to whom kings and princes commit their secrets are not to be envied" (*De regno* 9.7).

dum est illis quos reges in consilium adhibent.[21] In the first he quotes from Lucilius [1033]:

> Ille timendus erit semper, semperque verendus,
> Quem scis scire tuas omnes maculasque notasque.[22]

Such a feared man, Machiavelli knew, would probably be hated and might be ruined.[23] In the second chapter Patricius asserts that princes often attribute their successes to themselves, their failures to their ministers. As examples of ministers treated with complete ingratitude, Dante had written of Pier delle Vigne and of Romeo;[24] possibly Machiavelli had them in mind when he wrote in his *Capitolo dell' ingratitudine:*

> Onde che spesso servendo si stenta,
> E poi del ben servir se ne riporta
> Misera vita e morte violenta.[25]

Machiavelli also knew that a minister might ruin himself by acting otherwise—"altrimenti"—than prudently and unselfishly; the possibility is put as follows by Commynes:

[Le roy] une fois me dist, parlant de ceulx qui font grans services (et m'en allegua son acteur de qui il le tenoit), disant que avoir trop bien servy pert aucunes fois les gens et que souvent les grandz services sont rescompenséz par grandz ingratitudes, mais que il peult aussi bien advenir par le deffault de ceuls qui ont faict lesdictz services, qui trop arrogamment veulent user de leur bonne fortune tant envers leurs

---

[21] "Neither should they be envied whom kings employ to advise them" (ibid. 9.8).

[22] "He must always be feared, always be dreaded, whom you know to know all your affairs, both your sins and your secrets."

[23] See pp. 32, 47-8, 144, above. In the play of *Alphonsus Emperour of Germany* (attributed to George Chapman) is the following advice to the emperor by a supposedly Machiavellian minister:

> Be always jealous of him that knows your secrets,
> And therefore it behoves you credit few;
> And when you grow into the least suspect,
> With silent cunning must you cut them off (first episode, lines 173-6).

[24] *Inferno* 13.58-69; *Paradiso* 6.127-42.

[25] "Whence he often stints himself for the sake of his lord's advantage, and then for his good service receives for himself a miserable life and a violent death (lines 181-3).

In the preceding lines, however, Machiavelli has spoken less of ministers than of captains. One of his examples of ingratitude to successful soldiers was furnished by the career of Gonsalvo Ferrante, mentioned to the discredit of Ferdinand the Catholic (*Capitolo dell' ingratitudine* 164; *Discorsi* 1.29, p. 97a; cf. Guicciardini, *Istoria* 12.19, anno 1516). Cf. pp. 31-2, above.

maistres que leurs compaignons, comme de la mescongnoissance du prince.[26]

Guicciardini also recognized that ministers must conduct themselves wisely if they are to be rewarded:

Si vede per esperienzia che quasi tutti quelli che sono stati ministri a acquistare grandezza a altri, in progresso di tempo restano seco in poco grado: la ragione si dice essere, perchè avendo cognosciuto la sufficienzia sua, teme non possa uno giorno tôrgli quello che gli ha dato.[27] Ma non è forse manco perchè quello tale, parendogli avere meritato assai, vuole piú che non se gli conviene; il che non gli sendo concesso, diventa mal contento—donde tra lui e el principe nascono gli sdegni e le suspizione.[28]

[26] "The king once said to me, speaking of those who do great services (and he mentioned to me the man from whom he had it), that sometimes the performing of too good service was the ruin of men and that often great services are rewarded by great ingratitude, but that this ruin could also come about through the fault of those who have rendered the services in question, because they wish to use too arrogantly their good fortune both toward their masters and toward their companions, as well as from lack of proper recognition by the prince" (*Mémoires* 3.12, pp. 251-2).

Lorenzo the Magnificent presents what appears to the ruler too arrogant use of good services in his story of the emperor who instead of going to war in person, as Machiavelli advised, sends a general. On his victorious return the soldier asks the hand of his master's daughter. Indignant at such unheard-of pride—"superbia inaudita"—the emperor yet realizes that his refusal will put the state in great peril. His only resource is to temporize, hoping that the future may offer relief (*Rappresentazione*, pp. 80 ff.). Cf. *Discorsi* 1.39, p. 96b.

[27] Cf. the quotation from Machiavelli's *Capitolo dell' ingratitudine*, p. 32, above,

[28] "It is seen by experience that almost all who have been aids in acquiring greatness for others in the course of time stand low in their favor. The reason is said to be that the man raised up knows the minister's capacity and fears that he may one day take away what he has given. But perhaps as strong a reason is that the minister, thinking that he has merited much, wishes more than befits him; when this is not given to him he becomes discontented. As a result ill feelings and suspicions spring up between him and the prince" (*Ricordi* 52).

This *ricordo* is possibly an abridgement and adaptation of the chapter by Commynes part of which is quoted just above. The Frenchman speaks of ministers who cause fear to their masters; this theme also appears in Machiavelli's *Capitolo dell' Ingratitudine* 169-83; see p. 32, above. Guicciardini may have read the *Mémoires*, the first part of which was printed in 1524 and five times more by 1530.

These dates make it impossible that Machiavelli had seen a printed copy of the *Mémoires* before he composed *The Prince;* Part One was, however, complete in manuscript by 1493. Yet there is little evidence on its circulation in that form and the manuscripts now in existence are all probably later than the composition of Machiavelli's little book (see the *Mémoires* edited by Joseph Calmette, 1.xviii ff.). Commynes was at various times in Italy and visited Florence, and Machiavelli was in France, where apparently he heard a "detto" by Louis XI, Commynes' master, which he thought worth quoting (*Legazion seconda alla Corte di Francia,* let. 6, *Opere,* 1813, vi. 251). It is true that he does not quote Commynes, but he is not

Since Machiavelli spent most of his life as a public servant, this chapter on the qualities of ministers or secretaries should contain something of the autobiographical. An indispensable qualification of the man "che ha lo stato di uno in mano"[29] is fidelity to the interests of the prince and forgetfulness of self. As Guicciardini said, "è necessario [uno ministro] sia di grandissima fede e integrità."[30] Obviously the good minister, in the opinion of Machiavelli, would give his master such advice as is contained in *The Prince,* involving the subordination of everything to the well-being of the state. But such theories are applicable only to public affairs and the *bene commune;* they are not for the conduct of the minister himself. Any course designed for himself rather than his prince will be found injurious—"dannoso."[31] To be sure the wise king will give the minister reason to feel that devotion to the affairs of his employer is for his personal advantage; ingratitude to a sufficient and faithful secretary is damaging to the ruler. Machiavelli obtained no great rewards for his service of the state, but there appears to be no reason for thinking that in his official conduct he failed to carry out his program of devotion to his employers.

given to quoting recent authors; on the other hand, if he esteemed Commynes he could properly have mentioned him in *Prince* 22 along with Antonio da Venafro. The reference in the letter to Giovanni Ridolfi (June 12, 1506, *Lett. familiari* 11, p. 40) is colorless. The affinities with the French author apparent in various passages I have quoted (see *Commynes* in the index) are not proof of borrowing.

The age and their common interests perhaps explain all the similarities that the writings of Machiavelli and Guicciardini show to those of Commynes, yet it seems not impossible that there was direct influence of the older on the younger men.

[29] "Who has one's affairs in his control" (*Prince* 22, p. 45b).

[30] "It is necessary that a minister be of the utmost faith and integrity" (*Ricordi* 3). A little later Giraldi Cintio wrote: "I servitori dei re deono sempre loro servar lealtà."—"The servants of kings ought always to preserve loyalty to them" (*Gli Ecatommiti* 2.2). [31] *Prince* 22 (end), p. 46a.

Chapter 23

Quomodo adulatores sint fugiendi.
(How to escape flatterers.)

The first words of this chapter—"Non voglio lasciare indrieto
uno capo importante"[1]—perhaps reflect Machiavelli's consciousness
of the type of his work; it is as though he had said, "a heading
important in the works *de regimine principum,*" for hardly any
topic is more frequently treated in them than is flattery. Vincent
of Beauvais, for example, mentions it in the headings of five of
his twenty-eight chapters and alludes to it in still others. Hoccleve
speaks on the topic often, sometimes in connection with the taking
of counsel.[2] In dealing with the proper counsellors of the prince,
Beroaldus discusses flattery at some length:

Sit igitur princeps non solum ipse praeditus prudentia, verumetiam
consiliarios prudentes habeat, quibus bene consulentibus credere possit.
Nemo enim per se unquam solus ita sapit: nemo ita circumspectus ac
sagax: nemo ita linceus est: ut non aliquando labet atque caecutiat:
quod si genuina quadam excellentique prudentia praeditus princeps
aliquando reperiatur: ut alieno consilio non egeat: tamen id faciat quod
summi navium gubernatores qui in magnis tempestatibus a vectoribus
admoneri non recusant. Consilium bonum (ut inquit verissime Marcus
Varro) et ei qui consulit, et qui consulitur bonum habendum est. . . .
Melior est respublica et prope tutior, in qua princeps malus est; ea in
qua sunt amici principis mali. Siquidem unus malus potest a pluribus
corrigi. Multi autem mali non possunt ab uno quamvis bono ulla ratione
superari. . . . Sicut fidi consiliarii et prudentes audiendi sunt: ita
assentatores, adultoresque explodendi qui ad voluptatem loquuntur
omnia, nihil ad veritatem. . . . Sane adulatio (prout clarissimi scriptorum prodiderunt) res servilis ac perniciosa. In aula principum
prope peculiariter gliscens vigensque, perpetuum (ut inquit Curtius)
regum malum: quorum opes saepius assentatio quam hostis evertit.
Quocirca etiam atque etiam caveant principes, ne aures assentatoribus
patulas praebeant: neque se adulari sinant.[3]

[1] "I do not wish to leave out an important heading."
[2] *De regimine principum,* stanzas 635 ff., 703.
[3] "Therefore the prince should not merely be endowed with prudence himself,
but should also have prudent counsellors in whom he can have confidence as advising him well. For no one unaided is ever through himself so wise, no one so
circumspect and sagacious, no one so lynx-eyed, that sometimes he will not waver

Erasmus also devoted a chapter of his *Institutio* to the subject, using as a basis the work of Plutarch on how to distinguish a flatterer from a friend, the source of much that has been written on the matter.

This twenty-third chapter of *The Prince* is obviously a continuation of its predecessor, reinforcing in varied language some of its ideas, as that a foolish prince will not have good advisers. After the first paragraph the discussion of flattery is abandoned; it easily leads up, however, to a discussion of ministers because the prince has two possibilities in the men around him; either they will be honest, of whatever grade of ability, or they will be selfish, adapting themselves to the prince for their own ends. This is the opinion of Commynes:

Ne sauroie dire par quel lien on se puisse asseürer [de toute foy et loyaulté] les ungs des autres, et par especial des grandes, qui sont asses enclins à leur voulenté sans regarder autre raison; et, qui pis vault, sont le plus souvent environnéz de gens qui n'ont l'oeil à nulle chose que à complaire à leurs maistres et à leur louer toutes leurs oeuvres, soient bonnes ou mauvaises. Et si quelcun se treuve que vueille myeulx faire, toute se trouvera brouillé.[4]

Castiglione, asserting that princes "più che d'ogni altra cosa hanno carestia di quello di che più che d'ogni altra cosa saría bisogno che

---

and be blind. If a prince should be found endowed with such genuine and excellent prudence that he does not need the advice of others, yet he should act as do the best pilots of ships who in great tempests do not refuse to be admonished by passengers. Good advice (as Marcus Varro truly says) is to be esteemed both by him who counsels and by him who is counseled. . . . A state is better off and almost safer in which the prince is wicked than one in which the friends of the prince are evil, since one bad man can be corrected by several, but many wicked men cannot in any way be overcome by one however good. . . . Just as faithful and prudent advisers are to be listened to, so yes-yes men and flatterers, who say everything that is pleasing and nothing that is true, are to be driven away. . . . Flattery, indeed (as the most famous writers set forth) is a thing servile and pernicious. In the courts of princes it especially grows and flourishes, the perpetual evil of kings (as Curtius says), for flattery overturns their power more often than does the enemy. Therefore kings should watch continually lest they present open ears to flatterers; nor should they allow themselves to be flattered" (*De optimo statu*, folio 131).

[4] "I cannot say by what bond one man can make sure of himself with respect to the others in all faith and loyalty; this is especially true of the great, who are sufficiently inclined to their will without regarding any other reason; and, what is worse, they are often surrounded with people who have an eye for nothing except pleasing their masters and praising all their deeds, be they good or bad. And if there is any great man who wishes to do better, he will find himself completely confused" (*Mémoires* 2.6, p. 129). Cf. the quotations on pp. 86, 179 ff., above.

avessero abundanzia, cioè di chi dica loro il vero e ricordi il bene,"[5] wished his courtier to be a perfectly honest "institutor" of the prince. He knew, however, that even the friends of the sovereign spesso, per guadagnar grazia e favore, non attendono ad altro che a propor cose che dilèttino e dian piacere all' animo loro, ancora che siano male e disoneste: di modo che d'amici divengono adulatori, e per trarre utilità da quel stretto commercio, parlano e oprano sempre a compiacenzia, e per lo più fànnosi la strada con le bugie. Le quali nell' animo del principe partoriscono la ignoranzia non solamente delle cose estrinseche, ma ancor di sè stesso.[6]

Like Machiavelli, Commynes accepted the tradition that a conceited prince was unlikely to get the truth from his advisers: "Je me suys mys en ce propoz pour ce que j'ay veu beaucoup de tromperies en ce monde, et à beaucoup de serviteurs envers leurs maistres, et plus souvent tromper les princes et seigneurs orguilleux, qui peu veullent ouyr parler les gens, que les humbles et qui vulentiers escoutent."[7] This, like so many things concerning the

[5] "More than anything else princes lack that which they need more than anything else if they are to have abundance, that is, they lack some one to tell them the truth and remind them of what is good" (*Il cortegiano* 4.6).

[6] "Often, to gain grace and favor, they consider nothing except the proposal of things that may amuse and give pleasure to the spirits of their masters, though these things may be evil and dishonest. This they do in such a way that they change from flatterers to friends, and to obtain profit from their close association with the prince, they always speak and act with complacency, and for the most part make their way with lies. These lies bring forth in the mind of the prince ignorance not merely of extrinsic things but even of himself" (ibid.).

Something of the renaissance spirit appears in the following observations by a practical politician on an American president: "I [Mr. Cannon] have always thought that President [Theodore] Roosevelt was led into this serious error of judgment by listening to talebearers instead of continuing his policy of discussing legislative matters at first hand with those who had charge of legislation. Had he adhered to that policy he would not have had any friction with the house. . . . The agents of the Secret Service constructed for the edification of the President a fantastic story. . . . It was as ridiculous as taking seriously the opinions of the village gossip. But this affair illustrated better than anything that occurred during the Roosevelt Administration the danger of having the President surrounded by men attempting to poison his mind. . . . I hope we shall never have another such incident in this Government, for as I read history it was by such methods that some of the greatest mistakes were made by able and popular rulers in the past which led to demoralization, conflict, and their downfall. . . .

"It was remarked by many people that some of President Roosevelt's advisers were so deficient in political judgment that it was fortunate he had a weakness for doing things himself" (L. White Busbey, *Uncle Joe Cannon*, New York, 1927, 232-40).

[7] "I have come to this opinion because I have seen so much of the deceptions of this world and especially of those of ministers toward their masters. Proud princes and lords, who have little wish to hear men speak, are more often deceived than those who are humble and willing to listen" (*Mémoires* 1.10).

ruler, had already been observed by Egidio, who puts it as advice
to be humble:

Verum quia nullus homo sufficit ad excogitandum omnia quae possunt
esse utilia toti regno, cum hoc quod Regem expedit esse solertem ex se,
quae bona sunt regno utilia excogitando, oportet ipsum esse docilem,
aliorum consiliis acquiescendo. Possumus enim dicere de Rege, quod
dicitur de Magnanimo 4. Ethicorum, quod non decet ipsum fugere
commoventem. Non enim decet Regem in omnibus sequi caput suum,
nec inniti semper solertiae propriae: sed oportet ipsum esse docilem, ut
sit habilis ad capescendam doctrinam aliorum, acquiescendo doctrinis,
et consiliis baronum, seniorum, sapientium, et diligentium regnum.[8]

Machiavelli, however, feels that a prince can be too humble,
and points out a sort of Aristotelian middle path that enables the
ruler to obtain honest advice without allowing free speaking to
those who would develop contempt from their privilege. He is
to choose wise men as councillors and to them is to allow free
speech on matters submitted to them but on no others. This is
perhaps an attempt to make practical use in government of the
proverb, already applied to the ruler by Machiavelli's predecessors,
that "nimia familiaritas hominum honoris parit contemptum,"[9]
and to combine with it the common notion that it befits the king
"legiferos honorare, religiosos venerari, sapientes sublimare; et con-
ferre cum eis, dubitabiles movere questiones, honeste interrogare,
discrete respondere."[10] The prince is to be completely "facilis" only
to the "bonis, ac doctis viris"[11] who will not abuse their privileges.

[8] "Since in fact no man can adequately think out all the things that can be
useful to the whole kingdom, and also since it is well for the king to be expert
on his own account in thinking out good things to benefit the kingdom, he should
show himself teachable by yielding to the advice of others. For we can say of the
king, as is said of the magnanimous man in the fourth book of the *Ethics,* that it
is not proper for him to run away from any one who disturbs him. For it does not
become the king to rely on his own head in everything, nor to rely always on his
own ingenuity, but he should be willing to learn in order that he may be capable
of receiving the teaching of others and relying on the instructions and advice of
barons, old men, wise men, and those wishing well to the kingdom" (*De regimine*
1.2.8).
[9] "Too much familiarity by men of rank brings on contempt" (*Secretum
secretorum* 1.11).
[10] "To honor those who make laws, to venerate the religious, to exalt the wise
and confer with them, to raise doubtful questions, to ask honestly, to answer dis-
creetly" (ibid. 1.10).
[11] "Good and learned men" (Patricius, *De regno* 8.11).
Burd in his edition of *The Prince* (p. 349) refers to Isocrates (*Ad Nicoclem*
28), whose opinion on flattery is given by Patricius (*De regno* 4.2). In the translation of Isocrates by Phileticus (1514) the ruler is advised: "Eis vero tu tribue
potestatem atque licentiam apud te loquendi liberiorem, qui rerum gestarum ex-

Humility is recommended to the king by the moralists, who feel that truth is hated only by the proud.[12]

Like the Florentine, however, Commynes expected the king to make his own decisions, and vividly delineated the danger of the prince who puts his authority, which he ought to guard above everything else, in the hands of another.[13] He does not, however, suggest that the overtrusted minister is likely to usurp the throne, perhaps because he was influenced by his observations in France, while Machiavelli, because of his Italian experience, easily adopted the Aristotelian idea that one man should not be made great.[14]

In one respect Commynes' master was the ideal prince of Machiavelli, for "il aymoit à demander et à entendre de toutes choses,"[15] and the prudent prince will be a "largo domandatore."[16] The verbal similarity is probably not significant.

However good the advice that resulted from this questioning, the prince must still unite the varied suggestions he gets from his ministers. Long before Machiavelli, this was understood by the author of the *Secretum secretorum;* after having consulted his advisers separately, with precautions against allowing his own opinion to appear, the ruler is to act as follows: "Tempta ergo in anima tua eorum voluntates, sicut facit cerebrum ex hiis quae proveniunt ei ex sensibus, et declina ab eorum consiliis in eo quod contrariantur voluntati tue."[17] Commynes well understood the varieties of counsel that might come to a prince, and how each adviser might think "alla proprietà sua:"[18]

---

perientia, gravitate, sapientia, fide caeteris praestant."—"Give power and rather free license in speaking to you to those who excel in experience in practical affairs, in gravity, wisdom, and faith" (sig. B4 recto).

[12] Clichtoveus, *De regis officio* 9.   [13] *Mémoires* 1.10; 2.6.

[14] See p. 30, above. In the *Secretum secretorum* 3.12 we read: "Sollicite et diligenter moneo te et do tibi optimum consilium quod nunquam constituas unum bajulum solum in regimine loco tui, quoniam ejus consilium posset destruere et corrumpere regnum tuum et convertere subditos et proceres ad se et intendere propriis utilitatibus et excogitare declinacionem tuam."—"I zealously and diligently advise you and give you the excellent counsel that you never set up a single minister in the realm in your place, for the advice of such an one can destroy and corrupt your kingdom and change to himself the allegiance of your subjects and nobles, and it can be directed to serve his own interests and to devise a decrease in your power."

[15] "He always liked to ask and to hear about everything" (*Mémoires* 2.6, p. 130).

[16] "A great questioner" (*Prince* 23, p. 46b).

[17] "Therefore test in your mind the desires of your advisers, as the brain does those things that come to it from the senses, and turn away from their advice in that which is contrary to your will" (*Secretum secretorum* 3.9, p. 135).

[18] "Of what relates to himself" (*Prince* 23, p. 47a).

Est bien necessaire à ung prince d'avoir plusieurs gens à son conseil, car les plus saiges errent aucunes fois très souvent; ou pour estre passionnéz aux matières di quoi l'on parle ou par amour ou par hayne ou pour vouloir dire l'opposite d'un autre, et aucunes fois pour la disposition des personnes: car on ne doit point tenir pour conseil ce qui se fait après disner. Aucuns pourroient dire que gens faisans aucunes de ces faultes ne devroient estre au conseil d'ung prince. A quoy fault respondre que nous sommes tous hommes, et qui les vouldroit cercher telz que jamais ne faillissent à parler saigement, ne jamais ne se meüssent plus une fois que aultre, il les fauldroit cercher au ciel, car on ne les trouveroit pas entre les hommes. Mais en rescompense aussy, et y aura tel au conseil qui parlera très saigement et très bien qui n'aura accoustumé de ainsi le faire souvent; et ainsi les ungs radressent les autres.[19]

When such is the *verità effettuale,* no wonder the prince whose policy will be wise must be gifted with prudence!

But having made his decision the king is still not entitled to be praised as prudent unless he executes his plans; after his planning, it remains "andare drieto alla cosa deliberata ed essere ostinato nelle deliberazioni sua."[20] In thus holding that the king should beware lest

> enterprises of great pith and moment
> With this regard their currents turn awry
> And lose the name of action (*Hamlet* 3.1.86-8),

Machiavelli was again adopting a tradition.[21] Egidio had said:

Sexto est in consiliis attendendum, ut diu consiliemur; et si adsit oportunitas, cito in opere exequamur. Nam cum adest oportunitas operandi,

---

[19] "It is very necessary for a prince to have several men to advise him, for the wisest are frequently in error, either because they have strong feelings on the matters under discussion or because of love or hate or desire to say the opposite of what some one else does, and sometimes because of the way they are feeling, for one ought not to take as good advice what is said after dinner. Some will say that men committing these faults should not be on the council of a prince. To this one must answer that we are all men, and he who wishes to find men who will never fail to speak wisely and who will not be moved at one time more than at another must needs seek them in heaven, for he will not find them among men. But as some compensation there will be a man in the council who will speak very wisely and well who does not do so very often; so some will make up for others" (*Mémoires* 2.2, p. 103).

[20] "To go ahead with what he has decided on and to be firm in his decisions" (*Prince* 23, p. 46ab).

[21] Burd in his edition of *Il principe* (p. 350) quotes from Isocrates, *Ad Nicoclem* 38, the passage rendered thus by Phileticus: "Ea vero te hortor efficias, quae quom non temere considerata abs te atque provisa fuerint, optima videbuntur."—"I exhort you to do the things which, when you have considered them without haste and carefully, seem best" (*De regno gubernando,* sig. C2 recto).

et si recte volumus et non illud facimus, hoc est quia ignoramus an expediat illud fieri. Bene ergo se habet diligenter quodlibet negocium discutere arduum, an utile sit illud facere; sed post quam per diuturnum consilium est recte cognitum quid fiendum, si adsit operandi facultas, prompte operari debemus. Bene ergo dictum est quod scribitur 6. *Ethicorum* quod consiliamur multo tempore, operamur autem prompte: et quod oportet consiliari tarde, sed facere consiliata velociter.[22]

The same principle was well known to Lorenzo the Magnificent, whose successful general asserts:

> Pensata con maturo e buon consiglio,
> vuole aver presta poi l'esecuzione.[23]

In the light of the Emperor Maximilian's inability to carry a policy to completion, as explained in this chapter by his Florentine critic, it is somewhat ironical that Dürer represented the emperor as attended by Firmitudo, Oportunitas, Alacritas, and Velocitas, expressive of his ability to carry into execution.[24] But the artist has in mind the ideal emperor rather than the reality.

[22] "Sixth, attention must be given to getting advice, that we may consult a long time, and if opportunity offers quickly execute the plan we have made. For when opportunity for acting comes, if we properly desire to act and do not, it is because we are ignorant whether it is expedient that the deed in question should be done. It is therefore a good thing to discuss diligently any difficult affairs to see if it is useful to carry them on. But after through daily consultation we rightly know what ought to be done; then if there is a chance to act we should act promptly. It is therefore well said which is written in the sixth book of the *Ethics,* that we should consider a long time but act promptly, and that it is proper to be slow in making plans but to be rapid in doing what has been planned" (*De regimine* 3.2.17).

Patricius quotes the "proverbium vetus": "Tarde consulendum esse, celeriter autem agendum."—"Slow in counsel, swift in execution" (*De regno* 6.9).

[23] "What has been planned with mature and good counsel should be swiftly executed" (*Rappresentazione,* p. 85).

The importance of swift execution has not escaped modern writers on military matters, who, in presenting the qualities of famous generals of the past, consider themselves as advisers for the leaders of the present—quite in Renaissance fashion. Admiral Mahan writes of "the emphasis he himself [Lord Nelson] laid upon that direct, rapid, and vigorous action without which no military operations, however wisely planned, can succeed. In the want of this, rather than of great professional acquirements, will be most frequently found the difference between the successful and the unsuccessful general; and consequently Nelson, who had seen so much of failure arising from slowness and over-caution, placed, and rightly placed, more stress upon vigor and rapidity, in which most are found deficient, than upon the methods which many understand, however ill they may apply them. . . . Nelson carefully planned the chief outlines of operations" (*Admiral Farragut,* pp. 309-10). For Farragut's own careful planning and celerity, see pp. 311, 316, etc. Cf. Mahan's *Life of Nelson,* pp. 141, 205, 226. See also J. F. C. Fuller, *The Generalship of Ulysses S. Grant,* p. 143.   [24] See p. 79, n., above.

Guicciardini shared the tradition with Machiavelli, writing:
Non si può biasmiare gli uomini che siano lunghi nel risolversi; perché
se bene accaggiono delle cose nelle quali è necessario deliberare presto,
pure per lo ordinario erra più chi delibera presto che chi delibera tardi;
ma da riprendere è sommamente la tardità dello eseguire, poi che si è
fatta la resoluzione, la quale si può dire che nuoca sempre e non giovi
mai se non per accidente; e ve lo dico perché ve ne guardiate, atteso
che in questo molti errano, o per ignavia, o per fuggire molestia, o per
altra cagione.[25]

Considering both this tradition of advising vigor and promptness of action when once plans had been formed and the importance of such qualities in the *verità effettuale* of all times, one is inclined to wonder why Machiavelli did not write further on it.
The twenty-third chapter, however, is hardly the place for further
treatment of the topic, since the subject of flattery no more than
permits allusion to the persistence in policy proper to the ruler and
presentation of the result of bad advice in the uncertain conduct
of Maximilian. There might have been a chapter on vigor and
promptness, or the subjects might have been discussed in various
places where there is some hint of them; for example, in the chapter on avoiding contempt and hatred, contempt is said to result
from pusillanimity and irresolution, but respect from spirited conduct, strength, and the power of irrevocable decision.[26] Perhaps
the causal literary structure of *The Prince* made easy the omission
of a section devoted to vigorous action, yet it may be noted that the
topic does not receive deliberate treatment elsewhere in Machiavelli's
writings. It is, moreover, evident that he would hardly have advo-
cated promptness or celerity without relation to circumstances. On
the contrary he would have advised the policy most fitting to the

[25] It is not possible to blame men because they are a long time in making up
their minds, since if they well may be censured for it in relation to the things
on which it is necessary to make a quick decision, yet ordinarily he errs more who
decides quickly than he who decides slowly. But tardiness in execution is much to
be reprehended, when once a resolution has been made, for this conduct can be
said always to injure and never to avail except accidentally. I tell you this that you
may be on your guard against such tardiness, because many err in it, either through
sloth or to escape trouble or for some other reason" (*Ricordi* 191). Notable is the
opinion that through accident even ill-advised conduct may bring advantage.

In his edition of Guicciardini's *Storia d'Italia,* Toffanin cites in illustration Sallust,
Bellum Catalinarium, cap. 1: "Nam et prius quam incipias, consulto; et ubi con-
sulueris mature facto opus est."—"Before you begin, plan; and when you have ma-
tured your plans it is time for action."

Cf. also Xenophon, *Cyropaedia* 1.6.23.   [26] *Prince* 19, pp. 35b-36a.

times.[27] The cautious and delaying movements of a Fabius may at times be better fitted to gain success than the headlong impetuosity of Pope Julius, though on the whole the advantage is with impetuosity, since Fortune is likely to favor the violent rather than those who proceed sluggishly.[28]

But perhaps the chief reason why Machiavelli did not write on the policy of vigor is that his whole theory implies it and depends on it, though always under the control of prudence. Princes with no firmness—*mal resoluti*—are the opposite of his ideal ruler;[29] under *ignavia* can be summed up most of the defects of the ruler who loses his state, and reliance on oneself and one's carefully made preparations is the height of political wisdom.[30] Neutrality is a worse policy than action.[31] The ruler who must needs be severe should be able to act decisively and vigorously enough to secure his future, exercising his power "a un tratto"—at one fell swoop.[32] The words are fairly common in Machiavelli's writings, often with the connotation of approval.[33] The "rari esempli" or striking examples of his capacity on which the prince relies for part of his reputation may consist in actions for the common good.[34] If the ideal prince sees, he is even more one who acts.

In warfare the capacity of the good ruler is usually expressed in celerity rather than in Fabian conduct. Even its planning must be rapid: "I regni che hanno buoni ordini, non danno lo imperio assoluto agli loro re se non nelli eserciti; perchè in questo luogo solo è necessaria una subita diliberazione e, per questo, che vi sia una unica podestà."[35] On the plan action must follow: "Sapere nella guerra conoscere l'occasione e pigliarla, giova più che niuna altra cosa."[36] In fact, so important is rapid action that a leader should look for opportunity "potere, in uno subito e fuora di sua opinione, assaltare il nimico; la quale cosa sempre sarà cagione di darti la vittoria."[37] Especially is it advisable to be swift

---

[27] *Prince* 25, p. 48b; *Discorsi* 3.9.   [28] *Prince* 25, last paragraph, p. 49b.
[29] *Prince* 21, p. 44b.   [30] *Prince* 24, last paragraph, p. 47b.
[31] *Prince* 21, p. 44b.   [32] *Prince* 8, last paragraph, p. 20a.
[33] E. g., *Discorsi* 1.45, end, p. 116a; *Arte della guerra* 7, p. 362a.
[34] *Discorsi* 3.34, p. 248a.
[35] "Well regulated realms do not give absolute power to the king except in armies, because there alone is sudden decision necessary, and for the sake of this there must be a single leader" (*Arte della guerra* 1, p. 272a). Cf. *Discorsi* 1.33, first paragraph, p. 101a. Contrast *Discorsi* 2.15, p. 159a.
[36] "In war to understand how to recognize the right occasion and to take it is of more importance than anything else" (*Arte della guerra* 7, p. 362b).
[37] "To be able suddenly and unexpectedly to him to assault the enemy—something that will always be the cause of giving you the victory" (ibid. 4, p. 321b).

in pursuit of a beaten enemy, or if defeated to take the utmost advantage of any lack of enterprise on the part of the victors:

Quando si vince, si dee con ogni celerità seguire la vittoria e imitare in questo caso Cesare e non Annibale; il quale, per essersi fermo da poi ch'egli ebbe rotti i Romani a Canne, ne perdè lo imperio di Roma. Quello altro mai dopo la vittoria non si posava, ma con maggiore impeto e furia seguiva el nimico rotto, che non l'aveva assaltato intero. Ma quando si perde, dee un capitano vedere se dalla perdita ne può nascere alcuna sua utilità, massimamente se gli è rimaso alcuno residuo di esercito. La commodità può nascere dalla poca avvertenza del nimico, il quale, il più delle volte, dopo la vittoria diventa trascurato e ti dà occasione di opprimerlo.[38]

Since enemies are often blind, the general whose motto is *impigre* can hope to escape from desperate situations.[39]

Understanding of the relation between prudence and conduct appeared in the Florentine politics of his own day, for Machiavelli had heard Savonarola explain in San Marco the connection between them:

Mostrò per qual cagione egli si era ritirato indreto, e disse: *prudentia est recta ratio agibilium.* Dipoi disse che tutti gli uomini avevono auto e hanno un fine, ma diverso; de' cristiani il fine loro è Cristo, degli altri uomini, e presenti e passati, è stato ed è altro, secondo le sette loro. Intendendo adunque noi, che cristiani siamo, a questo fine che è Cristo, dobbiamo con somma prudenza e osservanza de' tempi conservare lo onore di quello; e quando il tempo richiede esporre la vita per lui, esporla; e quando è tempo che l'uomo s'asconda, ascondersi, come si legge di Cristo e di S. Pagolo; e così, soggiunse, dobbiamo far noi, e abbiamo fatto, perciocchè quando fu tempo di farsi incontra al furore, ci siamo fatti, come fu il dì dell' Ascensione, perchè così lo

---

Cf. ibid. 7, p. 363a: "Le cose nuove e sùbite sbigottiscono gli eserciti."—"New and sudden events bewilder armies." For Duke Valentino's use of rapid movement and surprise see ibid. 7, pp. 358b-359a, and for that of di Fois see *Discorsi* 3.44, pp. 258b-259a.

[38] "One who has conquered ought with all speed to follow up his victory, imitating in this situation Caesar and not Hannibal, for the latter by standing still after he had routed the Romans at Canne lost by it the empire of Rome. But Caesar after a victory did not stand still but followed the routed enemy with greater impetus and fury than he had assailed them when they were intact. But after a defeat a captain should see if any advantage to him can come from the loss, especially if some part of his army is left with him. The possibility of doing something can come from the heedlessness of the enemy, who usually after a victory become careless and give you occasion to overpower them" (*Arte della guerra* 4, p. 323a).

[39] *Discorsi* 3.39, p. 254b.

onor di Dio e il tempo richiedeva; ora che lo onore di Dio vuole che si ceda all' ira, ceduto abbiamo.[40]

The Frate's Latin is found in the *Summa theologica* (2.2.47.2) of Aquinas, where the idea is attributed to the sixth book of the *Ethics* of Aristotle. In a following article, St. Thomas explains that prudence in its concern with *agibilia* may be divided into three parts: (1) *consiliari,* (2) *judicare de inventis,* but as to the third, "practica ratio, quae ordinatur ad opus, procedit ulterius; et est tertius actus ejus 'praecipere'; qui quidem actus consistit in applicatione consiliatorum et judicatorum ad operandum. Et quia iste actus est propinquior fini rationis practicae, inde est quod iste est principalis actus rationis practicae et per consequens prudentiae. . . .

Bonitas consilii requiritur ut ea quae sunt bene inventa applicentur ad opus; et ideo praecipere pertinet ad prudentiam, quae est bene consiliativa."[41]

Without making Machiavelli a theologian, one may suspect that he knew the source of the unarmed prophet's doctrine.

[40] "He showed the reason why he had drawn back, and said: 'Prudence is right reason in practical matters.' Then he said that all men have had and have one end, but differing according to conditions. The end of Christians is Christ; that of other men, both present and past, has been and is something else, according to their religion. Since then we are Christians, whose end is Christ, we should with the greatest prudence and observance of conditions preserve the honor of that end, and when the circumstances of the time require us to expose our lives for it, we should expose them; and when it is time for a man to conceal himself, we should conceal ourselves, as may be read of Christ and St. Paul; and so, he continued, we ought to do, and we have done, for when it was time to move against the fury, we did it, as on Ascension day, because that was demanded by the honor of God and by circumstances. Now, when the honor of God demands that we yield to wrath, we have yielded" (to Ricciardo Bechi, March 8, 1497, *Lett. fam.* 3, p. 18).

[41] "Practical reason, whose function is execution, proceeds further, and its third activity is to forestall others; this activity consists in the putting into execution of what has been planned and judged. And since this activity is nearer the end of practical reason, it is therefore the principal activity of practical reason, and consequently of prudence. . . .

Excellence in planning is required that the things which have been well devised may be applied to the work in hand; hence forestalling pertains to prudence, which certainly has to do with planning" (art. 8).

While a distinction is made between the *factibilia* and the *agibilia* (*Summa theol.* 2.2.47.5), the latter may suggest the immediately practical; see Tommaseo's *Dictionary, s. v. agibile,* for a reference to Agnolo Pandolfini. Du Cange, with a hint of the demand for swift execution of what has been planned, defines *agibilis* as *industrius, acer, strenuus, velox. Agibilia* is not a classical word. It appears in Aquinas' discussion of prudence in his commentary on Aristotle's *Ethics,* lib. 6, lectio 4.

Chapter 24

Cur Italiae principes regnum amiserunt.
(Why the princes of Italy have lost their states.)

This chapter reiterates much that has already been said: the necessity of labor and prudence, of gaining both the people and the great, of military training, of preparation in time for the inevitable change of fortune, of choice of the plan most feasable in the given circumstances, and of dependence on one's own virtue. In fact, the purpose is to exemplify what has already been said, "le cose soprascritte."

To good laws and good arms, mentioned in chapter twelve, good examples—"buoni esempli"[1]—are added, without explanation. They are not, it appears, the "esempli rari" of chapter twenty-one, which were calculated to impress the imaginations of subjects, but rather examples that subjects are likely to imitate, such as those discussed in *Discorsi* 3.29, where in conclusion are the verses of Lorenzo the Magnificent:

> E quel che fa 'l signor, fanno poi molti;
> Chè nel signor son tutti gli occhi volti.[2]

Lorenzo was versifying a well-known idea. Cicero had asserted:

Nec enim tantum mali est peccare principes, quamquam est magnum hoc per se ipsum malum, quantum illud, quod permulti imitatores principum existunt. Nam licet videre, si velis replicare memoriam temporum, qualescumque summi civitatis viri fuerint, talem civitatem fuisse; quaecumque mutatio morum in principibus extiterit, eandem in populo secutam. . . . Ego autem, nobilium vita victuque mutato, mores mutari civitatum puto. Quo perniciosius de re publica merentur vitiosi principes, quod non solum vitia concipiunt ipsi, sed ea infundunt in civitatem, neque solum obsunt, quod ipsi corrumpuntur, sed etiam

---

[1] *Prince* 24, p. 47a.

[2] For the context see p. 44, above.

To the same effect Louis XI spoke: "Et pour ce que tous ont plus loeil sus un prince que sus un autre et que ce qui est sur un hault lieu est plus tost congneu et contemplé que ce qui est en bas lieu, le Prince doit estre mirouer et exemple aux autres de toutes vertus se doit maintenir et gouverner en toutes choses comme son estat requiert."—"And because all turn their eyes on a prince more than on any other and one who is in a high place is sooner recognized and gazed at than one in a low place, the prince should be a mirror and example to others of all the

quod corrumpunt, plusque exemplo quam peccato nocent. Atque haec lex dilatata in ordinem cunctum, coangustari etiam potest; pauci enim atque admodum pauci honore et gloria amplificati vel corrumpere mores civitatis vel corrigere possunt.[3]

Wycliffe wrote of the king: "Oportet regem defendere legem propriam, et obediendo ac implendo ipsam exemplare aliis quomodo parebunt eidem."[4] Beroaldus was of the same opinion: "Platonis[5] sententia est. Quales in republica principes sint, tales reliquos solere esse cives. Vita principis (ut Plinii panegyristae verbis utar) censura est, eaque perpetua.[6] Ad hanc dirigimur, ad hanc convertimur nec tam imperio nobis opus est, quam exemplo."[7]

virtues and should keep and conduct himself in all things as his estate requires" (*Le rosier des guerres* 7, near the end).

Nicephorus Blemmydes also held that the king should be a παράδειγμα or example, controlling first himself and then his people. The need for self-control is implied rather than stated by Machiavelli in such chapters as *Prince* 14, 17, and 19, where it appears that the prince should school himself to endure privation and control his lusts, as Nicephorus would have him avoid licentiousness— ἀσελγεῖς ἔρωτας (*Qualem oporteat esse regem,* coll. 613, 616). The position of the ethical writers *de reg. pr.* is represented by lines in Milton's *Paradise Regained* 2.466-72:

> He who reigns within himself, and rules
> Passions, Desires, and Fears, is more a King;
> Which every wise and vertuous man attains:
> And who attains not, ill aspires to rule
> Cities of men, or head-strong Multitudes,
> Subject himself to Anarchy within,
> Or lawless passions in him which he serves.

[8] "It is not so much that it is bad for princes to sin (though this is in itself a great evil) as that there are many who imitate princes. For it is easy to see, if you care to recall past times, that the state was of such a character as were its greatest men, and that whatever change of habits took place among the great was afterwards to be seen among the people. . . . I think that when the character and habits of life of the nobles are changed that the manners of states are changed. Therefore vicious princes are the more ill-deserving from the state because they not merely take up vices for themselves but infuse them into the state; they do damage not merely because they are themselves corrupted, but because they corrupt others, and injure more by their example than by the fault itself. And this law which has been spread out over the whole order can also be made narrow. For a few, indeed a very few, when made great by honor and glory, can either corrupt the morals of the state or correct them" (*De legibus* 3.14).

[4] "The king should defend his own law, and by obeying and fulfilling it exemplify to others how they should keep it" (*De officio regis* 5 D, fol. 130a, p. 94, lines 11-13).

[5] Patricius (*De regno* 1.7; 8.4) also gives Plato as his authority for the importance of the king's example.

[6] Pliny's *Panegyric,* sec. 45. See *Pliny* in the index.

[7] "This is the opinion of Plato: Of whatever sort are the chief men of a state, such are generally the remainder of the citizens. The life of the prince (to use the

Somewhat further on[8] he quotes the well-known lines of Claudian:

> In commune iubes si quid censesque tenendum
> Primus iussa subi: tunc observantior aequi
> Fit populus: nec ferre vetat quum viderit ipsum
> Auctorem parere sibi: componitur orbis
> Regis ad exemplum: nec sic inflectere sensus
> Humanos edicta valent quam vita regentis.
> Mobile mutatur semper cum principe vulgus.[9]

Many of the older writers are eager that the ruler shall furnish a moral example; Giraldus, for instance, would have him glorious in true doctrine and religion.[10] Machiavelli also obviously desired that the ruler should be morally good, or at least that he should present the appearance of goodness. Certainly he desired the people of his prince's state to have good habits—"buoni costumi"[11]— such as might be derived from imitation of Scipio, who

> tutte le provincie e le città,
> Dovunqu' e' fu, lasciò piene d'esempi
> Di pietà, di fortezza e castità.[12]

But the discussion in *The Prince* says little on that matter, since the first thing is to keep the ruler in his position. Such maintenance of the prince lies behind the statement that a bad example is fur-

---

words of Pliny the panegyrist) is a censorship, and a continual one. Toward it we are directed and toward it we are turned, nor do we so much need command as example" (*De optimo statu,* folio 132 verso). He then quotes, without acknowledgment, from the passage from Cicero I have just quoted. The opinion attributed to Plato is from Cicero, *Ep. ad Fam.* 1.9.12. Cf. Isocrates, *Ad Nicoclem* 31.

[8] Fol. 133 verso.

[9] "If you order something in general and think it should be observed, be the first to observe it, for then the people will be made more observant of what is just, nor are they unwilling to submit when they see that the maker of the law obeys his own orders. The world is arranged according to the example of the king, and edicts do not have such influence on the human feelings as do the lives of those in power. The fickle populace always shifts with the prince" (*De quarto consulatu Honorii* 296-302). Claudian is quoted also by Giraldus (*De principis instructione* 1.16, p. 54; 1.20, p. 141), Pontanus (*De principe* 19, p. 271), and Clichtoveus (*De regis officio* 5, folio 19 recto).

The idea is expressed by Diomede Carafa (*De regentis officiis,* pt. 2, p. 655). Castiglione puts it thus: "La vita del principe è legge e maestra dei cittadini, e forza è che dai costumi di quello dipendan tutti gli altri."—"The life of the prince is the law and master of the citizens, and it must needs be that his habits influence all other men" (*Il cortegiano* 4.23).   [10] *De principis institutione* 1.20.

[11] *Discorsi* 1.18, p. 87a. See Ercole, *La politica,* pp. 251 ff.

[12] "All the provinces and the cities where he was he left full of examples of piety, of fortitude and chastity" (*Capitolo dell' ingratitudine* 97-9).

nished by a prince who makes a law and does not observe it himself.[13] A magistrate who wrests the law to his own ends, instead
of preserving justice according to the recommendation of writers
de regimine principum, loses his reputation because the people do
not feel that his decisions are "irrevocabile" as they must be if he
is to avoid hatred and contempt.[14] Such a governor is in fact the
tyrant, who is distinguished by his failure to rule according to law.
In his chapter entitled *Quod principem legibus subditum esse decet:
et suo exemplo vitaeque probitate subditos ad virtutem inducere,*[15]
Clichtoveus writes:

Quinimmo hoc ipso rex a tyranno discrimen habet: secundum Aristotelis
sententiam. Quod rex vitam agit legibus subditus: quas ad unguem
observat. Tyrannus vero nullis legibus esse vult subjectus: sed leges
tantum aliis dare non accipere. Immo quicquid ei placuerit: id apud
ipsum vim legis habet. Quoniam recta ratione non ducitur tyrannus:
neque disquirit quid iustum sit vel quid iniquum.[16]

The self-command that enables the ruler to keep the laws is necessary if the prince is to present a good example to his subjects.
Clichtoveus quoted from Claudian:

Tunc omnia iure tenebis:
Cum poteris rex esse tui.[17]

In order to give a proper example the prince, according to Castiglione, must go beyond statute law: "Poi formi dentro a sè stesso
e osservi immutabilmente in ogni cosa la legge della ragione, non
scritta in carte o in metallo, ma scolpita nell' animo suo proprio,
acciò che gli sia sempre non che familiare ma intrinseca, e con esso
viva come parte di lui."[18]

---

[13] *Discorsi* 1.45, p. 115b.   [14] *Prince* 19, p. 36a.

[15] "That the prince should be subject to his laws; and by his example and the
probity of his life influence his subjects to virtue" (*De regis officio* 5, folio 18 verso).

[16] "This is the point in which, according to Aristotle, a king differs from a
tyrant: the king lives in subjection to the laws, which he observes to the utmost,
but the tyrant wishes to be subject to no laws; he wishes merely to give laws to
others, but not to receive them. Still further, whatever pleases him has for him
the power of law, for the tyrant is not guided by right reason and does not investigate what is just or what is unjust" (ibid., folio 20 recto).

[17] "Rightly you will have dominion over all things when you are able to be
king of yourself" (Clichtoveus, *De regis officio* 4, folio 18 recto; Claudian, *De quarto
consulatu* 261-2).

[18] "Then he should form within himself and observe immutably in every thing
the law of reason, not written on paper or metal, but engraved in his very mind,

In *Discorsi* 1.45 Machiavelli turns from the failure of a ruler to keep his own laws to the folly of daily injuries to subjects. The connection implicit in his mind is perhaps that tyrannical government—for the advantage of a ruler rather than the republic, and characterized by the breaking of the laws[19]—leads to such oppression. Continual injuries inflicted by a tyrant or a tyrannical party involve violation of law or improper enforcement of law or partisan legislation. With this example of injustice and selfishness, the subjects "in ogni modo si assicurano ne' pericoli"[20] without regard to law. When the ruler sets an example of violence, the subjects are induced by fear to attempt his overthrow.[21]

In yet another manner good examples preserve the state. As is well known, Machiavelli held the theory that a state at intervals must be brought back to its original good constitution if it is to endure. A good citizen and yet more, we may infer, a good prince, can accomplish this, if the corruption of the state is not too far advanced, merely through his example:

Nasce ancora questo ritiramento delle republiche verso il loro principio dalla semplice virtù d'un uomo, sanza dependere da alcuna legge che ti

---

that it may ever be to him not familiar but intrinsic, and that he may live with it as part of him" (*Il cortegiano* 4.23).

The relation of sovereignty to law has been recognized in modern times, for example: "The power to commit violence, perpetrate injustice, take private property by force without compensation to the owner, and compel the receipt of promises to pay in place of money, may be exercised, as it often has been, by irresponsible authority, but it cannot be considered as belonging to a government founded upon law" (Opinion of Mr. Justice Field of the United States Supreme Court in Juillard *v.* Greenman, 110 U. S., 467). In his comment on the case Laughlin thinks of the mediaeval monarch as without restraint: "Is it conceivable . . . that the founders of our government, or the people of to-day, ever intended or meant to reconvey to Congress such unlimited powers to abuse and destroy as belonged only to a mediaeval monarch? . . . The people of the United States are no longer protected from the mediaevalism of unlimited power over money by any guarantees, except those of an enlightened public opinion" (J. Laurence Laughlin, *The Principles of Money*, p. 490). The writers *de regimine principum* in showing that the good ruler keeps the law were endeavoring to secure both enlightened public opinion and recognition of responsibility by the monarch himself.

"Paying humble tribute in manner, though not in matter" to Queen Elizabeth, Sir Philip Sidney said to her "that place was never intended for privilege to wrong: witness herself, who how Soveraign soever she were by Throne, Birth, Education, and Nature; yet was she content to cast her own affections into the same moulds her subjects did, and govern all her rights by their laws" (Fulke Greville, *Sidney,* chap. 6, pp. 80-1).

[19] E. g., *Arte della guerra* 1, p. 271. See *tyrant* in the index.

[20] "In every way secure themselves in perils" (*Discorsi* 1.45, p. 116a).

[21] *Prince* 7, p. 17b.

stimoli ad alcuna esecuzione: nondimanco sono di tale riputazione e di tanto esemplo, che gli uomini buoni disiderano imitarle, e gli cattivi si vergognano a tenere vita contraria a quelle. Quegli che in Roma particularmente feciono questi buoni effetti, furono Orazio Cocle, Scevola, Fabrizio, i dua Deci, Regolo Attilio, ed alcuni altri; i quali con i loro esempli rari e virtuosi facevano in Roma quasi il medesimo effetto che si facessino le leggi e gli ordini.[22]

On the other hand, Niccolò entitled a chapter in the *Discorsi, Che gli peccati de' popoli nascono dai principi.*[23] The horrible state of the Romagna before its lords were overthrown by Pope Alexander VI was only in part the result of negligent government; the first cause of the wickedness of the people was imitation of rulers spotted with "simili errori." As Clichtoveus put it: "Enimvero quantum prodest ad virtutis prosecutionem populo boni principis vita: tantum officit et nocet pravi regis improbitas. Siquidem alios pertrahit ad consimilia scelera perpetrandi studium: redditque eos suo exemplo ad malum propensiores."[24] As might be expected, Erasmus spoke warmly in the matter:

Nullius pestilentiae neque citius corripit, neque latius serpit contagium, quam mali Principis. . . . Vulgus nihil imitatur lubentius, quam quod a suo Principe fieri conspexerit. Sub aleatore passim luditur alea, sub bellaci bellaturiunt omnes, sub comessatore luxu diffluunt, sub libidinoso lenocinantur, sub crudeli deferunt et calumniantur. Evolve veterum historias, reperies semper ejusmodi fuisse seculi mores, cujusmodi fuerat Principis vita. Nullus cometes, nulla vis fatalis sic afficit res mortalium, ut vita Principis rapit ac transformat mores et animos civium. . . . Princeps vel ob hoc ipsum cavere debet, ne malus sit, ne tam multos exemplo suo reddat malos.[25]

[22] "This retraction of republics toward their beginning rises also from the simple virtue of one man, without depending from any law that can stimulate you to carry out something; yet they are of such reputation and their reputations are so powerful that good men desire to imitate them and wicked men are ashamed of a course of life contrary to theirs. Those who especially produced these good effects in Rome were Horatius Cocles, Scevola, Fabricius, the two Decii, Regulus Attilius, and some others; these with their unusual and virtuous examples produced in Rome the same effect as laws and regulations" (*Discorsi* 3.1, p. 195a).

[23] "That the sins of the people spring from their princes" (*Discorsi* 3.29, p. 240a).

[24] "Indeed to whatever extent the life of a good prince furthers the pursuit of virtue among the people, to a like extent the wickedness of an evil king obstructs and hinders it, if he brings his subjects to a desire for perpetrating similar horrid deeds and renders them by his example more inclined to evil" (*De regis officio* 5, fol. 21).

[25] "There is no pestilence of which the contagion takes hold more quickly or spreads more widely than that of an evil prince. . . . For the multitude imitates nothing more willingly than what it has seen done by its prince. Under a dicer

In urging his prince to furnish good examples, Machiavelli uses the language of the tradition in an effort for good government, the antithesis of tyranny.

there is continual throwing of dice, under a warlike prince all are ready for war, under a spendthrift they give themselves over to luxury, under a licentious ruler they become panders, under a cruel one they tell tales and calumniate. Turn over the histories of the ancients and you will find that the manners of any age were of the same sort as the life of the prince. No comet, no fatal power so affects mortal things as the life of the prince seizes on and transforms the manners and spirits of the citizens. . . . For this reason the prince should beware lest he become evil and render many evil by his example" (*Institutio principis* 1, 568 F-569 B).

Chapter 25

Quantum Fortuna in rebus humanis possit, et
quomodo illi sit occurrendum.[1]
(The power of Fortune in human affairs, and
how she may be resisted.)

All of the mediaeval and renaissance writers *de regimine principum* were acquainted with the theories of Fortune, one of the topics
most familiar in Europe for centuries. Petrarch, for example, wrote
a work entitled *De remediis utriusque Fortunae,* and Pontanus
three books *De Fortuna,* as Machiavelli wrote his *Capitolo della
Fortuna.* In a work on princes Fortune appears with special propriety, because, as Gower remarks, it is the

> king, which on the whiel
> Fortune hath set aboven alle.[2]

A similar assumption dominates another poem which is a specialized example of the work *de regimine principum,* since its first
purpose is to warn rulers against wickedness through examples of
the misfortunes that deprive the unjust of their high estates—
Lydgate's *Fall of Princes.*[3] The figure sitting on the top of Fortune's wheel in graphical representations often wears a crown,
since the prince is *par excellence* the man lifted up by Fortune.[4]

Given such opinions, one expects to find references to Fortune
in books of advice to princes, and a few occur; Giraldus, for
example, asks at the beginning of his chapter entitled *De principis
audacia et animositate:* "Cum autem audaces fortuna juvet et
provehat, quem magis animositas et audacia quam magnos et
fortunatos decet?"[5] Egidio follows Aristotle's treatment of fortune,

---

[1] For Machiavelli's general view of Fortune, see Ercole, *La politica,* pp. 5 ff.

[2] *Confessio Amantis* 7.3172-3.

[3] 4.1996 ff.; 9.3239-302, and passim. Had Machiavelli seen the original of
Lydgate's work, the *De casibus virorum illustrium* of Boccaccio?

[4] See the illustrations in Patch, *Fortuna,* and the frontispiece of the present
volume.

[5] "Since fortune aids and exalts the bold, for whom more than for the great
and fortunate is spirit and audacity fitting?" (*De principis instructione* 1.14). Cf.
Prince 25, p. 49b: "Meglio essere impetuoso."—"Better to be impetuous." Cf.
p. 222, n. 2, below.

as does Patricius.[6] Beroaldus in *De optimo statu* touches on the famous debate concerning the influence of Fortune on the rise of the Roman power. But though the goddess is not forgotten, the number of references is smaller than might be expected. For this there are good reasons. "Quoniam fortuna principum in edito et praelustri sita est loco,"[7] their Fortune is likely to be discussed with relation to overthrow rather than rise; Lydgate, for instance, comparatively seldom speaks of the rise of Fortune's wheel.[8] But the conventional writer *de regimine principum* is advising a ruler in the full current of affairs, not one likely to fall; his ideal is the Utopian one of the happy father of a loving family. So far as he is among those who were accused by Machiavelli of presenting only imaginary states, serious reverse of fortune is not his concern. Or if he belongs to the highly moral school, his theory is that the good prince, docile to the advice he offers, will live in sanctified prosperity. The flattering adviser will avoid any suggestion that his virtuous patron may be overthrown; Boccaccio did not dedicate *De casibus* to a prince.

To be sure there were writers who realized that kings could be overthrown as punishment for their wickedness, as Lydgate and his originals so completely did. Such overthrow, however, is the work of Providence or the divine vengeance; Fortune as the avenger is subject to God and rational in her punishment of evil. But such a Fortune ceases to be Fortune, for mutability is of the essence of that goddess. If she is endowed with rationality, it is

> Oltre la difension de' senni umani: . . .
> occulto, come in erba l' angue.[9]

But Lydgate, in his confusion, gives her intelligibility. Sometimes, indeed, he quite forgets her and attributes the overthrow of the wicked directly to God.[10]

---

[6] Egidio, *De regimine* 3.2.16; Patricius, *De regno* 7.10; see also 1.12.

[7] "Since the Fortune of princes is seated in a lofty and magnificent spot" (Pontanus, *De principe,* p. 270).

[8] *Falls of Princes* 4.2640-2968; 5.2341-2403.

[9] "Beyond the power of defence against it by human thoughts: . . . hidden like a snake in the grass" (*Inferno* 7.81-4).

[10] *Falls of Princes* 9.1057. Commynes was unwilling to employ Fortune in political explanation: "Il fault bien dire que ceste tromperesse Fortune l'avoit bien regardé de son mauvais visaige. Mais, pour mieulx dire, il fault respondre que telz grandz mistères ne viennent point de Fortune et que Fortune n'est riens, fors seullement une fiction poetique et qu'il failloit que Dieu l'eust habandonné. . . . Il est vraysemblable et chose certaine qu'il estoit eslongné de la grace de Dieu de

Machiavelli believed himself quite unlike the writers alluded to. He did not set out to illustrate the righteous vengeance of God on the immoral, flattery was not his main business, and above all he did not hold a Utopian view, rather considering that in the *verità effettuale* there is no stability in human affairs, for Fortune is unpredictable and

Le sue permutazion non hanno triegue.[11]

As a result, Fortune pervades *The Prince* as she does no other similar work. She is ever present; few of the chapters are without references to Fortune or associated matters such as occasion, chance, time as the "mother of many mutations,"[12] or the variable things of the world. This dotting of the pages with references to mutability shows the author's preoccupation in his advice to the ruler; the work is, as it were, an exhortation to be ready against the uncertainty of the future. This is a world of flux and reflux; times of prosperity must be looked on not as normal but as opportunities in which the wise man will prepare for the deluge; no man knows the time of change; when it comes there is reasonable hope of survival only for him who is well prepared. The circumspect ruler, however, can do much to protect himself. Diomede Carafa is perhaps nearest Machiavelli in his sense of the uncertainty of the ruler's position. If the prince has leisure from domestic difficulties, he should look abroad to determine which rulers might in case of need be the best allies. "Propter incertos temporum casus"[13] expert generals and money for military purposes should always be ready. All the finances should be so administered, that the prince will be ready for sudden and unexpected events.[14] But even the writers most conscious of the uncertainty of the ruler's state are

---

se estre mis ennemy de ces troys princes et n'avoir ung seul amy qui l'eust osé loger une nuyct. Et autre Fortune n'y avoit mis la main que Dieu."—"It is certainly necessary to say that this deceiver Fortune had looked on him with her unfavorable countenance. But to put it better, one must say that such great mysteries do not come from Fortune at all, and that Fortune is nothing except a poetic fiction, and that it must needs be that God had abandoned him. . . . It seems to be and is a certain thing that he was separated from the grace of God when he was made an enemy of these three princes and did not have a single friend who dared to give him one night's lodging. No other Fortune than God had laid hand on him" (*Mémoires* 4.12, II, 86, on the ruin of the Count of Saint-Pol).

[11] "Her permutations offer no truces" (*Inferno* 7.88).

[12] Sidney, *Arcadia* 3.4, p. 373.

[13] "Because of the uncertainties that appear as time passes" (*De principis officiis*, pt. 1, p. 652).   [14] Ibid., pt. 3, beginning, p. 657.

much less concerned with it than is Machiavelli, who advises not the secure but the insecure ruler.

One defense against unfavorable Fortune is the internal one; though external goods, those vain goods which alone are under Fortune's sway, may fail, the mind of man is not subject to her power. According to Patricius, Hannibal was conquered by unfavorable Fortune, who shows her power more in war than anywhere else,[15] yet he did not yield, but "virtutem animi erigens,"[16] went on with his plans. By his example "monemur fortunae virtutem neutiquam cedere."[17] Still he finished his career as a suicide, wholly deserted by Fortune. The courageous attitude was approved by Machiavelli, as he shows in a chapter of the *Discorsi*

[15] Cf. Lorenzo il Magnifico, *San Giovanni e Paolo,* p. 85, where an outgoing general, uncertain of his return, says: "Fortuna nella guerra poter suole."—"Fortune is usually very strong in war." Patricius, *De regno* 7.3, attributes to Caesar the words: "Fortuna, quae in rebus bellicis semper plurimum potest."—"Fortune, which in matters of warfare is ever exceedingly influential." He applies it to the defeat of the skilful Hannibal at Zama. Caesar's words are: "Fortuna, quae plurimum potest cum in reliquis rebus tum praecipue in bello" (*De bello civili* 3.68). Polybius says substantially the same thing (2.4.5).

Fortune is still real to writers on military affairs. For example, Admiral Mahan writes of a naval engagement: "The loss of the head sails, and all that followed, is part of the fortune of war; of that unforeseeable, which great leaders admit may derange even the surest calculations. It is not, therefore, to be complained of, but it is nevertheless to receive due account in the scales of praise and blame; for the man who will run no risks of accidents accomplishes nothing" (*Sea Power in Its Relations to the War of 1812,* 2.141). Many such passages are to be found in his military writings. Of a mediaeval campaign Captain Nickerson writes: "This very reasonable plan failed through inaccurate timing and through Philip's combination of good judgment and good luck" (Spaulding, Nickerson, and Wright, *Warfare,* p. 348). In dealing with another mediaeval battle, the same writer attributes something to the aid of "good fortune" (*Oman's Muret,* in *Speculum* 6 [1931], 552). General Napier writes: "It can never be too often repeated that war, however adorned by splendid strokes of skill, is commonly a series of errors and accidents" (*Peninsular War,* bk. 12, chap. 5). Again and again he refers to Fortune by name (e.g., 14.6; 16.4, 7; 18.4). For other instances, including one from General Ludendorff, see Eugene S. McCartney, *Warfare by Land and Sea,* pp. 161-2, and Archibald F. Becke, "Waterloo Campaign," *Encyclopaedia Britannica,* 14th ed., 23.418. Guicciardini wrote with prophetic vision as well as historical truth when he asserted: "Quanto la fortuna possi nelle cose della guerra, . . . ne sono pieni tutti e libri, e testimonio infinite esperienze."—"All the books are full of the power fortune has in the affairs of war and many experiences testify to it" (*Discorsi politici* 13, p. 343).

In such matters the theory of warfare has not advanced beyond renaissance standards; knowledge of it, indeed, seems less generally disseminated than in the time of Machiavelli.

[16] "Arousing the force of his spirit" (*De regno* 7.3).

[17] "We are warned that virtue should never yield to fortune" (ibid.).

entitled *Le republiche forti e gli uomini eccellenti ritengono in ogni fortuna il medesimo animo e la loro medesima dignità.*[18]

Another type of defense is to stop in the mid-career of prosperity and refuse to tempt Fortune by further efforts. This, with its necessity for careful calculation of circumstances, smacks of Machiavelli's theory of proper adjustment to conditions.[19] It was the view of Budé who writes:

Les hommes prudents ne s'abandonnent du tout à icelle Fortune. Mais ilz se retirent de bonne heure, quand ilz veoient, qu'ilz ont assés esprouué les cas fortuits, ou quand ilz sentent, que le vent de prosperité & aspiration celestielle ne les veult fauoriser plus auant, & aussy quand ilz se doubtent, que celle puissance, qui les a esleués sur les aultres & sublimés, se lasse de les soustenir, & plus porter. Car aussy bien s'ilz n'y mettent ordre, & qu'ilz n'asseurent leur pied sur le degré de suffisance, auquel ilz veoient, qu'ilz se pourront maintenir & asseoir leurs garnisons de Prouidence: ilz tumbent & decheoient en grande ruine, sans qu'ilz y sçaichent mettre ordre, ou prouision conuenable: & s'ilz ne peuuent euiter un dangereux reculement, & honteux trebuchement du lieu, auquel ilz sont montés ou grauiz.[20]

Augustus Caesar, he says, paused in the expansion of the Roman Empire. The same sentiment is that of Costantino in the *San Giovanni e Paolo* of Lorenzo il Magnifico:

> Vittoriosa la spada rimetto,
> per non far piú della fortuna pruova,
> ché non sta troppo ferma in un concetto.[19]

As apparently a well-known sentiment, Machiavelli uses it in a humorous passage. One of the speakers in the *Art of War* com-

---

[18] "Strong states and praise-worthy men retain the same frame of mind and the same dignity no matter what their fortune" (3.31).

[19] *Prince* 25, p. 49b.

[20] "Prudent men do not entirely abandon themselves to Fortune. But they retire early, when they see that they have made sufficient tests of good luck, or when they perceive that the wind of prosperity and the breath of heaven does not wish to favor them more, and also when they suspect that the power which has raised them above others and put them in a high place gives up sustaining them and carrying them on. For if they do not attend carefully to it and make sure their feet on that rung of the ladder of satisfaction on which they see that they are able to maintain themselves and to make sure what they have received from Providence, they fall and tumble down in grand ruin, unless they know how to make suitable arrangements and provision, and unless they are able to escape a dangerous set-back and a shameful fall from the place to which they have mounted or climbed" (*De l'institution du prince*, chap. 33, p. 140).

[19] "I put up my victorious sword in order to make no further test of Fortune, for she does not long stand fixed in one opinion" (p. 101).

pares himself to a dictator: "Poichè sotto l'imperio mio si è vinto una giornata sì onorevolmente, io penso che sia bene che io non tenti più la fortuna, sappiendo quanto quella è varia e instabile. E però io disidero deporre la dittatura."[20] Machiavelli's serious view is not very different; the belief that a ruler could pause when he would rests on the assumption that he has full control of affairs. For Niccolò security of quiet, if it is possible, can be found only in retirement from the principate.

A relative security against Fortune is possible to the prudent man who foresees specific evils and takes measures against them, or who makes general preparation fitting to the conditions. As Patricius says, "Sicut optimus gubernator plagas omnes coeli circumspicit, ut ad omnem vim ventorum semper paratus sit, sic princeps se munit contra adversa omnia."[21] In the military or semi-military affairs where Fortune is especially important, rather more than in merely civil affairs, the value of such preparation is clear. The ruler who has prepared his town for a long siege can, if he remains courageous, hope to retain it "perchè le cose del mondo sono sì varie, che egli è quasi impossibile che uno potessi con gli eserciti stare uno anno ozioso a campeggiarlo."[22] A ruler who has carefully studied military affairs can as it were by industry lay up a store of capital which will enable him to resist Fortune when the change comes. As he leads his army he will seldom encounter an accident for which he will not have the remedy.[23]

In these parts of The Prince the author is concerned chiefly with defensive war. In offense the same preparation would enable the advantages furnished by Fortune to be siezed on. In the territory of the Samnites the experienced Publius Decius saw the hill left open by the mentally blind defenders and "impigre"[24] occupied it. Fortune gave the occasion and his experience fitted him to grasp it. As Fabrizio, the chief speaker in the work Dell' arte della guerra, said,

[20] "Since under my generalship a battle has been so honorably won, I think it will be well that I shall not tempt Fortune further, since I know how variable and unstable she is. Therefore I wish to lay down the dictatorship" (Arte della guerra, lib. 4, first sentence). Cf. Discorsi 1.26, p. 94b.

[21] "As the good pilot surveys all quarters of the sky that he may be prepared against all the violence of the winds, so the prince fortifies himself against all adverse circumstances" (De regno 6.11).

[22] "Because the things of the world are so various that it is almost impossible that any one will be able with his armies to remain in one place a year to besiege him" (Prince 10, pp. 22b-23a).   [23] Prince 14, p. 30a.

[24] Discorsi 3.39, p. 254b. On military promptness, see pp. 193 ff., above.

Gli uomini che vogliono fare una cosa, deono prima con ogni industria prepararsi, per essere, venendo l'occasione, apparecchiati a sodisfare a quello che si hanno presupposto di operare. E perchè, quando le preparazioni sono fatte cautamente, elle non si conoscono, non si può accusare alcuno d'alcuna negligenza, se prima non è scoperto dalla occasione; nella quale poi, non operando, si vede o che non si è preparato tanto che basti, o che non vi ha in alcuna parte pensato.[25]

Thorough preparation enables a leader not merely to give an acceptable excuse for failure, but also in some measure "signoreggiare" Fortuna,[26] "perchè le cose previse offendono meno."[27] The captain who guards against ambush in a region favorable to his enemy will give the hostile forces few opportunities to avail themselves of the aid of Fortune. Or when in battle a sufficient reserve is provided, Fortune is unlikely to favor the enemy:

Il maggiore disordine che facciano coloro che ordinano uno escercito alla giornata, è dargli solo una fronte e obligarlo a uno impeto e una fortuna. Il che nasce dallo avere perduto il modo che tenevano gli antichi a ricevere l'una schiera nell' altra; perchè, sanza questo modo, non si può nè sovvenire a' primi, nè difendergli, nè succedere nella zuffa in loro scambio; il che da' Romani era ottimamente osservato. [He then explains that they used three lines that could be brought successively into action.] Questo modo di rifarsi tre volte è quasi impossibile a superare, perchè bisogna che tre volte la fortuna ti abbandoni e che il nimico abbia tanta virtù che tre volte ti vinca.[28]

[25] "Men who wish to accomplish some action ought first of all to prepare themselves with great diligence, so that when the occasion comes they may be ready to carry out what they have planned to do. And because when preparations are made cautiously they are not known, no one can be accused of negligence if his preparation is not revealed before the suitable occasion. But if he fails to act when it does come, it is apparent that he has not made enough preparation or that he has not thought about it at all" (*Arte della guerra* 1, p. 269ab).

[26] "To be master of Fortune" (ibid. 2, p. 302b).

[27] "Because things foreseen do less damage" (ibid. 5, p. 335a).

[28] "The greatest violation of the correct principles for drawing up an army in order of battle is to give it a single line and limit it to one charge and one fortune. This rises from the loss of the ancient method of receiving one part of the army within another, for without this method the second cannot come to the aid of the first soldiers, nor defend them, nor go into the combat in their places; this was admirably attended to by the Romans. . . . This mode of renewing the combat three times it is scarcely possible to overcome, because it is necessary that fortune should abandon you three times and that the enemy should have so much power as to conquer you three times" (*Arte della guerra* 3, p. 304ab).

Wellington's cavalry tactics were not dissimilar: "A reserve must always be kept, to improve a success, or to cover an unsuccessful charge. . . . Normally a cavalry force should form in three lines. . . . The second line should be 400 or 500 yards from the first, the reserve a similar distance from the second line.

If Fortune does favor the enemy three times, there is no further defense; the wisest tactician, wholly abandoned by Fortune, will surely be ruined.

The defense against Fortune by foresight and careful preparation is not to be confused with over-caution. In fact, as the end of chapter twenty-five says, action and even violent action constitutes a defense against Fortune; for, as is written in the *Adagia* of Erasmus:

Cicero, Tuscul. Quaest. lib. 2. *Fortes enim non modo fortuna adjuvat, ut est in veteri proverbio, sed multo magis ratio. . . .* Admonet adagium fortiter periclitandam esse fortunam. Nam his plerunque res prospere cedere. Propterea quod id genus hominibus fortuna quasi faveat, infensa iis, qui nihil audent experiri, sed veluti cochleae perpetuo latent intra testas.[29]

Vigorous action is to be preferred to the laziness—*ignavia*—[30] that says: "Non fussi da insudare molto nelle cose, ma lasciarsi governare alla sorte."[31] To be sure there are times when one should adopt a policy of "temporeggiando per essere a tempo a potere pigliare la buona fortuna, quando la venissi,"[32] but this is only to get the right time for decisive action, according to the advice that Machiavelli late in life sent to Guicciardini: "Voi sapete quante occasioni si sono perdute, non perdete questa nè confidate più nello starvi, rimettendovi alla fortuna e al tempo, perchè col tempo non vengono sempre quelle medesime cose, nè la fortuna è sempre quella med-

---

. . . This is found not too great a distance to prevent the rear lines from improving an advantage gained by the front line, nor too little to prevent a defeated front line from passing between the intervals of its supports" (C. W. C. Oman, *Wellington's Army*, p. 111). Wellington's plan, "evolved from his Peninsular experience," from the *verità effettuale*, is intended to guard against bad fortune and improve the opportunities of favoring fortune.

[29] "Cicero, *Tuscul. Quaest.* bk. 2. For not merely does fortune aid the strong, as it is put in the old saying, but reason does still more. . . . This saying advises that fortune is to be tried with vigor; to men who do this, things often go prosperously. The reason is that fortune seems to favor men of this kind, but is hostile to those who do not dare to risk anything, but like snails always lie hidden in their shells" (1.2.45, col. 88 C). See *Tuscul. Disput.* 2.11.

[30] *Prince* 24, p. 47b.

[31] "One should not sweat much over things, but turn over the control of them to fate" (*Prince* 25, p. 48a).

[32] "Temporizing in order to be able at the right time to lay hold of favoring Fortune when she comes up" (letter to Giovanni Vernacci, Feb. 15, 1515, *Lett. familiari* 44, p. 180).

esima."[33] He who will in this way "on Occasion's forelock watchful wait"[34] must live in a state of mental alertness and be ready
for prompt and decisive action, if he is to approach the ideal presented by Machiavelli under the figure of the wheels of Fortune:

> Sarebbe un sempre felice e beato,
> Che potessi saltar di rota in rota.[35]

Since Fortune is unlikely to be overcome by the lazy, though she
may at times favor them, our author could have her habits in mind
when he wrote to Vettori: "Io credo, credetti, e crederrò sempre
che sia vero quello che dice il Boccaccio: che egli è meglio fare e
pentirsi, che non fare e pentirsi."[36] Such doing, to be sure, is that
of the man who has foreseen the tempest and, unlike the Italian
princes who have lost their realms, need not flee helplessly before
it; he has taken to heart the principle that "quelle difese solamente
sono buone, sono certe, sono durabili, che dependono da te proprio
e dalla virtù tua."[37] In a letter of advice for Pope Clement, Guicciardini concretely represents the conclusion of his school of Italian
thought on vigorous action and its implications:

Non concorro già con voi nella opinione che mi accennate per la
vostra, e me l'avete scritto etiam per altre, che noi di nostra natura non
siamo per muoverci, se non a partiti piani e bene sicuri ec.; perchè io
ho Nostro Signore per prudente, nè credo che si abbi appropriato tanto
il nome di Clemente, che si sia dimenticato che il naturale suo è Iulio,
e che non si ricordi che oggi dì il pontificato ha più riputazione dalle
qualità della persona sua, che da quella che gli dia per sè stesso il nome
della Sedia Apostolica; e però che da lui si ricerca e espetta molto più
che da ogni altro pontefice, e mancando a questa espettazione farebbe
grandissimo male agli altri, ma maggiore a sè con eterno carico. Né
dico questo perchè io desiderassi i partiti precipitosi, i quali non lauderò
mai se non per necessità; ma non manco biasimerei chi avessi deliberato
non si volere muovere se non a partiti sicuri e vinti; anzi quando fussi

[33] "You know how many occasions have been lost. Do not lose this one or
trust too much in keeping quiet, giving yourself over to fortune and time, because
the same things do not always come with time nor is fortune always the same"
(letter of May 17, 1526, *Lett. familiari* 65, p. 232).

[34] Milton, *Paradise Regained* 3.173. Cf. Machiavelli's *Capitolo dell' Occasione* 10.

[35] "He would be ever happy and blissful who was able to leap from wheel to
wheel" (*Capitolo di Fortuna* 116-7).

[36] "I believe, always have believed, and always will believe that Boccaccio was
right when he said that it is better to act and repent than not to act and repent"
(to Vettori, Feb. 25, 1513, *Lett. familiari* 32, p. 141).

[37] "Only those defences are good, certain, and durable that depend on
yourself and your own virtue" (*Prince* 24, p. 47b).

necessitato a uno de' dua, forse reputerei minore errore il primo; perchè
la fortuna fa qualche volta a chi la tenta miracoli, ma molto più rade
volte a chi non si muove. Credo in effetto che si ruinerà sperando ed
espettando: chi espetterà che la natura per sè medesima lo liberi da sì
gravi accidenti, e anche chi volesse accelerare di rompere il collo, troverà
facilmente il modo; però lauderei chi si deliberassi, venendo occasione,
che avessi speranza saltem pari al pericolo, pigliarla.[38]

This is like the opinion of Niccolò as expressed in this chapter on
Fortune, in that on the reputation of the prince,[39] and throughout
his writings.

Though a prudent captain will endeavor to secure himself
against misfortune by fighting only when he has the advantage of
position, numbers, and the like,[40] on the other hand he will sometimes, throwing himself on the support of Fortune, dare the risks
of combat against superior foes:

La necessità nasce quando tu vegga, non combattendo, dovere in ogni
modo perdere; come è: che sia per mancarti danari e, per questo, lo esercito tuo si abbia in ogni modo a risolvere; che sia per assaltarti la fame;
che il nimico aspetti de ingrossare di nuova gente. In questi casi sempre
si dee combattere, ancora con tuo disavvantaggio, perch'egli è assai meglio tentare la fortuna dov' ella ti possa favorire, che, non la tentando,
vedere la tua certa rovina. Ed è così grave peccato, in questo caso, in uno
capitano il non combattere, come è d'avere avuta occasione di vincere e

---

[38] "I do not agree with you in the opinion you indicate to me as yours and
have written to me by others, that we naturally should not be inclined to move,
except according to plans that are clear and certain; for I esteem our master as a
prudent man, nor do I think he has so taken to himself the name of Clement that
he has forgotten his earlier one was Julius and that it must not be every day re-
called that the pontificate has more reputation from his personal qualities than is
given it by the name of the apostolic seat in and for itself, and therefore that from
him is sought and expected much more than from any other pontif, and that if
he did not fulfil this expectation he would do great evil to others, but still more to
himself, with eternal discredit. I do not say this because I desire hasty plans, which
I would praise only in case of necessity; but nonetheless I should blame anyone
who had decided not to consent to move except according to secure and certain
plans. Indeed if it were necessary to use one of the two procedures, perhaps I should
think the first the lesser error, because Fortune sometimes does miracles for him
who tempts her, but much more rarely for him who does not make any move.
I truly believe that he who waits until nature herself liberates him from a difficult
situation can be ruined by hoping and waiting, and that he who wishes to hasten
on to break his neck will easily find a way to do it. Therefore I should praise him
who would decide, when there comes an occasion which offers hope at least equal to
its peril, to take it" (to Sigismondo Santo, May 28, 1525, *Opere inedite* 8.247-8).

[39] *Prince* 21, p. 45a.

[40] Also a principle of modern warfare. Admiral Mahan approves and justifies from
Napoleon the saying of Nelson: "Only numbers can annihilate" (*Nelson*, p. 688).

non la avere o conosciuta per ignoranza o lasciata per viltà.[41] I vantaggi qualche volta te gli dà il nimico e qualche volta la tua prudenza. Molti, nel passare i fiumi, sono stati rotti da uno loro nimico accorto.[42]

Our author is here making a special application of the principle that sometimes there can be no secure plan, and that the lesser evil must be embraced as a good;[43] with it he has joined the belief that Fortune favors the bold. To these proverbial ideas he has given clarity of his own. The material was also familiar in earlier writers on the art of war.[44] Egidio Colonna, following Vegetius, advised a leader to plan carefully "priusquam pugna publica committatur: melius est enim pugnam non committere, quam absque debita praevisione fortunae et casui se exponere."[45] In all respects he should endeavor to surpass his enemy, yet Egidio gives directions for combatting a large force with a small one. A good general will be alert for opportunity, as to attack his enemy when crossing a river; if the enemy expect reinforcements "vel non est bellandum, vel acceleranda est pugna."[46] All the elements must be

---

[41] For an opportunity lost to Venice through incompetence see *Arte della guerra* 4, p. 325b. Cf. a letter to Guicciardini of Nov. 5, 1526, *Lett. familiari* 69, p. 238: "Gli Spagnuoli hanno potuto qualche volta farci di gran natte, e non lo hanno saputo fare; noi abbiamo potuto vincere, e non abbiamo saputo."—"The Spaniards have some times been able to play us some clever tricks and have not known how to do it; we have been able to conquer and have not known how."

[42] "Necessity arises when you see that if you do not fight there is every probability that you will lose, as when you lack money and for this reason your army is certain to go to pieces, or when you are out of provisions, or the enemy expects to be reinforced by new soldiers. In these cases it is always necessary to fight, even at a disadvantage, because it is much better to tempt Fortune when she is able to favor you than without tempting her to see your certain ruin. And it is as grave a fault, in that case, for a captain not to fight, as it is to have had occasion for victory and not to have known it because of ignorance or lost it through baseness. Advantages are sometimes given to you by the enemy and sometimes by your own prudence. Many when passing rivers have been routed by a watchful enemy" (*Arte della guerra* 4, p. 324a).

To the same effect is *Discorsi* 2.10, p. 153a. This section is in harmony with modern opinion. Admiral Mahan often refers to the inevitable risks of war and makes proper taking of risk the mark of the great leader (*Armaments and Arbitration* 214, *Nelson* 227, *Farragut* 144). A decision of Nelson's to fight at a disadvantage is praised; secondarily to his decision Nelson was also looking for a good opportunity (*Nelson* 665). The brave Decatur is not praised for avoiding bloodshed when battle offered a possible opportunity of serving his country (*War of 1812*, 2. 403).   [43] *Prince* 21, p. 45a; see p. 176, above.

[44] Burd, *Le fonti . . . nell' Arte della guerra.*

[45] "Before engaging in general actions; for it is better not to join battle than without proper pre-consideration to expose oneself to fortune and chance" (*De regimine* 3.3.9).

[46] "Combat must either be given up or joined immediately" (ibid.).

taken into account, including audacity of spirit as well as externals, yet "forte enim nunquam contingeret omnes conditiones praefatas concurrere ex una parte: ubi tamen plures et meliores conditiones concurrunt, est pars potior ad bellandum."[47] Though Egidio sees that a leader cannot hope for all the advantages and must take some risk, he is far from rising to Machiavelli's conception that it is censurable to avoid combat, though without *meliores conditiones,* when inaction is dangerous.

It is not difficult to suppose that Machiavelli would have desired his captain to risk doubtful battle for political as well as strictly military reasons; something of the sort is implied in his assertion that a prince had better lose with his own forces than win with those of others,[48] or his praise of Philip of Macedon for carrying on war against the Romans in spite of his weakness;[49] the wise prince will defend himself, trust something to Fortune, lose gloriously, rather than show lack of enterprise—*ignavia* or *viltà*.[50] If he will have the reputation necessary to success, he must establish himself as one not too timid "con le arme in mano correre la fortuna sua."[51] This is illustrated by the career of Pope Julius; being in a situation where nothing could be gained without risk, he hazarded vigorous action and succeeded. A timid or over-cautious man, seeking a sure plan and an unexceptionable decision, would have attained nothing.[52]

Guicciardini is equally clear in this matter:

La fortuna volentieri favorisce chi si arrischia. Le istorie sono piene di infiniti esempli di persone che da estremi casi si sono liberati con la animosità e con lo entrare francamente ne' pericoli, de' quali non debbe spaventare chi è in caso di necessità; nè è temerità el pigliargli sanza vedere le cose troppo misurate; perchè ne' casi difficillimi non si può avere la sicurtà, nè si può una infermità di tanto pericolo cacciare sanza usare rimedi pericolosi; anzi la troppa prudenzia è imprudenzia nelle difficultà, e in fatto merita di essere chiamato prudente così colui che,

[47] "Perhaps it will never happen that all the aforesaid conditions will meet at one time, but when many and the more important of them come together, the better plan is to fight" (ibid.).

[48] *Prince* 13, pp. 27b-28a.   [49] *Prince* 24, p. 47b.

[50] *Prince* 24, p. 47b; *Discorsi* 3.10, p. 217b; 31, p. 244a; 37, p. 252b. See p. 68, above. In his *Discorsi politici* 14, p. 195, Guicciardini speaks with feeling on showing "nelle estremità la sua virtù, la sua generosità."—"In extremities his virtue, his nobility of feeling."

[51] "With sword in hand to put his fortune to the test" (*Prince* 21, p. 44a; see pp. 175 ff., above.   [52] Ibid., p. 45a.

quando la natura delle cose lo ricerca, sa rimettersi in qualche parte alla potestà della fortuna, come chi sa eleggere e partiti sicuri quando la sicurità si può avere.[53]

So far as Machiavelli in his treatment of the proper taking of risks improved on his predecessors, the reason is to be found in his observation of the particular and his power for combination of various elements in a principle of conduct. The similarities between him and other renaissance theorists on the one hand and recent writers on the art of war on the other suggest that sixteenth century concepts of Fortune as applied to the theory of warfare are founded on the *verità effettuale* of human nature and earthly conditions, such as those of topography.[54]

Evidently Machiavelli would not have been wholly satisfied with the internal victory over Fortune, commendable as is the virtue it requires. Like Pontanus,[55] he held the ancient doctrine that felicity demanded material as well as spiritual goods. But he is clearer than Pontanus in asserting that these external goods are not under the control of Fortune alone but are also subject to the human will.[56] Man can be in part the maker of his own destiny as absolutely as can Fortune. To be sure man's power is limited; as Patricius remarked, "Nemo enim inveniri potest, qui in rebus dubiis fortunam suam in consilio habeat; nec etiam quum de alienis deliberat futurum eventum divinare potest."[57] Fortune is in control of half or perhaps more than half of man's affairs, but the

[53] "Fortune is glad to favor him who takes risks. Histories abound with examples of persons who have been freed from desperate conditions by spirit and frank entrance into perils, which should not be feared by a man pressed by necessity. Nor is it temerity to enter into perils without measuring them carefully, for in difficult matters there can be no assurance, nor can so perilous a disease be cured without perilous remedies. On the contrary, when one is in difficulty too much prudence is imprudence, and in fact he who, when the state of affairs demands it, knows how in some fashion to give himself over to the power of fortune, deserves to be called prudent just as much as does the man who knows how to choose reliable plans when he is in security" (*Discorsi politici* 14, p. 196).

Much the same thing is said in Guicciardini's letter to Cesare Colombo, Dec. 24, 1525, *Opere inedite* 8.373; cf. also *Ricordi* 311. Remitting oneself to fortune here implies courageous taking of risks; in one passage from Machiavelli (p. 211, above) it implies sloth—*ignavia*. Cf. also pp. 176, note, and 214, above.

[54] See the footnotes on pp. 192 ff., 207 ff.

[55] *De Fortuna* 1.24: *Quantum bona Fortuna conferat ad felicitatem.*

[56] *Prince* 25, p. 48a.

[57] "No one can be found who in uncertain things can have Fortune among his advisers; not even when he deliberates on the affairs of other men is he able to divine what will come to pass" (*De regno* 7.10).

remainder can be mastered by the prudent, volent, and laborious man. Nor is the power of Fortune complete in certain instances and in others unexercised. Fortune is ever at work and man always may be. Duke Valentino could not have averted the death of his father or his own illness, but he could have provided against evil consequences from the first if Fortune had not used also the weapon of the second—perhaps an instance in which Fortune showed herself arbiter of more than half. Yet the evils of the second could have been abated had the duke been more prudent with respect to the election of the next pope. At the very worst there is left to man some opportunity for choice; under the control of Fortune the order of things will present no completely secure opportunity for action, but man still has opportunity for prudence in attaining "conoscere le qualità degli inconvenienti e pigliare il meno tristo per buono."[58] Thus at any and every moment man has opportunity to exercise his own will to modify the course of events. Because of the mutability of Fortune and the complete uncertainity of the future, the virtuous man never has reason to acknowledge himself beyond hope.[59]

Fortune also at times concurs with the plans of men, as in the instance of Julius II. "Gli uomini possono secondare la fortuna";[60] in fact Pontanus, in a chapter entitled *Fortunam et prudentiam interdum convenire*,[61] wrote:

Quanquam autem et dictum, et abunde probatum est, prudentiam rationemque fortunae prorsus adversari, nihilominus hac in parte, hocque in ipso munere videntur sibi quodammodo subblandiri. Namque ut prudentia ipsa rationis rectae praesidio et dirigit, et ducit ad finem incepta hominum, negotiaque suscepta: sic idem illud molitur ac praestat bona fortuna, impetusque ipse naturalis. Illud tamen interest, quod prudentia actiones dirigit et consilio susceptas, et ratione temperatas: fortuna vero secus, quippe quas ab impetu susceptas, ductu suo et perficit, et gubernat.[62]

[58] "To know the qualities of inconveniences and take the least objectionable one as a good thing" (*Prince* 21, p. 45a).   [59] Compare p. 143, above.

[60] "Men are able to aid fortune" (*Discorsi* 2.29, p. 187b).

[61] "Fortune and Prudence sometimes unite" (*De fortuna* 2.8).

[62] "Though it is said and abundantly established that prudence and reason are utterly opposed to fortune, none the less in this place and in this very matter they seem to aid one another. For as prudence by the help of right reason directs and brings to an end what has been begun by men and the business they have undertaken, so good fortune and natural impetus itself labors for and aids the same end. But there is this difference, that prudence directs actions that are undertaken after

In order to produce this agreement, a man must be prudent enough "variare co' tempi";[63] if he can do this, he will ever have good fortune, but of most men as of Pope Julius it must be said:

Se fossero venuti altri tempi che avessono ricerco altro consiglio, di necessità rovinava; perchè non arebbe mutato nè modo nè ordine nel maneggiarsi. E che noi non ci possiamo mutare, ne sono cagioni due cose: l'una, che noi non ci possiamo opporre a quello a che c'inclina la natura; l'altra, che, avendo uno con uno modo di procedere prosperato assai, non è possibile persuadergli che possa fare bene a procedere altrimenti: donde ne nasce che in uno uomo la fortuna varia, perchè ella varia i tempi, ed elli non varia i modi.[64]

This suggests the possibility of being born fortunate, of which Pontanus wrote in his chapter entitled *Fortunatos infortunatosque a natura esse institutos,*[65] where we read:

Quas ob res si natura quaedam irrationalis est fortuna, naturae huic ut adscribatur, necesse est, utque natura ab ipsa fortunati hi, illi vero infortunati et dicantur et sint. Qua in re illud etiam necesse est usuvenire ut hi quam illi natura ab ipsa magis minusve instituti sint ad fortunae fructus colligendos. . . . Videmus enim quosdam ita genitos, institutosque a natura, qualis Cato fuit is, qui cognomen habuit ab Utica, ut nullius eos suasio, nulla vis, impotentiaque, nullus etiam terror a proposito suo, suaque ab electione detorqueat: quos nesciam an fortunatos iudicem, etiam cum bene illis successerit, quando pertinaciae id, certisque eorum ac firmis propositis videatur prorsus adscribendum. Contra haec alios, qui ab incepto itinere et facile et statim dimoveantur, ac relicta ratione, prudentioribusque, admonitionibus atque consiliis, viam ingrediantur aliam, alienis minime vestigiis inhaerentes, ut qui vagi, palantesque ferantur. Qua e re, quod ita sors ferat, naturalis ille impetus praesidio illis est, ac favori, quod scilicet ratione relicta impetum sint secuti, ut videatur similitudo ipsa naturae simul eos conciliare, appareantque propter hanc conditionem, ab ipsa etiam natura fortunati:

---

consideration and tempered by reason, but fortune, quite otherwise, by its assistance makes perfect and governs what is undertaken impetuously" (ibid.).

[63] "To vary with the times" (*Discorsi* 3.9, title).

[64] "If there had come other times that demanded another plan, of necessity he would have gone to ruin, because he would not have changed his manner or rules for conducting himself. And there are two reasons why we are not able to change ourselves; one is that we cannot oppose that to which nature inclines us; the other is that it is not possible to persuade a man that he would do better by acting otherwise; thence it comes about that the fortune of a man varies because times change but his habits do not change" (*Discorsi* 3.9, p. 215a). Cf. the quotation from Alberti, p. 131, above.

[65] "The fortunate and the unfortunate are determined by nature" (*De fortuna* 2.13).

et quantum a ratione diversi ferantur, ac devii, tantum et fortasse amplius concilientur fortunae. Et qui, qua ratio vires extendit suas, parum ipsi prudentes videantur, parumque consulti, sint tamen ad fortunae promerendum favorem maxime appositi, et tanquam affabrefacti, naturalem ob levitatem, consimilesque impulsus.[66]

This suggests the remark in *The Prince* on the good fortune of Julius II, who, having adopted an imprudent plan, yet succeeded "fuora di ogni opinione e sua e d'altri."[67] The Machiavellian Fortune evidently has affinity with that of Pontanus. The Florentine's originality consists partly in his insistence on the power of Fortune in affairs of state and in his integration of his theory with practical advice to the ruler.

Machiavelli's concept of Fortune is of the essence of his theory of life and affairs. His world is not one ruled according to the intelligible decrees of a benevolent providence, but one in which man's well-being depends on his own efforts in a baffling medium. He emphasizes Fortune as do none of the other writers *de regimine principum* because of his desire to go to the *verità effettuale* of things, that he may write something genuinely useful to his readers. Seeing a world in flux, he cannot in honesty do anything other than advise men how to attain their ends in such a world. The first end of the prince is to maintain his state; if he will do this, he

---

[66] "Therefore if fortune is a sort of irrational nature, as it is said, it is necessary that by nature itself some are said to be and are fortunate, others are unfortunate. Accordingly it necessarily happens that the fortunate and the unfortunate are by nature herself more or less designated for gathering the fruit of fortune. . . . For we see certain ones so born and so formed by nature, as was Cato who had his surname from Utica, that the persuasion of no one, no force, no lack of power, even no terror can turn them aside from their determination and their choice. I do not know whether I should judge such men fortunate even when they are successful, since their success should certainly be ascribed to their sure and well-founded plans. On the opposite side we see others who are easily and immediately turned from the path on which they have set out and who, abandoning reason and more prudent admonitions and counsels, go another way, not at all following the steps of others, like those who go about uncertain and wandering. On account of this, since chance permits it to be so, their natural impetuousness is a protection and help to them, because, abandoning reason, they have followed their impulse; for this reason the very resemblance seems to unite them with nature, and at the same time for this reason they appear to be made fortunate by nature herself, and in proportion as they depart far from reason and wander about, they are perhaps the more closely united with fortune. And those who, where reason extends her sway, appear not very prudent and not very judicious, may yet be wholly fitted to obtain the favor of fortune, and as though ingeniously suited for it on account of their natural levity and their like impulses" (*De fortuna* 2.13).

[67] "Beyond every expectation, both his own and that of others" (*Prince* 13, p. 27b).

must in the turning of Fortune's wheels be able "saltar di rota in rota."[68]

This theory of the instability of human society leads to the quality of Machiavelli's exhortations. To be liberal today may win friends; tomorrow liberality may be "stracciata e rotta"[69] and usury and fraud may be powerful and rich. Nothing remains fixed and permanently calculable. Hence the inadequacy of the counsel of Budé for avoiding misfortune by ceasing to move in any direction.[70] Machiavelli might advise a ruler to restrict or enlarge his ambition, and might give precepts suited to different sorts of state, but security cannot be attained by mere limitation. Pause or retrograde movement may bring destruction, and safety rather than ruin may be found in expansion. Let the ruler shake off the old advice adapted to an unreal and static world and from the lessons of history and experience come to understand what Fortune is and does:

> Costei spesso gli buon sotto i piè tiene,
> Gl' improbi innalza; e se mai ti promette
> Cosa veruna, mai te la mantiene.
>
> E sottosopra e regni e stati mette,
> Secondo ch'a lei pare, e' giusti priva
> Del bene che agli ingiusti larga dette.
>
> Questa incostante dea e mobil diva
> Gl' indegni spesso sopra un seggio pone,
> Dove chi degno n'è, mai non arriva.
>
> Costei il tempo a suo modo dispone;
> Questa ci esalta, questa ci disface,
> Senza pietà, senza legge o ragione.[71]

Whether Machiavelli was right or wrong in his interpretation of man's condition is not to be decided here. We need only observe that his whole body of advice is founded on a world in which uncertainty prevails. Such a theory is in part the result of his own temperament, as are most theories of human affairs. Other writers

---

[68] "To leap from wheel to wheel" (*Capitolo di Fortuna* 117).

[69] "Broken and routed" (ibid. 90).   [70] P. 208, above.

[71] "Fortune often keeps good men under her feet and exalts the wicked; and if she ever promises you anything she never keeps her promise. She turns upside down kingdoms and states just as she likes and deprives the just of the goods that she freely gives to the unjust. This inconstant goddess and variable divinity often puts the unworthy in a seat the worthy man never attains. She arranges the time for things as she will; she exalts us, she undoes us without pity, without law or reason" (*Capitolo di Fortuna* 28-39).

saw the ultimate verity in another sort of world, in which, for example, a ruler should under all circumstances keep faith, as part of his adherence to a fixed norm of conduct essential to welfare here and hereafter. Machiavelli has been inexorably honest in presenting the results of his own philosophy, in which the felicity of the prince is dependent on prudence and strength in a turmoil of irrationality.

Chapter 26

Exhortatio ad capessendam Italiam in libertatemque a
barbaris vindicandam.
(An exhortation to take hold of Italy and restore her
to liberty from the barbarians.)

This last chapter presents the specific problem in the mind of
the author—that of free Italy. Yet occupation with some specific
condition is not out of harmony with the practice of writers *de
regimine principum*. Hoccleve, for instance, gives half his work
to his personal affairs, and may almost be said to have written to
encourage the king to display liberality and other princely qualities
that would lead him to pay the poet's pension. Giraldus Cambrensis wrote because of the wickedness of the kings of his day.
The second and third parts of his work constitute a bitter attack
on Henry II, and the first part is a norm of princely conduct with
which the wickedness of the king may be contrasted. Both Gilbert
of Tournai and Vincent of Beauvais wrote because of the special
interest of King Louis IX in the subject, and seemingly with his
preferences in mind. Egidio Colonna in writing for his pupil Philip
the Fair modified his Aristotelianism with reference to the French
monarchy. Erasmus, addressing Prince Charles, used the chapter
entitled *de bello suscipiendo,* which normally would have dealt
with military affairs, to attack all war and praise peace—one of his
own favorite ideas. Nor is this last chapter of *The Prince,* as an
exhortation, to be looked on as not an original and necessary part
of the work. Burd briefly shows the incorrectness of this superficial view.[1]

To chapter twenty-four it offers a contrast; if the princes of
Italy have lost their states, the new prince trained by Machiavelli
need not do so; the failure of the old princes has resulted from their
sluggishness—"ignavia"—strikingly shown in a "defetto quanto
alle armi"[2] which the virtuous and well-trained new prince will

[1] Burd's edition of *The Prince,* chap. 26, pp. 365-6. On the unity of *The Prince*
see Chabod, *Sulla composizione de "Il Principe" di Niccolò Machiavelli.*

[2] "Inadequacy with respect to arms" (*Prince* 24, p. 47b). Cf. Seneca, *Medea* 159:
"Fortuna fortes metuit, ignavos premit."—"Fortune fears the bold, but bears hard
on the slothful."

avoid. The first paragraph of chapter twenty-four, however, showing the glory of the new prince who gives his country good laws,
good arms, and good examples, is almost an antecedent part of
chapter twenty-six, in which also appears the glory of the prince.

Chapter twenty-five, following from its immediate predecessor
in order to show the extent to which Fortune, blamed by dispos-
sessed rulers, is properly responsible, leads up also to the last, where
we read that *The Prince* is set forth at this time—"al presente"—
because the author, having considered the matter, has concluded:
"Io non so qual mai tempo fussi più atto a questo."[4] Moreover
Fortune now favors the house of the Medici, which has also the
virtue seldom joined with Fortune, but necessary to a successful
issue.[5] Even in a world of flux and uncertainty largely controlled
by the fickle goddess, there is at the moment every probability
that a virtuous prince can establish in Italy a permanent government. Without consideration of the power of Fortune, Niccolò
could not properly have affirmed that the hour for Italy's salvation had come.

Of "tutte le cose di sopra discorse"[6] a number of others reappear
in this chapter. Military affairs receive their emphasis under the
expected heads: the prince as captain in person and citizen armies
with all the laws they imply. It is also repeated that weakness of
the leaders is what ruins the armies, with the implication that
good examples are needed.

There also appear matters less evident in preceding chapters.
While warfare has been often mentioned, its justice or injustice has
not been discussed, though something was implied in the account
of Ferdinand the Catholic in chapter twenty-one. In earlier chapters
the gaining of a principality by military conquest is repeatedly
spoken of, with little suggestion of approval or disapproval; it appears chiefly as a scientific fact which the political writer must
take into consideration. In chapter three it is recognized as natural:
"È cosa veramente molto naturale e ordinaria desiderare di acquistare; e sempre, quando gli uomini lo fanno che possono, saranno
laudati o non biasimati; ma quando non possono e vogliono farlo
in ogni modo, qui è lo errore e il biasimo."[7] This refers to complete

[4] "I do not know what time has ever been better suited to this" (*Prince* 26,
p. 49b).   [5] *Discorsi* 1.10, p. 75a.
[6] "All the things dealt with above" (*Prince* 26, p. 49b).
[7] "It is surely a thing very natural and ordinary to wish to acquire things, and
when men do it who can they will always be praised and not blamed; but when

conquest from which good government can follow; any other sort
is frowned on by Machiavelli. Yet a ruler is advised to fight rather
than "lasciare seguire uno disordine per fuggire una guerra."[8]
Under such circumstances war may be looked on as a necessity.
In the present chapter, however, the establishment of a new principate by military power is made a pious duty; never in history had
there been more just occasion for war. Machiavelli here echoes the
sentiment he assigns to Rinaldo degli Albizzi: "Sono solamente
quelle guerre giuste, che sono necessarie; e quelle armi sono pietose,
dove non è alcuna speranza fuora di quelle. Io non so quale necessità sia maggiore che la nostra, o quale pietà possa superare quella
che tragga la patria sua di servitù."[9] But though the conflict necessary to Italian liberty would be chiefly against the "barbaro dominio"[10] of foreign invaders, it is difficult to assert that Machiavelli's plan would not also have involved assaults on Italian princes
and even on free cities if they stood in the way of the deliverers or
seemed likely to offer footholds to further invaders; the powerful
foreigner must be in every way excluded.[11] To some extent, then,
the champion of liberty is a conqueror. Yet the prince by right
of the sword is not of necessity a tyrant; on the contrary, Castiglione, though deploring the lust of some princes "dominare ai
suoi vicini,"[12] yet writes:

Però debbon i principi far i populi bellicosi non per cupidità di dominare, ma per poter difendere sè stessi e li medesimi populi da chi
volesse ridurli in servitù, ovver fargli ingiuria in parte alcuna; ovver
per discacciar i tiranni, e governar bene quei populi che fussero mal
trattati; ovvero per ridurre in servitù quelli che fussero tali da natura,
che meritassero esser fatti servi, con intenzione di governargli bene e
dar loro l'ozio e 'l riposo e la pace.[13]

---

they are not able to and all the same wish to do it, here is their error and a reason
for blaming them" (*Prince* 3, p. 9ab).

[8] "To allow damage to result for the sake of escaping a war" (ibid., p. 9b).

[9] "Only those wars are just that are necessary, and those arms are piously taken
up aside from which there is no hope. I do not know what necessity can be greater
than ours, or what piety can be greater than that which delivers one's fatherland
out of slavery" (*Istorie Fiorentine* 5.8, p. 505a).

[10] "Barbarian dominion" (*Prince* 26, p. 51b).

[11] *Prince* 3, p. 7b.

[12] "To rule over their neighbors" (*Il cortegiano* 4.27, p. 382).

[13] "Therefore princes should make their people warlike not because of a desire
to rule over other states, but in order to be able to defend themselves and their own
people from any one who wishes to reduce them to servitude or to injure them in

This is not far from the position of Machiavelli in his last chapter; even in the earlier ones, though conquest is prominent, the first function of arms is the preservation of the state.

Such wars St. Thomas had in mind when he declared that "illi qui juste bella gerunt, pacem intendunt,"[14] and that if war is just, "requiritur uti sit intentio bellantium recta; qua scilicet intenditur vel ut bonum promoveatur, vel ut malum vitetur."[15] Though a friend of peace, Clichtoveus was willing to allow such wars:

Nunquam tamen ineatur bellum: nisi ut demum compositis rebus quiete tranquilleque vivatur: quod et Cicero in officiis faciundum monet. Suscipienda quidem (inquit) sunt bella ob hanc causam: ut sine iniuria in pace vivatur. Et rursum. Bellum autem ita suscipiatur: ut nichil aliud quam pax quaesita videatur. At vero ante omnia necessarium est: quod suscipitur bellum iustum esse et ex legitima causa initum: aut ad reprimendam malorum audaciam grassantium depopulationibus in regnum aut ad tuendam regionem atque rempublicam ab iis qui opprimere eam tentant.[16]

As an Italian patriot, Machiavelli found such a view of just warfare quite satisfactory. Nor is his present attitude a negation of his earlier chapters. Even a savior of Italy would have to walk in a difficult path and adopt at times methods superficially like those employed by tyrants.

---

some way, or in order to drive away tyrants and to govern well those peoples who were badly treated, or to reduce to servitude those who are slaves by nature and who deserve to be made slaves, with the intention of governing them well and giving them quiet and rest and peace" (ibid.).

[14] "Those who wage wars justly have peace in mind" (*Summa theologica* 2.2.40.1).

[15] "It is necessary that the purpose of those who carry on war should be just, by which is meant that either good is promoted or evil is shunned" (ibid.).

See also Alfred Vanderpol, *La Doctrine scholastique du droit de guerre*, pp. 15-158.

[16] "War never should be begun except with the purpose that at last, when things have been settled, life may be quiet and tranquil, as Cicero advises should be done in *De Officiis* [1.34]. Wars, he says, are to be undertaken only for this reason, that without injury life may be lived in peace. And again he says that wars should be so begun that nothing other than peace seems to be sought for. But in truth it is necessary before everything else that any war entered upon be just and begun for some proper cause, whether for repressing the boldness of wicked men who are growing into a formidable power by their ravages or for protecting the country and the state from those who attempt to oppress it" (*De regis officio* 16).

In the same chapter Clichtoveus approves the religious wars of Ferdinand which Machiavelli estimates as hypocritical and Guicciardini thinks not to have such a purpose as Clichtoveus demands. See pp. 166 ff., above.

With this view of warfare is associated an idea expressed in *The Prince* only here, though implied throughout;[17] the ruler of Machiavelli's dream will bring "bene alla università degli uomini"[18] of Italy. This is the *bene commune, utile publico,* or *bene publico* of which Machiavelli often speaks, and the consideration of which lies at the heart of his political theory. Its meaning appears in his enthusiastic description of Rome under good government:

In quelli [tempi] governati da' buoni, vedrà un principe sicuro in mezzo de' suoi sicuri cittadini; ripieno di pace e di giustizia il mondo: vedrà il Senato con la sua autorità i magistrati co' suoi onori; godersi i cittadini ricchi le loro ricchezze; la nobilità e la virtù esaltata: vedrà ogni quiete ed ogni bene; e, dall' altra parte, ogni rancore, ogni licenza, corruzione e ambizione spenta: vedrà i tempi aurei, dove ciascuno può tenere e difendere quella opinione che vuole. Vedrà, in fine, trionfare il mondo; pieno di riverenza e di gloria il principe, d'amore e sicurtà i popoli.[19]

This is immediately followed by a still more vigorous picture of the horrors of life under a tyrant, who regards not the *bene commune,* but the *bene particolare.* The two are often contrasted by Machiavelli as when he says that what Piero did was "per salute della patria e non per ambizione sua,"[20] and that the good Camillus labored "ad utile publico e non a propria utilità."[21] In Machiavelli's time his readers would have understood that in specifying the *bene commune* the author was implicitly excluding the *bene proprio* of the tyrannical ruler. Mediaeval authors had reiterated it; for ex-

[17] See p. 168, above.

[18] "Good to the generality of the men" (*Prince* 26, p. 49b). See, for example, *Discorsi* 1.16, p. 83b; 58, p. 131b; 2.2, p. 142a; 19, p. 169b; 3.1, p. 196a; 16, p. 225a; 24, p. 235b; 28, p. 239b; 30, p. 241b; *Arte della guerra,* proemio; *Istorie Fiorentine* 7.1, p. 562a. For discussion see Ercole, *La politica,* pp. 45 ff. Machiavelli sometimes spells *commune* and *publico* in the Latin fashion of his time.

[19] "In those ages governed by good men will be seen a prince secure in the midst of his secure citizens, and the country full of justice and peace; the senate will be seen to have its authority and the magistrates their honors; the rich enjoy their riches, nobility and virtue are exalted; every sort of quiet and good will be apparent; on the other hand, all rancor, all license, corruption, and ambition have disappeared; it will be a golden age, where every man is able to hold and defend whatever opinion he wishes. In short, the country will appear completely happy, with the prince abounding in reverence and glory, and the people in love and security" (*Discorsi* 1.10, p. 75b). Cf. *Discorsi* 1.16, p. 83b; 2.2, p. 142a; *Istorie Fiorentine* 4.33, p. 498a).

[20] "For the safety of his fatherland and not because of his own ambition" (*Discorsi* 3.3, pp. 197b-198a).

[21] "For the public benefit and not for his personal benefit" (*Discorsi* 3.30, p. 241b). Cf. *Discorsi* 1.2, pp. 60b-61a; 8, p. 73a; 58, p. 132b; 2.2, p. 139b; 3.16, p. 225a; *Istorie Fiorentine* 7.1, p. 562a.

ample, Gilbert of Tournai had said that the king exists "non ad commoditatem propriam sed ad sibi subditorum utilem gubernationem."[22] Coluccio Salutati had asserted that it was the nature of the tyrant "suisque non subditorum utilitatibus providere," and to conduct himself "secundum finem, cuius est que sibi conduxerint maxime sequi facultatesque proprias ampliare."[23] A little later Leon Batista Alberti had said: "Se tu hai atteso, mediante il regno ad accumularti ricchezze, tu hai pessimamente esercitato il magistrato tuo, e ti sei portato non da Re, ma da tiranno, se tu le hai accumulate per bene del publico, hai fato quel che ti si aspettava."[24] In a passage of advice to a ruler from the pen of Lorenzo il Magnifico, evidently familiar to Machiavelli, is a touch of verbal similarity to some of his statements of the idea:

> Non pensi a util proprio o a piacere,
> ma al bene universale di ciascuno.[25]

While *The Prince* lay in manuscript, Niphus wrote in his *Libellus de principe:* "Ut enim medicus languentis utilitati non suae consulere debet, ita Rex eorum, quibus imperat: aliter ne utique rex habendus esset sed tyrannus qui pecuniis et divitiis studens, omnia pro utilitate sua metitur."[26] Nor was the idea then forgotten. Some years after the death of Machiavelli, Pigna wrote: "Il Tiranno ama anchor esso il popolo, ma tratto dal proprio particolare l'ama per dispogliarlo e per distruggerlo, come la meretrice ama il suo drudo, e il lupo la pecora."[27] And in the next century Cardinal Bellarmine

[22] "Not for his own benefit but for the useful rule of those subject to him" (*Eruditio regum* 3.7, p. 90).

[23] "To provide for his own convenience and not for that of his subjects" and "according to the end of a man who desires to follow the policies that conduce to his own benefit and to increase his own resources" (*Tractatus de tyranno* 1.7). For further mediaeval examples see the edition of the *Tractatus* by Ercole, pp. 46-7.

[24] "If you have given your attention to accumulating riches for yourself by means of your kingdom, you have exercised your authority badly and conducted yourself not as a king but as a tyrant; if you have accumulated riches for the good of the public, you have done what was to be expected of you" (*Del principe* 4, p. 116).

[25] "You should not think of your own good or of pleasure, but of the good of each one of all your people" (*Rappresentazione,* p. 100). See p. 197, above, and for another use of "bene universale" in the same passage, p. 44, above.

[26] "Just as the physician should consider the benefit of the sick man, and not his own, so the king should consider the good of those he rules; otherwise he is to be considered not a king but a tyrant, who, desiring wealth and riches, measures all things by his own profit" (cap. 4, p. 1 verso).

[27] "The tyrant also loves his people, but since he is influenced by his own profit, he loves them to despoil them and destroy them, as the harlot loves her gallant and the wolf the lamb" (*Principe* 1, folio 9 verso).

went back to Aristotle for it: "Charitatem paternam esse Principi in primis necessariam, docet Philosophus in libro de moribus octavo: ubi ponit differentiam inter Regem et Tyrannum, quod Tyrannus in omnibus quaerat quae sua sunt; Rex vero quae sunt populi; sive quod finis propositus Tyranno sit utilitas propria; finis propositus Regi sit utilitas Reipublicae."[28]

By exhorting his ruler to consider the common good, then, Machiavelli is using a well-known and commonly accepted formula which excludes tyranny and expresses the aspiration of all writers *de regimine principum* for good government conducted by an ideal monarch.[29]

The same conventional conception of good government appears in the suggestion, in the same sentence of *The Prince,* that the *forma* which will produce the common good will also give the prince honor.[30] Such a reward is about the only one possible to the laborious prince of Machiavelli and the other writers; he must, for example, live a life not of luxury but one that will fit him to bear the hardships of a military campaign.[31] Some suggestion of this reward of the ruler has already been given: Agatocle, as a tyrant, could not attain the glory proper to the lawful ruler, but Marcus, as the father of his people, was deservedly glorious.[32] Among the writers *de regimine principum* glory was assumed as the only earthly reward of the ruler. Aquinas discussed the matter at some length:

Quoniam autem secundum praedicta, regis est bonum multitudinis quaerere, nimis videtur onerosum regis officium, nisi ei aliquod proprium bonum ex hoc proveniret. Oportet igitur considerare, quale sit boni regis conveniens praemium.

[28] "Paternal charity is one of the first things needful to the prince, as the Philosopher teaches in the eighth book of the *Ethics,* where he lays down the difference between the king and the tyrant, indicating that the tyrant in everything seeks what will be of benefit to himself, but the king what will be of benefit to the people. The end set before the tyrant is his own utility; the end set before the king is the utility of the state" (*De officio principis* 1.7).

[29] See *tyrant* in the index.

[30] *Prince* 26, first sentence.

[31] Patricius, for example, writes: "Nihil enim difficilius esse potest (ut saepe iam diximus) quam bene imperare. Adeo ut non insulse dixisse videatur Tiberius Caesar, quum ait: *Nescitis quanta belua sit imperium.*"—"As I have often said, nothing can be more difficult than to rule well. So true is this that Tiberius Caesar seems not to have spoken foolishly when he said: 'You do not know how great a monster the empire is'" (*De regno* 5.18). See also pp. 27, 73, above.

[32] *Prince* 8, pp. 18b-19a; ibid. 19, p. 41a; *Discorsi* 1.10, p. 75a.

Quibusdam igitur visum est non esse aliud nisi honorem et gloriam. . . . Sed quantum ex dictorum sapientum intentione apparet, non ea ratione honorem et gloriam pro praemio principi decreverunt tamquam ad hoc principaliter ferri debeat boni regis intentio; sed quia tolerabilius est si gloriam quaerat, quam si pecuniam cupiat, vel voluptatem sectetur. . . . Hoc autem satis exprimitur per id quod Aristoteles de magnanimo in *Ethicis* dicit, quod non quaerit honorem et gloriam quasi aliquid magnum, quod sit virtutis sufficiens praemium, sed nihil ultra hoc ab hominibus exigit. Hoc enim inter omnia terrena videtur esse praecipuum ut homini ab hominibus testimonium de virtute reddatur. . . .

Nec igitur terrenum aliquid est praemium regis sufficiens. . . . Solus igitur Deus est qui hominis desiderium quietare potest, et facere hominem beatum, et esse regi conveniens praemium. . . .

Sic igitur verificari potest quod regis praemium est honor et gloria. Quis enim mundanus et caducus honor huic honori similis esse potest, ut homo sit civis et domesticus Dei, et inter Dei filios computatus, et hereditatem regni coelestis assequatur cum Christo?[33]

Having shown that king and tyrant are opposed in their attitude to the *bonum commune,* Egidio explains further: "Ex hac autem differentia prima sequitur secunda, videlicet quod tyrannus intendit bonum delectabile: Rex vero bonum honorificum. Nam sicut inenarrabile est quanto quis delectatur in bono proprio, sic quasi inenarrabile est quantus honor sequitur, et quanto honore

[33] "But since according to what has been said above, the function of the king is to seek the good of the multitude, the office of the king seems too onerous, unless something good for himself comes out of it. It is therefore proper to consider what sort of reward is suitable to the good king.

"To some it has seemed that his reward is nothing other than honor and glory. . . . But as far as appears from the intention of wise writers, they do not assign honor and glory as the reward of the prince to such an extent that the attention of the good king should be directed principally to them, but only as it is more easily borne if he seeks glory than if he covets wealth or pursues pleasure. . . . This is sufficiently expressed by what Aristotle in the *Ethics* says of the magnanimous man, namely that he does not seek honor and glory as great things, which are sufficient rewards for virtue, but that he exacts from men nothing in addition to them. For it seems to be the chief of all earthly things that testimony of his virtue should be given to a man by other men. . . .

"Nothing earthly, therefore, is a sufficient reward for a king. . . . God alone remains, therefore, as able to quiet the desire of man and make man happy, and to be the reward fitting to a king. . . .

"Thus it can be established that the reward of the king is honor and glory. For what worldly and fading honor can be like this honor, namely that a man be a subject and servant of God, and counted among the sons of God, and should obtain the inheritance of the celestial kingdom with Christ?" (*De regimine* 1.7-8).

est dignius intendens commune bonum."[34] Much later Patricius asserted: "Optimi Regis praemium, quod pro rectis actionibus expectare debet ab his quibus praeest, sola est gloria, et honestus honor, qui a multitudine hominum et diversis populis celebratus, in rumorem primo deinde in famam illam crescit, quam neutiquam omnino aboleri Homerus sentit."[35] Lorenzo the Magnificent has Julian the Apostate declare that "rappresentano il tutto i signor veri";[36] for all his labors the emperor obtains no material reward:

> L'onore ha sol di tal fatica frutto;
> l'onor, che fa ogn' altra cosa vile,
> ch' è ben gran premio al core alto e gentile.[37]

Such was the common opinion, with emphasis on the earthly or heavenly quality of the fame in proportion to the piety of the writer. Often, too, this emphasis on the king's reward of honor was, as by Machiavelli, put late in the work; Niphus, for instance, devotes to the subject the last three chapters of his *De principe libellus*.

Niccolò emerges, then, in agreement with the writers of other works of advice to rulers, who desire to benefit the people by securing good government. The new method that he announced was not calculated to produce for the people a result unlike that desired by his predecessors. On the contrary, his objection to the works *de regimine principum* that he had read is based on the means they advocate for the attainment of the end. The theoretical writers had failed because it was impossible for any state to be made happy by a ruler who followed their precepts; the felicity of the people required a ruler in contact with the *verità effettuale,* who without hesitation on ethical grounds will adopt any procedure likely to assure the well-being of his country. The proper methods for avoiding tyranny and carrying on in the real world a government for the good of the people as a whole Machiavelli believed that he set forth in *The Prince.*

[34] "From this first difference a second follows, to wit that the tyrant has in view a good that is pleasing, but the king a good that brings honor. For just as it cannot be told how much any one is pleased by his own good, so it is almost unutterable how much honor follows him who has in view the common good and how much more worthy of honor he is" (*De regimine* 3.2.6).

[35] "The reward of the excellent king, which he should expect for his just acts from those whom he rules, is glory alone, and becoming honor, which, after it has been sung by a multitude of men and by diverse peoples, first increases to rumor and then grows to that fame which Homer thought never would be abolished (*De regno* 9.19).

[36] "True lords represent the whole people" (*Rappresentazione*, p. 111).

[37] "He has honor alone as the fruit of such effort, honor, which makes everything else vile, and is the great reward of the noble and gentle heart" (ibid.).

THE ORIGINALITY OF *THE PRINCE*

A S IN the preceding pages I have dealt with Machiavelli's similarities to his predecessors, I have not been influenced by the purpose of making him appear a smaller man than he was; I have merely pointed out what he knew about himself and knew that his contemporary readers would know, namely that he was adding another little book to the long list of works *de regimine principum*. How astonished the Florentine secretary would have been to be told that a time would come in which princes would have so little importance that his opuscule would appear not as one of a familiar type, but *sui generis!* It is a type that accompanies the rule of the irresponsible—at least the highly influential—prince. As kings ceased to control the destinies of Europe, books showing how they should do it ceased to appear. In countries where the prince ruled personally they lingered longest. This perhaps explains the vigor of the type in Spain after 1600.[1] Because of the lingering power of the Bourbons in Italy, the Spanish work of Mendo was translated into Italian in 1816. James I of England wrote such a book for his son Henry because he took himself seriously as a divinely appointed ruler, as had Saint Louis when he gave instructions to his son. As a curiosity, Anthony Hope in recent years gave the title of *The King's Mirror* to a novel dealing with a mythical state where the ruler still was in a strong position. A work with such a title must in the present age be fictitious, for when the prince began to submit to parliaments, men of ability abandoned the attempt to improve government by improving the morals or intellect of the monarch. With the reason for the book of advice to the prince passed also the vitality of the type. Thinkers turned to the discussion of matters suited to the spirit of the age.

The similarities of Machiavelli with his predecessors may be supposed to reveal his genius at its lowest point. But so far from its being a sign of weakness to depend on the past, it is rather a mark

[1] See Vicente García de Diego's introduction (pp. 19 ff.) to Saavedra Fajardo, *Idea de un principe Político cristiano*.

of genius—certainly indispensable to the exhibition of genius—to make use of earlier work. Advance is produced not by completely rejecting the old but by transcending it; the genius masters the old, observes its weaknesses, selects its valuable parts, breathes into the result a new spirit and adds his own invaluable contribution. The result is both like and unlike the old. In one aspect it is the best representative of the old because the great man has a power over the old that the mere student cannot possess. So *The Prince* may be called the best representative of the thousand books *de regimine principum* because of the mastery the author's mind had attained over the type. To understand is to see both defects and virtues; in proportion as Machiavelli understood the type, he was fitted to attack and destroy it. Certain it is that without the old moulds the metal of *The Prince* could not have received form. Machiavelli is known as the author of that work rather than of the *Discorsi* partly because it is traditional in form; if instead of relying on formulas developed for centuries he had attempted to work *ab ovo, The Prince* would perhaps now be one of those pitiable books known only to scholars.

Its typical character is to be strongly asserted. While comparisons with a great political work such as Dante's *De monarchia* are valuable in assisting one to grasp the conceptions of either,[2] there should be no confusion between the differences in spirit inherent in the authors themselves, or between the differences in the nature of the work that each is attempting. Had Dante attempted a book of advice for a ruler, it would have been, one may infer from the eighteenth and nineteenth cantos of the *Paradiso,* in the tradition of Aquinas and Egidio Colonna; the observance of the Christian virtues would have been inculcated rather than the policy of expediency. Associated ideas found in *The Prince* might also have been treated, such as the power of Fortune, and the proper reward for the ministers of a sovereign.[3] The world-wide sweep of the treatise on empire and papacy would have been lacking. Though more idealistic than *The Prince,* such a work would have more resemblance to it than to the *De monarchia.* Some, but only a small part, of the matter of the treatise on monarchy would appear in such a composition; it would be a more spirited version of the *De regimine principum* of Egidio Colonna, a more vigorous rend-

[2] Ercole, *La politica,* pp. 289 ff.
[3] Cf. *Inferno* 7.67-96, *Paradiso* 6.127-42, 8.139.

ering of Petrarch's *De republica optime administranda.* The type of Machiavelli's work is quite unlike that of the political treatise actually written by Dante, and must be judged according to the limitations of the type as Machiavelli submitted himself to them.

Of the supposed parallels with or anticipations of passages in *The Prince* that have been cited, some may be challenged as presenting ideas that occurred quite independently to Machiavelli. Generally, however, the similarity between works *de regimine principum* is so great that no large number of unusual ideas is to be found in any one; if a thought occurs in one of the predecessors of Machiavelli, it will usually be found in several of them. That Niccolò developed what earlier writers had suggested, perhaps without realizing the full significance of what they said, is probable; indeed I should consider the assertion of such development one of my theses. On the other hand, it may be supposed that Machiavelli had access to many works on the conduct of the prince that I have not seen; if I could cover his circle of reading in works belonging to and related to the type, I probably should be able to find more adequate parallels and to discover anticipations of what seems original; yet in view of the homogeneity of the type, the amount of wholly new matter would, I suspect, not be large.

While I have given some attention to parts of *The Prince* that, so far as I know, were not derived from earlier examples of the type, I have not always attempted to show the derivation of these new conceptions. Something, it is generally agreed, he derived from the classical historians, Tacitus and Polybius. Other parts of his theory were perhaps well-known to the diplomats of the time and appeared in their conversations without being written down.[4] Guicciardini, for example, may be suspected to have lived in an atmosphere akin to that of *The Prince* even when not in the company of his neighbor, Machiavelli; if we may judge from certain of his *Ricordi,* his early mission to Spain was especially fruitful in stimulating Machiavellian reflection.[5] Vettori too we may suppose to have sympathized with his correspondent because he was already a Machiavellian rather than because he became a convert to doctrines he learned from his friend. Possibly manuscripts, now lost, of writings in some way comparable to *The Prince* were

[4] For such a suggestion by Tommasini, see p. 10, above.

[5] *Ricordi* 77, 105, 142, 144, 273, 351. See Roberto Palmarocchi's *nota* in Guicciardini, *Scritti politici e Ricordi,* p. 373.

in circulation; the work of Diomede Carafa, more nearly anticipative of Machiavelli than anything else we know, was to be read only in manuscript for many years after its composition.[6]

As has appeared throughout this volume, few of the ideas expressed in *The Prince* are altogether novel; most of them are to be found in mediaeval and renaissance works belonging to the type of books of advice to kings. Possibly a complete reading of the treatises belonging to this class would leave Machiavelli with nothing wholly new. With such a limitation in mind, one may tentatively give a number of ideas that are novel, at least unconventional, though concerned with the old subjects. The Machiavellian ruler is not sure of the value of fortresses; he need not feel obliged to keep faith against the interest of his principate; he need not fear the reproach of stinginess, for liberality is not always a virtue; he may feel that good military measures will secure good laws of other sorts; cruelty is not denied to him as a ruler; he is not to regard the bonds of moral conduct that restrain individuals; he must beware of hatred brought upon him because of good works. There are also a number of topics of which no aspect is normally discussed by Machiavelli's predecessors, such as mercenaries; conquered states obtained in various ways, good and bad; fear of and even dependence on other rulers; ecclesiastical princes; the possibility of losing a realm completely; the power of Fortune. The presence of these topics and the views expressed on them are the result of Machiavelli's philosophy of government, in which his true originality inheres; this is quite different from any particular opinion that may be new, and dominates the entire work. He asks in effect: What will secure immediate good government in Italy as it is? To this all is subordinate. Abstract theology or morality is well enough, but is it applicable? The new ruler, seldom considered by the older writers, is a fact; he must be dealt with, and dealt with as he is and as he came to his high position, by means fair or foul, and as he is able to retain it. The rulers Machiavelli knew were seldom independent agents; what advice is to be given to a prince who fears his neighbors? In a world of wickedness good character furnishes no assurance of success; the means must be sought out with care and applied with energy. A benevolent *pater patriae,* a king of Yvetot, may find circumstances too hard for him; the ruler must be a strong man, who can hold the respect of his

[6] Persico, *Diomede Carafa,* p. 148.

subjects and of other princes by his ability and power, even his ruthlessness. In a world of uncertainty, where even the good may be miserable, no single and simple policy is adequate; the prince must adapt himself to the day as it is. In these things lie the true originality of Machiavelli; all may be summed up in his conviction that government is an independent art in an imperfect world; it is practical, and the only true theory is that derived from and returning to practice.

But however Machiavelli may be explained, in his achievement he overshadows all who may be compared with him. With the old he fused the new and to the product thus formed he gave a cutting edge. Something of the offense caused by his work resulted from the combination. The new ideas would have been attacked under any circumstances. But to state them not as a history of tyrants worthy of condemnation, but in a form that had hitherto been altogether moral—the book instructing the prince in his *governi*— this was more than could be endured. Here was an enemy within the fortifications. Part of the reputation of *De principatibus* and part of its greatness may be accounted for by means of this new and daring combination, conspicuous beyond all present estimation in a time when every reading man was familiar with the moral advice to princes consecrated by the centuries. On taking up this new example, he was shocked by finding that the chapter on liberality or on faith was no longer what Aristotle and the church had taught, but that a new guiding principle was used.

This new moral principle was Machiavelli's theory of the state. Like all political writers, he saw that for the good life of man a settled order was indispensable. But such a condition was not possible in a land where a city could not for a year be sure of security from revolution or invasion or both. At all costs there must be firmly established government; there rests the morality of nations. The great question for republic or prince is: how can turmoil and confusion be permanently avoided? Nothing else mattered in comparison, either present morality or hope of life hereafter. To this theory of the settled state all was subordinated. It has been noted that Machiavelli is not always accurate in fact, that he magnifies and belittles as his theory leads him to do, that if the *verità effettuale* consists in accurate details he fails to attain it. But without this neglect, even perversion, he could not have given so impressive presentation to his great idea of the importance of the life of the state. Details yielded to an overmastering conviction, itself presented with complete intellectual honesty. In the unshrinking truth with which he formulated and expressed his conception of the state has been found an important part of his greatness.[7]

Yet in this adaptation of facts to a theory, that direct contact with life which Machiavelli considered one of his qualifications as a political writer does not disappear. The roots of his belief are fixed in his life of political negotiation. From what he had seen, meaning had come to him, even though not the meaning that history now declares should have come. To be sure men who knew the world had addressed princes before. Simon Islip had seen plainly enough the condition of the English common people in the reign of Edward III, but he lacked theoretical power; Egidio Colonna was not inexperienced in affairs, but his mental life was prevailingly that of the Aristotelian philosopher; Pontanus was an observer of politics, but first of all a humanist. Machiavelli was essentially politically minded, with possibly the greatest amount of detailed experience in affairs of state possessed by any writer of advice to a ruler, if we except the kings themselves who became authors. On the whole it may be said that the writers of treatises *de regimine principum* were literary men in politics; Machiavelli was a politician in literature. Perhaps the dominant interest explains the loose literary construction of *The Prince,* inferior to that normal in works *de regimine principum* composed more temperately by literary men. Yet through this disorganization speaks a greatness of spirit before which criticism can only admire.

The ability of the author to make politics live in his own mind, though at the price of alteration of fact, which underlies the vigor of *The Prince,* extends beyond contemporary Italy to Greek and Roman history. Even in the renaissance Niccolò is exceptional for the liveliness with which the statesmen and generals of the past came before his mind's eye. The Cyrus of Xenophon was a hero to many a literary man of the sixteenth century, but for Machiavelli he lived, and Machiavelli's pages live for us.

In addition to the qualities that may be assigned to Machiavelli for *virtù,* he had also the aid of fortune. The world was ready to listen to a discussion of *ragione di stato.* Machiavelli first formulated and presented to all Europe the new and characteristic thought of his age on matters of public administration. For some

[7] Mosca, *"Il Principe" di Machiavelli,* pp. 67-84.

hundreds of years men had been writing *de regimine principum*. In the early part of the sixteenth century, when the books issuing from the circle of Alphonso of Naples were still recent, the type was in high favor. Yet all that could be done for its perfection according to the old ideas had been done. Though it was to enjoy wide popularity for another century, it was not to develop; it had done its work and its decline was imminent. Into the old form Machiavelli threw the new conception of the state that was appearing. Had he attempted a treatise of a kind wholly new, his abilities would not have had a clear road, but working according to a method thoroughly understood, and supplied with vital matter from his own reflections, he came at a juncture when time in its changes permitted him to produce one of the books we can call permanent, the sole living representative of the great type of works *de regimine principum*.

BIBLIOGRAPHY

PRIMARY WORKS

Agapetus *De officio regis ad Iustinianum Caesarem,* Graece et Latine. Basel, 1518.

The work was composed in 527 and first printed in 1509, at Venice.

Leon Batista Alberti *Momus* or *Del principe,* in *Opuscoli morali.* Venetia, 1568.

Composed in Latin about 1444, and printed at Rome in 1520.

Alfonso X, el Sabio See *Las siete partidas.*

Scipio Ammirato *Discorsi sopra Cornelio Tacito,* ne i quali si contiene il fiore di tutto quello, che si trova sparto ne' libri delle attioni de' Principi, e del buono, ò cattivo loro governo. Notando trà i movimenti delle guerre, e trà i conducimenti de gli esserciti e trà gli altri capi dell' Istoria, alcuni avvertimenti notabili ad utilità di essi Principi per inducer ne i popoli la desiderata felicità. Venetia, 1607.

First printed in 1574.

Anonymous *Lancelot of the Laik from Cambridge University Library MS.* Edited by Margaret Muriel Gray *(Publications of the Scottish Text Society).* Edinburgh, 1912.

Translated probably before 1500 from the French prose romance of *Lancelot du Lac,* printed in 1488.

Anonymous *Secretum secretorum.* Vol. 5 of *Opera hactenus inedita* Rogeri Baconi. Oxford, 1920.

In the Middle Ages attributed to Aristotle. In the thirteenth century it was translated into Latin from the Arabic. It was widely circulated and translated into Italian and other languages. Several Latin editions were printed before 1500.

Aquinas See St. Thomas.

Aristotle *Works,* translated into English. Oxford, 1908-31. See Anonymous.

Francis Bacon *De sapientia veterum,* in *Works,* vol. 12. Boston, 1864.

Matteo Bandello *Novelle.* London, 1792.

Cardinal Bellarmine *De officio principis Christiani.* Cologne, 1619.

Philippus Beroaldus *De optimo statu libellus,* in *Varia opuscula.* Basel, 1513.

Printed as early as 1497.

Petrus Bizzarus *De optimo principe,* in *Varia opuscula.* Venice, 1565.

Nicephorus Blemmydes *De regis officiis,* in Migne, *Patrologia Graeca,* vol. 142. Paris, 1885.

Composed in the thirteenth century.

Giovanni Boccaccio *I casi degl' huomini illustrati* (a translation of *De casibus virorum illustrium*). Florence, 1598.

First Latin edition about 1473.

Iacopo di Messer Poggio Bracciolini *Xenophonte della vita di Cyro re di Persi tradotto in lingua Toscana.* Tusculano, 1527.

Made before 1478, from his father's translation into Latin (1447).

Poggio Bracciolini *De infelicitate principum,* in *Opera.* Basel, 1538.

Finished in 1440.

Historia disceptativa de avaritia. Ibid.

Henrici de Bracton *De legibus et consuetudinibus Angliae,* edited by Sir Travers Twiss. London, 1879.

Bracton died about 1268.

Guillaume Budé *De Linstitution du prince,* livre contenant plusieurs histoires, enseignements, & saiges dicts des anciens tant Grecs que Latins. Paris, 1547.

Completed about 1519.

Caius Julius Caesar *De bello civili.* Leipzig, 1893.

De bello Gallico. Leipzig, 1935.

Giraldus Cambrensis *De principis instructione,* in *Opera,* vol. 8. London, 1891.

Completed about 1217.

Ioannes Antonius Campanus *De regendo magistratu,* in *Opera.* Rome, 1495 or 1502 (the date of the volume in the Biblioteca Nazionale in Palermo is uncertain).

Composed about 1460. Also in *Opera selectiora,* Leipzig, 1734.

Diomede Carafa *De regentis et boni principis officiis,* in Fabricius, *Biblioteca Latina.* Florence, 1858.

A translation by Guarini of the following work.

I doveri del principe, in Tommaso Persico, *Diomede Carafa, uomo di stato e scrittore del secolo XV,* con un frammento originale dei *Doveri del principe.* Naples, 1899.

Composed a few years before the death of the author in 1487.

Baldessar Castiglione *Il libro del cortegiano.* Milan, 1928.

Michele Scherillo, the editor of this edition, believes the author worked on this book as early as 1508; it was finished in 1524 and printed in 1528.

George Chapman *Alphonsus Emperor of Germany,* in *Tragedies.* London, 1910.

Traditionally assigned to Chapman but probably not by him. Performed in 1636 and printed in 1654.

Marcus Tullius Cicero *De legibus*, in *De re publica*, etc. London, 1928.
    De officiis, London, 1928.
    Correspondence, Dublin, 1886-1904.
    De oratore. Leipzig, 1914.
    De re publica. London, 1928.
    Brutus. Leipzig, 1914.
    Tusculanae disputationes, Cambridge, 1905-34.
Giovanni Battista Giraldi Cintio *Gli Ecatommiti*. Torino, 1853.
    First edition in 1565.
Claudius Claudianus *De quarto consulatu Honorii Augusti pane-gyricus*, in *Opera*. New York, 1922.
Egidio Colonna (Aegidius Romanus, Egidio Eremita) *De regimine principum*. Rome, 1556, 1607; Venice, 1498.
    Composed before 1286; first printed in 1473.
    Del reggimento de' principi. Florence, 1858.
    An Italian translation of a French translation from the Latin, completed in 1288.
Iodocus Clichtoveus *De regis officio opusculum,* quid optimum quemque regem deceat, ex sacris literis et probatorum authorum sententiis historiisque depromens. Paris, 1519.
    Apparently the first edition.
Philippe de Commynes *Mémoires,* edited by Joseph Calmette with the collaboration of Chanoine G. Durville. Paris, 1924-5.
    This work was probably commenced in 1489 and completed in 1497 or 1498. It was first printed in 1524 but circulated in manuscript in earlier years. The edition used is based on the manuscripts; they are, however, all copies of MSS now lost.
Lambertus Danaeus *Aphorismi politici et militares,* ex diversis auctoribus Graecis et Latinis collecti. Utrecht, 1603.
    First edition 1575.
Dante Alighieri *Convivio,* in *Le opere.* Oxford, 1924.
    Divina commedia. Ibid.
    De monarchia. Ibid.
Dionysius Carthusianus *De vita et regimine principum,* in *Opuscula insigniora.* Cologne, 1559.
    Composed before 1471.
Albrecht Dürer *Des Meisters Gemälde, Kupferstiche und Holzschnitte,* ed. by Friederich Winkler. Berlin, fourth edition.
Sir Thomas Elyot *The boke named the governour.* London, 1880.
    First edition in 1531.
Desiderius Erasmus *Adagia,* in *Opera,* vol. 2. Leyden, 1703.
    Apophthegmata lepideque dicta principum, philosophorum, ac diversi generis hominum, in *Opera,* vol. 4.
    Xenophontis Hieron sive tyrannus. Ibid.

Institutio principis Christiani saluberrimis referta praeceptis. Basel, 1516. The first edition.

>Also in *Opera,* vol. 4, Leyden, 1703. Translated into English by Lester K. Born, *The education of a Christian prince.* New York, 1936.

Praecepta Isocratis de regno administrando ad Nicoclem. Basel, 1516.

>In the same volume as the work listed just above.

Diego Saavedra Fajardo *Idea de un principe político Cristiano representada en cien empresas,* edited by Vicente Garcia de Diego. Madrid, 1927.

>First printed in 1640. I have used also the Italian translation, Venice, 1678, the German translation, Amsterdam, 1665, and the Latin translation, Amsterdam, 1659.

Felice Figliucci *De la politica overo scienza civile secondo la dottrina d'Aristotile.* Libro non sol utilissimo, ma necessario a chi desidera saper il modo & l'arte de' governi de' popoli, regni & stati. Venice, 1583.

>Composed before 1551.

Girolamo Frachetta *Il prencipe,* nel quale si considera il prencipe & quanto al governo dello stato & quanto al maneggio della guerra. Venice, 1647.

>First printed in 1597.

>*Il seminario de' governi di stato, et di guerra,* nel quale sotto cento dieci capi si comprendono intorno à otto milla massime, ò propositioni universali, & regole, ò insegnamenti di stato, & di guerra. Venice, 1647.

Aulus Gellius *Attic nights.* New York, 1927.

Gilbert of Tournai (Guibertus de Tornaco) *Eruditio regum et principum,* edited by A. de Poorter. Louvain, 1914.

>Completed in 1259.

Bernardo Giustiniano *De institutione principis* (a translation of Isocrates' *Ad Nicoclem*). Paris, 1511.

>First published in 1492.

John Gower *Confessio amantis,* in *Complete works.* Oxford, 1901.

>Completed by 1393.

Fulke Greville (Lord Brooke) *The life of the renowned Sir Philip Sidney.* London, 1652.

Francesco Guicciardini *Discorsi politici,* in *Opere,* vol. 8. Bari, 1933.

>*Dialogo del reggimento di Firenze,* in *Opere,* vol. 7. Bari, 1932.

>*Storia d'Italia,* edited by Costantino Panigada. Bari, 1929.

>*Istruzione delle cose di Romagna a suo fratello Iacopo,* in *Opere inedite,* vol. 8, pp. 393-420. Florence, 1866.

Ricordi politici e civili. Florence, 1929. See also *Opere,* vol. 8. Bari,
    1933.
Hildebert of Le Mans   *Epistolae,* in Migne, *Patrologia Latina* 171.
    Paris, 1893.
Thomas Hoccleve   *The regement of princes.* London, 1897.
    Composed 1411-1412.
Anthony Hope   *The king's mirror.* New York, 1904.
Simon Islip   *Speculum regis.* Paris, 1891.
    This work, addressed to Edward III, was composed and re-
    vised from 1337 to 1345.
Isocrates   *Ad Nicoclem,* in the *Orations* of Isocrates. New York, 1928.
    Translated by Erasmus, Giustiniano, and Philecticus, q. v.
James I   ΒΑΣΙΛΙΚΟΝ ΔΩΡΟΝ or *His majesties instructions to his
    dearest sonne, Henry the Prince.* Edinburgh, 1603.
Justinian   *Institutiones,* in *Corpus iuris civilis.* Berlin, 1928-9.
D. Junius Juvenalis   *Satirae.* Cambridge, 1931.
Lancelot of the Laik   See Anonymous.
Titus Livius   *Ab urbe condita.* Leipzig, 1898-1901.
Lorenzo de' Medici il Magnifico   *La rappresentazione di San Gic
    vanni e Paolo,* in *Opere.* Bari, 1914.
    First printed in the first decade of the sixteenth century.
Louis IX (Saint Louis)   *Enseignements a son fils.* Bibliothèque de
    l'École des Chartes, XXXIII (1872), 424-42.
    Texts in both Latin and French. Presented by the king to his
    son just before his death.
Louis XI   *Le rosier des guerres,* enseignements de Louis XI Roy de
    France pour le Dauphin son fils. Paris, 1925.
    First printed in 1521. It seems probable that the work was
    composed by Pierre Choisnet, possibly with the king's assistance,
    certainly with his approval.
Lettres. Paris, 1883-1909.
John Lydgate   *The fall of princes.* Washington, 1923.
    Probably finished by 1439.
Niccolò Machiavelli   *Tutte le opere storiche e letterarie,* a cura di
    Guido Mazzoni e Mario Casella. Firenze, 1929.
    Most references are to this text; the columns are indicated by the
    letters *a* and *b.*
Opere. Florence, 1782-3.
Opere. Italia, 1813.
Il principe. Edited by L. Arthur Burd. Oxford, 1891.
Lettere familiari, a cura di Cerolamo Lazzeri. Milano, 1924.
    References to the letters are to this edition.
Scritti inediti risguardanti la storia e la milizia. Florence, 1857.

Ammianus Marcellinus *Rerum gestarum libri qui supersunt.* Berlin, 1910.

Juan de Mariana *De rege et regis institutione,* translated as *Del rey y de la institucion real,* in *Obras.* Madrid, 1854.
First printed in 1598.

Menander Protector *Historiarum excerpta,* in *Corpus scriptorum historiae Byzantinae.* Bonn, 1829.

Andres Mendo *Principe perfecto y ministros ajustados.* Lyons, 1662.
First edition in 1657.

John Milton *Works.* New York, 1931 ff.

Eutychus Augustinus Niphus (Nifo) *Libellus de his quae ab optimis principibus agenda sunt,* ad Ludovicum atque Elveriam Ferdinandos a Corduba principes Suessanos. Florence, 1521.
De regnandi peritia. Naples, 1523.
A great part of this work is a Latin rendering of *The prince.*

Hieronymus Osorius *De regis institutione et disciplina,* ad serenissimum et invictissimum Portugaliae regem Sebastianum. Lisbon, 1571.

Antonio Beccadelli, il Panormita *De dictis et factis Alphonsi Aragoniae.* Basel, 1538.
Composed in 1455.

Franciscus Patricius Senensis *De regno et regis institutione.* Paris, 1531.
Composed before 1492. Apparently first printed in 1519.
De institutione reipublicae. Paris, 1534.

Guillelmus Peraldus *De eruditione principum,* in St. Thomas Aquinas, *Opera,* vol. 27. Paris, 1875.
Composed before 1275.

Franciscus Petrarchus *De remediis utriusque fortunae,* in *Opera.* Basel, 1554.
De republica optime administranda. Ibid.

Martinus Philecticus *Isocratis de regno gubernando ad Nicoclem liber.* Vienna, 1514.

Giovanni Battista Pigna *Il principe.* Venice, 1561.

Baptista Saccus Platina *Principis Διατύπωσις.* Frankfurt, 1608.
Composed about 1470.
De optime cive. Paris, 1530.
First printed in 1505.

Caius Plinius Caecilius Secundus *Panegyricus.* Leipzig, 1933.
Epistolarum libri novem. Ibid.

Plutarch *Apophthegms,* in *Varia scripta,* vol. 2. Leipzig, 1829.

Polybius *Histories.* New York, 1922.

Joannes Jovianus Pontanus *De principe*, in *Opera*, vol. 1. Basel, 1556.
    First printed in 1490.
    De fortuna. Ibid.
    De magnificentia. Ibid.
    De obedientia. Ibid.
The Proverbs of Solomon in the *Bible*. New York.
Francis Quarles *Enchyridion*, in *Complete Works*, vol. 1. Edinburgh, 1880.
    Observations concerning princes and states. Ibid.
Egidio Romano See Egidio Colonna.
Mambrino Roseo *Institutione del prencipe Christiano*. Venice, 1562.
    Finished by 1543.
St. Thomas Aquinas *De regimine principum*, in *Opera*, vol. 27. Paris, 1875.
    In decem libros ethicorum ad Nicomachum (commentary on the *Ethics*). Ibid., vols. 25-26.
    In libros politicorum (commentary on the *Politics*). Ibid., vol. 26.
    Summa theologica, in *Opera*, vols. 1-6. Paris, 1871-3.
Caius Sallustius Crispus *Bellum Catilinae*. New York, 1920.
    De republica ordinanda. New York, 1920.
Coluccio Salutati *Tractatus de tyranno*, edited by Francesco Ercole. Berlin, 1914.
    Composed in 1400.
Joannes Saresberiensis (John of Salisbury) *Policratus sive de nugis curialium et vestigiis philosophorum*. Oxford, 1909.
    Completed in 1159. First printed about 1476; two editions in 1513.
Lucius Annaeus Seneca *De beneficiis*, in *Opera*, vol. 1. Leipzig, 1900.
    De clementia. Ibid.
    Medea, in *Tragedies*. New York, 1927.
    Oedipus. Ibid.
William Shakespeare *Hamlet*, in *Tragedies*. Oxford, 1912.
    Macbeth. Ibid.
James Shirley *The traitor*. London, 1635.
Sir Philip Sidney *Arcadia*. Cambridge, 1922.
    First printed in 1590.
Las Siete Partidas del Rey Don Alfonso el Sabio. Paris, 1843.
    Compiled in the thirteenth century.
Smaragdus Abbas S. Michaelis ad Mosam *Via regia*, ad Ludovicum Pium, in Migne, *Patrologia Latina*, vol. 102. Paris, 1865.
    Composed in the ninth century.
Edmund Spenser *Veue of the present state of Ireland*, in *Works*. London, 1907.
    The Faerie Queene, in *Works*. Baltimore, 1932 ff.

Secretum Secretorum. See Anonymous.

Stobaeus *De regno.* One of the sections in the Latin translation of his *Sermones.* Sermo 147 in *Loci communes sacri et profani sententiarum* . . . Congestarum per Ioannem Stobaeum, etc. Frankfurt, 1581.

Tacitus *Annals.* New York, 1931.

Giovan Giorgio Trissino *Poetica,* in *Tutte le opere.* Verona, 1729.
    Composed by 1529.

Flavius Vegetius Renatus *Epitoma rei militaris.* Leipzig, 1885.

Francesco Vettori *Sommario della storia d'Italia dal 1511 al 1527,* in *Archivio storico Italiano,* Appendice, vol. 6. Florence, 1848.

Vincent of Beauvais *De morali principis institutione,* from a photographic copy of MS Merton 110.
    Composed in the thirteenth century.

Jacobus Wimpfelingus *Agatharchia;* id est bonus principatus vel epithoma condicionum boni principis ad Ludovicum Philippi comitis Rheni Palatini primogenitum. Strassburg, 1498.

John Wycliffe *De officio regis.* London, 1887.
    Composed in 1378.

Xenophon *Cyropaedia.* London, 1914. See also Bracciolini.
    First printed in the Latin version of Francis Philelphus in 1476.
    It was also circulated in manuscript in the fifteenth century.

SECONDARY WORKS

F. Alderisio *Machiavelli.* Turin, 1930.

Jozsef Balogh "Rex a recte regendo," in *Speculum* 3 (1928), 580-2.

Archibald F. Becke "Waterloo Campaign" in *The Encyclopaedia Britannica,* 14th ed.

Biographie Universelle. Paris, 1811-62.

Lester K. Born "Erasmus on political ethics," in the *Political Science Quarterly* 43 (1928), 520-43.
    "The perfect prince," in *Speculum* 3 (1928), 470-504.
    See Erasmus in the first part of the bibliography.

Arthur Boucher *Les lois éternelles de la guerre.* Paris, 1922-5.

L. Arthur Burd "Le fonti letterarie di Machiavelli nell' *Arte della guerra,*" in *Atti della reale accademia dei Lincei,* memorie della classe di scienze morali, storiche e filologiche, vol. IV, parte I. Rome, 1897.
    See Machiavelli *Il principe.*

L. White Busbey *Uncle Joe Cannon.* New York, 1927.

Delio Cantimori "Politics and rhetoric in Italian humanism," in *Journal of the Warburg Institute* I (1937), 83-102.

Federico Chabod "Sulla composizione de *Il principe* di Niccolò Machiavelli," in *Archivium Romanicum* XI (1927), 330-83.

"Del principe di Niccolò Machiavelli," in *Nuova Rivista Storica* IX (1925).

Separate volume, Milan, 1926.

Pierre Champion *Louis XI*. Paris, 1927.

Chauncey M. Depew *My memories of eighty years*. New York, 1922.

John Dickinson "The mediaeval conception of kingship as developed in the *Policraticus* of John of Salisbury," in *Speculum* 1 (1926), 308-37.

G. Ellinger "Die antiken Quellen der Staatslehre Machiavelli's," in *Zeitschrift für die gesamte Staatswissenschaft* 44 (1888), 1-58. Tübingen.

Francesco Ercole *La politica di Machiavelli*. Rome, 1926.

See Coluccio Salutati.

Giuseppi Ferrari *Gli scrittori politici Italiani*. Milan, 1929.

Francesco Flamini *Il cinquecento*. Milan, n.d.

John F. C. Fuller *The generalship of Ulysses S. Grant*. New York, 1929.

Allan H. Gilbert "Notes on the influence of the *Secretum Secretorum*," in *Speculum* 3 (1928), 84-98.

Everardo Gothein *Il rinascimento nell' Italia meridionale*. Florence, 1915.

Martin Grabman *Thomas Aquinas,* translated by Virgil Michel. New York, 1928.

J. Lawrence Laughlin *The principles of money*. New York, 1903.

Eugene S. McCartney *Warfare by land and sea*. Boston, 1923.

Alfred Thayer Mahan *Armaments and arbitration*. New York, 1912.

Admiral Farragut. New York, 1901.

The life of Nelson. Boston, 1899.

Sea power in its relations to the War of 1812. Boston, 1905.

Gaetano Mosca *"Il principe* di Machiavelli," in *Saggi di storia della scienza politica*. Roma, 1927.

William F. P. Napier *History of the war in the Peninsula*. London, 1835-40.

Achille Norsa *Il principio della forza nel pensiero politico di Niccolò Machiavelli,* seguito da un contributo bibliografico. Milan, 1936.

C. W. C. Oman *Wellington's army*. New York, 1912.

André Otetea *François Guichardin,* sa vie publique et sa penseé politique. Paris, 1926.

Howard L. Patch *The Goddess Fortuna in mediaeval literature*. Cambridge, 1927.

Mark Pattison *Isaac Casaubon*. Oxford, 1892.

L'Abbe Pierre-Louis Pechenard *Jean-Juvenal des Ursins*. Paris, 1876.

Tommaso Persico *Gli scrittori politici napoletani dal' 400 al' 700.* Naples, 1912.

See Diomede Carafa.

L. Petit de Julleville *Histoire de la langue et de la littérature française.* Paris, 1896.

Ch. Petit-Dutaillis *Charles VII, Louis XI, et les premières années de Charles VIII,* vol. 4, part 2, of Ernest Lavisse, *Histoire de France.* Paris, 1911.

John Ruskin *Modern painters,* in *Works.* London, 1904.

Walter B. Scaife "Commerce and industry of Florence during the Renaissance," in the *Annual report of the American Historical Association for 1891.* Washington, 1892.

Don C. Seitz *Lincoln the politician.* New York, 1931.

G. Solari Review of Federico Chabod, *Del "Principe" di N. Machiavelli, in Rivista Storica Italiana* 44 (1927), 42-7.

Oliver L. Spaulding, Hoffman Nickerson, and John W. Wright *Warfare;* a study in military methods from earliest times. New York, 1925.

Arpad Steiner "Petrarch's optimus princeps," in *The Romanic Review* 25 (1934), 99-111.

Giuseppe Toffanin *Machiavelli e il "Tacitismo."* Padova, 1921.

Oreste Tommasini *La vita e gli scritti di Niccolò Machiavelli.* Rome, 1883-1911.

Niccolo Tommaseo and Bernardo Bellini *Dizionario della lingua Italiana.* Turin, 1924.

Alfred Vanderpol *La doctrine scolastique du droit de guerre.* Paris, 1925.

Pasquale Villari *Niccolò Machiavelli e suoi tempi.* Milan, 1927.

INDEX

Index

rulers, works on conduct of, see *De regimine principum*
Ruskin, John 66
ruthlessness 235

S

Saavedra 50, 231, 241
Saint Louis, *see* Louis IX
Saint Paul 196
Saint-Pol, Count of 206
Saint Thomas, *see* Aquinas
Sallust 100, 150, 161, 163, 193
Salutati, Coluccio 227, 244
San Miniato 159
Santa Croce 128
Sardanapalus 153
savageness 155, attribute of tyrant 105
Savonarola 67, 195
sayings, of Cosimo 130, striking, of rulers 168-9, *see also* proverb
Scaife, Walter B. 85
Schuster, Mauritius 161
Scipio, imitation of Cyrus 75, humanity 75, 102, and Hannibal 106, 110, virtues 199
Scevola 202
Scottish History Society 4
secrets 130, known to minister 182, 183
Secretum secretorum 5, 238, Middle English translation 7, on foresight 26, military affairs 63, liberality 87, translations 88, known to M 88, Machiavellian 114, faith 122, spectacles 169, ministers 179, advice 180, 190, rewards 182, familiarity 189
securitas 79
security, how gained 80, in ruler's own hands 110, assumed 117, mutual 150, and gratitude 174, against Fortune 208-9
Seitz, Don C. 155
self-control 198, 200
self-defence 224
self-interest 57
self-reliance 68, 111, 112, 117, 145, 194, 197
self-sufficiency 175
selfishness 78
Seneca, on the ruler as physician 28, injuries 48, *De clementia* 98, 113, fear 149, 150, love 160
service, good, ruin of minister 184
servitude, Florentines cannot endure 102

severitas 104
severity 52, 79, 99, 100, 104, 105, 106, 162, *see also* cruelty
Severus 141, 145, 168
Sforza, Francesco 72
Sforza, Galleazo 107, 110, 131
Shakespeare 88, 191
Shirley, James 168
Sidney, Sir Philip 3, on importance of prince 3, praise of good ruler 45, value of history 74, severity 99, 100, the prince and law 201, time 206, *Arcadia* 244
siege 209
siete partidas, Las 244
simulation 126, 129, 132
simulatione 132
single ruler 43
Sinigaglia 111, *see also* Valentino
sins, confidant of to be feared 183, of people derived from rulers 202
sixteenth century, and the classics 5
slaves, by nature 225
Sloan, Matthew S. 32
sloth, see *ignavia*
Smaragdus 79, 244
social animal 121
society 220
Socrates 139
Soderini, Piero 25, 49, 226
Soderini, Tommaso 21
Solari, G. 37
soldiers, mercenary 62, functions 63, training 69, masters of state 158, *see also* mercenaries, military, war
solertia 79
Solomon, King 167
sources of *Prince* 5-15, 16, 233
sovereign, mediaeval 3, renaissance 3, *see also* ruler
sovereignty 201
Spain 37, 38, 48, 231, 233
Spaulding, Oliver L. 207
spectacles, public 91, 169, 177, *see also* festivities, sports
speech, care in 130, errors 131, brief 171
Spenser 41
sports 177, *see also* spectacles
Stanton, Edwin M. 155
state, perfect 4, kinds of 19, mixed 24-32, new 35-50, unjustly gained 51, badly-ordered 67, imaginary 77, 83,

THE first purpose of this book is to present an important and neglected part of Machiavelli's intellectual environment; its higher purpose is to interpret and, to some extent, evaluate the work. The Machiavelli who emerges is no mysterious figure, but one who had read, observed, and thought, and at the end poured into an old form ideas new and old such as his critical judgment approved. His standards are not abstract but immediate and practical. He respects morality, but no moral code is so high as that founded on the common good. He contemplates the well-being of the state and above all a united Italy; and to that end is directed all the advice his experience enabled him to offer to the ruler.

Studies of Machiavelli in the last forty years have been so numerous that the bibliography requires a volume by itself, yet slight attention has been given to his affinities with other writers of somewhat the same sort such as Thomas Aquinas, Petrarch, Erasmus, and Guillaume Budé. With the decline of kingly power, books of advice to the king declined too; only a production with intrinsic vigor such as that possessed by Machiavelli's

(Continued on back flap